A HISTORY OF MODERN WALES

In preparation

A History of Medieval Wales
Huw Pryce

A History of Modern Wales 1536–1990

Philip Jenkins

LONGMAN
London and New York

Longman Group UK Limited,
Longman House, Burnt Mill, Harlow,
Essex CM20 2JE, England
and Associated Companies throughout the world.

Published in the United States of America
by Longman Inc., New York

First published 1992

British Library Cataloguing in Publication Data
Jenkins, Philip, *1952–*
   A history of modern Wales 1536–1990
   1. Wales, history
   I. Title
   942.9
ISBN 0–582–48925–3 PPR
ISBN 0–582–48924–5 CSD

Library of Congress Cataloging in Publication Data
Jenkins, Philip, 1952–
   A history of modern Wales, 1536–1990/Philip Jenkins.
   p.   cm.
   Includes bibliographical references and index.
   ISBN 0–582–48924–5 (cased): £28.00 (est.).–ISBN 0–582–48925–3
   (paper): £13.99 (est.)
   1. Wales—History.   I. Title.
DA720.J47   1991
942.9—dc20
                                                                90–20643
                                                                       CIP

Set in Linotron Bembo 10/12pt

Produced by Longman Singapore Publishers (Pte) Ltd.
Printed in Singapore

Contents

Contents

List of Maps

List of Tables

Preface

Writing a general history of any nation over a lengthy period is a
foolhardy venture, and choosing terminal dates is particularly
difficult. Given the ancient continuity of the Welsh nation, it seems
inappropriate to begin an account at any point after the Roman
occupation. It is especially difficult to understand the impact of the
Tudor reforms in Church or State without knowing the late
medieval background, at least as far back as the Glyndŵr rising; so
beginning this history in the 1530s may appear eccentric or
inconvenient. On the other hand, the present book has to be seen as
the second of a pair of complementary volumes, which between
them will describe the history of Wales from earliest times to the
present.

This book is meant to be suitable for readers without any previous
knowledge of Welsh history, though it is hoped that it might also be
of value for those who already have some background. The general
nature of the book means that references have not been provided
quite so abundantly as in a more technical work; and it should be
noted that chapter twenty, 'Historical Writing in Wales' serves a
multiple purpose. In addition to exploring the traditions of Welsh
historiography and offering suggestions for further reading, the
chapter also lists the sources that have been consulted in writing the
book.

Names and dates

Welsh place names pose a particular problem. There was for example
an ancient region known as Meirionydd, which was anglicised to
'Merioneth', and gave its name to the later shire. The tendency in

reent years has been to return to the older Welsh forms, which are seen as more 'authentic', and where such forms are not available, they are invented. 'Merionethshire' is now part of the modern parliamentary constituency of Meirionydd Nant Conwy, while the borough of Aberavan is known as *Aberafan*.

This issue of linguistic purity attracts remarkable passions, but it is difficult to share the enthusiasm. One could for example refer throughout to *Sir Gaernarfon*, but from the sixteenth century to the twentieth, the county was 'Caernarvonshire'; and a form like 'Cacrnarfonshirc' is a monstrous hybrid. (The present writer has even seen instances where the English peers are described as the 'Earls of Caernarfon'!) It would be bizarre for an English-language text to refer to Swansea as *Abertawe*, Cardiff as *Caerdydd* or Newport as *Casnewydd*. Why then apply a different principle to lesser places with equally well-established names? We might spell the name of the Monmouthshire town as *Blaenau*, though its residents have always known it as Blaina, and that is the name used here. Similarly for Llantwit Major (*Llanilltud Fawr*) or Holywell (*Treffynnon*).

Perfect consistency is not claimed, but this book tends to follow the traditional English usage, as represented in the Ordnance Survey maps of the 1960s – before the outbreak of linguistic 'correctness'. In the south and borders especially, this has the virtue of following local usage.

All dates before 1752 are old-style, except that the year is taken as beginning on January 1.

To Liz
Catherine and Alexandra

CHAPTER ONE
Introductory: Which Wales?

For a thousand years, English and other writers have been in no doubt of the existence of a distinctive Welsh people, originally demarcated by language, but also by real or alleged ethnic traits. The Welsh were strongly attached to their homeland, which at various times had a separate political identity. In 1536, Henry VIII's Act of Union spoke of a 'dominion, principality and country of Wales'; a century later, Milton assumed that the Council in the Marches exercised control over 'an old, and haughty nation proud in arms'. But exactly what was this nation?

The land of Wales is clearly defined as a political entity, comprising the 13 traditional counties formed under the Tudors, and reorganised in 1974 into eight new units.[1] Beyond this, almost any statement about 'Welshness' or the nature of Wales is likely to be controversial. In history and social science, it is common to use phrases that seem to assume clear distinctions within the geographical unit. One area might be 'more Welsh', while another is part of the 'anglicised lowlands'; and language is only one factor in this division. This makes it appear that there exists an ideal 'true Wales', *pura Wallia*, which different regions can resemble to a greater or lesser degree. On the other hand, a survey of the modern history of Wales suggests a more complex picture. Within the small area of Wales, there are important regional and cultural distinctions, and it is a matter of debate whether any one region or cultural pattern can claim a greater correctness or authenticity. These divisions have provided an essential context to the development of every aspect of Welsh life, especially in matters of politics and religion.

1. Except where otherwise stated, 'Wales' will be taken to refer to the thirteen historic counties, including Monmouthshire.

A WELSH NATION?

Can we speak of 'Wales' as anything more than an expression of geographical convenience? Henry VIII had officially snuffed out any legal distinctions or peculiarities that Wales might formerly have possessed, leaving a mere component of England, 'incorporated, united and annexed'. Does 'Wales' mean anything more than a term like 'East Anglia' or 'Wessex', both geographical terms that preserve distant recollections of ancient statehood?

It is useful here to compare the experience of the three Celtic nations that would ultimately form part of the United Kingdom. Scotland, Ireland and Wales were all inhabited by people of largely Celtic stock, and in all three, there were substantial populations speaking Celtic languages. When that has been said, we have exhausted the common Celticity of the three societies. Of the three, Wales is the least understood by English historians, perhaps precisely because it was less visibly alien than Scotland or Ireland. The two latter countries were undeniably foreign in their social makeup. Scotland was clearly a different society, with its traditions of Roman law and feudalism; and the establishment of the Presbyterian religion for most of the period. The Scottish highlands were the home of a Gaelic society strongly derived from ancient Celtic traditions; but the Lowlands too demonstrated social and political features that left no doubt that this was a distinct national culture. Ireland was shaped by the conflict of race, religion and language, and was ruled by a colonial framework very different from England. In neither was language the sole criterion of identity: no rational observer would use the scarcity of Gaelic speech to justify calling Glasgow an 'anglicised' city; still less Dublin.

Yet in Wales, it was the Welsh language that gave the country what unity it possessed. As we will see, Welsh survived remarkably well through the political changes of the sixteenth and seventeenth centuries, and Wales entered the years of industrial revolution with perhaps 80 or 90 per cent of its people using Welsh as the normal medium of communication. Language was a substantial distinguishing mark, but it corresponded little with social or legal arrangements; and the vexed question of defining Wales politically meant that linguistic unity was not transformed into activism.

The lack of national unity was not counteracted by centralising institutions, either administrative or religious. Unlike Scotland, Wales had never been united under a Welsh kingdom or government – with the possible exception of short-lived conditions in the thirteenth century, or the time of the Glyndŵr rising. In early modern times, a Council of Wales and the Marches survived until 1689, but this impinged little on the everyday affairs of any section of Welsh society after 1640. There was a Welsh Great Sessions, used by judges as a forum for presenting their views on society and politics; but it never produced a glittering local bar with its attendant culture, on the lines of Georgian Dublin or Edinburgh. In education, there was from Tudor times something like a Welsh 'University College'; but this was Jesus College, Oxford, rather than any local institution.

REGIONS

Early modern Wales therefore lacked most of the characteristic features of nationhood, even those of a nation in subjection. Moreover, one of the most obvious and powerful facts about Wales in this era was the force of regionalism. It may seem remarkable to apply such a concept to such a small territory, but geography and communications made such local divisions quite inevitable. One of the most powerful and persistent of these themes was the distinction between north and south Wales, a separation recognised by many administrative devices. The division seemed obvious after the Acts of Union, which created 12 Welsh counties (Monmouthshire was detached): what could be more natural than to create two symmetrical halves, each with six shires? In the early modern period, each region had its own Vice-Admiral, its own structure for the collection of taxes and excise; while legislation in the interregnum clearly saw the two halves as separate missionary territories.

But the administrative division between north and south also reflects fundamental geographical factors, based above all on ease of transport and communication. The civil war in Wales involved two distinct and barely related series of campaigns. In more recent times, schemes for national structures in Wales generally envisaged a twin structure for north and south. The Methodist seminaries of the nineteenth century were established at Bala in Merionethshire and Trefecca in Breconshire. In the 1870s, most schemes for the proposed University of Wales suggested twin colleges, on the model originally proposed by Owain Glyndŵr. The location of the national eisteddfod alternates between north and south.

Wales was in fact an agglomeration of different societies and regions, and there was no urban centre to unite disparate areas. Wales had no natural capital, and until the mid-eighteenth century, the largest centres were market towns with populations of about three thousand. The only administrative centre of substance was Ludlow, the headquarters of the Council under the Tudors and Stuarts. Without a Welsh city, the country's regions looked towards metropolitan centres across the border. Roughly, there were three regions, which had little contact with each other. Even less promising for any prospect of national development, these regions were defined and maintained in terms of English towns and trading patterns.

For north Wales, the vital capitals were Chester, and later Liverpool, while even Dublin was more familiar than any southern Welsh town. In the south, Bristol played a similar role as the centre of commerce, finance and social life. It acted as a real metropolis, an urban centre that drew into its orbit the surrounding counties of England as well as the shires of the south Wales coast. Shrewsbury was the regional capital for mid-Wales, and it dominated the crucial woollen industry. The three-fold division of Wales was reinforced by the nature of roads within the principality. There were traditionally three great roads. One led from Chester to Caernarvon; one from Hereford to Brecon and Carmarthen, and thence to St David's. A third was the southern coastal route, through Cardiff and Swansea. The glaring inadequacies of most road transport in Wales put a premium on coastal traffic, where the routes also radiated from Bristol and Chester.

Marriages and social contacts occurred within such a metropolitan area, rather than on a 'Welsh' basis. Obviously, it was the upper ranks of society who tended to look further afield for marriage partners; but this suggests little awareness of a Welsh context. In Monmouthshire or Glamorgan, no gentry family in the century after 1660 formed a marriage alliance with anyone from the six counties of north Wales. By contrast, there were dozens of such links with the squires and ladies of Somerset, Gloucestershire and Wiltshire. Squires of Caernarvonshire and Denbighshire were equally close to the gentry communities of Cheshire or Staffordshire.

Over the years, this naturally meant that landed estates in Wales tended to pass to owners from elsewhere within these larger Anglo-Welsh regions. Thus we find Bagots and Pagets among the gentry of north Wales, Wyndhams in the south. In landowners' correspondence of the seventeenth and eighteenth centuries, we rarely find any suggestion of acquaintance with other Welsh families beyond the adjacent county. In contrast, they were part of widespread networks in England, within the wider metropolitan region. Below the level of the gentry, Bristol, Shrewsbury and Chester were the indispensable market towns, centres for trade, recreation or shopping; and marriage ties or migration often followed social contacts. The early industrialisation of south Wales was financed by capital from Bristol; the north looked to Cheshire and Lancashire.

These trends were accentuated rather than reduced by the improving communications of the nineteenth century. Major railways ran from east to west, and the vital communication routes of this era were three rail lines running westwards from Newport, Shrewsbury and Chester. These facilities provided the basis for growth in communications and urbanisation, but again these developments were conditioned by the needs of the English metropolitan regions. Tourism from the English midlands and north-west created a holiday coast from Conway to Prestatyn, which in turn permitted the emergence of urban centres like Llandudno and Colwyn Bay. Naturally enough, these new towns looked east to the English heartland, rather than south into Wales. By the nineteenth century, Liverpool had become perhaps the greatest Welsh city of all: the culmination of a trend at least as old as the middle ages.

COUNTIES AND HUNDREDS

These economic regions can be seen as the essential building blocks which made up the Welsh nation; but other views are possible. For a Welsh person living in, say, 1700, there were other units which might be taken to mark the boundaries of life and experience, and 'Wales' was probably not one of them. As we have seen, there were rudimentary 'national' institutions like Jesus College, but these were as nothing in prestige or significance besides those of the county. The Welsh county might have been an upstart creation of the 1530s, but it rapidly acquired real significance.

Quarter Sessions, the county Bench and lieutenancy, the Grand Jury – all were county events and institutions, deciding issues central to the life of the landed community, of clergy and burgesses, and to the making of policies that affected virtually everyone within the shire. Even the 'Welsh' Great Sessions manifested themselves as a county event, when the assizes were the scene of local pageantry and festivities; and the assize sermon was a high point of local ecclesiastical society. The power of the county is also suggested by negative evidence, in that religious and political dissent grew on the fringes of the shires, far from the agents of justice. In the seventeenth century, the greatest Jesuit centre stood on the boundary between the shires of Monmouth and Hereford; while the headquarters of one widespread Baptist network was at Rhydwilym, on the frontier between Pembroke and Carmarthen. In this sense, the experience of Welsh people in the early modern period was essentially identical to those of their English neighbours.

But we can refine our vision still further. Wales was made up of fundamentally different economic regions. Each region comprised different counties; and furthermore, even the county might be too gross a unit for accurate perception or analysis. Most counties included at least two sharply distinct regions that were physically separated by only a few miles, though they were sharply demarcated by economy, population structure, social arrangements and sometimes language. One region might be 'anglicised', another 'pure Welsh'. Each had its own community, often with natural linkages lying beyond the official boundaries.

Even the island county of Anglesey, which seems to have the best-defined natural boundaries, has in its southern tier a very distinctive social and economic unit: the hundreds of Menai and Dindaethwy are strongly linked to the northern coastal strip of Caernarvonshire to form a 'Menai region'. Again in Caernarvonshire, the eastern part of the county was sharply differentiated from the western regions of Llŷn and Eifionydd. Denbighshire politics were long shaped by the need to reconcile the divergent interests of eastern and western halves, with their respective capitals at Wrexham and Denbigh. In Glamorgan, the river Ogwr marked the internal border between east and west. The central government had to exercise care in allotting patronage so that neither region felt slighted.

Which territorial area best defined people's awareness? Even for the greater gentry like the Mansells and Mostyns, their correspondence suggests that the truly local community was an area within a radius of only five to ten miles around the great house: that is, well below the scope of the county. Between the parish and the county was the hundred, an often neglected unit that fitted rather well with Welsh realities. Hundreds were rarely formed in a wholly arbitrary way under Henry VIII. They usually followed some traditional Welsh boundaries, or else the model of a feudal lordship, and their limits were often natural frontiers. In northwest Wales, the hundreds were usually the ancient commotes; while in the south, a special commission decided boundaries under Henry VIII. In Pembrokeshire, the hundreds followed the old cantref boundaries, with finer divisions being drawn according to manors and lordships rather than parishes. In the whole of Wales and Monmouthshire, there were 90 hundreds with an average size of about 89 square miles. The average hundred in the later seventeenth century had about 4500 people, rising to 6500 in 1801. For the historian, it is the hundreds which perhaps offer the most manageable units for examining the diversity of local communities and cultures.

To illustrate the distinctions in social structure, let us briefly compare two hundreds within the single county of Glamorgan: Ogmore in the lowland 'Vale', and the upland area of Llangyfelach.[2] Both hundreds had similar populations in the seventeenth century – Ogmore had three thousand people, Llangyfelach closer to 3600 – and both used Welsh as their normal means of communication. (English had made somewhat more progress in Ogmore, but it was not a dominant force until the later eighteenth century). Neither had a town or city of any size, though both stood near moderate market towns: Swansea in the west, Cowbridge in the Vale. Both had coastlines, though neither had a major port; and major roads passed through both.

The two hundreds were separated by barely 20 miles, but in social structure they were different worlds. Llangyfelach was a hilly area with a pastoral-industrial economy, and from about 1700 it was a prominent centre of rapid industrialisation. Most of Ogmore depended on mixed agriculture, and was little affected by industry. The economic contrast was clearly reflected in social stratification. In 1670, the hundred of Llangyfelach had at most four gentry by customary English standards of wealth or income, while 90 per cent of the people lived in houses of one or two hearths. The largest house in the hundred had only six hearths, and no family had an income in excess of £300. However, there were many other people who were viewed as gentlemen by local and traditional standards. They often acted as leaders of the community in struggles with the feudal lords, the Dukes of Beaufort; who in turn condemned these 'Welch ragamuffins'. Llangyfelach fits closely with the experience of upland societies throughout Europe as portrayed by scholars like Braudel: this was a world of poor clergy, religious dissidence, weak

2. The hundred of Ogmore was the survival of an old lordship which included a separate and sparsely populated upland 'Welshry'. I have excluded this anomaly from the figures presented here.

A History of Modern Wales 1536–1990

political control, a variety of economic resources, and (above all) an absence of landed nobility.

By contrast, Ogmore was a wealthy gentry-dominated society. In 1670, about 80 per cent of people lived in houses of one or two hearths. At the other extreme were 16 or so gentry families, several living in houses with ten or more hearths. The richest magnate was Sir Edward Stradling with seats at St Donats Castle (30 hearths) and Merthyr Mawr (13). There were probably eight families in the hundred with incomes in excess of £500, and these would certainly have been recognised as gentry by any contemporary English observer. By the nineteenth century, the area was dominated by the Earls of Dunraven, with their seat at Dunraven Castle.

The presence or absence of a gentry decides the means by which historians can study that area. History is shaped by the nature and availability of sources, and the attitudes of historians attracted to that kind of material. In Ogmore, the gentry have left abundant estate records and correspondence, and our historical view is a story of squires, ladies, castles, and 'high' politics. Llangyfelach strikes us through the institutions and facilities that tended to leave their records there, and it thus appears to be a land of nonconformist chapels, copper-works and coal mines. Tourists and travellers went to Ogmore as a haven of the picturesque, and their records provide much evidence of social life and landed society. They went *through* Llangyfelach, usually cursing its roads and gradients. Through the nature of the sources alone, one area appears much more like the Welsh stereotype than does the other.

Differences between the regions could be listed at length. In the seventeenth century, there were usually five or so resident Justices to administer the hundred of Ogmore. The local houses of St Donats, Dunraven and Ewenni were generally represented on the Bench and the lieutenancy, as well as in most parliaments from 1550 to 1800. By contrast, the political history of Llangyfelach can be written in terms of negatives, in discussing the offices they did not hold. Except during the interregnum, men from this hundred never served as Members of Parliament, and rarely as Justices or lieutenants. A few individuals made an impact during the 1650s, but that was precisely what made this a 'revolutionary' decade. Giving power to families like these, from a region like this, was almost as subversive in county terms as regicide was to the nation as a whole. Ogmore politics tended to be shades of Toryism, characterised by an extremist streak of high royalism, Jacobitism and nonjuror sympathies. Llangyfelach hundred was more often Whiggish, with

8

strong evidence of the survival of ideas and sympathies from the republican years.

Ogmore and the many areas like it were far more tightly controlled than an upland region like Llangyfelach, in religious affairs as much as secular. Twelve parishes occupied the 36 square miles of the southern portion of Ogmore, where parishes often coincided with villages. Each parish had a clergyman, or at least a vicar residing nearby. In 1763, there were eight resident clergy in the hundred, with two more living elsewhere in the county: excellent figures for Georgian Wales. There was virtually no tradition of religious dissent before 1780, and no meeting house for most of the eighteenth century. There were never more than 20 nonconformists out of 3000 people.

Llangyfelach, naturally, was different. An area larger than Ogmore, it was covered by only four parishes, and decentralised settlement made ecclesiastical supervision as difficult as secular control. In the century after 1660, this was a heartland of nonconformity, with Anglican clergy regularly estimating the number of dissenters at 20 to 30 per cent of the people. In the seventeenth century, the hundred produced Puritan soldiers like Philip Jones and clergy like Marmaduke Matthews. The eighteenth century chapels had a flourishing intellectual life, but one wholly removed from the assumptions of the established Church.

It would be over-simple to equate gentry dominance with Tory and Anglican views. An area could be as tightly controlled as Ogmore, and yet its rulers might vary greatly in political outlook. Indeed, one interesting point that emerges from intra-county studies is the existence of distinct elites and gentry communities within the county whole, made separate by family ties, economic interest and political outlook. In perhaps the most extreme case, in Monmouthshire, the contrast was not between gentry and non-gentry hundreds, but between two distinct gentries, one high Tory with Catholic sympathies, the other Whiggish and friendly to dissent. Both the hundreds of Raglan and Caldicot were in a sense 'Ogmore'-type hundreds, with well-established gentry; but the rivalry and indeed enmity between the two was intense.

In terms of historical stereotypes, Llangyfelach and Ogmore seem like separate and rival nations rather than regions. Llangyfelach is quintessentially 'Welsh': a land of democratic and independent freeholders and industrial workers, nonconformists owing little respect to squire or parson. Ogmore represents a type of social structure far different from what is usually perceived as the Welsh

9

norm, almost a piece of Somerset mistakenly appended to Wales; but it is not perhaps as exceptional as it may appear.

Call them what we may – part of 'Anglo-Wales', manorial Wales, or whatever – hundreds like Ogmore formed a significant part of the country. There were many such odd regions of mixed agriculture, often on the banks of a great river like the Clwyd, Severn, Wye or Tywi. There would sometimes be a gentry on the English pattern; and social relations revolved around a great house on the familiar model. It is not difficult to find these areas of manor houses, nucleated villages and great medieval churches, as in the Vale of Clwyd, the border country of Flintshire and eastern Denbighshire; the eastern fringes of Radnorshire and Montgomeryshire; the southern parts of Glamorgan, Monmouthshire and Pembrokeshire. Perhaps 20 Welsh hundreds, over a fifth of the total, represented this 'untypical' Ogmore pattern.

The terms used for such zones are themselves of interest, as we tend to describe them as 'anglicised', or even English. Historically, this has a little justification, as the prosperous lowland hundreds had been profoundly influenced by patterns of landownership and agriculture derived from England, from the villa society of Roman times to the manorial practices introduced by the Anglo-Normans. But these 'English' regions had social arrangements quite as authentic and long-grown as many upland areas. It is only in retrospect that they have been denaturalised by changing concepts of Welshness and nationhood. Far from being alien, such areas were for many years the centres of wealth, power and influence within Wales. To a remarkable extent, the great houses of these areas were the vital centres of Welsh literature and scholarship.

INDUSTRIALISATION

Early modern Wales was therefore marked by important regional distinctions: the principality and the march; the regions of the English metropolises; pastoral uplands and arable lowlands. Some of these divisions are ancient, but the coming of industry after 1700 created a new and starker fracture. Before this point, there were certainly areas of Wales that were more wealthy and populous than others, but no one county stood out as strongly dominant. From the Industrial Revolution, however, the south-eastern shires of Glamorgan and Monmouth did take the lead, to such an extent that we might almost talk of two distinct nations. The enormous disparity in population can be illustrated by this table:

Table 1:1   The Growth of Regional Disparities in Population

Region	Population (thousands) in:		
	1670	1801	1901
Gwynedd	62(16.5)	106(18)	225(11.1)
Clwyd	63(16.8)	100(17)	213(10.6)
Powys	78(20.7)	100(17)	132(6.6)
Dyfed	89(23.7)	167(28.3)	284(14.1)
south-east	84(22.3)	117(19.8)	1157(57.5)
(Glamorgan and Gwent)			

(Figures in parentheses give the proportion of the total population of Wales living in each region)

During the sixteenth and seventeenth centuries, the population of Wales was fairly evenly distributed between the various regions. In the nineteenth century, the two south-eastern counties began to assume massively greater importance. They represented about 20 per cent of the population in 1801, 33 per cent by 1851, and 57.5 per cent by 1901. Since 1921, the proportion of Welsh people living in these two counties has fluctuated between 60 and 65 per cent of the whole. In the mid-nineteenth century, there also began to be urban centres in the south, at Cardiff, Newport, Swansea and Merthyr Tydfil. In the twentieth century, the first three of these have all come to exceed 100,000 people, providing the urban development so conspicuously lacking in earlier centuries. Alongside 'Welsh Wales', therefore, we now find 'American Wales', the land of the booming polyglot metropolitan centres. Nor have subsequent depressions erased the division. In 1990, Wales had 38 Members of Parliament, 23 of whom represented seats in the historic shires of Glamorgan and Monmouth. And under the 1974 government reorganisation, four of the eight new counties were within the borders of the old south-eastern giants.

IN QUEST OF WALES

It has always been difficult to define Welshness or the Welsh nation in such a way as to take account of these regional factors. Problems of definition have become acute since the widespread decline of the

Welsh language, which has also accentuated older regional divisions. In fact, some would argue that 'true' Wales might be confined to only a part of geographical Wales, perhaps a very small portion of that territory. This issue might be illustrated from a remark of the nineteenth century radical MP, Henry Richard, who used the cultural 'Welshness' of the common people as a rhetorical weapon against the Anglican and Anglophone social elite. For Richard, the Welsh speakers and nonconformists of Wales could say to 'this small propertied class': 'We are the Welsh people and not you'. In other words, Welshness was to be defined by language, culture and religion, as opposed to birth or heredity. This would be a powerful idea in the present century, and it is strong today among nationalists and Welsh-language activists.

But who were the 'Welsh people' of Richard's phrase? About 1910, there were 2.4 million people in Wales, of whom 40 per cent were Welsh speakers, and 23 per cent were dissenting communicants. About a fifth of the total population lived in the 'core', those counties of the north and west where at least 80 per cent of people spoke Welsh, and 40 per cent or more were nonconformists. These were the shires of Anglesey, Caernarvon, Merioneth, Cardigan and Carmarthen, and they would long retain their identity as a heart of 'Welshness'. Richard's generalisation about the people of Wales would seem to have considerable force here, and this area would also fit the Welsh stereotype of a remote and pastoral nation. In the 1970s, radical defenders of the language sought to create here the *Bro*, a Welsh monoglot bastion.

But if this was the true Wales, what became of the rest of 'geographical' Wales? Against the five 'heartland' shires, we might set the five counties where in 1910 the proportion of Welsh speakers was under 40 per cent, and where dissenters made up less than 25 per cent of the population. These counties – Glamorgan, Monmouth, Flint, Radnor and Brecon – included the economic heartland of Wales; and this 'Anglo-Welsh' area included four times as many residents as the heartland. If the Welsh language and dissent are taken as the touchstones of Welshness, then most modern history in Wales was simply not 'Welsh'; an insupportable paradox. By the 1980s, the proportion of Welsh speakers in the country as a whole had fallen to little more than a fifth, and the decline in the south-east had been precipitous. Even in the *Bro*, the number of Welsh speakers had fallen closer to 70 per cent. Does Wales still exist? Did it ever?

A historian therefore has to give due attention to the diverse social and cultural strands that make up the fabric of Welsh history. The modern writer must also understand the origins of the powerful historical traditions that have tried to define 'Welshness' in their different ways. Over the centuries, it has been argued that true Welshness was expressed in resistance to the Protestant Church establishment; in monarchist enthusiasm; or in nonconformist Liberalism. Each of these contradictory claims has been buttressed with a sizeable historical literature, to claim the past in the interests of whatever cause is currently at issue. We will therefore find Welsh history littered with the products of centuries of myth-making, and it is only in recent years that many of the most cherished tales have been accorded their proper value. The new maturity and insight that have characterised Welsh historical study in the last three decades have been reflected by diligent attention to this work of reassessment; though much still remains to be done.

PART ONE
Welsh Society

CHAPTER TWO
Early Modern Society

Wales is a land of barely 8000 square miles, which had perhaps 400,000 people in 1700 (see appendix at end of this chapter). Five of the 13 shires had populations below 25,000, a level paralleled among English counties only by Westmorland and Huntingdonshire. Even these unimpressive levels were recorded at the end of a period of rapid growth. In 1500, the population was only some 200,000, probably little more than before the Black Death. This figure then began a steep rise, to perhaps 230,000 in 1550, 317,000 in 1601, and to almost 400,000 by 1650: estimates vary considerably.

Of course, there were major fluctuations within these limits, but the general direction was clear. Between 1540 and 1640, the average rate of increase was 6.3 per cent per decade; though between 1561 and 1586, growth exceeded 10 per cent in each decade, almost equal to the extraordinary rates achieved during the nineteenth century. Growth was especially rapid in Gwynedd under the Tudors and early Stuarts, reflecting the colonisation of new lands. The rate of increase then slowed after the civil war years, and the early eighteenth century figure may well have fallen below that of 1650. The pace of growth soon resumed. The population was about 480,000 in 1750, and it can reliably be fixed around 587,000 in 1801.

THE GEOGRAPHICAL CONTEXT

Wales has survived as a distinctive linguistic and cultural entity despite immediate proximity to expansive and often hostile neighbours. At its broadest point, it is little more than 100 miles from the

English border to the western sea, but that short distance includes some forbidding and inaccessible territory. The country is a protuberance from western Britain which features at its heart a rugged central upland massif. About 60 per cent of the country is above the 500 foot level, and a quarter is over 1000 feet. The Cambrian mountains cover some two-thirds of the area of Wales, and in the north they rise to steep peaks. In the centre and south, the range becomes flatter, and it is characterised by large plateaux cut deeply by valleys. In this Welsh heartland, the uplands are marked by 'rich pastures, grassy plains, and forbidding bogs', where mean annual rainfall exceeds 60 inches. For much of the period covered by this book, the Welsh mountains were regarded by most outsiders as undesirable – in fact, repulsive – countryside. Defoe in the 1720s exhausted his vocabulary of horror and disgust on the relatively slight hills of south Wales, and could find no words adequate to describe a monstrosity like Cader Idris. Not until the late eighteenth century would tourists begin to see positive features in such a landscape.

This monstrous heart would for centuries be the preservation of Wales and its language, but of course, Wales was more than hills. Around the mountainous core are a number of lowland regions of varying fertility and prosperity, including important coastal plains and river valleys. In addition, this small land has over 600 miles of coastline, offering abundant opportunities for trade and communication; but also presenting the threat of seaborne incursions. To understand the nature of Wales, we must therefore begin with the mountains; but we must also appreciate the other regions clustering around the fringes of the mountains like islands around an ocean.

The geographical contrast would have powerful social implications, as the upland areas so often provided the basis for dismissive accounts of Welsh backwardness and poverty. Pre-industrial Wales is thus seen as an isolated and primitive backwater. It was 'a pastoral economy, freckled with sleepy market towns' and some industrial villages; '. . . the province was in the hands of a native hayseed squirearchy'.[1] This picture of remoteness and stagnation is by no means a modern invention. Many English writers of the seventeenth and eighteenth centuries have left accounts which support this view of a benighted and impoverished land, isolated from the civilised (that is, English) world by its Celtic speech. Of course, this critique had in part a political and religious bias, as Anglican Tory Wales was

1. Roy Porter, *English society in the eighteenth century* (Penguin 1982).

thus stigmatised for its apparently backward and superstitious loyalism. When Methodist and Evangelical movements arose, they found useful this characterisation of the *ancien régime*. The portrayal of Wales as primitive also appealed to later Romantics, delighted to find noble savages and unspoiled landscape so conveniently close to home.

The poverty of Wales also seems confirmed from the evidence of taxation, where very low assessments were common.[2] In 1691, the whole of Wales produced only £5700, of which an eighth came from the three shires of Gwynedd. Of the taxable wealth 55 per cent was to be found in the four shires of the southern coast, together with Breconshire. To place this in context, the southern counties appear less desperately poor than the northern, but they were still humble compared to English shires. Glamorgan was the richest county, with an assessment greater than the whole of Gwynedd; but even so, it was only equal to that of northern English shires like Northumberland. North Wales counties found their closest parallels in the wealth attributed not to English shires, but to individual cities like Exeter and Chester.

THE PASTORAL UPLANDS

There was an extensive satirical literature on the beggarly 'Taffy', remote in his mountain fastnesses, surviving on cheese and leeks, surrounded by goats and unpronounceable names. Confirmation of such an account came for instance from the land between Tregaron and Builth, 'for the most part pasture, mountainous, heathy, rocky, barren; but breeds great plenty of good sheep'.[3] Inventories even show the popularity of non-wheeled forms of transport like sleds and sleighs, necessitated by the lack of good road transport. The sparsely populated uplands were also areas of weak administration and control, as is suggested by the vast parishes that prevailed here. The average size of Wales' 850 parishes was roughly 6000 acres, but some were far larger than this. This table gives nineteenth century acreages, but the essential picture had changed little for centuries:

2. Sir Walter Scott, ed. *The Somers Collection of Tracts* (London 1809–1820), x, 596–597.

3. The account of agrarian life and rural society is derived from volumes four and five of Joan Thirsk, ed., *The agrarian history of England and Wales*.

19

Table 2:1 The Large Upland Parishes

County	Parish	Acres
Denbigh	Henllan	14,334
	Llanfair Talhaiarn	11,114
	Tir yr Abad Isaf	11,264
Merioneth	Llandrillo	28,200
Caernarvon	Beddgelert	26,716
	Llandegai	15,477
	Penmachno	13,000
Montgomery	Llangurig	50,000
Radnor	Llansantffraed	32,000
Glamorgan	Cadoxton juxta Neath	31,155
	Ystradyfodwg	24,515
Monmouth	Bedwellty	16,210
	Mynyddislwyn	15,938
Brecon	Merthyr Cynog	21,278
Cardigan	Caron	39,138
	Llanfihangel Geneu'r Glyn	30,136
	Llanbadarn Fawr	52,420
Carmarthen	Llanfair ar y Bryn	23,567
	Llandeilo Fawr	26,000
	Llangadog	23,472

This rather arbitrary list provides a remarkable picture. Three huge
Cardiganshire parishes took up a total area of almost 190 square
miles, while Llangurig covered almost 80. By the nineteenth
century, some of these huge areas were experiencing rapid industrial
and urban growth; but in earlier times they were little populated. In
the 1560s, most such parishes had only 40 or 50 households, with
perhaps 200 individuals. Llangurig had 60 households, Beddgelert
52, Llandegai only 32. Even in the nineteenth century, Llangadog
had only 2600 people.

Trawsfynydd in Merionethshire suggests the economic implications of this barren and depopulated setting. This was a remote and
desolate landscape, a parish that spread over 20 square miles, with
only 70 households in 1563. Even in the twentieth century, it
remained so desolate that it was felt to be an appropriate site for a
nuclear power station. In the 1690s, a report on its economy found
'oats the grain generally sown, some rye and barley'.[4] There were
800 cattle, 2000 lambs, 100 goats and 100 horses. The people were
'used to hard labour and a milk diet'. Travel and communications

4. Joan Thirsk ed., The agrarian history of England and Wales (Cambridge 1967), iv,
116.

20

were appalling. Society was organised on comparatively simple lines, with few tradesmen or professionals, and no local residents who would qualify as gentlemen by English standards of wealth or standard of living. Settlements were usually isolated farmhouses, perhaps with occasional nucleated hamlets. In the severe winters which characterised the 1690s, snows might cause dramatic losses among sheep herds, which made agricultural survival even more tenuous.

LOWLAND COMMUNITIES

But Trawsfynydd was only one aspect of Wales, the extreme face of the stock-raising pastoral uplands. As we have already seen in the case of Ogmore, there was much else to the Welsh economy. In south Pembrokeshire, for example, we find the hundred of Castlemartin, noted by George Owen as yielding

the best and finest grain and most abundance, a country of itself naturally fit and apt for corn, having lime, sand, weed of the sea, and divers other principal helps to better the soil, where need is; this country yieldeth the best wheat and the greatest store.[5]

Defoe found little good to say about much of Wales, but of south Pembrokeshire he remarked that 'this part is so pleasant and fertile and is so well cultivated that 'tis called by distinction, Little England, beyond Wales.'

There were several regions which bore closer resemblance to Castlemartin or Ogmore than to Trawsfynydd. Parishes here were likely to cover 3000 acres or less, markedly different from the upland communities of four or five times this size. Their geographical location provided them with relatively good communications – by road, but also by sea through the numerous small ports which dotted the coastline. There were areas of mixed agriculture like Anglesey, known as 'the Mother of Wales' for its wheat exports. Camden found in the Vale of Clwyd not merely green meadows and yellow cornfields but 'fair houses standing thick'. By the late seventeenth century, such areas were reporting an impressive mixture of products: wheat, barley, oats; plenty of bread and malting corn for local needs, and probably a surplus for sale; as well as peas and

5. H. Owen ed., *George Owen's description of Pembrokeshire* (Honourable Society of Cymmrodorion 1892).

beans. No less than 14 of Wales' 60 market towns specialised in the sale of corn, including Brecon, Builth, Presteigne, Tenby and Denbigh. Land was often 'good for corn, pasture and hay', with excellent grazing for cattle and sheep.

In individual terms, the hill country might be symbolised by a man like David ap Griffith of Dolwyddelan (Caernarvonshire), who died about 1635. He left a solid inheritance of £40, mainly comprising herds of 28 cattle and 28 sheep as well as two horses. This was a typical upland inventory, and it contrasts sharply with the property of a Denbighshire contemporary like Magdalen Puleston of Gresford, whose goods (1606) included cattle, sheep, pigs, poultry and horses; but also rye, wheat, barley, oats, malt, vetches, peas, buckwheat and hemp.[6]

Against the sort of landscape and economy associated with Dolwyddelan or Llangurig, we might also consider a central Monmouthshire farm of *c.* 1700, that of William Prichard of Place Evor, which lay between Abergavenny and Monmouth. The property included 294 acres, distributed as follows[7]

Type of land	Percentage of farm
arable	60
pasture	20
meadow	7
woodland	8
apple orchards	3
clover	2

In southern Monmouthshire, there was a rich mixed agriculture based on fertile arable soils, and rich grazing, with meadows on reclaimed salt marshes.

Economic differences were reflected in demographic patterns. Average population density for Wales as a whole was about 40 per square mile in 1600, rising to 73 in 1801. However, richer mixed farming areas might have between 50 and 70 people per square mile in the seventeenth century. This was the figure for Castlemartin, and similar densities may be found in hundreds like Painscastle (Radnorshire), Dinas Powis (Glamorgan), Mold (Flintshire) or Creuddyn (Caernarvonshire). At the opposite extreme were upland

6. Thirsk, *Agrarian history*, iv, 132–139.
7. Joan Thirsk ed., *The agrarian history of England and Wales* (Cambridge 1984) v, 1, 413.

hundreds with 10 to 20 people per square mile. Such were Defynnog in Breconshire, Nantconwy in Caernarvonshire, Ardudwy in Merionethshire (the last of these contained Trawsfynydd).

RURAL SOCIETY

The sixteenth century marked a fundamental division in the legal and social structures which shaped rural life. In the middle ages, manorial farming had prevailed in parts of the south and border country, while a tribal-based land system could be found through much of Wales. In the latter, families shared common lands, but also had *cytir* rights which entitled them to a portion in pastures, woods and water. From the fifteenth century, parts of the clanlands increasingly fell into the sole possession of individuals and families. There was also a decline in the system of seasonal movement or transhumance. Summer settlements (*hafod* pl. *hafotai*) now became permanent residences, and there were encroachments on the hill pastures and open moorlands beyond. Demand for grazing land became acute as population grew in the sixteenth century, and the cattle trade developed in scale. The crises and depopulation of the fifteenth century had far-reaching effects in the manorial lowlands. As in the hills, land tended to become more widely available, and traditional structures were disrupted. Bond hamlets were broken up, demesne land was leased, villein holdings were abandoned.

From the early sixteenth century, there was a general movement to absolute possession on the English model, and the creation of substantial consolidated estates. This accelerated after the Acts of Union abolished *cyfran* (gavelkind), the partible inheritance of lands. Legislation could not entirely shape local practices, and we find gavelkind common well into the seventeenth century, in Builth, in Gower, even in manors around Monmouth and Abergavenny; but the trend was clear. Through purchase and exchange, enterprising landowners consolidated separated and hitherto uneconomic units, and were able to pass these holdings intact to their heirs. There was also extensive colonisation and settlement of new lands, in the barren uplands (*ffridd* land), as well as the fringes of the sea. *Ffridd* land that technically belonged to the lords became thoroughly confused with *cytir*, and was thus claimed by local freeholders.

Claiming new land could be regarded as socially useful work, but the century after 1560 also witnessed much conflict over the extent of the nationwide assault on common land and waste. Much of the process went unrecorded, but the records of the Council in the Marches permit us an unusually detailed insight into the enclosure battles before 1640. Typical was the effort by a new gentry family, the Williams' of Llangibby, to seize common lands at Trefgrug in Monmouthshire, thus excluding some 800 freehold tenants. The war continued throughout the reigns of Elizabeth and James I, culminating in a gentry victory through the use of force in the 1620s. Such encroachments were regularly met with vigorous opposition, by riots that involved the destruction of fences and gates. This was especially likely when the encloser was a newcomer with not even the shadow of a claim on local obedience or sentiment. This was the background to the opposition to the enclosures by the Earl of Leicester in Denbighshire in the 1560s; and to the efforts of Thomas Myddelton to improve his new estate at Chirk after 1595.

In the early eighteenth century, Ellis Wynne summarised a long tradition of social criticism when he asked, 'What is the tailor who steals a piece of cloth besides the great man who, out of the mountain, steals the half of a parish?'. Enclosure was thus the most egregious of the many sins committed by the wealthy against the wider community:

> We remember hardly one estate not founded by some oppressor or murderer or arrant thief, leaving it to others as oppressive as themselves, or to lazy blockheads or drunken swine. And to maintain their prodigal pride, vassals and tenants must be crushed.[8]

But the process was more complex than might appear from the endless suits and petitions. Landed estates became bigger, and below them, so did the farms of their tenants. In lowland Monmouthshire or Glamorgan, a normal seventeenth century farm might be 30 to 50 acres, in contrast to a medieval villein holding of only 14 or so. In the uplands, farms of 40 to 100 acres were common. Such substantial holdings lent themselves to rationalised land use, and enclosed fields became common in the lowlands by the late sixteenth century. Enclosure and encroachment were thus the work of all classes, including cottagers. Especially in the upland regions, there was a strong tradition of *ty unnos*, by which cottagers established rights to common land by building a dwelling and lighting a fire in the span of a single night; and the practice remained common into Victorian

8. Ellis Wynne, *The dream of the sleeping bard* translated by T.Gwynn Jones, (Gregynog Press, 1940), 134–135.

times. Obviously, some outrageous abuses were committed in the process of encroachment, but enclosure as such was not at fault.

TENURE

Historically, freehold tenures were common in Wales, especially in upland regions; but manorial survivals in the south meant that there were many copyholders in the more fertile regions of mixed agriculture. In the coastal plain, manors usually included a mixture of freeholders, copyholders and leaseholders. In the seventeenth and eighteenth centuries, freeholders of manors owed dues that were broadly similar to those of copyholders. A farmer holding by 'socage tenure in perpetuity' would pay homage and fealty to the lord; he owed suit of court; and he would pay heriots of the best beast, apart from small money rents. Customary tenants would owe the same obligations, as well as fines on admission to tenure. They would have to grind at the lord's mill, and even owed labour services connected with the upkeep and repair of the mill.

This gives a rather archaic feel to documents portraying Welsh agriculture as late as the early nineteenth century. Under the Stuarts, the records of manorial courts and surveys almost suggest the conditions of the high middle ages, even to the survival of the ancient division between Welsh and Norman zones, the 'Welshry' and the 'fforenry' ('foreignry'); and this is as true of Monmouthshire as of west or north Wales. Squires held their position as manorial lords, often controlling several manors with their attendant courts and feudal structure. Individual manors also differed in their farming practices, and intense localism prevailed. One of the nightmares for the historian of the period is the very diverse nature of the weights and measures used throughout early modern Wales, where local equivalents of acres and bushels were used. In Monmouthshire, the old Welsh *cyfar* ('cover') was used to measure land into the eighteenth century.

From the seventeenth century at least, landlords attempted to transform customary tenures into leases, but these often incorporated many of the old dues. Leases specified for example that tenants would pay food rents, and even labour services. These were often commuted by the eighteenth century, but there is no doubt that they were far more than legal fictions when originally conceived. Some leases even require the payment of cymorthas, unofficial taxation bordering on blatant extortion, that had been specifically forbidden by the Acts of Union.

Though essentially similar, copyhold tenure did not give the right to vote, and there was a great temptation for landlords to transform their tenures into leasehold when they needed an infusion of voters at the time of a contested election. In addition, customary tenants were not permitted to exploit minerals found under their lands. This posed a problem in areas such as Gower or east Carmarthenshire, where coal rights might be enormously profitable. For lords and their tenants, it was essential to defend manorial privileges, and there were constant battles to prevent encroachments on the commons by unauthorised making of bricks or burning of lime. The building of cottages was particularly contentious, as industrial enterprises attracted workers who found homes by squatting on common or waste land.

By the early seventeenth century, there was essentially a four-fold division in rural society. At the top of the pyramid were the gentry, the *uchelwyr*, of whom more in the next chapter. This class shaded imperceptibly into the yeomen, the better-off farmers whose main sphere of action and influence lay at the level of the parish. The great majority of the population were husbandmen, ordinary farmers; and beneath them were labourers and servants. There were also paupers, into whose ranks the husbandmen and labourers would fall on occasion.

These broad divisions were found throughout Wales, though as we might expect, regional distinctions were pronounced. In housing, the chief division was between the pastoral uplands and the regions of arable and mixed farming. There was also an east-west division, resulting from the relative strength of English influences; and of course, another factor was the availability of building materials. Two extremes might be cited. In the Vale of Glamorgan, the presence of fine building stone permitted the building of quite excellent limewashed rural cottages and farmhouses from the early seventeenth century, and the tradition often drew favourable remark from later travellers. A Glamorgan yeoman almost certainly lived in considerably greater comfort than many a gentle contemporary in a county like Cardiganshire or north Carmarthenshire, where the 'great rebuilding' in permanent materials can be dated to the railway age. In the central borderlands, meanwhile – in the counties of Montgomery or Brecon – half-timbered houses of great quality were commonplace.

IMPROVEMENT

Feudal survivals would often be accused of hindering agricultural progress. In stock-breeding, the practice of seizing the best beast naturally acted as a disincentive to improvement. But the archaic character of legal arrangements certainly did not imply that rural society in Wales was unusually primitive. As we will see, the rural economy was a complex affair with a strong market orientation, and Welsh agriculture was remarkably open to improvement, notably in the most traditionally 'manorial' areas of the south and borders. This resulted from the close economic ties with English regions in the south-west and west midlands. Practices were imported, became popular, and would be disseminated by landlords and their stewards. The great landed estates of the south were often headed by individual gentlemen who looked favourably on new methods, and they had the capital to indulge their enthusiasms. In the north too, there were progressive farmers like Henry Rowlands of Llanidan in Anglesey, who explored the new methods in the proposed book *Idea Agriculturae* (1704).

One problem throughout the period was the lack of winter fodder for the cattle who were so fundamental a part of the local economy. In Welsh, the month of November still bears the name *Tachwedd*, from the general 'slaughter' that occurred at that time. From the sixteenth century, it became common throughout south Wales to use lime as a fertiliser, which improved grazing, and permitted the use of new grasses. Denbighshire and Flintshire followed a little later. Clover was much used after the Restoration, while in the eighteenth century, the southern coastal counties experimented extensively with sown grasses like sainfoin and lucerne. Already in the mid-seventeenth century, Bristol imported its turnips from south Wales; but it would be another century before the crop entered common use, through the encouragement of the influential agricultural societies. The Breconshire society established in 1755 marked a major step towards the progressive restructuring of Welsh agriculture. It was turnips which provided the long-needed winter fodder. New grasses and rotations allowed improvements in arable farming, and south Wales became a significant corn exporter by the 1660s.

Progress can be measured in terms of the new crops, but more significant in the long run may have been the administrative and managerial changes of the century after 1660. Estate stewards often achieved a high degree of professionalism, and sought to improve estates by consolidating holdings, promoting larger farms, and by encouraging the use of leases. They were aided in this by the stabilisation or decline of population, which promoted a concentration of landownership.

DEFENDING THE LAND

The enclosure of common lands also played some part in this era of improvement, but less so than in parts of England. The enclosure of much of the wealthier south had been undertaken before 1640, leaving little conflict for the eighteenth century. The acquisition of enclosed land benefited some estates; but for much of Wales, the real danger was that this new land would not be exceeded by the loss of other land to sea and sand. In the sixteenth and seventeenth centuries, this was largely a losing battle; and in the eighteenth, land reclamation and coastal defence were of great interest to the improvers. It is often easy to forget how vulnerable much of Wales was to coastal incursions. There were several regions where folk tales told of lost lands once overwhelmed by the sea: in Swansea Bay, off the northern coast, and most dramatically, in Cardigan Bay, where the tale was confirmed by sunken forests. As John Wesley observed, 'Nay, it is not at all improbable that formerly it was dry land from Aberystwyth to St David's Point'.[9]

Throughout the early modern period, frequent floods and incursions struck the lowlands, and thus the most prosperous areas. In 1607, southern Monmouthshire fell prey to a flood which devastated 26 parishes, and killed hundreds. Much further inland, heavy rains might also cause a river to flood, with lethal consequences. Less dramatic, but more harmful in the long run, was the regular invasion of sand and dunes in areas like south-western Anglesey, west Glamorgan and south Carmarthenshire. The ruins of the medieval borough of Kenfig were a striking monument to the danger that threatened if coastal defences were not maintained. We can only speculate about the impact that the battle with the sea may have had on the minds of men and women. At the least, it encouraged a continual sense of vulnerability to nature and providence, and discouraged any belief in the possibility of progress.

Reclamation and coastal defence were constant preoccupations from monastic times, but it was only in the eighteenth century that

9. A.H. Williams, ed., *John Wesley in Wales* (Cardiff: University of Wales, 1971), 94.

decisive progress was made. In the north, the most visible triumph occurred in the old Traeth Mawr that separated the counties of Caernarvon and Merioneth; and where there now appeared a whole reclaimed landscape, centred on the new town of Tremadoc. At the end of the century, the coastal shipping routes were protected by the building of lighthouses, part of the same atmosphere of 'improvement', that had become almost a general ideology.

Further from the coasts, this was also the age in which the area of workable land was extended into what had once been inaccessible uplands. The high farm prices after 1793 provoked an enclosure boom, and the massive exploitation of marginal lands. This is the period that marks the rapid colonisation of the heartland:[10]

Table 2:2 The Process of Enclosure

Date	Number of Awards	Acreage enclosed (thousands)
1730–1792	18	35
1793–1815	85	213
1816–1845	26	12
1846–1885	102	121

Between 1793 and 1815, a minimum of 59,000 acres was enclosed in Montgomeryshire, 40,000 in Breconshire, 23,000 in Caernarvonshire, 20,000 in Cardiganshire. Though not as dramatic as the contemporary growth of industry, this expansion of inhabitable Wales was of enormous importance for rural society.

TRADE AND INDUSTRIES

Developments like these remind us that the Welsh countryside was not a complete backwater: this was in many ways a dynamic society. This is also indicated by the trading and commercial activities which linked local communities with major provincial towns. Welsh localities were increasingly integrated into the wider economy, with its structure of cash and credit. Industrial development began early, and contributed to making a diverse and powerful economy. Mineral

10. Colin Thomas, 'Colonization, enclosure and the rural landscape', *NLW Journal* 19 (1975) 132–146.

exploitation dated back to the middle ages, but accelerated sharply between 1560 and 1630. There were ironworks at Pontypool and Wrexham, brass and wire works at Tintern; coal was mined in Flintshire and west Glamorgan; slate quarried in Caernarvonshire; copper was smelted at Neath. Under James I, Hugh Myddelton emerged as the precursor of the Welsh industrialists of a later day, with his coal enterprises in the north-east, and his exploitation of the lead and silver of Cardiganshire. When reserves of timber began to be depleted, it was found that coal could be used for smelting most ores, with the important exception of iron; but that problem would be resolved after 1700. The enterprises were often tiny in scale, and some were ephemeral, but every region of Wales was affected to some extent. We will examine this in much greater detail in chapter eleven. At this point, we will just note that industrial development reached a new scale and sophistication under the later Stuarts.

TRADE AND SHIPPING

The commercial orientation of most of rural Wales is suggested by the extensive trading networks and the abundance of fairs and markets. In the Elizabethan period, there were over 240 fairs in Wales, and it was said that there was a fair somewhere in the country four days of each week. As so often appears, the south was much more prosperous and economically active, with almost 60 per cent of the fairs in the southern coastal shires, together with Cardigan. Northern fairs were fewer, but some (like Machynlleth) were very large, and served an enormous rural area. About 1600, the four counties of the south coast also had half the weekly market days.

The Welsh coasts were dotted with numerous small ports or creeks which participated in a lively trade with other regions of Wales, or with English towns. About 1780, Iolo Morganwg wrote of his home county of Glamorgan:

> There are many harbours on the coast, the most frequented are those of Rumney Bridge, Cardiff, Penarth, Sully, Barry, Aberthaw, Newton, Aberafan, Briton Ferry and Neath, Swansea, Port Eynon, Burry etc. Most of these places trade with Bristol etc and Swansea and Neath with London etc, and being so frequent on the coast afford a cheap conveyance of corn, coal, butter etc outwards and of whatever they want inwards.[11]

11. G.J. Williams, *Iolo Morganwg* (Cardiff 1956), I, 30.

Aberthaw in particular had a substantial trade with Minehead. Pembrokeshire had famous ports at Pembroke, Tenby and Haverfordwest. Between 1550 and 1750, there are records of coastal shipping using Fishguard, Newport, St Dogmaels, Abercastle, Dinas, Solva, and Porthclais. Milford Haven had 'sixteen creeks, five bays and thirteen roads'. Around Cardigan Bay, the coastal trade in the eighteenth century was felt to be so profitable as to justify the creation of a new planned town at Aberaeron. In Caernarvonshire too, ships could be found at a dozen locations besides Caernarvon itself. Shipping on the coastal routes was usually small, rarely over 40 tons. Anything over 100 tons was sufficiently noteworthy to be thought fit for ventures further afield, to France or Ireland.

Some of the ports had a specialised trade, but most carried the general produce of neighbouring farms for sale in some convenient town. In the south, this meant Bristol above all, and cattle and wool were the main items in the sixteenth century. Corn was a leading item of trade by the 1650s, reflecting the progress of agricultural improvement in the region. In the seventeenth and eighteenth centuries, these ships often carried dairy produce, notably butter and cheese, and Bristol continued to serve as a major market for Welsh farmers into Victorian times. In the north, Chester and Liverpool exercised a similar magnetic attraction for local enterprise until the railways ended these ancient coastal links.

Throughout Wales, the wool trade was of great importance from the middle ages into the early nineteenth century. From the fourteenth century, the technology of the water-wheel had been applied to power fulling mills. This use of water exploited a resource that Wales was known to possess in large quantity, and such mills (*pandy*, plural *pandai*) became common features in the landscape. The industry boomed, as a suitable activity for a society based on isolated homesteads, where every family member could participate in the process of production and preparation for sale. It was also crucial for fully exploiting the labour of girls and women. By the sixteenth century, there was an elaborate structure of spinners, weavers, dyers, fullers, tuckers and knitters.

At first, the wool trade was a southern speciality, but in the sixteenth century, the guilds of towns like Carmarthen attempted to dominate production. The industry thereupon moved to north and mid-Wales, to Merionethshire, Montgomeryshire and parts of Denbighshire. By the later sixteenth century, control of Welsh wool production was firmly in the hands of the drapers of Shrewsbury; and for the next two centuries, market day in that town would

31

resemble a Welsh invasion. The Huguenot settlement in the 1680s assisted the growth of industrial centres at Newtown, Llanidloes and Dolgellau. Some areas had their own specialities, like the stockings of Merionethshire, which found their outlet in the local market at Bala. Montgomeryshire was a flannel centre. The wool trade supported many local fairs and markets, as well as minor industrial centres like Caerphilly and Bridgend.

Apart from wool, the major trading activity of the Welsh interior was in livestock. Welsh horses were much sought after; but it was the activities of the cattle-drovers which brought the local economy what little cash it ever saw. In seventeenth century Caernarvonshire, the drovers brought 'the Spanish fleet of Wales, which brings hither the little gold and silver we have'. Northern drovers used routes through the Wrexham and Chester areas; mid-Wales herds crossed near Shrewsbury; the southern drove routes generally entered England through Herefordshire.

The drovers were able to use their access to a cash economy to act as moneylenders and bankers for the surrounding community. In Carmarthenshire and Breconshire, official banking activity from the end of the eighteenth century owed its origins to the activity of the drovers. This is neatly symbolised by the name of the Black Ox bank at Llandovery (1799). Hides provided the basis for a substantial leather industry in south Wales, in towns like Swansea, Cardiff and Brecon. In Tudor times, leather was much in demand for furniture, while saddles were a perennial product.

The archetypal inhabitant of Stuart Wales would be a hill farmer. Many thousands fitted this description, but the reality of Welsh society was much more complex. The range of agricultural activities was far wider than the emphasis on the pastoral zones might suggest; and there were other more specialised groups, like miners, quarrymen and workers in the smelting industries. There were drovers and sailors, weavers and drapers, tanners and saddlers, schoolmasters and alehouse keepers. Throughout Wales, there were also miscellaneous craftsmen like smiths, carpenters and masons, who would frequently be represented among the leaders of Welsh culture and religious dissent. A glance at the pages of the *Dictionary of Welsh Biography* will soon produce numerous examples of the eighteenth or nineteenth century craftsman or drover who earned fame as a poet or preacher, often both. It was a Glamorgan stonemason named Edward Williams, *Iolo Morganwg*, who launched a revolution in the study of Welsh culture and antiquities.

An individual might become involved in several occupations during an average lifetime, and might either rise or fall in the process. One vital source for this is a remarkable and little used diary kept between 1762 and 1794 by a Glamorgan schoolmaster, William Thomas. He provided vignettes of hundreds of his plebeian contemporaries, and frequently describes careers which alternated between village craftsmanship, petty enterprise, and outright vagabondage. Some also had sidelines in preaching or (surprisingly often) magic and conjuring. How for example can we classify Thomas of Llanharry, who died in 1767

> a religious self-conceited man, walking here and there in fairs, exhorting people as a preacher in churchyards on Sunday evenings and about houses singing some scriptural songs of his own composing, of a very strong memory in scripture, but gave himself to a fugitive life, almost naked, working rough straw work, being but a slothful sort of a man.

A similarly varied career is recorded of Thomas Edwards (*Twm o'r Nant* 1739–1810), a celebrated author, promoter and actor in the dramatic 'interludes' that were so popular throughout late Georgian Wales. He earned money by these efforts, as well as by poems that were presented at the eisteddfodau of the 1790s; but he was anything but a full-time professional writer. By trade, Twm was a timber hauler and carter, but problems with debt caused him to flee his native Denbighshire for south Wales. While never giving up the hauling business, he ran a tollgate on one of the numerous turnpike roads, and built an alehouse to support his daughters. He became a stonemason, learned bricklaying, and ventured into the construction and upkeep of iron stoves and ovens; 'and not unfrequently I have practised as a smoke doctor'. About 1808, he was employed in the land reclamation projects around Portmadoc.

All social groups might well alternate between such activities and spells in farming. Well into the mid-nineteenth century, with a slate boom in progress, many Gwynedd quarrymen would take time off to maintain their smallholdings. It was also likely that many farmers and other workers would find themselves in need of poor relief during extreme crises like those of the mid-1690s, 1727–1731 or of 1739–1741. They thus became 'paupers' for at least part of their lives. There were also the chronic poor, abundant in the years of population expansion after 1540, less so by the eighteenth century. Even so, it is in the mid-eighteenth century that we hear of the *bobl gerdded*, the 'walking people', 'a set of vagabonds {who} used to traverse the country, begging with impunity to the disgrace of the

33

law of the land'.[12] In the 1670s, roughly a third of the population throughout Wales was regarded as too poor to be expected to pay the hearth tax; and were thus, at least technically, 'paupers'.

TOWNS

This was essentially a rural society. In 1550, there were at most four towns with 2000 people or more. Even by 1801, there were only 12 in this category, and the largest community in Wales had less than 8000 people.

In 1550, there were over 50 towns in Wales, but we reach this figure only by including communities with two or three hundred people. Using more exacting standards, we find only 12 towns with a thousand people or more, a small increase from the nine which met this criterion in 1400. The largest communities were Carmarthen, Wrexham, Brecon and Haverfordwest, all of which had lengthy histories and proud corporate traditions. Haverfordwest had eight guilds in the sixteenth century, including glovers, feltmakers, tailors and saddlers. Between 1569 and 1583, nine guilds incorporated in Carmarthen. All the towns were important as regional centres serving an agricultural hinterland. In Brecon, this pastoral environment reflected in the town's trades: in 1664, tanners, curriers and related crafts made up 37 per cent of the tradesmen, followed by tuckers, weavers and dyers (27 per cent). Denbigh had an abundance of tanners, corvisors and glovers.

There were perhaps another seven centres with 1000 or more people. These were Tenby, Swansea, Cardiff, Kidwelly, Monmouth, Caernarfon, and Denbigh. Of the 11 largest towns, seven were thus in the southern shires, and six of these relied on the Bristol Channel trade for their survival. We find another three in the far north. There were few centres in the heartland, which looked to the English midlands.

The fortunes of the towns fluctuated over time. By the mid-eighteenth century, the leading towns of Wales were still the four that had held this position in 1550, though their populations had now swelled somewhat to 3000 or so. In addition, new centres were challenging the old. Wrexham was displacing Denbigh, while

12. A.J. Johnes, *An essay on the causes which have produced dissent from the established Church in Wales* (London 1832).

Brecon was giving way to Glamorgan communities like Swansea; and the metal industries were supporting the rise of Aberystwyth to dominate Cardigan Bay. In mid-Wales, Dolgellau was prospering on the strength of the wool trade. But there certainly had not been dramatic urban growth before the 1790s: even the larger conglomerations were scarcely cities, and to speak of any 'urban' history in Wales prior to the nineteenth century is perhaps to misuse the term. Even if we include the very small towns (200 people or more), the 'urban' proportion of the population of Wales at this time was barely 11 per cent. It is likely that the Welsh town population was little greater in the early eighteenth century than 400 years previously.

Despite their small size, the towns had a considerable impact on the surrounding regions. This is apparent in religious matters, where towns like Carmarthen, Cardiff and Haverfordwest were long the only centres where definite Protestant teaching had made much headway. This was in large part a reflection of Bristol influence. In the 1560s, it may have been the Carmarthen merchant and tanner Humphrey Toy who financed the publication of the first Welsh translation of the New Testament and Prayer Book. In the civil war, the parliamentarian loyalty of Pembroke, Tenby and Haverfordwest made Pembrokeshire oppose the King, with serious consequences for the Royalist war effort throughout Wales. Puritan sympathies will be discussed below, but there was a long tradition that associated 'fanaticism' with towns and tradesmen. In 1687, a satire on one of James II's new Dissenting Justices concluded:

> What say you to see
> Such fellows as he
> To act where did men of renown?
> I think you had rather
> To see him still gather
> The calves skins about Swansea town[13]

Also, these relatively small communities supported an influential social elite. The nature of social hierarchy is suggested by the case of Neath under Charles II, where there were some 212 households, perhaps 900 people in all. Of these families 120 lived in small houses with only one hearth, and this included most of those judged too poor to pay the hearth tax. Only 16 households had five or more hearths. The poor were chiefly to be found in Water Street, while High Street was a prestigious area containing nine of the largest

---

13. Philip Jenkins, 'Two poems on the Glamorgan Gentry', *NLW Journal* 21 (1979) 159–178.

houses.[14] The elite of such a town was largely made up of tradesmen. In Haverfordwest, testamentary evidence in the early seventeenth century suggests that the wealthiest citizens included mercers, tailors, glovers, butchers and merchants, as well as a general category listed simply as 'aldermen'.[15]

There was also a strong gentry contingent. Many of the greater gentry maintained town houses, for example the establishments of the Herberts and Matthews in Cardiff; and sometimes, a town was dominated by a mansion or castle, as at Montgomery. The Plas Mawr in Conway (built by a Wynn of Gwydir) is one of the few surviving examples of these town houses, which could be quite imposing. Younger sons were likely to be found in the nearby boroughs. In early Stuart Haverfordwest, we find scions of the local gentry like the Bowens and Voyles. William Walter was the younger son of the Walters of Roch, and became Mayor of Haverfordwest under Elizabeth. His son Roger Walter was thrice Mayor, and left £689 on his death in 1626, the largest estate in the town at this period. There were many in the towns described as 'gentlemen', some well-born, others being upwardly mobile professional or commercial families.

One such was the Gibbs family of Neath. In the century before 1540, they had been active in coal exploitation. Under Charles I, two sons attended the Inns of Court, and John Gibbs was an active lawyer in mid-century. His nephew Marmaduke Gibbs was spectacularly successful: a lawyer, he served most of the great Whiggish families of Glamorgan in the 1670s and 1680s. He acquired a landed estate, and moved the family home from plebeian Water Street to genteel High Street. Marmaduke Gibbs was a Justice, a deputy-lieutenant and a Welsh judge; and only demographic accident prevented him from establishing his family among the gentry elite.

The Welsh towns were small, and politically controlled by the local gentry. On the other hand, there were still opportunities for professional and commercial families to gain great wealth and power within this apparently restricting framework. In fact, gentry politics created opportunities for such groups, who were usually associated with the towns. The lords and squires needed stewards to run their estates, they needed financial and legal advisers, and it was common for these professional groups to become rich on the strength of this service. The intense party conflicts that were endemic from the later

14. Philip Jenkins, 'The Gibbs family', *Morgannwg*, 25 (1981) 100–111. 15.
15. B.G. Charles, ed., *Calendar of the records of the borough of Haverfordwest*, (Cardiff: Board of Celtic Studies 1967).

seventeenth century placed a new premium on the wealth and expertise of these town allies, especially in matters affecting elections. Successful gentry factions needed the support of prominent families, like the Wells', Purcells and Richards' in Cardiff.

From the early eighteenth century, these local elites combined with neighbouring gentry in developing the social facilities of the provincial towns, which became centres of leisure and cultural life. Commonly, the towns would promote horse races, balls and assemblies. They might acquire theatres, book societies, substantial inns, rebuilt or improved town halls and public buildings. Montgomery offers a good surviving instance of the degree of provincial elegance that now became possible. This general improvement was partly a result of greater familiarity with London and its fashionable ways. It was also a response to the greater wealth produced by industrial development in and around towns like Neath, Swansea, Llanelli, Wrexham and Aberystwyth.

A MIDDLE CLASS?

The concept of a 'middle class' is nebulous, and it may be anachronistic before the nineteenth century. On the other hand, there certainly were 'middling' groups in early modern Wales, below the level of the gentry, but richer and more powerful than even the substantial farmers. There were lawyers, stewards and merchants, often (but not inevitably) connected with the towns. During the eighteenth century, they were increasingly likely to prosper from expanding industrial enterprises. In Glamorgan, there were 'rich and proud' attorneys like Anthony Maddocks, whose political support had to be courted by local gentry and even peers.

Most of the more successful, like the Gibbs', attempted to enter the landed elite, but some remained firmly connected with trade. In eighteenth century Anglesey, the central figure in industrial development was the attorney Thomas Williams, whose family established much of the local banking network. In the south, the banking pioneers were the Wilkins family, from a professional house who had for many years produced clergy and lawyers. Terms like 'middle class' might not be appropriate, but professional and 'moneyed' groups did exist; and like the towns they inhabited, their influence was out of proportion to their numbers. Early modern Wales was far from being the simple peasant land of legend.

Appendix to chapter two: population summary[16]

	1545–63	1670	1801	1851	1901	1976
Gwynedd						
Anglesey	9.8	16.2	33.8	57.3	50.6	62.0
Caernarvonshire	14.9	26.2	41.5	87.9	125.7	122.8
Merioneth	10.5	19.4	29.5	38.8	48.9	34.7
Dyfed						
Cardiganshire	17.3	20.0	43.0	70.8	61.1	55.4
Carmarthenshire	34.4	37.2	67.3	110.6	135.3	162.8
Pembrokeshire	20.1	31.5	56.3	94.1	87.9	98.8
Clwyd						
Denbighshire	22.5	40.8	60.3	92.6	131.6	187.8
Flintshire	12.6	22.9	39.6	68.2	81.5	183.7
Powys						
Breconshire	21.2	27.2	32.3	61.5	54.2	52.7
Montgomeryshire	19.0	34.9	48.2	67.3	54.9	43.6
Radnorshire	14.2	16.3	19.1	24.7	23.2	18.7
Gwent						
Monmouthshire	22.6	34.2	45.6	157.4	298.1	462.2
Glamorgan	29.5	49.9	71.5	231.9	859.9	1264.2
Total	248.6	376.7	588.0	1163.1	2012.9	2749.4

16. Population figures before the 1801 census are obviously controversial. The figures given here for 1545–63 and 1670 are taken from the work of Leonard Owen. However, Wrigley and Schofield would suggest rather lower figures – a national total of 220,000 in 1546, rising to 241,000 in 1566, and 393,000 by 1641.

CHAPTER THREE

Yr uchelwyr: the Welsh gentry

The traditional view of the poverty, backwardness and 'otherness' of
Wales was influential in shaping attitudes to the landed elites of the
country, the 'high ones' or *uchelwyr*. It could even be asked whether
Wales had a gentry on anything resembling the English model. The
stereotypical 'Welsh squires' were proverbially poor, but they
puzzled English commentators by their claims to gentility. In the
words of a modern historian, 'claims to gentility inhered in blood,
not necessarily in economic competence'.[1] This tendency was
allegedly reinforced by the practice of partible inheritance, by
allowing frequent subdivisions of already small estates.

A 'Welsh gentleman' might therefore have far less than the
income required to maintain this sort of status in England, but his
descent from noble or even royal stock cemented his position; and he
might well look down on his far richer (but worse descended)
nouveau-riche neighbour. It was the Jacobean genealogist John Jones
of Gellilyfdy who explained in lofty terms the aspirations of the
'gentle', *bonheddig*:

> There is no man admitted by the law to be called *Gûr Bonheddic*, but he
> that paternally descendeth from the kings and princes of this land of
> Britain, for *bonheddic* is as much as *nobilis* in Latin . . . Common persons
> of late years have taken upon them the title of *bonhedd* or generosity, but
> they are not really *bonheddic*, but are so called or termed for fashion's sake
> by reason of their wealth, offices or behaviour which are but transitory
> things and *bonhedd* consisteth in no transitory thing but in a permanent.[2]

1. See for example the work of Major Francis Jones in *Wales in the eighteenth
century* (Swansea: Christopher Davies, 1976).

2. NLW Llanstephan MS 144.

39

In the Wales of 1600, there were thousands who could plausibly claim descent from post-Roman kings or aristocrats like Maelgwn Gwynedd or Meurig ap Tewdrig. The status of *bonheddig* was thus widely diffused in rural society, giving rise to a characteristic egalitarianism of outlook. Generations of intrigued comment on the hill gentry are neatly summarised by Thomas Pennant's description of his visit to a Merionethshire squire about 1780. Among 'a wild horizon of rocks', he found Mr Evan Llwyd of Cwmbychan, eighteenth in descent from Bleddyn ap Cynfyn, who had plotted against William the Conqueror. The Llwyds had for centuries lived in isolated splendour in a characteristically 'ancient seat of a gentleman of Wales', a house little changed for two or three centuries. In a Merionethshire parish like Llanuwchllyn, there were several recognised *uchelwyr* living in one-hearth houses, and owning property essentially indistinguishable from their yeoman neighbours.

Twentieth century Welsh historians have often treated sympathetically this concept of a peculiarly Welsh view of gentility. Francis Jones, for example, stresses the much greater homogeneity that existed between the Welsh squires and their social inferiors, in comparison to England. He attributes this to the survival of the ancient royal and noble families of Wales. Unlike in England, there never was a single catastrophic act of conquest to establish a new ruling class. There had been intruders (*advenae*), but these soon merged with the older stock. Of course, there were 'leviathans' of wealth, like the Bulkeleys of Anglesey or Mostyns of Flintshire, but Wales never had a real local squirearchy on the English model: or at least, not until the late eighteenth century, when the idealised native gentry faded into oblivion. Some squires lost their lands to English or Scottish heirs, who had newer and more commercial attitudes. Others forfeited their Welsh heritage, and became effectively indistinguishable from their new neighbours, the Smiths or Campbells. This portrait of the wealthy landowner as an alien innovation would be a common weapon in the Liberal and nonconformist polemics of the nineteenth century.

The issue of the number and power of local gentry is important because the distribution of powerful landowners had an immense impact on everyday life. Wealthy squires tended to be major employers of rural labour, both agricultural and domestic; they were key sources of capital and investment, and vital markets for goods and produce; they promoted (or restrained) agricultural and industrial development. They did much to shape towns, landscape and architecture. As sources of money and patronage, landowners provided the local populace with opportunities for education and social mobility. A landowner with political contacts could begin a local client or neighbour on a path to advancement that might even bring him to prosperity in a bishopric, an Oxford college, or a London trading company. A community with powerful gentry was simply a different society from one that lacked squires. Given the central importance of religious developments in Welsh histori- ography, it is also notable that the attitudes of squires did so much to shape the beliefs and practices of their tenants and neighbours.

If Wales did lack a gentry on the English model, then this was a fact of great moment for every aspect of social and political history. It was the middling gentry of English counties who were so active in promoting the commercial facilities and leisure activities of their provincial capitals from the late seventeenth century, thus providing an impetus to economic growth, and ensuring the prosperity of local shopkeepers, entrepreneurs and artisans. The absence of such a prosperous gentry would have had far-reaching consequences on issues such as urbanisation, consumer demand, building activities, and the provision of capital for economic development; to say nothing of the impact on politics, both local and national.

The Welsh stereotype certainly existed, for instance in Radnor- shire. In a much-quoted account, a Cromwellian Major-General complained that it was easier here to find ten squires of fifty pounds a year, rather than five of 100; when even 500 pounds would be paltry by English standards. In Cardiganshire, similarly, there were just a handful of great houses that might be recognised as gentry seats by an English observer: Nanteos, Peterwell, Gogerddan and Crosswood. The county was 'pitiful poor'; the squires were 'a shocking prospect of poverty and idleness, neglect and ignorance'; the clergy were universally poor; and 'the vulgar here are most miserable and low'. This would be a representative selection of comments of the sort regularly applied to the counties of north and west Wales. Obviously, this relative poverty had political conse- quences. Central government faced a perennial nightmare in filling key offices such as JP or deputy–lieutenant. By the eighteenth century, they found a solution of sorts in the mass employment of clerical justices, the only device which permitted the administration of justice to continue in a county like Merionethshire.

But as we will see, this picture was not universal. There were indeed few squires in the counties considered as a whole, but certain regions of Wales were highly gentrified, as will be recalled from hundreds like Ogmore or Castlemartin. Intensive magnification to the level of the hundred suggests that distinctive societies were united (or rather federated) within the larger county. Some of these building-blocks were in effect gentry-free, pure 'Welsh' landscapes of independent freeholders; other regions were as subject to elite control and dominance as the most placid shires of eastern England. Combined, the two societies yield an inaccurate county-based index of gentrification.

This can be illustrated from the county of Pembrokeshire. In 1673, Blome's *Britannia* listed 65 gentry here, a list that corresponds closely to the owners of large houses (those with six or more hearths according to the 1670 hearth tax). We might therefore conclude that Restoration Pembrokeshire had about 60 or 70 squires, by no means an impressive number. However, this would give a highly misleading picture of the real nature of gentry power in the county, as will be seen if we break down these figures by hundreds:

Table 3:1 Pembrokeshire Houses in 1670

Hundred	Number of Parishes	6–9 hearths	10 or more hearths	6+ hearths
Dewsland	20	1	0	1
Cilgerran	8	1	0	1
Cemais	25	5	1	6
Roos	21	6	4	10
Narberth	21	16	2	18
Castlemartin	18	15	2	17
Dongledy	21	5	4	9
Total	134	49	13	62

Of the greatest houses (ten or more hearths), only one stood in the three northern hundreds of Cilgerran, Cemais (Kemes) and Dewsland. Twelve were in the four southern hundreds, where the lands between Pembroke and Haverfordwest now emerge as a real gentry heartland. Around Pembroke, there were great mansions like Orielton, Stackpole, Lawrenny and Picton Castle, where we often find not only squires but knights and baronets. The towns in this region also had sizeable houses of wealthy burgesses and urban 'pseudo-gentry'. In the hundreds of Castlemartin and Narberth, about half of all parishes included a substantial house with at least six hearths. In Dewsland and Cilgerran, there were only two such houses in 28 parishes, and neither hundred had gentry in anything like the English sense. In 1575, it was lamented that 'There dwell not continually any justices of the peace in the hundreds of Dewsland or Cemais'.[3]

Pembrokeshire, in summary, was not exactly one moderately gentrified county. It was made up of some squire-ridden areas, and others largely squire-free, with all that implied for social, political and religious history. Pembrokeshire's divisions are well-known, with the landsker representing an ancient geographical and linguistic frontier; but several shires have obvious boundaries between north and south, or between hills and coastland. In Carmarthenshire, the social division was essentially east–west, with gentry seats heavily concentrated in and near the Tywi valley; while squires were hard to find in western hundreds like Elvet and Derllys. The prosperous shores of the Menai Straits formed a magnate-dominated region quite remarkable for Gwynedd: this is the landscape of mansions like Baron Hill and Plas Newydd, of Vaenol and Penrhyn, Llanidan and Llanfair-is-gaer, Plas Coch and Coed Helen.

The fallacy of county averages for social stratification is particularly apparent in Glamorgan, the most gentrified shire. In the later seventeenth century, there were in Glamorgan 182 houses with six or more hearths; 49 of these had ten or more hearths. Half of the greatest mansions (24) were to be found in only three of the county's ten hundreds, those of Ogmore, Dinas Powis and Cowbridge: that is, the Vale of Glamorgan. Only three houses on this scale could be found in the western upland hundreds of Neath, Newcastle and Llangyfelach. In the Vale, the gentry made up perhaps 2.5 or 3 per cent of the population, as against 1 per cent or less in the upland areas. By this sort of coarse measure, the hundred of Dinas Powis was about seven times as gentrified as that of Llangyfelach.

The gentry can be located by criteria like titles, offices held, or the size of their houses. On the other hand, the fundamental issue was ultimately one of wealth. In the later seventeenth century, an income of £1000 marked a family as belonging to the landed elite on English standards; while £500 certainly qualified its owner for inclusion in the upper gentry. Cardiganshire in 1660 had only one gentleman credited with £1000 a year, Edward Vaughan of Crosswood, but this was a poor and highly polarised county. Flintshire, in contrast, had at least six squires with between £1500 and £4000, with the Hanmers and Mostyns as wealthy as many English peers.

By the end of the century, Sir Roger Mostyn valued his estate at

3. Quoted in H.A. Lloyd, *The gentry of South West Wales 1540–1640* (Cardiff, University of Wales, 1968).

43

about £5000 a year, and the scale was perhaps less impressive than
the geographical power suggested. His lands were spread over
Flintshire, Caernarvonshire, Cheshire, Anglesey and Denbighshire
(in decreasing order).[4] Apart from agricultural wealth, Sir Roger was
an active industrial entrepreneur: in 1700, the Mostyn coalworks
contributed some £2000 to the total value of the estate. Nor was
Flintshire unique. Under Charles II, Glamorgan probably had a
dozen or more squires with 'great gentry' incomes on the English
scale, at least £1000 a year, and so the county was unusually
gentrified. The southern squires too were deeply interested in
exploiting a wide range of sources of income, including minerals and
industry.

Below the dozen or so elite families, there were in seventeenth
century Glamorgan another 30 or 40 who might aspire to important
offices like Justice of the Peace; and another group of some 40 mere
'gentlemen', recognised by the title of 'Mr.' The gentry community
therefore incorporated some 90 families with incomes ranging from
£250 upwards. Their influence spread from the highest reaches of
national and parliamentary politics to the most strictly local affairs of
the hundred and parish. In other words, Glamorgan did indeed have
the 'middling' gentry long believed to be absent from Welsh affairs.
Such a group was present in counties like Pembrokeshire, in
Denbighshire and Flintshire, and in regions of several other counties.

THE EMERGENCE OF THE GENTRY 1500–1640

The Welsh gentry emerged in the century before the Reformation
and the Acts of Union. Some were *advenae*, English or Norman
families settled in the regions where manorial farming had become
established. Although their names were English, families like the
Bulkeleys and Salusburys had usually intermarried with neighbouring houses, and had adopted the Welsh language and customs.
Others were of purely Welsh origin, descendants of free clansmen of
the later middle ages, who had settled in ancient clan-lands,
consolidated holdings, and established property rights there. They
also built up these estates by marriage and inheritance. By the
fifteenth century, they were emancipating themselves from the
structure of the kindred, the Wynns of Gwydir in Caernarvonshire

4. NLW Wynnstay MSS C106.

offering one of the most famous instances. In the sixteenth century, they gave up their traditional patronymics and adopted surnames, often choosing the name of the family seat. Thus we find the Bodvels of Bodvel in Caernarvonshire; the Mostyns of Mostyn in Flintshire. It was John Wyn ap Maredudd (died 1555) who was the first 'Wynn of Gwydir' in Caernarvonshire. In Cardiganshire in 1547, Richard ap Moris Fychan or Vaughan settled at the 'Place at Trawsgoed'. He thus began the establishment of the 'Vaughans of Crosswood' (*sc.* Trawsgoed), an estate that survived into the twentieth century.

A real lay landed elite was apparent in much of Wales by Tudor times. Already by the Wars of the Roses, there were Salusburys in Denbighshire, Philipps in Pembrokeshire, Morgans of Tredegar in Monmouthshire, Mansells in Glamorgan. The strength of this new elite is suggested by a study of the 64 Welsh landowners knighted by the Tudor monarchs between 1485 and 1558. Only the greatest families obtained this honour, and the list is a muster-roll of the leading Welsh gentry of the next two centuries – Pulestons and Hanmers in the north-east, Carnes, Mansells, Stradlings and Mathews in Glamorgan and numerous and widely dispersed Herberts.[5]

But most striking is the geographical concentration of these knights in the south-east. Twenty-eight were to be found in what would become the shires of Glamorgan and Monmouth, 14 more in Carmarthen and Pembroke. There were no knights in Cardigan, Radnor, or Merioneth; and the one name from Montgomery represented an offshoot of the Monmouthshire Herberts. The distribution helps to explain the despairing words of Bishop Rowland Lee in 1536, when he wrote that 'there are very few Welsh in Wales above Brecknock who have 10 li. land, and their discretion is less than their land.'[6] This suggests a country with few substantial landowners; but matters were quite different 'below Brecknock', as well as in the north–east.

The century after 1540 was an age of great expansion for the gentry class. The Acts of Union prescribed primogeniture as the means of inheritance, permitting the consolidation and transmission of landed estates. The Reformation also benefited lay landowners with access to Crown favour, permitting the establishment of some

5. W.R.B. Robinson, 'Knighted Welsh landowners 1485–1558', *Welsh history review* 13 (1987) 282–298.

6. Quoted in Trevor Herbert and Gareth E. Jones, eds., *Tudor Wales* (Cardiff 1988), 23.

immense holdings that often remained powerful into the present century. In the south-east, the Dissolution marked the beginnings of great prosperity for entrepreneurial families like the Lewises of Y Fan or the Vaughans of Crosswood, who now began a century of barely interrupted land accumulation. Also, the heavy sales of Crown lands throughout the sixteenth century accelerated this process, but only for those with the right political connections. For many, Royal service was the philosopher's stone that allowed the generation of enormous wealth. In addition, the political divisions of the sixteenth century assisted a few families to achieve entry into the peerage, and to dominate Welsh politics for a century and more.

THE NEW ARISTOCRACY

The Tudor regime faced many threats, and there were periods when it seemed impossible to contemplate a future without war and civil catastrophe; but treason and dissent had their uses, and the dynasty made great use of them. An enemy dispossessed meant the potential to reward a loyal servant, or to purchase the allegiance of the half-hearted. The dissolution of the monasteries was only one of several examples that assisted the creation of a powerful local peerage. In 1531, the execution of Sir Rhys ap Gruffydd for treason brought the Crown lands said to be worth £10,000 a year. Much of this estate passed to Rhys' rival Walter Devereux, a trusted servant of the dynasty, and Chief Justice of South Wales. Walter (Lord Ferrers) founded the fortunes of what became a great aristocratic family, with a Welsh seat established on what had once been the episcopal estate of Lamphey. His grandson was the first of the Devereux Earls of Essex, who led a powerful party or 'interest' in Wales well into the Stuart period. Another branch of the Devereux became Lords Hereford, whose influence in the counties of Montgomery and Brecon continued into the present century.

Royal service also established the power of other great houses like the Somersets, Earls of Worcester. In 1492, Sir Charles Somerset married the heiress of the fifteenth century Earls of Pembroke. By 1514, he had acquired both the title of Earl of Worcester and, much more valuable, the castle of Raglan which gave military dominance of much of south Wales. Through the century, the Earls occupied many royal offices, including that of Lord Chamberlain; and the openly Catholic fourth Earl (1553–1628) served as Master of the

Horse to Elizabeth and James I. The family became immensely wealthy, securing Tintern Abbey (among much else) at the Dissolution. In 1682, the Somersets became Dukes of Beaufort.

In the first half of the sixteenth century, the Somersets and Devereux represented the greatest aristocratic families in Wales, but political turmoil permitted the establishment of a third and still greater house. William Herbert (1500–1570) was by no means a 'new man', as he was descended from some of the most powerful men in fifteenth century Wales; but his career demonstrates the opportunities opened to the ambitious by the wars and crises of the mid-Tudor years. Originally a follower of the Somersets, he created a vast landed estate in his own right. This was crowned by the triumphs of 1550 and 1551: his elevation to the Earldom of Pembroke, and the presidency of the Council in Wales and the Marches. A host of royal offices and patronage in Wales followed, permitting the displacement of the Somersets.

These rewards he owed to his military skill, and to his consistent loyalty over three decades, in the wars with France, and against internal insurrections: the west in 1549, Wyatt's rising in 1554. When he did plot, as in the case of Lady Jane Grey, he was sufficiently adroit to avoid the consequences of defeat. Like Devereux, he benefited from the misfortunes of the less successful. He received monastic lands (at Wilton and Llantarnam), and rapidly accumulated lands formerly held by others fallen into disfavour, including Anne Boleyn and Protector Somerset. Under Elizabeth, the Herberts formed a powerful Protestant faction at Court, together with the Dudleys and Sydneys. The second Earl of Pembroke married a daughter of Sir Henry Sydney, President of the Council in the Marches; who was in turn brother-in-law to the Earl of Leicester.

In Wales, the political history from 1550 to 1640 can almost be described as the Age of the Herberts. The second Earl succeeded Sydney as Lord President in 1586, and both the second Earls were Vice-Admirals of south Wales, with responsibility for defence and naval matters. Meanwhile, the family spread its influence. By the end of the sixteenth century, there were powerful Herbert gentry established at half a dozen seats in Glamorgan, Monmouthshire and Montgomeryshire. Edward, son of the first Earl, established his own dynasty at Powis Castle, and these would ultimately become Lords Powis. Edward's steward and chief ally here was another Edward Herbert, a close kinsman who would in turn become the ancestor of other peers: in this case, the Herberts of Cherbury.

The three great southern families were the social and political elite

47

of Wales in the sixteenth and seventeenth centuries. Only under Charles I were more native gentry raised to the peerage, with the grant of (Irish) titles to Lord Bulkeley in Anglesey, the Earl of Dungannon in Denbighshire and the Earl of Carbery in Carmarthenshire. By 1714, there were other Welsh Lords: Mansell, Trevor and Lisburne. The next wave of creations occurred in the 1770s and 1780s, with the ennoblement of Lord Dynevor, and the grant of Irish peerages to Lords Kensington, Milford, Penrhyn, Llandaff and Newborough.

THE GENTRY AND THE STATE

Families like the Herberts and Somersets were at the peak of the social hierarchy, but there were numerous wealthy gentry throughout Wales. After the Acts of Union, they colonised the new offices such as sheriff, Justice of the Peace and Member of Parliament. In the seven constituencies that make up the present Dyfed, 90 individuals were elected between 1540 and 1640, representing 48 families. Some were courtiers or outsiders, often English, but the majority were a true native gentry, often risen to power within recent decades. The most frequently represented were the Jones' of Abermarlais, Vaughans of Golden Grove, both from Carmarthenshire; the Pembrokeshire Perrotts and the Pryses of Gogerddan in Cardiganshire. These positions enhanced their prestige, but they also gave real power that helped the process of accumulating and defending wealth.

One of the most successful exploiters of the new opportunities was Sir Rice Mansell of Glamorgan, a soldier who served on the commissions that undertook the dissolution of the monasteries. He created a great estate on old monastic lands at Margam Abbey. His son, Sir Edward, married a daughter of the second Earl of Worcester, and represented Glamorgan in Parliament in 1554. He was sheriff in 1576, Justice of the Peace from 1555 to 1595. His eldest son was Sir Thomas Mansell, one of the first to obtain the rank of baronet. He was MP in 1597 and 1605, and served as sheriff three times between 1594 and 1623. Between 1670 and 1710, four of Sir Edward's descendants dominated the representation of both the county and the borough; and the family entered the peerage in 1712.

Another instance would be the Mostyns of Flintshire, a purely Welsh house who assumed a surname only in the mid-sixteenth century. William Mostyn was county Member in 1554, and again from 1572 to 1576. He was three times sheriff of Flintshire; his son and grandson would frequently serve for this county, in addition to Anglesey and Caernarvonshire. Sir Thomas was a member of the Council in the Marches under James I; his son Sir Roger was active as a deputy-lieutenant. The same story could be told of the Wynns of Gwydir, who dominated the first 80 years of Caernarvonshire's parliamentary representation. Sir John Wynn (1553–1626) served as sheriff of his own county, as well as Merionethshire and Denbighshire; he was MP for Caernarvonshire, and a member of the Council in the Marches.

Houses like Gwydir and Margam symbolised a gradual rise to power over centuries. However, there were many new families establishing themselves in the century after 1540, and indeed long afterwards. This was and long remained an open elite, into which entry could be gained through the proceeds arising from royal service, from landownership and speculation, or from the law. Richard Myddelton was so far from being a social upstart that he represented the borough of Denbigh in Parliament in 1542. However, it was his sons who transformed a respectable house into one of spectacular wealth. These were Hugh and Thomas Myddelton, both of whom were involved in London trade and colonial enterprise, and who sponsored the New River project under James I. Their successes allowed the family to dominate Denbighshire politics for many years after the Restoration. In the south, dramatic successes were possible for the descendants of Dr William Aubrey (1529–1595), a civil lawyer and judge whose service to the Crown allowed him to lay the foundation for a substantial fortune. He was a sheriff, MP and a member of the Council in Wales. Originally a Breconshire house, the Aubreys would be baronets in seventeenth century Glamorgan, where they were among the greatest landowners.

Also in Glamorgan, the Thomases of Bettws accumulated land in the hill country from the mid-sixteenth century. By the 1640s, the wealth of the house permitted Edward Thomas to play a central role in county politics, and to achieve a baronetcy. After the Restoration, his son Sir Robert Thomas would be one of the leading political figures in south Wales, but political adventurism and accumulated debts caused the ruin of his family in the 1680s. He was replaced by the Edwins, a family founded by a Lord Mayor of London. They may appear upstarts in the landed community, but they were only imitating what many of their neighbours had done in the previous century. Within a generation, the Edwins were firmly established as Welsh squires, as confident of their ancient power as any Mansell or Mostyn.

49

THE HOUSES OF THE GENTRY

The rapid creation of new estates after 1540 was symbolised by a building boom. Each new family needed a great house according to the latest fashion, and architectural orthodoxy was reflected in dozens of great mansions that now appeared across Wales. Initially, these buildings showed strong signs of their medieval and castellated origins, but the later sixteenth century witnessed the emergence of new domestic styles. The great houses tended to have two storeys, with masonry fireplaces, chimneys and permanent staircases. Stone houses were common in the south-east and north-east, while half-timbered traditions were influential in the central borderlands. In the 1560s, Sir Richard Clough's house of Bachegraig (Flintshire) marked the introduction of brickwork and Flemish tastes.

The concentration of this building activity under Elizabeth and the early Stuarts is well known, but it is rather concealed by the frequency of subsequent alteration and rebuilding. In fact, it is almost inevitable that the greatest houses do not survive, as the richest families generally replaced their older mansions with still newer houses in the eighteenth or early nineteenth centuries. An existing Tudor or Jacobean structure must have survived by some freak circumstance, usually the move of a gentry line to some newly acquired property, or else the early extinction of the founders. In the Vale of Glamorgan, the Tudor house at Llantrithyd survives only because the eighteenth century Aubreys moved to their lands in more fashionable Buckinghamshire; and even Llantrithyd is now in ruins. Nearby Llansanwyr Court escaped remodelling because its masters moved to Dorset. However, there is some visual evidence of what the new gentry-ruled landscape must have looked like, from Denbighshire mansions like Trefalun or Bodelwyddan. We might also note houses like Plasteg in Flintshire, Treowen in Monmouthshire or Old Gwernyfed in Breconshire; or Glamorgan mansions like Beaupré or Rhiwperra. There are also narrative accounts, and a few paintings: most strikingly, some panoramic studies of Margam.

To understand the full impact of the new houses, it is necessary to imagine them in their proper context, surrounded by outbuildings, by gardens and parks, The house often towered over a nearby church, where the finest art-work would no longer be connected with worship or liturgy, at least after the depredations of the Reformation. By 1600, the greatest splendour was rather found in the magnificent tombs that effectively turned the churches into mausolea and temples for the lay ruling elite. Llantrithyd again offers excellent illustrations, and the Herberts left superb monuments in the churches of 'their' towns, like Cardiff and Montgomery. The early Stuart Mansell tombs in Margam Abbey are quite overwhelming. They offer a series of fine figure sculptures as well as what amounts to a narrative of the family's kin and marriage links. Future archaeologists could well be forgiven for seeing the religion of this time as a return to ancestor worship.

THE IMPACT OF RISING POPULATION

The sixteenth century was a time of rapid population growth, which affected the gentry class in a number of ways. One consequence was a surfeit of young men for whom there was no adequate employment. This encouraged the traditional habit of keeping large households, which could be cheaply staffed with young servants and retainers; and which resembled royal courts in miniature. In 1630, 150 people dined daily at Raglan, where there was an elaborate ritual and procedure, together with a hierarchy that included offices like steward, comptroller, sewer, master of the horse, gentlemen waiters, pages, purveyor of the castle, ushers, wardrobe master, master falconer, gentlemen and ladies of the chamber, and so on.

Sixteenth century peers like Pembroke would assuredly have had comparable (or larger) establishments, while great gentry like the Mansells or Wynns would have exercised only a little more restraint. Of the Jacobean Sir Richard Bulkeley, we read that

> he kept many servants and attendants, tall and proper men; two
> lackeys in livery always ran by his horse; he never went from home
> without 20 or 24 to attend him.[7]

Keeping such a household was more than a tribute to the vanity of the newly great. Servants maintained and defended the family honour, and could be used in faction fights with rival gentry. In fact, we will see that riots and disturbances of the Elizabethan period were often initiated by the quarrels of rival groups of gentry retainers. Once a feud was under way, it would be prosecuted by using large armed gangs of 'tall and proper men', who were expected to risk their lives and health for their masters. Demographic factors may help to explain the endemic gentry feuds of Tudor Wales.

7. Quoted in Trevor Herbert and Gareth E. Jones, eds., *Tudor Wales* (Cardiff 1988), 21–22.

51

Large families had their impact in other ways. Particularly after the restriction of gavelkind, there was more likely to be an abundance of younger sons who were expected to seek their own fortunes. In the 1590s, the Earl of Essex was able to accumulate a large Welsh faction from the ranks of the well-born and desperate, many of whom followed military careers. The wars in Ireland and the Netherlands attracted many younger sons, including Sir Thomas Morgan. Some of their contemporaries saw their best hope in political adventurism, and were well represented among the Catholic plotters of the age.

Others found more conventional avenues to advancement, for example in the naval adventures of the age. The most successful was Sir Robert Mansell, son of Sir Edward of Margam. He was a naval commander who achieved success as a courtier and a monopolist under the early Stuarts, and became Vice-Admiral of England. He sat in most early Stuart Parliaments for constituencies that included Glamorgan and Carmarthenshire. Other 'sea-dogs' were Sir Sackville Trevor and Sir Thomas Button, younger sons of gentry houses in (respectively) Denbighshire and Glamorgan. The Golden Grove family produced Sir William Vaughan of Llangendeirne, whose Newfoundland settlement of 'Cambriol' (c. 1617–1619) was the first of many attempts to establish a distinctively Welsh colony overseas. Both Hugh and Thomas Myddelton were younger sons who had entered 'trade' and colonial enterprise, with success far above the average.

The ideal solution was however to find an heiress, and thus to create a new estate that might even rival the ancestral property. In the century after 1540, some prolific families expanded into several new estates, often in other counties. As they customarily maintained their link with the original line for generations, this had the effect of extending still further the sway of a great house. We have already witnessed the spread of the Herbert family, but the seventeenth century Mansells provide another illustration. Another son of Sir Edward Mansell's was Francis, whose several children founded some of the wealthiest gentry estates in Carmarthenshire, at Muddlescwm, Stradey and Trimsaran. Some went on to establish cadet lines in Ireland. Well into the eighteenth century, these distant Mansell kin clearly looked to Margam as in a sense the centre of the family. A younger son of Sir Thomas Mansell had married the heiress of the wealthy Briton Ferry estate in Glamorgan, and their son was Bussy Mansell, one of the key figures in South Wales politics in the Interregnum. Under the later Stuarts, the combined Mansell families of Margam, Briton Ferry and eastern Carmarthenshire constituted a potent political bloc.

THE DEMOGRAPHIC CRISIS

The reforms of the 1530s consecrated the new regime of the lay landowners. In the sixteenth century, aristocratic families dominated several counties, but this power waned under the Stuarts. Some, like the Earls of Pembroke, withdrew to their English estates; others, like the Earls of Worcester and Powis, were crippled politically by their adherence to losing causes in Church and state. From the seventeenth century to the nineteenth, it was the gentry who held political power in Wales, who dominated every aspect of the society, who effectively controlled the fortunes of the Church, who manipulated borough affairs. Except for the political crisis of the mid-seventeenth century, they remained unchallenged until the rise of radical Liberalism under Victoria. Their ancient mansions and parks provided a visual symbol for this long continuity, and helped give gentry rule an aura of inevitability.

And yet this would be deceptive. Gentry rule flourished, as did the gentry as a class; but in the century after 1660, the individual families changed far more than might be suggested by the continuity of names and estates. In contrast to the demographic explosion of an earlier age, there was now a period of real contraction and decline that resulted in the extinction of gentry both great and merely middling. Like the earlier period, these changes also had far-reaching social consequences.

The problem is suggested by the case of the eighteenth century Morgans of Tredegar, whose political ties to the Whig regime gave them a vast influence even beyond what might have been expected from their landed wealth. Thomas Morgan headed the family from 1731 to 1769. In the 1740s, there was every reason to believe that the succession to Tredegar was secure, as he had four sons and two daughters. In addition, there were two nephews. But of the six males in this generation, none produced successors. Brother succeeded brother, until finally in 1792, the death of another John Morgan marked the end of the male line. Tredegar thereupon passed to a sister, Jane, who married a Kentishman named Charles Gould. Their son adopted the name of Morgan, and thus the break in the succession was concealed.

53

There were many reasons for this failure to produce heirs. An increasing number of squires remained unmarried. If they did marry at all, it was usually much later, quite possibly in their thirties or forties. If they married, there were far fewer children born; and often, the children did not survive to adulthood. In summary, the squires born in the early eighteenth century were between a third and a half as likely to have surviving sons as their counterparts a century earlier. There may well have been cultural or social reasons for these changes. Perhaps the decline of conventional religious sanctions from the later seventeenth century reduced the moral pressure to marry and procreate. Alternatively, new concepts of childhood and child-rearing led some to have fewer children, who could receive greater attention and personal care. New patterns of marriage settlements may have made it advantageous to wait longer for a valuable match. Any of these reasons might have had their impact, as may more speculative causes like homosexuality or a greater availability of contraception.

The fate of the Morgans was typical of what befell hundreds of gentry families across eighteenth century Wales. It was the generation born between about 1640 and 1720 that was most likely to commit the gravest sins against family continuity, above all by simple failure to marry. The likelihood of an estate 'ending in an heiress' was greatest between about 1720 and 1760. In Glamorgan, many of the richest families died out in the male line between 1720 and 1760: Hensol in 1721, Dunraven in 1725, Cefn Mabli in 1735, Fan in 1736, St Donats and Friars both in 1738, and Margam in 1750. The end of the Mansells was similar to the story at Tredegar. The first Lord Mansell died in 1723, leaving two surviving sons, and a grandson born of a third. The grandson died unmarried at 25, to be succeeded in the title by his two uncles. Neither left sons, so the title became extinct in 1750. The property was divided between the heiress of the fourth Lord, and the descendants of his sister. This permitted the creation in the county of two new families, respectively the Earls of Jersey and the Talbots of Wiltshire.

Sometimes a property remained in the family, but passed to the husband or successor of an heiress. On other occasions, the last squire would die without any obvious successor, so that many years of litigation would follow, or the estate would be sold or broken up. In both cases, there would be a real and dramatic break in continuity. This was the fate of a great majority of the estates of Glamorgan and Monmouthshire in the eighteenth century. Similar trends operated throughout Wales at this time. Brother succeeded brother as head of the Philipps' of Picton, the estate eventually passing to a cousin who adopted the name of Philipps. It was an early nineteenth century Williams who took the name of Bulkeley to feign unbroken continuity in that Anglesey estate. The northern house of Brogyntyn concluded with William Owen, who died in 1768. Marriage with the heiress eventually produced the powerful Ormsby-Gore family, who would become Lords Harlech in the next century.

These changes contributed to the concentration of landed wealth in the early eighteenth century, as surviving landlords inherited the property of one or more relatives and neighbours. In the 1740s, the fourth Lord Mansell controlled not only the traditional Margam estate, but also the properties of Briton Ferry and St Donats; though these would in themselves have supported a gentleman in considerable state. In north Wales, the chief beneficiary of such trends was the Williams-Wynn family of Denbighshire, who used their new wealth to secure enormous political power. In Caernarvonshire, the Wynns of Boduan now acquired the estate of Glynllifon, laying the foundation for what would become the aristocratic house of Newborough. Great families were fewer but wealthier, with all that implied for increased oligarchy in the political structure, and for electoral stability.

Sometimes, these changes would affect several counties. In 1708, Charles Talbot married a woman who would become heiress to the great Glamorgan estates of Castell-y-Mynach and Hensol. Their son would himself die without male issue, and leave another heiress. In 1756, she married the Carmarthenshire Whig leader, George Rice of Dynevor. Their son was George Talbot-Rice, Lord Dynevor, whose landed inheritance enhanced still further the traditional Rice power in the south-west.

But there were other consequences. The lack of adult heirs made it likely that estates would experience long minorities, in which time great power would be exercised by stewards and lawyers serving the gentry. This gave new power to such professional groups, who often used the opportunity to establish the fortunes of their own families. Some took advantage of the 'age of heiresses' to make their own matches in society; and in the early nineteenth century, it was common for traditional legal and professional families to enter the gentry in their own right. Presumably such a nouveau-riche community would be more likely to welcome alliances with rising industrial families, or at least not to unite against them. The demographic changes of the eighteenth century may thus have contributed to the relative ease with which the industrial tycoons established themselves among the Welsh elite.

But the most significant impact of demographic change may have been in the area of Welsh culture. Seventeenth-century squires had followed the medieval tradition of providing munificent patronage to the bards and harpists; they had spoken Welsh, and had sponsored the publication of Welsh books. After the 1680s, this support was much less in evidence, and it failed utterly by the 1720s. One reason was that resident squires were fewer, and many manor houses functioned chiefly as the administrative centres of estates. Also critical was the nature of the new gentry established on the ruins of the old. The frequency of marriages between the Welsh gentry and rich English houses meant that the new heirs were themselves more likely to be English in language and culture. And unlike the time of medieval newcomers like the Mansells, there was now no incentive to assimilate into the Welsh-speaking community. Support for the aristocratic bardic culture thus withered. Henceforward, Welsh culture would have to seek new sources of support, which it found in humbler levels of society.

In concluding, let us return to the problem posed at the beginning of this chapter. In economic terms, we can say that the picture of the impoverished Welsh squire is relevant only to certain areas of mid-Wales. In the richer shires, like Glamorgan or Denbighshire, there was an elite gentry community of real substance, together with a hierarchy of middling and lesser squires who formed a broad continuum, extending down to the substantial yeoman farmers. There were indeed 'leviathans' and 'alien squires', but both were relatively late creations resulting from the demographic crisis. Such figures may have been a major presence in nineteenth century life, but it would be misleading and anachronistic to apply this pattern to earlier centuries. Early Modern Wales was ruled by a landed class that was largely resident, and overwhelmingly native.

CHAPTER FOUR

Welsh Language and Culture

In the last two decades, historians have devoted much attention to the concept of the 'British world', the network of very different societies united by their subjection to the British Crown. This approach has been fruitful for the history of countries as diverse as Scotland, Ireland, America and the West Indies. All were dominated to a greater or lesser degree by English political power, modified by local considerations such as foreign threats and hostile aboriginal populations. In each society, language and culture were gradually drawn into common British patterns. It is curious that Wales, the oldest colony, has received relatively little attention from the new British historians. If Wales in the seventeenth or eighteenth centuries was what it initially appeared, a radically different Celtic society with a distinctive hierarchy, language and customs, then this is a fact of considerable importance for the realm as a whole. England would have faced an essentially alien colony across a long and indefensible border, with a constant danger of foreign foes capitalising on nationalistic sentiment. Also, the Welsh were sufficiently numerous to pose a threat. They made up perhaps eight per cent of 'England-and-Wales' in 1700, compared to a modern five per cent. In political terms alone, the degree of Welsh cultural assimilation or separateness would seem important.

'OTHERNESS'

In reality, Wales represents a rather curious model of a Celtic society within the larger British world. On the one hand, it was in a sense the most alien and 'Celtic' of the three societies that composed the British Isles, the one which best preserved the ancient language. But at the same time, it is surprisingly difficult to locate distinctively Welsh characteristics in many areas of prime interest to social historians. Some apparent differences result from the failure to compare like with like. Merionethshire, for example, was a thinly populated and mountainous area with a pastoral economy, and social patterns here would differ enormously from those of Norfolk or Hampshire; but those counties would in turn be different from Westmorland. Inappropriate comparisons underlie the myths about the peculiar nature of 'Welsh gentility'.

To identify the problem, let us begin with the question of folk culture, the subject of considerable scholarly attention precisely because Wales seems to preserve so many archaic practices and beliefs. In reality, there is surprisingly little that differed significantly from the beliefs and practices of a comparable area of western or upland England. The later eighteenth century was a watershed here. As we will see below, this was a fertile time of creativity in the invention of traditions and allegedly ethnic rituals and practices. Modern druids, *eisteddfodau*, 'Welsh' costume, all owe their foundation to this proto-Romantic period, as do the modern cults of folk heroes like Owain Glyndŵr or Twm Sion Catti. It is thus important to observe matters before this age of invention.

There were certainly legends and practices that appear Welsh, and which struck contemporary tourists as charmingly Celtic. But these were often local manifestations or survivals of what had once been generic to the British Isles; or indeed, common in western England. A good illustration would be the *mapsant*, the feast-day on which villages commemorated the local saint. This was identical with the customs of England (wakes) and of Ireland, and it may represent either medieval or pre-Christian practice. So did the maypoles, bonfires and 'summer birches' which travellers found so characteristic a part of Welsh village life.

Again, there appears to be something distinctively Welsh about the wandering bards and harpists, and indeed bards did itinerate between the homes of the gentry well into the eighteenth century. Others served as resident 'family bards', an office found in the early middle ages. But John Aubrey, the antiquary, describes a pre-civil war Wiltshire that resembles this stereotypical Wales in many details: 'When I was a boy,' he wrote, 'every gentleman almost kept a harper in his house; and some of them could versify.' Of course, this was on a different cultural level to the rich tradition of the Welsh bards, but the similarities are suggestive. At the same time, Wiltshire had many semi-pagan rural customs, almost identical to those later seen as peculiarly Welsh. According to Aubrey, these customs were irrevocably ruined by the civil wars, but some survived in Wales long enough to become a source of delight to antiquaries.

Wales' rich archaeological heritage attracted its share of local customs and lore; but the country has no sacred wells, white ladies, fairies, or golden warriors that cannot be paralleled in England. There were some peculiarities about Welsh lore, including survival of the pagan Celtic veneration of the salmon, and vestiges of animal sacrifice connected to the cult of local saints; but once again, the differences from English customs or beliefs are so slim as to be almost negligible. When peasants rioted, they demanded the rights granted to them under the laws of Hywel Dda, rather than demanding the overthrow of the Norman Yoke; but beyond the issue of names, the traditional values to which they referred were much the same.

At higher social levels, it is equally difficult to discern what was characteristically Welsh. Unlike Scotland, Wales did not have a distinctive legal code, and it is often hard to tell how far traditional native law survived in popular practice. Some surviving customs which bore Welsh names were in fact the common practice of pastoral communities throughout the British Isles. Also, 'traditional' Welsh law had been deeply influenced by English practice at least as far back as the laws of Hywel Dda, with their extensive borrowing from West Saxon models.

THE LANGUAGE

Where Wales deviated most sharply from a 'British' norm was of course in the question of language. Welsh was the customary medium of communication until well into the nineteenth century. As late as 1890, perhaps 60 per cent of the inhabitants of Wales spoke the traditional language, as opposed to the 10 or 15 per cent of Scottish people who spoke Gaelic. In the sixteenth or seventeenth centuries, the proportion of Welsh speakers in Wales was probably around 90 per cent, and many border areas that would later be thoroughly anglicised were then bilingual. Of course, the hill areas were the real monoglot strongholds, above all remote territories like Trawsfynydd, or Ystradyfodwg in Glamorgan.

But Welsh was the ordinary language of virtually every parish even of coastal Monmouthshire and Glamorgan, areas in almost daily contact with Bristol or Minehead. Some eighteenth century travellers reported difficulty in finding English speakers in such later areas of anglicisation as New Radnor, Cardiff or Llantwit Major. Indeed, the contemporary Glamorgan term for broken English was *Saesneg Llan Illtud*, Llantwit English. The chief division was less between Welsh and English speaking regions, than between bilingual areas and those of monoglot Welshness.

In the central borderland, between Chirk and Crickhowell, the real transition from Welsh to English appears to have come as late as the century after 1750, with Welsh prevailing before that date in most of Denbighshire, Breconshire and Radnorshire. There were also substantial pockets of Welsh speakers in English counties like Herefordshire and Shropshire: Welsh was strong in the Forest of Dean, the Clun Forest, in Oswestry, and in many parishes west of Shrewsbury. In the 1560s, the work of translating the Scriptures and Prayer Book into Welsh was entrusted to the four Bishops of Wales – and their colleague of Hereford. Conversely, the only English speaking areas of Wales were strictly confined: to Gower, south Pembrokeshire and around Chepstow. Nor was the decline of Welsh a simple linear process. In fact, the combined influence of the Welsh circulating schools and of the Old Dissent may have caused a minor revival in some areas well into the eighteenth century.

The Welsh language was spoken in many geographical regions, and in most social strata. At least until after 1700, it would have been remarkable to find a Welsh squire or even peer unable to read or converse in Welsh. This was true of the greatest families, not merely the obscure hill gentry. We find evidence of a knowledge of Welsh in surprising quarters until the end of the Stuart period, among aristocrats like the Somersets, Herberts, even the Harleys. The real change here seems to have coincided with the demographic crisis of the Georgian era. Welsh proved to be resilient, resisting successive attempts to diminish its use. At different times, national governments hoped to integrate Wales by means of the Church, of boroughs, and the universities. But by the Restoration, most boroughs were bilingual, with a preference for Welsh; Welsh-language Anglican services were commonplace throughout the country; and Jesus College probably did more to spread Welsh influence in Oxford than to transmit English culture back to the principality.

The evidence for these generalisations comes from a wide range of sources: from the accounts of tourists and travellers, from incidental stories by local writers, from diocesan records of court proceedings and the language prevailing in church services; but the general picture is quite overwhelming. Until 1700, Welsh was the language of all classes in Wales. By 1800, the gentry and clergy might have moved away from this consensus, but without much immediate effect on the linguistic character of the nation as a whole.

TRADITIONAL CULTURE

The Welsh language was the vehicle for an ancient culture, which survived and even flourished in the century following the Reformation and the Acts of Union. Welsh literature was so successful in part because it was fundamental to the values of the new social and political elites that triumphed under the Tudors, especially the gentry. They patronised the class of professional bards, who kept alive the complex metrical and poetic forms evolved over the previous millenium. In fact, some of the Tudor and early Stuart poets were of the highest quality, including northerners like Wiliam Llŷn, William Cynwal and Siôn Tudur. Glamorgan bards like Lewys Morgannwg and Dafydd Meurug received the patronage of the greatest families, the Herberts, Lewises and Stradlings. This support faltered with the civil wars, but it perished only with the demographic crisis of the early eighteenth century.

Bards were required to serve a lengthy apprenticeship before they could earn the rank of *pencerdd*, which entitled them to itinerate between the great houses. The period of study was necessary in order to learn the elaborate rules of rhyme and metre that made much Welsh poetry of the time as richly ornate as a Renaissance jewel. The fifteenth-century poets had decided on a canon of 24 strict metres that had to be mastered. Poetic forms were categorised according to line-length, rhyme and stress, with the device of *cynghanedd* adding to the complexity. This involved 'rhyming' words with like consonants, so that an English cynghanedd would permit the matching of *leaves* and *lives* (Wilfrid Owen undertook such experiments). Aspiring bards also had to study the works of the masters, the pantheon of earlier poets dating back to the sixth century.

Welsh poetry of the period was not 'literature' in the sense that it needed to be written or read: it was a social phenomenon, to be

61

declaimed in a public setting, usually before a patron. There were several major forms. Highly venerated was the long *awdl*; but the *cywydd* was in widespread use between the fourteenth and seventeenth centuries. This will serve as an example of the nature of the different metres. A cywydd consists of rhymed couplets, with each line having seven syllables. One line has a masculine rhyme, one feminine; while alliteration and cynghanedd are much used. Poets employed the *cywydd mawl*, or poem of praise, the *cywydd gofyn*, or request, and the *cywydd marwnad*, the elegy or lament. The shorter *englyn* was popular in the early modern period, particularly for compliments. (Free verse forms were also much in use, but they were less esteemed.)

Much of the poetry is predictable in its choice of subject matter: most patrons tended to be praised as nobly bred, courageous, patriotic, munificent, charitable, and so on. The interest and novelty of the work lies rather in the imagery, the handling of the complex metres, and the detail in the *cynghanedd*. Here is a fairly standard *cywydd*, in praise of an Elizabethan squire in Pembrokeshire:

> *Y pur Cymro, pêr gynnydd,*
> *Pen stôr, post o aur rhudd,*
> *Pingal wyt, pan glyw'r iaith,*
> *Pêr frau iôn, pur Fryttaniaeth*

> (Thou pure Welshman, of fair increase,
> Of the greatest wealth, a pillar of real gold,
> But thou art a pinnacle when the nation hears
> The pure British language, sweet, tender lord.)
> (H.A. Lloyd's translation)[1]

(The sense of national identity and pride indicated here is quite typical).

There were always those who felt that contemporary bards fell short of the rigorous standards demanded of them, and could not approach the halcyon days of the later middle ages. In the sixteenth century, bardic skills were much in demand to glorify the many parvenu gentry who needed to justify their newfound wealth and authority. It was Siôn Tudur who wrote a *cywydd* to the bards, denouncing their willingness to prostitute their talents to praise any upstart who could fee them. The new men were serfs (*taeog*) and churls, drawing their power from usury and extortion. Such complaints grew common in the century after 1640, and it seems that

---

1. Quoted in H.A. Lloyd, *The gentry of South-West Wales 1540–1640* (Cardiff, University of Wales) 201.

the guild structure of apprenticeship and examination fell into disuse. The Jacobean poet Morys Berwyn was one of many who denounced the unsettling decline:[2]:

> *Oer yw'r sâl ar yr oes hon*
> *Oes heb urddas i'r beirddion*
>
> Chill is the reward in this age
> An age which offers no status to the poets

The ancient musical traditions similarly entered a period of crisis about this time, with a surge of English and French influences. In 1694, Henry Vaughan the Silurist was asked by the English antiquary John Aubrey for an account of the organisation and work of the bardic order. In reply, Aubrey was referred to the account by Siôn Dafydd Rhys in a book published as long ago as 1592.[3]

On the other hand, it would be wrong to imagine a sudden eclipse. At least into the 1680s, there were prominent gentry families patronising poets of real merit: Huw Morys was supported by the Myddeltons and a number of other northern houses; Edward Dafydd by the Mansells of Margam; Owain Gruffudd by the Mostyns. Siôn Dafydd Lâs, in fact, is commonly regarded as the last resident household *bardd teulu*. He lived at Nannau in Merionethshire until his death in 1694, but wrote and sang for a dozen north Wales families. The Phylips, *Phylipiad Ardudwy*, were a Merionethshire poetic dynasty that kept the tradition alive from the 1540s into the 1680s. In the eighteenth century, we can still find a resident bard of sorts with Dafydd Nicolas at the remote house of Aberpergwm in Glamorgan; though his official title was family tutor.

This brief sketch will suggest the opulence of the oral culture, and the constant vigilance on the part of bards and patrons that was required to prevent the degeneration of these elaborate forms. When this system decayed, the old values were preserved for a generation or so by amateurs, often squires or clergy themselves. On the other hand, there was a great deal more to Welsh poetry than this aristocratic world. Poetry was created and used at every level of society, with wonderful consequences for the social historian. Scholars like Glanmor Williams can trace popular reactions to the Reformation or to early Puritanism in Glamorgan by referring to the

2. Quoted in Glanmor Williams, *Recovery, reorientation, Reformation* (Oxford/University of Wales 1987), 448.
3. Quoted in Gwyn Jones ed., *The Oxford book of Welsh verse in English* (Oxford 1977), 291–292.

cwndidau, religious verse that gives unparalleled insight into the minds of ordinary Welsh people.

Political attitudes can also be studied from the numerous surviving prophecies, which enjoyed a massive and apparently unstoppable circulation. From the fifteenth century to the time of the Republic, every major crisis found an echo in some new prophecy, attributed to an ancient sage, and drawing on immemorable Welsh tradition. This was essentially a popular form, though prophecies were often linked to particular aristocratic houses and families. From the later seventeenth century, *baledi* (ballads) became popular, as did religious verse, the *halsingod*. There was also a popular dramatic tradition in the form of the *anterliwt* (interlude) of the sort made famous by ∙ *Twm o'r Nant*, though the genre died in the chillier religious climate after 1800, with the rise of Methodist and Evangelical opposition. Literacy was of little relevance in the survival of this culture, as verses enjoyed a fairly accurate oral transmission over decades.

For high and low, there were collective gatherings for the celebration of the traditional culture in verse and song. Under Elizabeth, the chief concern was the contamination of the bardic art by strolling rhymesters who could not fulfil bardic standards. Partly in order to reassert 'guild' regulation, an *eisteddfod* (session) was held at Caerwys in 1528 and 1567. But poetic and musical meetings occurred at humbler social levels:

> Their harpers and crowthers sing them songs of the doings of their ancestors . . . and then they rip up their pedigrees at length how each of them is descended from their old princes. Here also they spend their time in hearing some part of the lives of . . . the intended prophets and saints of that country.[4]

The traditional culture of the seventeenth and eighteenth centuries emphasised the long continuity of Welsh society, and proudly recalled the memories of many heroes, lay and religious. In addition, this popular historical awareness was closely linked to the surrounding landscape, where a massive corpus of legendary lore gave significance to almost every stream and hill, each standing stone and tumulus.

4. Quoted in A.H. Dodd, *Studies in Stuart Wales* (Cardiff 1971), 13.

KINSHIP AND GENEALOGY

The importance of continuity explains the inordinate popularity of genealogical study in the early modern period. Early Welsh society had placed a high value on what seem today to be distant relationships, up to the ninth generation. Although the tribal system had generally fragmented by the sixteenth century, there is abundant contemporary comment to suggest that the Welsh continued to esteem kin relationships. In 1755, Philip Jones wrote to the great Glamorgan squire Robert Jones of Fonmon to request help during a crisis arising from debt and illness. He cited his exact relationship to the current squire, for the two men had a common ancestor who was probably born about 1570. This placed him no less than six generations before the squire to whom he was applying. That is a remote relationship, but it was sufficient to lead Philip Jones to make the request; and to let the squire (or his family) decide to grant it.

The enthusiasm for kinship was reflected in the cultivation of genealogy by families of any pretension to social status, at least up to the mid-eighteenth century. In part, this reflected a practical need, in light of the naming practices which prevailed in early modern Wales. The son of John ap Robert was David ap John, and his son might be William ap David. The greater gentry replaced patronymics with surnames under the Tudors, but they were not followed in this by many lesser squires until the eighteenth century. Among the lower classes, the change was not general until Victorian times. It was thus difficult to know the exact relationship of (say) David John and William Probert, in the absence of a family name. On the other hand, the exact history of a family might need to be established in order to secure a claim on property, for instance, during an interrogation before a manorial court. The genealogist was thus a socially necessary individual.

As with bardic poetry, genealogy was so popular because it was closely connected with the pride and élan of the gentry class, who were anxious to prove their worth by demonstrating their connections with earlier nobles and princes. This work was time-consuming and expensive in terms of travel and correspondence; but it helped to develop a network of local historians and antiquaries with a fine sense of the nature and limits of the county community, and its origins in a specifically Welsh antiquity. In the seventeenth century, the most prominent genealogical scholars were gentry or clergy themselves, like David Edwardes and William Lewes of Carmarthenshire, John Davies of Denbighshire; and the circles around them. Such highly cultivated gentlemen collected manuscripts of Welsh poetry in addition to genealogical materials. Robert Vaughan (1592–1667) of Hengwrt in Merionethshire, was the greatest collector of Welsh antiquities before Victorian times. The Hengwrt/Peniarth collection, which included treasures like the Black Book of Carmarthen, formed the priceless core of the collection of the modern National Library of Wales.

There is no way to quantify the importance of this kind of study, but repeated comments over the centuries stress the central importance of noble descent for the ruling elite. In the early eighteenth century, Ellis Wynne's *Dream of the sleeping bard* provided a comprehensive critique of the sins of each social class; and the gentry suffered above all from the sins of pride in self and family. In the lowest level of hell, we find 'Cain, Nimrod, Esau, Tarquin, Nero, Caligula, and the others who first kept pedigrees and devised family arms.' The Treasury of Pride, meanwhile, is filled with weapons of war, as well as 'all manner of armorial bearings, banners, escutcheons, books of pedigrees, poems of antiquity, *cywyddau*.'[5]

NATIONHOOD?

Wales had neither a flag, a capital, an army, or a government; but contemporary writings show a powerful sense of Welshness, expressed above all through linguistic and cultural patriotism. It is not difficult to find assertions of fervent Welsh loyalty in contemporary books or correspondence: exiles clamouring for one clod of good Welsh earth; juries giving biased verdicts against English plaintiffs; Glamorgan clubmen in the 1640s protesting the presence of English gentry; genealogists lamenting that a family of good stock hitherto had made a marriage in England. Wealthy and sophisticated squires described themselves proudly as 'mountainous Welshmen'.

National and local pride found expression in antiquarian research and scholarship, usually written in English, but demonstrating a strong sense of Welsh identity. The Elizabethan squirearchy in particular left many historical works of the first quality: the *Description of Pembrokeshire* of George Owen, the *Morganiae Archaiographia* of Rice Merrick, the copious writings of Sir Edward

5. Ellis Wynne, *The dream of the sleeping bard* translated by T. Gwynn Jones, (Gregynog Press, 1940), 21.

Stradling of St Donats. Sir John Wynn of Gwydir chose to write a history not of his county but of his own family, and in so doing produced one of the treasures of Welsh historical scholarship. Among the greatest achievements of the Elizabethan antiquaries was the *Historie of Cambria now called Wales . . .*, published in 1584 by David Powell, but drawing on the work of several predecessors lay and clerical. Humphrey Llwyd was one of the best antiquaries of this talented group.

This sort of manifestation can be attested at great length from any period before the mid-eighteenth century, but it emerged particularly strongly at the Restoration. In 1661, Percy Enderbie published *Cambria triumphans*, which emphasised the ancient Welsh roots both of the English monarchy, and of the leading aristocratic families. This intensely patriotic work was patronised by an impressive list of magnates: Lord Powis, Lord Herbert of Cherbury and the later Marquess of Worcester, as well as great gentry like the Monmouth-shire Morgans, the Glamorgan Stradlings and Lewises.

A few years later, a similarly prestigious group of west Wales gentry (like John Barlow and William Wogan) led a campaign to secure the appointment of a royal printer for the Welsh language. These men came from south Pembrokeshire, historically one of the most anglicised parts of Wales, but they still seem to have joined unequivocally in the movement. Also in this area, in the very anglicised hundred of Castlemartin, we find complaints in the 1680s that powerful local gentry like the Meyricks persecuted clergy and merchants of English origin explicitly on the grounds of their nationality.

Alongside the great squires of the south, we might consider Thomas Mostyn of Mostyn in Flintshire, a highly cultivated gentleman with an estate less than 20 miles from Chester. This man was far from being a country bumpkin or an impoverished hill squire, but he was lauded by the bards in Welsh poems that he presumably understood and appreciated. He collected Welsh manu-scripts, and pursued genealogy. A similar portrait could be drawn at this time of any significant landowner in any part of Wales, up to and over the English border.

If the gentry were so positive about their Welsh heritage, the academics and the antiquaries were still more extreme, as they regularly asserted the superiority of Welsh culture, and extolled its long continuity. Could not contemporary Welsh speakers understand Taliesin's work (*c.*600AD) better than the English could comprehend relative moderns like Chaucer and Gower? And what were upstarts like these compared to their fourteenth century contemporary, Dafydd ap Gwilym?

THE POLITICS OF WELSHNESS 1540–1760

All this would tend to suggest that Wales was in fact a thoroughly different and alien Celtic society quite as much so as Scotland. It might seem natural that such an elaborate and self-confident culture would inevitably find political expression, and provide a firm footing for nationalism. In reality, pride in Wales and its culture did indeed have political implications, but there is virtually no evidence of serious or overt nationalism between the sixteenth and late eighteenth centuries. There was no organised movement, and it would be anachronistic to expect one. However frequently the lords and squires were praised for their ancient British blood, they saw no conflict between Welsh loyalty and the benefits they received in the greater Britain. The very strength of Welsh culture was a sign that the language and all it signified were safe enough in this political environment, even if the bardic system may have disintegrated.

When Welshness was employed as a polemical weapon in political and ideological argument, the goal was as likely to be the assertion of British unity as of Welsh separatism. Under the Tudors, Welsh history and Arthurian precedent were enlisted into the cause of asserting the imperial independence of the Tudor Protestant state, which even took its 'British' title from Welsh lore. The term 'British Empire' may have been an invention of that amazing Welsh European, the occultist John Dee. In this view, the Tudor coup of 1485 marked the Welsh absorption of England, rather than the reverse. Welsh achievements, like the mythical Welsh settlement of the medieval Prince Madoc, gave legal precedent for British adventures in the New World.

Religious history was similarly mined for the purposes of contemporary debate, with Celtic Christianity a favoured topic. It was commonly agreed that the Celtic church was of ancient origin, possibly even of apostolic foundation, and it had had certain distinctive practices that had earned it the condemnation of the papal mission to Britain. After the Reformation, the precise nature of the Celtic difference was of great interest. Catholic and recusant writers asserted that the Welsh, with their ancient Christian heritage, were the true inheritors of the island of Britain; while the Anglican church was another foreign imposition. In contrast, Protestant writers like Bishop Richard Davies noted that the apostolic Celtic church had been suppressed by Rome, presumably because its authentic proto-Protestantism had offended the papists. But this argument too sought to justify current realities with reference to early history. Both sides also tried to annex the great medieval poets. Catholics admired their catholicity and Marian devotion; Protestants and Puritans stressed their social and moral criticisms, which were seen as having laid the foundations for the Reformation.

After the civil wars, the historical debate shifted to new ground. In England, there was a long-lasting theory which justified radical rhetoric and popular rights with reference to ancient Anglo-Saxon precedents overwhelmed by the Norman invaders. At least by the seventeenth century, Welsh Whigs and radicals had evolved a parallel view, asserting that popery, tyranny and arbitrary government were all part of a Saxon yoke, imposed upon free Welsh people. The nationalistic implications of this widely disseminated theory might appear obvious in retrospect; but they were all but ignored at the time, as the 'Saxon Yoke' continued to be used only in the battle between Whig and Tory.

We will often find this apparent paradox. Welsh patriotism was used in a remarkable variety of political causes, often employing a rhetoric with strong nationalistic undercurrents; but these were ignored in practice. In terms of practical politics, a theme of Welsh nationhood *can* be followed from Tudor to Georgian times, but it is a thin skein. In the sixteenth century, there was clearly a fear that Catholic propagandists might be able to evoke nationalistic resentment, which might provide the background for a rising or invasion. If this were ever planned, then there was a ready-made propaganda network in place in the form of the bards, whose inclinations were generally Catholic. But the day for such a poetically-inspired rising never came. The only possible manifestation of nationalism came in 1592, and it is controversial. This was the trial and execution of the Pembrokeshire magnate Sir John Perrott, on charges involving an alleged plot to secure his power over an autonomous Wales; but the background to this is uncertain.

Far from seeking independence, it was rare for Welsh politicians to act in a way that recognised any Welsh dimension at all. One rare exception was the Parliamentary struggle to end the importation of Irish cattle, which provided the only serious competition to Welsh produce, and Welsh MPs struggled vigorously for the economic interests of themselves and their tenants. After this campaign succeeded in 1666, 'Wales' as an entity would be a ghostly presence at Westminster; although individual Welshmen might achieve high rank at court or in national parties and factions.

In the next century, the tradition grew faint. In 1695 and 1696, there was intense opposition to William III's grant of Crown lordships in north Wales to his favourite, the Earl of Portland. A particularly daring contribution to the debate was made by Robert Price, who was hailed in opposition pamphlets as a 'Bold Briton', the 'patriot of his native country', whose speeches defended *Gloria Cambriae* against a tyrannical monarchy. Once again, the rhetoric is suggestive, but it is noteworthy precisely because it is so unusual. The same applies to partisan attempts to annex St David's Day, a popular holiday from Tudor to Georgian times. It was celebrated even by the Royal Family, and especially the circle of the Prince of Wales. But who exactly was this Prince? Jacobites naturally had their own views on this question after 1688, and held appropriate pro-Stuart celebrations on the first of March. The political rhetoric was predictable, but it is interesting that the Jacobites felt that the festival was of sufficient popularity and importance to be worth stealing. In response, Whig groups like the London-based Society of Ancient Britons (1715) held their own counter-demonstrations to assert Hanoverian claims. Welsh causes and issues were therefore subsumed in the political divisions of a wider Britain.

THE EIGHTEENTH CENTURY RENAISSANCE

Welsh culture changed fundamentally during the eighteenth century, although the political significance of this transformation would not become fully apparent until the 1790s. We have already noted the decline of gentle or noble patronage in the century after the Restoration. At the same time, Welsh scholars and literati were increasingly influenced by methods and theories emanating from England or the European Continent. Poetry and antiquarianism were both regenerated; but both were now under the auspices of very different social groups than before, with a quite different political and religious outlook. The cultural developments of this age were the work of 'middling' or plebeian groups, often nonconformist, and increasingly radical.

By the 1720s, it was increasingly apparent that the old 'high' culture was in grave danger. Old musical notations were already incomprehensible, the instruments were all but extinct, and the ferociously difficult metres were fading from memory. This was of great concern to a number of patriotic activists, often clerics or minor government servants. Most famous was the Morris family of Anglesey, four brothers born in the first decade of the century; and incidentally, this was the first generation of the family to abandon the patronymic. The greatest were Lewis Morris (1701–1765) and Richard (1703–1779), both government servants. Lewis was a customs searcher and a steward of Crown lands in Cardiganshire; Richard was a clerk in the Navy Office, which brought him to London.

For decades, they sought out and catalogued the remnants of the old poetry and music, ransacking gentry libraries, as Petrarch before them had searched the decaying monasteries of Europe. They developed a network of correspondence among the poets and historians of the day, and attempted to disseminate their findings, which were often exciting. It was in 1758 that Lewis Morris became aware of the sixth-century poem, *Gododdin*, which he compared to the best of Homer or Milton. Richard in particular was a leading figure among the London Welsh, and in 1728, he had been a steward at the dinner of the Society of Ancient Britons. In 1751, he was the prime mover in creating the first Cymmrodorion Society, under the presidency of a Merionethshire squire, William Vaughan of Cors-ygedol. This society, which lasted until 1787, was a focus for intellectual and literary activism in London and Wales. It also attempted to preserve links with Wales overseas: that is, Pennsyl-vania, where a St David's Society dated from 1729. More important, the Cymmrodorion was the model for many other cultural and political organisations in the next century.

The loss of the oral tradition of bardism meant that any revival would have to rely on the printed word. Fortunately, the work of the Morrises coincided with an upsurge of publishing in the Welsh language. Between 1546 and 1660, at least 108 titles appeared; from 1660 to 1710, the figure was 215; between 1710 and 1730, there were an impressive 330. Dr G.H. Jenkins has identified 140 authors of such books between 1660 and 1730, so there was a literary public prepared to become involved in scholarly debate. Before 1730, the vast majority of this literature was religious in nature, but there were some auspicious exceptions. In 1730, there appeared William Wotton's edition of the Laws of Hywel Dda, the *Leges Wallicae*, that would be so fundamental for the study of medieval society. This was edited by Moses Williams, a former assistant of Edward Lhuyd who published extensively between 1711 and 1730. At a much humbler level, the ubiquitous Welsh Almanacs produced from the 1680s onwards regularly included sections of poetry. The Welsh printing industry began in Shrewsbury in 1688, and there was a printing shop in south Cardiganshire by 1718. Thereafter, Carmarthen emerged as the main centre.

Perhaps the greatest problem faced by the Welsh language in this period was the lack of set forms and grammar, so that local dialects grew further apart, and loan-words crept in. In 1632, the *Dictionarium Duplex* of John Davies of Mallwyd had attempted to provide a Welsh–Latin dictionary, and Davies also produced a Welsh grammar. This work was the basis for several similar efforts in the following century. Activity intensified between 1720 and 1780, when modern Welsh acquired a stability and an academic respectability it had not hitherto possessed. In 1725, John Rhydderch produced an *English and Welsh Dictionary*; he followed this in 1728 with his *Gramadeg Cymraeg* (Welsh Grammar), which summarised bardic rules about metre and rhyme. In 1727, William Gambold published a *Grammar of the Welsh language*; and in 1753 the Rev. Thomas Richards offered his *Thesaurus Antiquae Linguae Britannicae*. In 1770, the Rev. John Walters of Llandough, Glamorgan published his *Dissertation of the Welsh language, pointing out its antiquity, copiousness, grammatical perfection . . .*; and over the next quarter of the century, he would follow this work with yet another *Dictionary*.

Walters' *Dissertation* offers an explicit statement of the vital necessity of the language as the basis of Welsh patriotism. As such, it marks a new and more aggressive stage in the revival. Welsh was one of the oldest languages in existence, with a superb literature. It was despised by some who 'being Welshmen by birth, have lately commenced Englishmen.'[6] There were those who tried to exterminate the language (a striking and novel concept), but he denies that they could be true Ancient Britons. They were rather 'aliens (Normans, Flemings, etc.) that have by intrusion formerly got footing in the country'. Arguing that a plurality of languages harmed a society was nonsense, as diversity harmed only 'a few mercenary tradesmen, a few triking drovers, etc.'. Walters also reflected the realism of the language reformers. Though anxious to preserve the purity and correctness of Welsh, they also wanted to ensure that it was a practical and functional language, and they invented words and structures with the abandon of an English playwright of the age of

6. John Walters, *Dissertation of the Welsh language* (Cowbridge 1771), 60–61.

Shakespeare. Many of these neologisms successfully entered main-stream usage.

Also successful was the endeavour to codify poetic rules. It was from the pages of a book that Goronwy Owen of Anglesey learned the skills of metre and *cynghanedd* that he used to become one of the greatest poets of the age. But the tradition was meaningless if the ancient works were destroyed or contaminated, and high priority was given to publishing the poetry of earlier masters. In 1764, Evan Evans (*Ieuan Fardd*) produced *Some specimens of the poetry of the antient British bards*, which earned the notice and respect of English writers already in quest of the medieval and proto-Gothic. This was after all the decade of 'Ossian', Chatterton and Percy's *Reliques* (and Gray's *Bard* had been published as early as 1757). It is the 1770s that marks the beginning of the tourist invasion of 'picturesque' Wales, when the country attracted the attention of English antiquaries like Thomas Pennant, H. Penruddocke Wyndham, William Gilpin and Lord Torrington. These were often antiquaries in their own right, and their travels stimulated interest in things Celtic. In 1770, Daines Barrington published the *History of the Gwydir family*, written by the Jacobean Sir John Wynn.

By the 1760s, Welsh poetry and culture had become fashionable once more, and the Cymmrodorion became quite gentrified in its membership. The group still carried on their work of providing the patronage which was no longer forthcoming from the gentry: in 1773, they supported Rice Jones' collection of 'Masterpieces of the British bards', *Gorchestion beirdd Cymru*. The society also began the defence of Welsh culture through the law and the courts, a tactic that has been so common in our own century. In 1766, a controversy erupted when an English parson named Bowles was presented to an overwhelmingly Welsh-speaking parish in Anglesey. After all, in the words of his counsel: 'Wales is a conquered country; it is proper to introduce the English language, and it is the duty of the bishops to promote the English, in order to introduce the language.' The Cymmrodorion Society mobilised the Welsh gentry in defence of the parishioners and their linguistic rights, and raised over £250 from a group that included six Welsh MPs. £100 came from Sir Watkin Williams-Wynn, £30 from Lord Bulkeley and £20 from William Vaughan of Corsygedol.

The case established the precedent that language should be a factor in such appointments; but other activists were unimpressed. It was charged that the Cymmrodorion had become less serious in its fight for Wales and its language, and the more committed drifted away to new organisations. Most significant was the Society of Gwyneddigion, founded in 1770 for a north Wales membership, and meeting regularly at the Bull's Head Tavern. Among its most important members was Owen Jones, *Owain Myfyr*, the true intellectual heir of the Morrises. Under his auspices, the year 1789 became the annus mirabilis of the Welsh Enlightenment. There finally appeared an edition of the poems of Dafydd ap Gwilym; and the society sponsored cultural competitions at Llangollen, Bala and Corwen. Far more than the aristocratic gatherings of earlier eras, these would be the precursors of the modern *eisteddfod*. It was also at this time that the first literary and cultural magazines appeared in the Welsh language The rediscovery of music and harp song had already been given a fillip by Edward Jones' book of 1784, *Musical and poetical relicks of the Welsh bards*.

But the work of collection and editing was far from over. In 1792, there appeared *The heroic elegies and other pieces of Llywarch Hen*, edited by William Owen Pughe. Between 1801 and 1807, Myfyr and his collaborators attempted the ambitious project of publishing all the major literary texts of early Wales, together with some of the historical *Bruts*. Three volumes appeared as the *Myvyrian archaeology*.

BARDS AND DRUIDS

Owain Myfyr and his companions had been wonderfully successful; but their work was blighted by the influence of one of the editors of the *Archaeology*, Iolo Morganwg, and his distinctive views on Celtic antiquity. In order to understand this, it is necessary to trace the development of antiquarian and historical scholarship over the previous century. In the 1690s, Edward Lhuyd had emerged as one of the finest archaeological and linguistic scholars in British history. In 1707, his *Archaeologia Britannia* had confirmed that Welsh was one of a Celtic family of languages, a point made earlier by the French scholar the Abbé Pezron. As such, the Celts could claim literal and cultural descent from the Gauls and Britons described by Caesar, with their warriors and druids. Lhuyd's theories were popularised in the *Drych y prif oesoedd* (Mirror of the Early Ages), of Theophilus Evans, which also rehearsed the legends associated with Geoffrey of Monmouth. Some argued moreover that the Welsh language itself was many thousands of years old, perhaps the oldest living language: did the *Cymry* not bear the name of the Biblical Gomer, son of Japhet (Gen. 10:2)?

In the early eighteenth century, the discovery of the roots of Wales became associated with contemporary theories about ancient societies and their religions. Classical literature asserted that druid priests had been vital in early Celtic society; and through the work of scholars like John Aubrey and William Stewkeley, druids came to be associated with sun worship, and with stone circles like Stonehenge.[7] They also enjoyed a vogue as worshippers of Nature and Reason, precursors of the rational religion of the Enlightenment. As contemporaries of the Patriarchs, they had equal authority. To quote Blake, 'Adam was a druid, and Noah'. About 1710, it was the radical Whig and deist John Toland who wrote *The critical history of the Celtic religion and learning, containing an account of the druids or the priests and judges, of the vaids (sic), or the diviners and physicians, and of the bards, or the poets and heralds . . . with the history of Abaris, the Hyperborean, priest of the sun.*

Druids made their first significant appearance in modern Welsh historiography in 1723, in the *Mona antiqua restaurata* (1723) of Henry Rowlands, a correspondent of Lhuyd's. Rowlands argued that druidical remains could be seen throughout the island of Anglesey, in the form of 'mounts, pillars, heaps, altars and other appurtenances of their superstitious worship' – essentially, any prehistoric site, but most spectacularly stone circles. The druids were a hierarchical priesthood, who were expert in 'the theory of Nature, astronomy, geometry, medicine, and natural magic'. Among their ranks, we find not only priests but *vates* and bards. The metropolitan authority of the sect was based at the *Gorsedd*, 'a Tribunal or Judicature'.[8] Rowlands was thus the source for most of the druidical fantasy that would saturate Welsh culture over the next two centuries. Incidentally, the work also foreshadowed a distressing number of later antiquaries in seeking Welsh etymologies for Classical or Hebrew words – in this case, the names of the Greek and Roman deities.

IOLO MORGANWG

The Welsh revival found both its culmination and its nemesis in the work of Edward Williams, *Iolo Morganwg* (1747–1826). Iolo was an

7. Some of the most valuable writing on the origins of the druid myth has been undertaken by Stuart Piggott, in books like *William Stukeley* (Oxford 1950) or *Ancient Britons and antiquarians* (London: Thames and Hudson, 1989).

8. Henry Rowlands, *Mona antiqua restaurata* (Dublin 1723), 61, 87 etc.

enthusiastic student of all things Welsh, poetic and ancient, and we have already seen that the Wales of his youth offered many opportunities to indulge these interests. He was a pupil of John Walters and Thomas Richards, both of whom were neighbours in the Vale of Glamorgan; and he made contact with poetic circles in the Glamorgan hill country. They were not, as he claimed, the last survivors of the ancient bardic tradition, but they were an able and interesting group of political and religious radicals like Edward Evans and Lewis Hopcyn, who cared deeply about preserving the traditional poetic skills in their full rigour. They also held poetic competitions from the 1730s, to which we might apply the general title of local *eisteddfodau*. One such poet was John Bradford, a weaver and dyer from Tir Iarll, who was a correspondent of Lewis Morris and a member of the Cymmrodorion.

By the 1780s, Iolo was making spectacular claims about what he had learned from such men, and found in their libraries. He claimed that the bardic order had maintained its traditions in areas like Tir Iarll, and that he had been initiated into it. In support of this, he offered written accounts of bardic meetings and decisions tracing back over the centuries, and involving people of undoubted historicity. In reviving the bardic craft, he also attempted to show its druidical roots, and plundered Rowlands mercilessly. He devised the whole farrago of robes, sun worship and stone circles that are so powerful a component of the modern eisteddfod movement. In 1792, he began initiating enthusiasts into his druidical circle, the *Gorsedd*.

In part, he wished to assert the glory of south Wales against the predominantly northern membership of the Gwyneddigion; and the druids were only part of a one-man industry of forgery and invention that offered helpful evidence about every aspect of Glamorgan history from prehistoric times into the eighteenth century. His influence is much in evidence in works like the edition of Llywarch Hen and the *Myvyrian archaeology*. Welsh history and literature did not liberate themselves from the influence of this remarkable charlatan until well into the present century.

We will return to Iolo and his influence in a later chapter, when we consider the radical political environment of the 1790s; but his career is a notable illustration of how sharply Welsh poetry and antiquarianism had deviated from their aristocratic roots. Both had originally been associated with the world of the gentry and nobility, and both had been employed in the service of the established order. By the late eighteenth century, the leading defenders of the culture constituted a new clerisy, a generation of patriotic scholars whose nationalistic rhetoric sought a fundamental redefinition of the Welsh community: one that all but excluded the higher ranks of society. It was natural that political radicals should find such a synthesis at once attractive and invigorating.

In other words, the possession of a distinctive language did not in itself make Wales a particularly recalcitrant or ungovernable province of greater Britain. From the eighteenth century, however, the language acquired social and class connotations that made nationalist resistance possible. Politics were a lively pursuit in Tudor and Stuart Wales; but a distinctively Welsh politics had to wait until the 1780s.

PART TWO

Church and State 1536–1800

CHAPTER FIVE
The State

THE COUNTIES AND THE NATION

In the early sixteenth century, Wales was divided politically into three major regions. First was the principality, chiefly the area that held out longest against conquest, where Edward I had introduced a substantial measure of English administration. This included the counties of Anglesey, Caernarvon, Merioneth, Flint, Cardigan and Carmarthen. There were also the Marcher lordships, most of which had over the years become subject to the King as the greatest Marcher lord. Finally, there were some independent lordships, chiefly in Montgomeryshire and parts of the south.

This patchwork of territory was commonly regarded as beset by crime, violence and the lack of effective and equitable means for enforcing the laws. Typical of many comments from this time was the remark of Sir Edward Croft in 1533 that 'Wales is far out of order and there have been many murders in Oswestry and Powys'.[1] Criminals could easily find refuge by fleeing into other jurisdictions; and much worse was the role of great lords and gentry in defending or abetting the criminals. Throughout the century, it would be remarked how the great were surrounded by followers who used their position to escape the consequences of their actions. Between 1536 and 1543, a series of Parliamentary statutes created a new legal and administrative framework for Wales. Collectively, these measures are known as the Acts of Union, which remain controversial in both their intent and their consequences. Nationalist writers lament the termination of the legal identity of Wales. Others would follow

1. Trevor Herbert and Gareth E. Jones, eds., *Tudor Wales* (Cardiff 1988), 147.

W. Llewelyn Williams in seeing the measures as (in a sense) the 'grant of a constitution', to a Wales whose legal subjugation dated back at least to the Statute of Rhuddlan in 1284. For contemporaries, however, such grand aims were scarcely in view. The new legal settlement of Wales was emergency legislation, strictly an ad hoc response to the public order crisis.

Initially, the reforms sought to end the jurisdictional problems that permitted criminals and bandits to escape punishment by fleeing to an independent Marcher lordship. Soon, however, more sweeping changes were effected: Justices of the Peace were appointed, on the English model, and the whole of Wales was to be divided into counties. This involved sewing together the new Welsh shires that became Glamorgan, Pembroke, Brecon, Montgomery, Radnor and Denbigh. In addition, Monmouthshire was to become an English county. All counties were to have the appropriate institutions, including the right to return Members of Parliament. English was to be the language of the law and of a reorganised court system, and the inheritance practice of gavelkind was to be replaced by the English pattern of primogeniture. Also prohibited were the customs of *cymortha* (the exaction of payments from neighbours or tenants) and *arddel*, or the ability of a fleeing offender to take refuge with a lord. The final Act, of 1543, consolidated the previous measures, and also gave statutory authority to the prerogative council in Wales and the Marches. Not initially connected with the reforms were the changes associated with the Reformation, but these also affected the hierarchy of government in Wales by transforming the parish into another arm of secular administration. As in England, the county and the parish would define the structure of government in Wales for the next three centuries.

However the new counties were to be structured, it was essential to have some higher organ with the power to oversee local administration, and to prevent local officeholders from flouting the law. This authority was properly known as 'The Lord President and Council of the Dominion and Principality of Wales and the Marches of the Same', with its headquarters eventually fixed at Ludlow. It had a civil and criminal jurisdiction extending over the whole of Wales and the English border shires, though the latter made strenuous efforts to secede under James I. The Council enforced the administration of justice, supervised local officials, struggled against vagabondage and piracy, and oversaw defence and internal security. In the context of the time, these last functions naturally gave the Council wide scope in matters of religion and belief.

Originally formed under Edward IV and Henry VII, the Council flourished for a century after the grant of a new legal mandate in the 1530s, and it gained real stature under the presidency of Rowland Lee, Bishop of Lichfield (1534–1543). It probably reached its height in the time of Sir Henry Sydney (1559–1586), with his powerful Court connections. The position of the President approached that of viceroy, and the Christmas festivities at Ludlow under Elizabeth and James I were those of a provincial Court. This authority was most directly felt when the presidents were themselves great landowners in Wales, as with the first two Earls of Pembroke. The Council themselves included some of the greatest Welsh magnates, major gentry like Sir John Perrott of Pembrokeshire, Richard Pryse of Cardiganshire, Sir Thomas Mansell of Glamorgan, or Sir Richard Trevor of Denbighshire. There was also a considerable legal and administrative apparatus with all that implied for powers of patronage.

THE COUNTIES

The Council was dissolved in 1641, but it was the only one of the regional prerogative courts restored after 1660; though without its criminal jurisdiction, Thereafter it enjoyed a curious afterlife until final abolition in 1689. Other aspects of the Henrician legislation shaped government and administration in Wales until the end of the nineteenth century and beyond. A series of powerful local offices were either created, or else extended to the whole of Wales. In the social context of the time, it was inevitable that these would become the preserve of the new lay landowners, the gentry. They used this official power to reinforce their growing position as masters of the county community.

In the long run, the most valued of the new prizes was election to Parliament, the county constituency being the richer plum. Wales and Monmouthshire together had 27 constituencies, a rather meagre representation that reflected official recognition of the nation's poverty: it simply could not afford to support more idle hands. Each county had a single Member of Parliament, except for the 'English' shire of Monmouth, which had two. Every county also had a single borough representative, with two exceptions. Merioneth, poorest and least populous of shires, had none; while Pembrokeshire had an additional member for the borough (technically, 'county') of

Haverfordwest. By the later seventeenth century, the total electorate was probably about 20,000, which meant that perhaps a fifth of the adult male population was entitled to vote.

In the century after the Acts of Union, the new social elite of Tudor Wales could be recognised by the firm grip that the various gentry families had secured on parliamentary representation of both county and borough. Only slightly less prestigious at this time was the office of sheriff. Though burdensome, the shrievalty involved real power, above all during a contested parliamentary election. It is scarcely an exaggeration to say that sheriffs decided most such elections in the century after 1540. Sheriffs were rarely even notionally neutral: in Montgomeryshire in 1588, the sheriff actively canvassed for one candidate, who was his father-in-law. A sheriff received the writ ordering a new election, which he was quite capable of concealing or delaying. On the election day itself, it was common for Elizabethan sheriffs to perpetrate a sudden change of venue, that was announced only to his political allies. In Denbighshire in 1588, the election was secretly shifted to the well-defended house of one of the allies of the sheriff and his candidate, although the property did not even lie within the boundaries of Wrexham, which the writ had specified as the legal venue.

Even if the opposition detected the ruse and forced an entry, it was still possible for a biassed sheriff to overturn a vast majority with which he did not concur. He determined the victor by his highly subjective perception of the number of voices cast on each side. If the contest went to a ballot, there was infinite flexibility for selectively qualifying the voters of each faction. It is likely that many of those casting their votes in an Elizabethan or Jacobean election represented social categories so humble that they would not receive the franchise legally until the age of Gladstone.

Less critical than sheriff, though still important, was the characteristic gentry office of Justice of the Peace. By the 1530s, Justices were already central to the enforcement of law in England, and their administrative importance would grow steadily over the next century. By 1600, they were theoretically charged with the enforcement of over 300 statutes. Acting singly or in pairs, Justices were responsible for suppressing and investigating a wide range of criminal activity, while the legislation of the 1560s made them central to the organisation of the Poor Law. At Quarter Sessions, the Justices acted in effect as the local parliament, with a greater abundance of 'devolved' powers than have been suggested in most recent schemes for Welsh provincial 'assemblies'. The President and

Council played an important role in choosing and continuing Justices; particular attention was paid to the key office of Custos Rotulorum in each county.

At the Great Sessions – held twice yearly, for a period of six days – the circuit judges tried the accused committed by the Justices. The Great Sessions provided a real focus for county solidarity and public festivities, when there were important opportunities for the expression of official policies in the judges' speeches. In addition, a leading cleric presented an assize sermon which often stated the religious or political views of the county community, or at least of whichever faction was in the ascendant at the time. There were four Welsh circuits, each containing three shires (Monmouthshire was connected to the Oxford circuit). From the 1570s, there were two Justices for each circuit, as well as an inferior hierarchy of prothonotaries, chamberlains, criers and so on; with all appointments heavily influenced by the President of the Council. Until their abolition in 1830, the Great Sessions were the only distinctively Welsh legal or political institution. However, the judges themselves rarely had local roots: between 1542 and 1830, only 14 per cent of the incumbents were of Welsh origin.

The Justices were drawn from the great and middling gentry, and by the late sixteenth century, there were normally 15 to 20 in each county. After the Restoration, both offices, Justice and sheriff, were increasingly devalued. By the 1730s and 1740s, appointment as sheriff was a fate inflicted on farmers and petty landowners lacking the connections to escape the burden. More serious was the fate of the Bench of Justices, where there were desperate efforts to find men really willing to undertake the work in addition to holding the honour of the post. From the early eighteenth century, petty gentry and urban professionals were increasingly drafted to fulfil this function, and the county Benches grew dramatically in number: a typical Welsh county might have over 100 Justices by 1750, over 200 by 1800.

Justices and sheriffs were at the apex of the civil administrative hierarchy, which also included lesser positions like coroner, and the constables of hundreds or parishes. However, there was also a distinctive and separate military hierarchy in charge of the militia and the armed forces. The existence of the Council gave Wales distinctive arrangements in this area. In England, the crucial figures were the Lords-Lieutenant, but in Wales, the presidents initally held this position for all the counties. This responsibility forced the delegation of functions like recruitment and military preparations, originally through the selection of special commissioners. From the 1580s, however, deputy-lieutenants were appointed. Every county had at least one, while most had two, often selected to take acount of internal divisions within the shire. This was a sensitive and prestigious office, held by the greatest gentry. In Caernarvonshire, this meant men like William Maurice of Clenennau and Sir John Wynn of Gwydir, respectively serving the western and eastern regions.

The numbers of deputy-lieutenants increased during the seventeenth century, chiefly to accommodate ambitious gentry. Even so, the lieutenancy was always a more select body than the Bench, and inclusion was a valuable guide both to political loyalty and to economic status. In a typical county by the later seventeenth century, Justices outnumbered deputy-lieutenants by roughly three to one. In 1663, each county had nine or ten deputy-lieutenants, and a list of the lieutenancy includes the cream of county society. In Cardiganshire, the group was headed by Sir Richard Pryse of Gogerddan, Sir Francis Lloyd of Peterwell and Sir Edward Vaughan of Crosswood. In Caernarvonshire, we find elite names like Sir John Owen of Clenennau, Sir Richard Wynn of Gwydir and William Griffiths of Cefnamwlch.

INVASION

The select nature of the lieutenancy draws attention to the central importance of defence and security as paramount considerations for early modern regimes; though in fact, this emphasis also affected every arm of government. From ancient times, social and economic conditions in Wales had been much affected by the nation's trade routes across the western seas, to Ireland and south-western Britain, and beyond to western France and Spain. Under the Tudors and Stuarts, this geographical context was of major political concern, because it made Wales a likely entry point for raiding or invasion; particularly when the country had so many promising ports and landing sites.

In a sense, the early modern period both begins and ends with maritime incursions of a type that contemporary governments had to view with deep concern. In 1485, Henry Tudor began his march to Bosworth Field from Milford Haven, in Pembrokeshire; while in 1797, a French expeditionary force landed in the same county, at

Fishguard. Between the two dates, fears of landings were endemic. In turn, dissidents and exiles often viewed Wales as hopeful territory in which to launch an invasion. If Henry VII had come to Milford, why should not the Old Pretender begin a victorious campaign at Milford or Swansea? It was in the 1690s that a perceptive if inaccurate historian attributed the wealth of castles in Wales to the ancient threat of foreign invasion.

In the 1540s, the chief danger appeared to be the French, but the events of the Reformation presented new dangers. Anglesey was felt to be a prime target for naval occupation, with at least one scare in every decade from the 1530s through to the civil wars. Spanish threats were naturally paramount under Elizabeth, but it was the fear of Irish incursions that dominated the seventeenth century. Ireland was Catholic, populous and hostile, so there was a perennial fear that an Irish rebellion would lead to invasion. The Irish situation was a pressing reality in the 1590s, when the wars required the conscription of thousands of Welsh soldiers. Between 1594 and 1604, 6611 men were forcibly enlisted: almost three per cent of the total population. In Caernarvonshire, the levies represented perhaps 15 per cent of the adult male population.

If the Irish struck back at Wales, they would no doubt be assisted by an insidious fifth column drawn from local peers and gentry, who could offer both ports and castles. Once Wales was secure, the towns of the English midlands were open to assault. The potential alliance between local subversives and Irish invaders was a fear that shaped Welsh history for over a century. In the civil war, the hopes of the Royalist cause were gravely damaged by the negotiations conducted by the Earl of Glamorgan, son of the Marquess of Worcester, with the Irish rebels. In 1688, a fear of Irish invasion led to panic and rioting in many centres, notably at Bala and Dolgellau.

Irish landings were rumoured, or feared to be imminent, in 1641, 1678, 1688 and 1691. When the Irish threat became implausible after the Williamite wars, it was rapidly submerged into the similar danger of French Catholic invaders allying with local Jacobites. However, this new version of 'the threat from the seas' retained the same basic cast of characters, the same gentry families at the same castles and mansions; and the Somerset family continued to play a central role. A French landing was actually believed to have occurred in Glamorgan in 1708; while Jacobite-assisted landings were feared in 1722 and 1745. At least from the sixteenth century to the eighteenth, Welsh politics were rarely free of the danger of conspiracy and sedition, always linked both to foreign perils and religious dissidence.

Even when the coasts appeared to be relatively secure from political threats, they still posed significant problems for the enforcement of law and order. Wales in the seventeenth century possessed literally hundreds of small ports and creeks, and there were many remote islands and beaches which could serve as landing places. There was enormous potential for piracy and smuggling, while celebrated pirates like John Challice frequently allied with the authorities. In the late sixteenth century, a major target of such charges of connivance was Edward Kemys of Cefn Mabli in Glamorgan, who held the office of sheriff no less than four times. Nothing better illustrates the dilemma of early modern administration, the impossibility of ensuring equitable law enforcement in face of upperworld criminality.

In sixteenth century west Wales, it was widely believed that pirates were succoured by gentry, who sheltered them in their houses. In face of such a threat, the only solution was concerted action by other Justices: but who would be prepared to commit such a deadly sin against the harmony of county society? Richard Davies, the Bishop of St Davids, attempted to eliminate this scandal, but found it impossible when those tainted were said to include some of the most prominent men in the royal regime, like Richard Vaughan and even Sir John Perrott. In Caernarvonshire, there were gentry in sixteenth century Llŷn who grew rich without visible means of honest improvement, and piracy and smuggling are both likely explanations for their success. Such pirates might well be semi-political in nature, or at least they represented organised groups like the Barbary pirates. In the mid-seventeenth century, Dutch privateers were felt to be a constant danger, in part because of the fear that they might ally with local Puritans or Roundhead veterans. Where there were iron forges, squires were said to engage in the illicit manufacture and export of heavy weaponry.

Finally, wrecks were a rich source for additional income for coastal communities. Riots frequently occurred when Justices or squires attempted to safeguard the goods of a wrecked ship from plunder by the country people. On the other hand, it is important to define 'wrecking' with some care, and there are few well-authenticated incidents before the eighteenth century where a ship was deliberately lured to ruin by false beacons. Conflict arose rather over differing legal definitions over who had the rights to the goods of a ship once it was ashore. In the 1770s and 1780s, judges and magistrates inflicted severe penalties in an attempt to deter coastal plunder. The enduring maritime threat gave a real importance to the positions of Vice-Admiral of North and South Wales; while the opportunities provided by wrecks made these worthwhile offices, held only by the most powerful lords and squires.

RISINGS AND CONSPIRACIES

Alongside foreign threats, there was also felt to be a constant danger of internal political subversion, often to a puzzling extent. It often seems as if Justices and deputy-lieutenants grew disproportionately excited at the prospect of a plot or conspiracy, and the discovery of a sinister letter or a few weapons drove them to what may appear to be heights of paranoia. To understand the nature of government and administration in this period, it is essential to comprehend the power of this conspiracy tradition.

As to its plausibility, it is useful to recall the enormous impact that only a few leaders with a handful of weapons could have in the civil war era. By modern standards, armies were small affairs. In the first civil war, most of the key battles fought in south-west Wales probably involved only 1000 or so men on each side, and the loss of 850 men (killed or taken prisoner) at the battle of Colby Moor in 1645 crippled the Royalist cause in the region. 4000 men under Prince Maurice staved off Royalist collapse throughout north Wales. At St Fagan's in 1648, the total involved in both sides was perhaps 11,000; but this was quite exceptional.

More typical was the rising in 1648 when Sir John Owen raised 150 horse and 120 foot in the King's service. With this tiny force, he was able to stage a vital diversion for the main Royalist rising in south-east England. He operated for several weeks, confining the Parliamentarian commander Mytton to his stronghold at Caernarvon castle. Properly led, a force of a few hundred could dominate two counties. Owen's short-lived success helps to explain why activists were jailed so readily at the faintest suspicion of trouble. This was also why loyalists grew so disturbed at the news of dissenting religious meetings that attracted hundreds of supporters, whether the dissidents in question were the recusants of 1590, the Puritans of 1670 or the Methodists of 1760.

Vulnerability to plots, to surprise attack by small armed forces, helps explain the continuing importance of those ancient bastions of power, the medieval castles. They were vital to the preservation of order in Wales at least to the end of the Stuart era, and they suggest the limitations of the changes achieved by the Tudors. In the fifteenth century, south Wales had been dominated by the lords of great castles like Raglan, who undertook expeditions on behalf of the King against the strongholds of his enemies. But all through the sixteenth and seventeenth centuries, Raglan continued to be the essential centre for royal security in Wales, and the castle itself would be refurbished and modernised until the traumatic capitulation of 1646, which marked the fall of royal authority in the south.

The importance of the castles was most apparent during the civil war, which was in Wales largely a contest of castles and sieges. The changing balance of political power can be traced through observing the fate of the castles and garrisons, and the loyalties of the men placed in charge of them. In 1659, the success of the extreme religious radicals was marked by their takeover of the key fortresses of north and mid-Wales, as at Caernarvon, Conway and Beaumaris. Meanwhile, south Wales was dominated by the garrisons at Swansea and Cardiff, making a political landscape that would have been quite familiar to Edward I. In the 1670s, it was the Marquess of Worcester's garrison at Chepstow Castle that was seen as the dominant military reality in the Bristol Channel area. In addition, these royal castles served as political prisons. Henry Marten the republican was long an inmate of Chepstow, but many humbler radicals were incarcerated in the 1660s. Even in the nineteenth century, with castles thoroughly obsolete, it often appeared that the army garrison at Brecon would be the last redoubt against insurrection in the industrial areas.

ORTHODOXY AND OFFICE-HOLDING

For the central government, the twin threats of invasion and subversion made Wales an important area, in which official policies were shaped by events far afield. The attitude of the government to dissidence often depended on international affairs as much as the character of the individual administrators. At times of perceived threat, there was a high premium on religious and political orthodoxy, and on ensuring that there was a powerful network of key government supporters in each shire.

In the Tudor period, it was common for patronage to be concentrated in the hands of one trusted servant, who might receive copious official rewards. In Pembrokeshire, so exposed to invasion and piracy, this function was exercised by Sir John Perrott (1530–1592); his counterpart in mid-Wales was Edward Herbert of Montgomery (1513–1593). On the other hand, this great power might readily be abused, and it inevitably tended to attract jealousy or resentment. Attacks on the royal servant tended to become directed against the regime which he represented. In the 1570s, Perrott was constantly under attack by a powerful faction led by the Philipps of Picton, and including the great squires of Slebech, Orielton, Prendergast and Henllys.

In addition, dissidents had to be excluded from important administrative positions like the lieutenancy or the Bench of Justices. Between 1642 and 1725, partisan appointments and ejections were a common and controversial phenomenon; but a balance had to be struck. Alongside the need for security and political correctness was a rival concept which held that county institutions like the Bench or the lieutenancy were offices held of right by the leading men of the community. Those excluded might well be insulted, and even driven to opposition or active sedition. As we will see, in the later seventeenth century, there were occasions when the royal government determined to rule an area only through one loyalist faction or network, to the exclusion of moderates. The ensuing conflict effectively made shires like Monmouthshire ungovernable. Again under Anne, the frequent official purges gave a fierce intensity to party conflict.

THE NATURE OF POWER IN EARLY MODERN WALES

Politics and government in early modern Wales differed radically from modern practices, and the extent of these differences is often masked by the apparent similarities. In the seventeenth century, we find factions that bear superficial resemblance to modern political parties, and these groups struggle for control of local office-holding or parliamentary representation in what appears a recognisably modern way. Having said this, there were fundamental differences in both the nature of politics and the substance of power; and the workings of government cannot be understood without recognising these different assumptions.

To illustrate this, consider Sir Edward Mansell of Margam (1636–1706), one of the most powerful figures in late Stuart south

Wales. Mansell's power can be recognised from his successful tenure of all the elite local offices of the time, and by the comments of contemporaries. However, explaining this power is a more complicated matter. In examining this one case, we can also sketch the political foundations of pre-industrial Wales: what was true for Mansell of Margam was equally true for Mostyn of Mostyn, Philipps of Picton Castle, Wynn of Gwydir, Bulkeley of Baron Hill, or 50 other elite families.

The power of a family like the Mansells was ultimately based on local wealth and landholding. By the 1670s, he was the lord of 11 manors, and the annual income of the Margam estate was probably some £4000, which made Sir Edward one of the wealthiest individuals in Wales. This landed power also provided him with hundreds of tenants, dependants and servants, who could all be useful in asserting Mansell power, for instance in faction fights with other gentry. The estate dominated a large swathe of the western Vale of Glamorgan and of west Gower. This economic power made it unthinkable for a central government to attempt to govern the county of Glamorgan without using Margam and its lords. In turn, authority in the locality was consolidated by generations of intermarriage with the neighbouring gentry.

Power was therefore firmly rooted within the shire, but there was also a crucial national dimension. Authority would have been meaningless without the administrative and political positions that permitted the exercise of power in the community. Sir Edward was thus a Justice and a deputy lieutenant; he served as sheriff; and he and his family long retained a hold on the representation of both the county and borough seats of Glamorgan. His position was thus reinforced by alliance with the central government that dispensed offices and patronage. Sir Edward Mansell used his personal and family power to gain access to the regime. His relative, the Earl of Manchester, was probably responsible for securing his appointment as Vice-Admiral of south Wales; and also several successive Secretaries of State, especially Sir Joseph Williamson. Courtiers and bureaucrats depended on Mansell and his like to maintain the loyalty of the localities; Mansell enhanced his power and standing by serving as a conduit for government favours and patronage. The relationship between local and national government was thus both essential and reciprocal.

THE MEYRICKS

This interchange between local and national affairs also helps to explain the nature of factional or party politics in the early modern era, when national issues and ideologies were complicated by the role of service or clientage to great families. We will see in chapter seven that aristocratic clientage played a vital part in shaping loyalties during the civil war and interregnum, as local gentry followed the lead set nationally by peers like the Earls of Pembroke, Leicester, Essex and Worcester. This relationship to a wealthy family might extend over generations, which means that it is rarely possible to understand a specific incident or conflict without appreciating the historical background and the family context. Studying the genealogies of the great families in this period is no mere snobbish indulgence: it provides an essential tool for historical analysis.

The nature and endurance of clientage is suggested by the case of a gentry house that served the Devereux Earls of Essex. This was the Meyrick family, that came to be based in Pembrokeshire. Gelly Meyrick was a follower of the Earl of Essex from 1583, and served as steward of the Earl's household. However, he was executed following Essex's coup attempt in 1601. Gelly's nephews also served the Devereux, and another Gelly Meyrick would be adjutant general of the Earl's forces in the civil wars.

But the relationship lasted even longer than this. In the 1670s, a high Anglican cleric named Francis Godwyn complained of his maltreatment at the hands of Pembrokeshire Whigs. Foremost among these was Essex Meyrick, son of the second Gelly, and said to be a fanatical supporter of 'conventicling liberty'. Meyrick led Whig factions both in Haverfordwest, and among the gentry of south Pembrokeshire. Godwyn explains the relationship of the Meyrick family to that Earl of Essex 'who led presbyterian villainy into the field armed'.[2] Appropriately, Godwyn himself could also be taken as a representative of the enduring character of politics in the era. He counted several Anglican bishops among his ancestors, and his grandfather and father had served the Royalist cause with as much loyalty as the Meyricks had served parliament.

Clientage and long-standing loyalties to a noble house might thus be associated with the powerful force of kinship and family tradition, and this could cause conflicts with ideological or religious belief. When an Anglican became head of the Somerset family in 1667, it

---

2. Thomas Godwyn, *Phanatical tenderness* . . . (London 1684).

assuredly did not mean that the house lost the support of its Catholic adherents, or that the Somersets regarded themselves as less obligated to support and defend those neighbours and friends. When an aristocratic house lost its primary association with an area, it might take many years for residual loyalty to that house to fade.

THE VAUGHAN INTEREST

One of the key concepts in the politics of the age was that of 'interest', a more useful concept than the anachronistic 'party'. The Mansells and Devereux both had celebrated interests; but we might also take a third example, the Vaughan family of Golden Grove, who were descended from 'the blood royal of Carmarthenshire'. Under James I, Sir John Vaughan was accused of maintaining a body of liveried retainers, contrary to laws over a century old. A strong Catholic, Vaughan prevented other Justices from enforcing the recusancy laws against his people. His son, the Earl of Carbery, commanded Royalist forces in west Wales in the early phase of the first civil war, and was President of the Council in the Marches from 1661 to 1671. His son John, Lord Vaughan, was also a Member of Parliament. He commanded the army regiment that bore his name, and served as governor of Jamaica from 1674 to 1678. The Vaughans were therefore a wonderful channel of official patronage. Despite this official favour from the Stuarts, the Vaughans were by no means Royalist fanatics, and the Earl's mother was a Meyrick. They used their Devereux connections to make an easy exit from the war, and enjoyed much official favour under the Commonwealth.

By the 1650s, Carbery effectively ruled Carmarthenshire, in part through his access to the house of Essex. Moreover, 'he (Carbery) hath set up and maintaineth an interest in most counties of Wales': an interest that would survive for a generation, under a very diverse series of regimes. This power originated with landholding and the wealth and prestige that gave, together with family connections, but 'interest' implied far more. An interest involved a network of loyalties that extended from wealthy landowners to lesser squires, to professionals and clergy, and ultimately to the tenants and farmers who would provide the footsoldiers for the great.

The course chosen by the Carbery family (or the Mansells) was important not only for the attitudes of the Earls and their immediate families, but for hundreds or even thousands of others in their 'interest'. In the seventeenth century, it was likely that this service to a great lord or squire would involve following him into literal combat, if not in a battlefield then in the streets of a nearby town at election time. By the eighteenth century, an 'interest' normally began with the accumulation of a landed estate, and was followed by the consolidation of electoral power.

As Carbery went politically, so followed his kinsmen and neighbours, even if this involved serpentine changes in loyalty, from Catholic and Anglican Royalist, to civil war neutral and later Whig. Of course the Earl would be followed by great squires like Harry Vaughan of Derwydd or John Vaughan at Derllys, all 'principled and actuated by their kinsman', the Earl. We also hear of another Carmarthenshire gentleman named Harry Middleton who was in principle a firm monarchist, but in practice he too was 'necessarily subservient to the Earl of Carbery's will'.[3]

Kinship ties could obviously affect the administration of justice. In 1656, William Williams of Carmarthenshire published an account of his maltreatment at the hands of Carbery and his relatives, who had (he claimed) repeatedly swayed courts and juries in their favour. In England, he wrote,

> you will have no respect of persons; but we [in Wales] being
> descended from the ancient Brute, and so truly noble, do and will make a
> difference, and will make you know that he that toucheth anyone within
> the ninth degree of our prince, or any of our cousins, allies, or
> confederates, it were better for him to take a bear by the tooth; yea,
> though the thing were true, it shall cost all that he can procure to spend[4]

The Carbery interest therefore did much to shape the attitude of a whole county towards national issues, but quite humble local controversies were linked ultimately to national 'high' politics. The Earl's will was expressed through the clique's control of the instruments of justice, the holding of offices like sheriff and Justice of the Peace; and these positions depended on maintaining government favour. If a family lost these offices, an interest might well crumble; but once this favour was secure, anything was possible, and an interest could dominate whole counties. Opposing a friend or favourite of Golden Grove might mean having to deal with the extensive powers available to hostile Justices, with false charges tried before thoroughly partisan juries and biassed judges. Loyalty to a

3. NLW Llanstephan MS 120.
4. William Williams, 'A mystery of iniquity, or a remarkable relation of a Carmarthenshire cause. . . .' (1656), copy in Cardiff Central Library.

great family – gentle or noble – was a matter of survival more than sentiment.

LOCAL AND NATIONAL POLITICS

In early modern Wales, it is exceedingly difficult to draw a dividing line between the politics of the county or locality and those of the nation, to divide issues from self-interest. Under Charles II, local Whigs like Essex Meyrick were part of the Pembrokeshire county community, but they were also part of the national connection or interest that looked to Whiggish aristocrats and courtiers like Lords Wharton or Holles. Within the county, they in turn controlled their own interests or factions, cemented by whatever patronage, whatever moneyed or landed power was available to them. An individual might thus be part of a nationwide chain of common interests, ideologies and allegiances; and at the summit of that faction were lords or parliamentary leaders with the power to shape policy by securing the favour or goodwill of the monarch.

The 'interest' of Carbery (or of Lord Mansell, or of Sir Watkin Williams-Wynn) thus merged into national politics and parties, a fusion that found one expression in parliamentary politics. Membership in a national faction also offered the opportunity of election outside the normal confines of the Welsh seats. In 1640, there were five Caernarvonshire squires in parliament, though the county's own quota was only two. Throughout the century after 1660, there were normally five or six MPs of Glamorgan origins. This made it all the more likely that local feuds would be projected on to the national stage.

The public nature of parliamentary affairs makes this impact easy to trace. Less visible for the modern historian was the eternal quest for office at court or in the central government, where success could put an invaluable seal on local power. In the early seventeenth century, tenure of local offices symbolised the stature of great Welsh gentry like the Mansells of south Wales or the Wynns of Gwydir in the north; but this authority was also cemented by Court positions that ultimately depended on personal access to the monarch or those around him. Between 1617 and 1643, the 'high politics' of north Wales must take account of the personal whim and favour of magnates like Lord Keeper John Williams, or the Duke of Buckingham. For the winners in these competitions, there were rich offices to be had, and more power to be dispensed to followers. Sir Richard Wynn of Gwydir was a successful courtier who held many offices; one brother was solicitor to Queen Henrietta Maria; another held a position in Chancery.

FEUDS AND FACTIONS

Personal and family power therefore became inextricably linked with the use and abuse of official position. For much of the sixteenth and seventeenth centuries, the political history of Wales revolved around conflicts or feuds between family-based gentry factions, with the spoils of office as the highest reward. Struggles that apparently could have little more than a county or local significance came to involve magnates and courtiers on a national scale. These battles were not devoid of political or religious content, and in the century after 1540 it was common for rival parties to espouse different religious causes. However, not until the crisis of the mid-seventeenth century did these considerations become paramount. It is the civil war era that marks the increasing role of religion and ideological politics in faction feuds; though the case of Golden Grove indicates that 'interest' long coexisted with party. Conflicts on the Elizabethan model were by no means extinct in Georgian Wales.

The complexities of sixteenth-century politics are suggested by the case of Denbighshire.[5] There was a sizeable Catholic interest here, and a tradition of clandestine organisation that ultimately led to the execution in 1586 of one of the greatest men in the shire, Thomas Salusbury of Llewenni. On the other hand, the political divisions reflected other priorities: of family pride and precedence, Court factions, and office-holding. In the 1580s, there was a marked division between the gentry of the eastern and western halves of the county, with their respective capitals at Wrexham and Denbigh. Also crucial were personal rivalries that developed into lasting feuds. The roots of such antagonism are difficult to locate, but they usually arose from petty insults, often imagined. Commonly, blame could be placed on the tavern or street altercations of servants or retainers, each vaunting the glory of their respective masters. In 1576, Dr David Lewis wrote a famous account of conditions in Wales which noted that

5. J.E. Neale, *The Elizabethan House of Commons* (London 1949).

> The great disorders in Wales specially in south Wales have grown much of late days, by retainers of gentlemen, whom they must after the manner of the country bear out in all actions be they never so bad[6]

In 1588, the 'western' candidate was one William Almer, who had become engaged in conflicts with several of the most powerful easterners, including the families of Edwardes, Trevor, Puleston and Brereton. These personal feuds led to an electoral contest, in which Almer was defeated through the creative procedural abuses of the sheriff. The contest suggests the scale and importance of the respective 'interests'. At election time, each squire led his followers to Wrexham for the poll, with the consequence that the town was filled with two or three thousand well-armed men ready to fight for their respective faction. A typical Elizabethan election represented an armed gathering little smaller than many civil war engagements in Wales. In the Montgomeryshire contest of 1588, we specifically hear of crowds armed with 'swords, bucklers, forest-bills, long staves, and glaives'. There was real menace in John Salusbury's remark in 1601 that he would be elected county member if it took 500 deaths to achieve his end; and it is remarkable that such gatherings so rarely resulted in open warfare.

The 1601 contest also demonstrates the importance of national factions in local feuds. In the 1590s, the Earl of Essex had systematically built up a strong interest in Wales, with Sir Gelly Meyrick as his local 'manager'. Devereux followers already held the borough seats of Cardigan, Carmarthen and Radnor. The east Denbighshire families had generally attached themselves to this rising star. Their initial rewards included offices like deputy-lieutenant, and the knighthoods that gave social precedence to easterners like Sir Richard Trevor of Trevalun and Sir John Lloyd of Bodidris. The patronage proved especially valuable at this time, when the urgent demand for fighting men in Ireland permitted the lieutenants to conscript their political opponents, or to extort money by threat of such coercion. On the other hand, alignment with national factions also carried its perils, and the fall of Essex in 1601 threw his whole interest into jeopardy. In 1601, there was an election even more bitter than that of 1588, with the eastern deputy-lieutenants using a militia muster as the excuse to stockpile arms in readiness. The ensuing assembly was so contentious, and the danger of bloodshed so great, that the election was postponed.

Denbighshire was notoriously factious, and the tenure of key

6. Trevor Herbert and Gareth E. Jones, eds., *Tudor Wales*, (Cardiff 1988), 153.

offices was consequently of the greatest importance. On the other hand, all the Welsh shires had their legendary feuds and struggles in this period, with the commonest motive being resentment of the hegemony of one great family. In the Montgomeryshire contest of 1588, it was the Herberts of Montgomery who were defending their supremacy. In Caernarvonshire in 1620, the target of gentry resentment was the house of Gwydir under its patriarch, Sir John Wynn. His son Richard was defeated for the county seat by John Griffiths of Cefnamwlch, from a rising family that succeeded in mobilising the western regions of Llŷn and Eifionydd. This affair naturally drew in protagonists from other shires, including Sir Richard Trevor of Denbighshire, and it involved Court interference. In addition, the Griffiths had the support of the President of the Council, the Earl of Northampton. The ramifications of such conflict were by no means confined to the secular establishment. The Wynns were supported by the Bishop of Bangor, Lewis Bayly, who was in turn subverted by his own Dean, a Griffiths of Cefnamwlch. A contested election might be only one manifestation of unrest and division that could paralyse effective administration for years.

These were some of the great 'set-piece' battles of the period, but conflicts of this kind were endemic. They often turned into street riots, duels or even sieges. We have to exercise great care in reading such accounts. Often, we hear about them from only one side, from victims anxious to depict their opponents not only as wrong but as guilty of riotous acts worthy of the attention of Star Chamber. But the widespread use of violence in such feuds is beyond doubt. Also notable is the kaleidoscopic diversity of the conflicts in evidence: rarely was there one single family feud dominating a region over a generation.

In Glamorgan, for example, the dominant reality of political life was the power of the Earls of Pembroke, and of the several branches of the Herbert family established in the county. From the 1550s onwards, the major conflicts set the Herberts against great local gentry like the Mansells and Stradlings. In 1557, a dispute over the seizure of a wreck led to a riot at Oxwich castle, with the death of a Mansell lady. Through the next decade, Mansells and Stradlings affected to defend royal interests against the alleged abuses of Pembroke within the lordship of Glamorgan. In the 1570s, however, the Mansells and Stradlings themselves became the leaders of rival factions, each being followed by half a dozen lesser gentry. In 1576, a riot at Cowbridge set William Herbert against two of these lesser families attached to the Mansells. None of these conflicts were involved in the most violent and enduring battles of the period, the Cardiff riots of the 1590s. These set the Herberts and Lewises against other local gentry, the Mathews.

In such a balkanised situation, control of the machinery of government and the administration of justice was critical, in that it allowed a faction to bypass legal procedures to achieve their ends. In 1595, the bailiff of Cardiff jailed some followers of Sir William Herbert, only to be attacked by some 18 Herbert followers sent to liberate the prisoners. In turn, the burgesses of Cardiff were roused to attack the Herbert men, with consequences of death and mutilation. Sir William Herbert then persuaded his relative, the sheriff, to pack the coroner's jury in the case, and thus find no grounds for criminal proceedings. Local malpractice could only be countered by attracting the sympathetic intervention of the central government, and the state papers of the Tudor and Jacobean periods are littered with petitions accusing local Justices and sheriffs of the most heinous deeds. These are obviously partisan documents, which can only be read with the greatest scepticism. On the other hand, such petitions do serve to illustrate the necessity of buttressing local interest with influence in the central government.

Glamorgan offers another example of this interplay of interests. In 1584, the death of a local landowner left Barbara Gamage of Coity as a highly sought heiress. It was natural that rivals should have competed for her hand, but the contemporary political context also ensured that this became an affair of national politics. One of the suitors was Herbert Croft, grandson to the Comptroller of the Royal Household, who was also a friend of Lord Burghley. On the other hand, the victor in this great matter of state proved to be even better placed in terms of Welsh politics: this was Robert Sydney, son of the current President of the Council in the Marches, with his connections to the Herberts and Dudleys. The courtship therefore could be seen as another stage in the running battle between the Cecil and Dudley factions at Court. In Welsh terms, the consequence was the creation of a new aristocratic interest, and Robert Sydney twice represented the county of Glamorgan in Parliament.

It is easy to see how family conflicts over office and patronage might achieve national political significance. In Caernarvonshire, there was a serious and lasting struggle between the two gentry families based at Cefnamwlch and Glynllifon. In 1626, the Griffiths' of Cefnamwlch succeeded in obtaining the position of Vice Admiral of North Wales, much to the displeasure of the Glynnes of Glynllifon, who now emerge as opposition leaders – a rare enough phenomenon in Caernarvonshire. By 1640, Thomas and John Glynne were both prominent in the Parliamentary opposition, against the courtier family of Cefnamwlch. In 1642, Thomas Glynne and his allies were arrested as likely insurgents against the Crown. Though all initially served the King, Glynne and his clique were among the first Caernarvonshire defectors to the parliamentary side in 1646. He was a mainstay of the parliamentary committees, and he also received the long coveted position of Vice-Admiral of north Wales. Not until the Restoration did Cefnamwlch return to official prominence.

The official records of Tudor and early Stuart Wales portray a deeply split society with extensive lawlessness and partisan conflict, with divisions extending into every aspect of the new political settlement – parliament, the Bench and Lieutenancy, offices like coroner and sheriff. On the other hand, the sheer wealth of the documents is misleading. The new organs of government and administration were not the cause of division, so much as the arena in which existing grievances were fought out. Also, the situation was almost certainly improving by the late sixteenth century. Whereas earlier Welsh magnates had carried on their private battles with little need to consider central intervention, the Elizabethan squires were clearly well aware of the chance of action by the Council in the Marches or by Star Chamber, and this did have a restraining effect. Even the worst affairs, like Denbighshire in 1601, usually fell short of the overt violence that was ostensibly feared. Riots and duels did continue, but on a much smaller scale than the real bloodshed of the fifteenth century; and even this local violence was on the wane after 1600. And while electoral malpractice continued unabashed into the eighteenth century, the subterfuges were less likely to be as flagrant as under the Tudors.

In the century after 1660, there were many riots in Wales, often directed against specific religious groups, or else arising from electoral conflict, and some involved the use of weapons, even firearms. On the other hand, it was the first half of the seventeenth century that saw the end of the armed band of followers or retainers as a characteristic tool of Welsh politics. Whatever their original goals, Thomas Cromwell and his contemporaries would have been satisfied at the achievement. This was a relatively stable political order, based on the common self-interest of the central government and the great local landowners.

CHAPTER SIX
The Religious Revolution

The new political order also faced novel religious challenges which threatened this hard-won stability. Even as the new propertied class was establishing its wealth and political power, so there was increasing evidence of disaffection. This was very noticeable among those gentry who had done so well from the Reformation. The landowners welcomed the opportunities to plunder the Church, though within a generation they were usually manifesting strong Catholic sympathies. For a century, successive governments would see a persistent Catholic challenge.

In Wales, the religious transformation was less a response to internal pressures or conflicts than an act of state imposed by the central government; and there is little early evidence of overt resistance, or even dissatisfaction. The most immediate impact came less in matters of doctrine or liturgy than in the confiscation of Church property, offering an immediate prize to predatory landowners. Initially, the chief loss was the religious houses, a blow less severe than it might have been because of the condition of the Welsh monasteries. It was not that the religious were especially sinful or slothful, but they were few in number, and their houses were of little financial value. There were 47 houses in all, the great majority with between three and seven religious: in the whole of Wales, there were only some 250 religious. A strong monastic tradition could only be observed at Tintern, and at the Augustinian and Franciscan houses of Carmarthen. No Welsh monastery was worth over £200, which meant that all were candidates for early dissolution. In Glamorgan, for example, there were only three houses of any note, the monasteries of Margam, Neath and Ewenni; but even these were worth less than £200. In other words, dissolution was not a revolutionary act in the sense of removing some great religious rival who might be seen as an enemy of the lay magnates.

After the fall of the monasteries, it was uncertain how much further the government might go. Would all episcopal lands be seized? The parish churches demolished? In the event, there were two further confiscations: of chantries, in 1548; and of the goods of parish churches, in 1552 and 1553. As with the monasteries, neither act netted much in financial terms: even the chantries, so long the beneficiary of charitable donations, were worth perhaps £950 in the whole of Wales. Also, both seizures tended to enrich the familiar body of lay servants. Removing Church lands was achieved with little difficulty. It was a different matter to create a new Church order, with all that implied for doctrine, ritual, and the enforcement of new standards in everyday life. The major ecclesiastical reform of the era for Wales might have been the abolition of shrines and pilgrimages in 1538, a traumatic move that closed such cherished sites as Penrhys in Glamorgan, Llandderfel in Merionethshire and the statue of Our Lady of Cardigan.

Also, the practical effects of the Reformation were limited because so often the gentry who now acquired monastic lands were the same families who had long leased them. Characteristically, Sir Richard Bulkeley was steward of Penmon priory long before acquiring the lands. And the dissolution in itself did not create a new class, though it strengthened the men who were already establishing themselves by other means. In a time of war and fiscal crisis, the monasteries offered a cheap way for Henry VIII to distribute largesse to his servants, to soldiers, diplomats and lawyers. Naturally enough, those servants and officials most directly involved in dissolving the monasteries often did best when the lands were redistributed. When the great Border monasteries were dissolved by a commission of four men, no less than three of these would found gentry families with seats at secularised religious houses: Sir John Price at Brecon Priory, Sir Edward Carne at Ewenni Priory and John Arnold at Llanthony Abbey. Again in Glamorgan, the dissolution generally benefited an emergent group of gentry who were already in the process of consolidating landed estates, in most cases with enormous success. Families like the Mansells, Herberts, Matthews, Stradlings, Carnes and Turbervilles would be the core of county society for 200 years.

On the other hand, there was no necessary correlation between monastic landholding and Catholic sympathies. Many of the families who reaped the richest harvests from Church lands would also demonstrate pronounced Catholic sympathies under Elizabeth or even much later. The Glamorgan Carnes and Turbervilles would long entertain priests in their houses, though these had once been Church estates. In Caernarvonshire, families of Catholic inclination included the Wynnes of Melai, who had acquired the monastic property of Maenan; and the house of Bodvel, who held the lands of Bardsey Abbey. Even the Somersets, Earls of Worcester, had benefited greatly from the lands of Tintern. Most striking, the Welsh gentry who served the Catholic Queen Mary so enthusiastically after 1553 were often in the process of establishing their new estates on abbey land: Rice Mansell at Margam, the Earl of Pembroke at Wilton, Sir Edward Carne at Ewenni. Among Mary's Welsh servants, we also find the notorious Ellis Price of Merionethshire, a leading henchman of Thomas Cromwell's, and an apparently staunch Protestant under Elizabeth. The ultimate opportunist, he would serve as sheriff for different counties on no less than 14 occasions.

There is little evidence of active Protestant sentiment in Wales before the 1530s, or indeed for some years afterwards. Between 1530 and 1558, there were only four known executions for Protestantism, and one of these was the political execution of the Bishop of St Davids. Elsewhere, there was an execution at Haverfordwest under Mary; and only at Cardiff is there any suggestion of an authentic popular tradition, evidenced by martyrdoms in 1543 (Thomas Capper) and 1555 (Rawlins White). In addition, the chance of creating a native Protestant movement was limited by the weakness of the Welsh towns. Even if they had been stronger or more populous, we should perhaps recall that there was currently much acrimony between the boroughs and the surrounding countryside over the burgesses' attempts to monopolise the cloth trade. Even such towns as did exist were not centres of ecclesiastical power: the Bishops were at St Davids and St Asaph rather than Carmarthen or Wrexham.

It was in the diocese of St Davids that the government was most concerned to establish a Protestant cause, by appointing as Bishops William Barlow (1536–1548) and Robert Ferrar (1548–1554). Barlow attempted unsuccessfully to transfer his diocese to Carmarthen, though he did move his residence to Abergwili, near the town; and he stripped the lead from his old cathedral. He created schools at Brecon and Carmarthen, and moved his collegiate church from Abergwili to Brecon. Usually, the progress of Protestantism depended initially on the appointment of such bishops, who were

both resident and activist. There were several such, especially
Rowland Meyrick in Bangor. St Davids was successively headed by
two Marian exiles, Thomas Young (1559–1561) and Richard Davies
(1561–1581).

Welsh Protestantism was handicapped by the question of
vernacular translation. In England, the translation of the Bible and
the creation of the prayer book marked real breakthroughs in
popular access to the Church. In much of Wales, however, the early
years of the Reformation were characterised by a shift from
incomprehensible Latin to barely understood English. When Bishop
Meyrick took the Protestant step of requiring the use of the new
prayer book, he was commanding the use of an English work. The
process of translating the fundamental documents of the faith was
therefore particularly vital. In 1547, Sir John Pryce of Brecon
sponsored the publication of *Yn y llyvyr hwn* . . . (In This Book
. . .), the first book printed in Welsh. This contained Welsh versions
of the ten commandments, the Lords Prayer, and the creed. The
greatest name in the work of translation was William Salesbury, a
true Renaissance scholar, who in 1551 published *Kynniver llith a ban
o'r ysgrythur lân*, with the epistles and gospels used in services. These
entered regular use in the 1560s. In 1563, Parliament ordered the
publication of the Bible in Welsh. The work was sponsored by
Bishop Davies, who invited Salesbury to his palace at Abergwili. In
1567, through their work, the Welsh had access to a prayer book and
New Testament in their own language.

The movement culminated in 1588 with the publication of a
complete Bible in Welsh, an event commonly taken as one of the
crucial moments in Welsh culture. Apart from making possible a
truly autonomous Protestantism, the language of the new Bible also
had an incalculable influence on Welsh literature and poetry. In
Welsh history, it is this event rather than the Armada which gives
the year its real significance (although a popular edition had to wait
until 1630). The publication of the new Bible also suggests that the
Reformation Church had come into its own: the translator was
William Morgan, a native Welshman who had held firmly Protestant
doctrines since his university days in the 1560s. Appointed to the see
of Llandaff in 1595, Morgan moved to become Bishop of St Asaph
in 1601. Morgan was assisted by several other ecclesiastics, including
Richard Vaughan, who would become Bishop of Bangor in 1595.

Little less important than the availability of books was the creation
of a college in which potential clergy could learn to use them. In
1571, Jesus College, Oxford was established following a gift from

Hugh Price of Brecon. This was an important event in the history of Wales, as it marked the creation of the first real Welsh university college, a position not challenged until the 1870s. Only briefly in the interregnum was there even the possibility that Jesus might be replaced by a new university actually located in Wales. The institution gained a Welsh identity that it has never lost, and which was reinforced by the college's revival under Leoline Jenkins in the 1660s.

For the Welsh clergy, Jesus College was by far the most common place for higher education. Jesus also served this purpose for the gentry and lay aristocracy, who flocked to the universities in the century after 1540. Two thousand Welshmen attended a university in this time, showing an eight to one preference for Oxford colleges. Many attended Jesus, and gave generously for the upkeep and expansion of the house. In the 1630s, it flourished under the benefactions of south Wales gentry like the Mansells, Aubreys and Kemys's. This link continued until the end of the seventeenth century, when the richer families began to choose other and more fashionable colleges, above all Christ Church, at which they would not be forced to rub shoulders with their humbler compatriots.

The decades after the Reformation were also important for the provision of secondary schools, where godliness could be imbibed along with the English language. We have already noted Barlow's foundation of grammar schools at Brecon and Carmarthen (the latter was refounded in 1576). The school at Abergavenny also dates from the 1540s, while later foundations included the 'Friars' School' at Bangor (1561) and Goodman's school at Ruthin (1574). These last were probably the largest, but there were many smaller creations across Wales, at Presteigne, Caerleon, Trelech and so on. The later seventeenth century brought other important names, such as Bishop Gore's school in Swansea, and the grammar school at Cowbridge. This was founded in 1608, but fundamentally restored under Leoline Jenkins.

Throughout the next century, the Welsh Church was desperately hampered by the extreme poverty of the sees. The dioceses had never been rich, but they were extensively plundered in the Reformation years. The situation was particularly bad in the south, where there were so many powerful and rapacious gentry, often connected to peers like Pembroke. Sometimes, Bishops who put up little opposition to this could easily be seen as corrupt or cowardly time-servers. Bishop Kitchen of Llandaff (1545–1563) has this reputation, and he certainly granted episcopal lands to powerful laymen on such extremely generous terms as to approach an outright gift. 'A bad *Kitchen* did for ever spoil the good meat of the bishops'. At Bangor in 1638, 'Everything is let for lives by his (the bishop's) predecessors, to the very mill that grinds his corn'.[1]

Commonly, very long leases were used to benefit allies or relatives. One of the worst offenders was William Hughes of St Asaph (1573–1600), a spectacular offender who held 16 livings and an archdeaconry *in commendam*. However, the ardent reformers also participated in questionable actions. William Barlow's brothers created great estates from the Church lands at Slebech and Haverfordwest; and even Richard Davies provided for his relatives from St David's estates. The value of the diocese fell from £458 in 1535 to £263 by 1583, and that in a time of ferocious inflation.

Whatever the causes, the sees were poor and inconveniently placed. There were regular proposals (as in 1720) to move the sees to more logical urban centres, like Wrexham or Denbigh in the north-east, Carmarthen or Brecon in the south. It took a heroic soul to live in his diocese rather than resorting to the common practice of absenteeism; but some remained, and did work of real substance. The northern Bishops in particular were often excellent. Such was Lewis Bayly, Bishop of Bangor from 1616 to 1631, and author of a highly regarded *Practice of piety*. His successor Humphrey Humphreys (Bishop 1689–1701) was a fine administrator active in educational schemes, and a notable scholar, described by the Oxford scholar, Edward Lhuyd as 'incomparably the best skill'd in our antiquities of any person in Wales'. Few of the Bishops achieved this quality, but most were at least adequate. In view of later criticisms, it is also striking that most Welsh Bishops under the Tudors and Stuarts were themselves native Welshmen, and usually Welsh-speakers. Not until the time of George I were the Bishops customarily English, and non-resident. Bishop John Wynne (1715–1727) was the last Welsh incumbent at St Asaph until 1870.

The impoverished sees also contained a great many poor parishes, which could barely support an incumbent. This became still more glaring as various reformers attempted to demand higher standards for parochial clergy. Without pluralism, survival simply was not possible in much of the south. In the 1530s, the *Valor ecclesiasticus* suggested that 558 of 795 livings in Wales, or 70 per cent, were worth less than ten pounds, and 192 only brought in five pounds. In

1. Christopher Hill, *Economic problems of the Church* (Oxford 1956) 26–27, 234, 314–315.

the diocese of Llandaff, over a third of livings fell into this pitiful category. The tithes of many parishes had been impropriated by the monasteries, and passed to the gentry who acquired their lands at the Reformation.

The problems associated with this poverty were often discussed from the sixteenth century into the nineteenth, and they were described in detail by Erasmus Saunders in his *View of the state of religion in the diocese of St Davids* (1721), one of the most quoted works on early modern Wales. Saunders depicts a desperate situation, where poor curates held the most perfunctory services in the many parishes where they were paid to minister. In consequence, the religious knowledge of the common people was almost non-existent, and Catholic or pagan practices flourished. Later Methodist critics drew heavily on such an account for their portrait of the age of spiritual 'sleep' that preceded the evangelical 'awakening' of 1735.

However, it is in the early seventeenth century that we find evidence of a parish clergy of real merit. One of the most famous was Rhys Prichard, vicar of Llandovery from 1614 to 1644, generally known as 'the Vicar' for two centuries after his death. Prichard earned his fame from the Welsh verses he created to explain Christian doctrine to the unlettered. His device was so successful that his verses circulated for decades before eventually being compiled and published in the 1660s, in what became a Welsh classic, *Canwyll y Cymry* (The Welshman's candle).

There were other first rate parish clergy who belie the traditional image of the ignorant and impoverished Welsh parson. One of the finest was John Davies, rector of Mallwyd in Merionethshire from *c.* 1604 to 1644. Davies was a notable Welsh grammarian who participated in the new Welsh translation of the Bible and prayer book published by Richard Parry in 1620 and 1621 (Parry himself was a learned and conscientious Bishop of St Asaph). From 1576 to 1623, the Archdeacon of Merioneth was Edmund Prys, a Welsh poet who undertook a metrical rendering of the psalms. He also engaged in controversies with the traditional bards, in which he asserted the merits of the new learning.

A Merionethshire cleric of a later generation was Ellis Wynne, author of one of the finest works of Welsh prose, *Gweledigaethau y bardd cwsc* (The dream of the sleeping bard), published in 1703. That Wynne was not altogether an isolated genius is suggested by the work of Edward Lhuyd, who undertook an extensive antiquarian survey of Welsh parishes in the 1690s. Many of the responses to his questionnaire were undertaken by local clergy, who often reveal enormous intelligence and observational skill, together with considerable scholarship. Many incumbents were from clerical 'dynasties', often petty gentry who entered the priesthood generation after generation, and who tended to receive patronage from the same group of their wealthier cousins. Such men could rarely be described as spiritual leaders, but they were usually respectable, and they had the time and inclination to undertake intellectual work of substance. It is to such men that we owe the preservation of many of the most important manuscripts of Welsh history and poetry.

Other clerical circles left their mark chiefly in the English language. From the 1640s onwards, the work of Henry Vaughan the Silurist indicates the existence of such a cultured elite in Breconshire, in parishes like Llanfigan and Cantref, as well as Llansantffraed itself. Another friend was John Williams, Archdeacon of Cardigan, who was one of Lhuyd's best contacts; and there were lay associates like Katherine Philipps of Cardigan, the 'matchless Orinda'.

In the sixteenth century, supporters of the established Church had tended to regard it as a compromise with more thoroughly Protestant arrangements. In the early seventeenth century, however, we find an increasing number of the Welsh laity demonstrating real enthusiasm about the new Church as presently constituted. In 1595, the layman (and soldier) Morris Kyffin translated into Welsh Bishop Jewel's *Apology* for Anglicanism, a work that would have great popularity in Wales for three centuries. Even before the civil wars, the influence of high Church doctrines is indicated by the construction of new churches or chapels at Llanfair Dyffryn Clwyd, near Ruthin (1619–23); Gwydir (1633–4) and Rûg, Corwen (1637). In Merionethshire, the lively clerical scholarship and piety found a lay counterpart in the work of Rowland Vaughan of Caergai, a squire of poetic and antiquarian bent, whose loyal churchmanship was quite impeccable.

The collapse of the established Church in the interregnum convinced some that the Anglican compromise had failed, and they turned to Catholicism. This was the course taken by gentry like the Carne family in Glamorgan, or by Thomas Bayly, son of the Bishop. Defections like these were deeply troubling. Others, however, supported the high Church traditions they had usually acquired at Oxford, often at Jesus College itself. They maintained the Anglican tradition in clandestine services at gentry houses, where they also protected high and Laudian clergy: in the war years, there were sometimes several Bishops in residence at the Glamorgan castle of St Donats. At Oxford, Leoline Jenkins and others maintained a virtual 'Welsh College' in opposition to the Puritan regime in the university at large. After the Restoration, there was thus a core of high Anglican gentry in south Wales, who were close to the establishment in both Church and state. Anglicanism had not only matured, it had become inseparable from the family pride and tradition of some of the wealthiest houses in Wales. It also had political significance, as the high Anglicans were determined to avoid a return to the religious subversion that had almost destroyed their Church. This lay tradition became a mainstay of the Tory cause in Wales over the next century; it was manifested in occasional support for Nonjuror and Jacobite movements; and it helped the growth of educational movements like the Society for Promoting Christian Knowledge.

Lay enthusiasm for the Church cause was of such importance because the gentry and peers controlled most of the patronage to livings, and their appointments decided the tone and political outlook of the clergy. In Glamorgan, lay magnates controlled two-thirds of the livings in the early eighteenth century. Some of the patrons were 'ecclesiastical capitalists' on a large scale: Lord Mansell appointed to 24 livings, Lord Windsor to 14, and any squire of stature would probably have the patronage of two or three parishes. Gentry of 'high-flying' inclination chose clergy of like mind as their domestic chaplains, and would gradually appoint them to better livings. By the time of Anne, there might have been many parsons who were lukewarm pluralists; but there was also a core of real enthusiasts, who sought the defence and extension of Church interests.

The improving status of the clergy is suggested by the growth of clerical power in secular government, and the spread of clerical magistrates in the Welsh counties. Clerical Justices were a rather controversial novelty in Wales in the early eighteenth century, and they smacked rather of Laudian attempts to secure Church domination of the secular world. Some gentry also despised the clergy as social inferiors. The high Tory regime of 1710–1714 appointed a number of highflying clergy, who were usually purged by the Whigs after 1714; but from the 1730s, clerical Justices began to be appointed in large numbers. Glamorgan had six in 1743, 37 in 1793. In most Welsh counties, clergy represented between a quarter and a third of names on the Commission of the Peace by the 1790s, and a far higher proportion of the JPs who actually served on a regular basis.

CATHOLICS

Religious movements outside the established Church have long been a popular subject with Welsh historians, in part because of the extensive available documentation. Because maritime Wales posed such a strong security threat, the central government devoted much attention to the position of Catholics there, and in consequence there is abundant correspondence with local Justices and lieutenants; and the persecution of recusancy has left many legal records. But in addition, emphasising the strength of the Welsh religious resistance has a partisan appeal, in that it confirms the foreign nature of the new establishment. In the words of the Tudor poet Twm ab Ifan ap Rhys[2]

> *Ny ni droyson gan ffydd Sayson*
> *Ni ddaw ein kalone ni byth yn y lle*
>
> We have been changed by the faith of the Saxons
> Our hearts are not sympathetic towards it
> (translated by J.Gwynfor Jones)

Nonconformist writers could argue that the Anglican church was from the first an alien importation which made little impact on the Welsh people, who thus wandered in darkness until the Puritan and Evangelical revivals. For Catholic or High Church writers, there is the additional agenda of showing that contemporary practices and beliefs formed part of a long and patriotic Welsh continuity.

Wales was celebrated as a Catholic heartland under Elizabeth and James I, a political and theological 'dark corner' . Catholic practices were pervasive in Welsh culture; and Catholic memories long endured in popular poetry. Nicholas Robinson, the Bishop of Bangor, wrote in 1567:

> I have found since I came to this country images and altars standing in churches undefaced, lewd and indecent vigils and watches observed, much pilgrimage-going, many candles set up to the honour of saints, some relics yet carried about, and all the country full of beads and knots[3]

In 1593, the Earl of Pembroke wrote of the counties around Milford Haven that the people:

---

2. Quoted by J.G. Jones in 'The Reformation bishops of Llandaff', *Morgannwg* 32 (1988) 46.

3. Quoted by Martin Cleary in 'The catholic resistance in Wales', in *Blackfriars,* (1957), 111.

are in religion generally ill-affected, as may appear by their use of popish pilgrimages, their harbouring of mass priests, their retaining of superstitious ceremonies and the increase of recusants[4]

There were many such comments over the next century. For a century after the Reformation, popular piety involved the extensive use of rosaries and the sign of the cross, while churches were slow to give up their old altars, over which the host was duly elevated. In the 1590s, deputy-lieutenants throughout Wales were strenuously attempting to suppress the many local shrines and holy wells. Some centres were on a much larger scale, especially Holywell, which continued to be a well-frequented pilgrim shrine until the present century. There were also new shrines and alleged miracles, where the cult inevitably had a powerful political message. At St Donat's in Glamorgan, there were reports in 1559 that a tree struck by lightning had been formed into the shape of a cross, to the excitement of the visiting faithful, and to the deep concern of the government. In the Catholic heartland of Monmouthshire, visitors in the late seventeenth century were shown the place where Skirrid mountain had been cleft at the moment of Christ's death on the cross.

As late as 1721, Erasmus Saunders commented that the people of rural west Wales

many times in their ejaculations . . . invoke not only the Deity, but the Holy Virgin and other saints; for Mair-Wen, Jago, Teilaw Mawr, Celer, Celynnog and others are often thus remembered as if they had hardly yet forgotten the use of praying to them. And there being not only churches and chapels but springs and fountains dedicated to those saints, they do at certain times go and bathe themselves in them, and sometimes leave their small oblations behind them either to the keeper of the place or in a charity box prepared for that purpose by way of acknowledgment for the benefit they have, or hope to have thereby[5]

Cultural Catholicism might have withered over the decades, but a different challenge was posed by Catholic exiles, and the missionary priests they trained. By 1570, leading exiles at Douai included William Morys of Clynnog, and Owen Lewis of Anglesey, both Oxford graduates. Both were close to St Charles Borromeo at Milan, whose confessor was another Welshman, Griffith Roberts. Lewis even became the titular Bishop of Cassano. Catholic activists saw Wales as a fertile recruiting ground, and a rich field for missionary endeavours. In the 1570s, Morys Clynnog developed an

4. Quoted by Lloyd in *Gentry of South-West Wales*, 187.
5. Erasmus Saunders, *View of the state of religion in the diocese of St David's* (London 1721).

elaborate plan for a Catholic rising in Wales, supported by invasion fleets landing at Menai. But other forms of invasion appeared more feasible in the immediate future. Between 1574 and 1578, 52 priests were sent from Douai to Britain, and 11 of these were Welshmen; while between 1568 and 1642, over 119 Welsh students went to the seminaries.

These priests were usually patronised by gentry, whose seats became long-enduring centres for Catholicism in neighbouring regions. At Plas Du in Llŷn, there were up to six priests at various times under Elizabeth, and the local Catholic circle was believed to number as many as 80. The squire here was Thomas Owen, who had two exile brothers, one of whom was a seminary priest. Hugh Owen was involved in the Ridolfi plot of 1571, as was Thomas Morgan of Llantarnam. The Plas Du group was linked to other centres throughout north Wales in a recusant network that appeared to the regime to represent a deeply dangerous conspiracy.

This extended to Plas Newydd, the seat of the Edwardes family in Denbighshire, and to Penrhyn Creuddyn in Caernarvonshire. The latter house produced Robert Pugh, who appears on many government lists as a much-wanted fugitive. He was involved in the dramatic incident in 1587 when a secret printing press was discovered during a search of Rhiwledyn cave on the Little Orme (near the present Llandudno). This may have been where Griffith Roberts' work, *Y drych Cristionogawl* (The Christian mirror) had been printed in 1585. The north-east seemed dangerous under Elizabeth: as many as 1200 recusants were convicted in Flintshire between 1581 and 1624. In 1586, the Babington plot led to the execution of two Denbighshire squires, Thomas Salusbury of Llewenni and Edward Jones of Plas Cadwgan.

Catholicism was often cited as an underlying factor in faction feuds. This charge must be treated with scepticism, as it was an obvious device which one side could use to stigmatise its opponents; but the religious dimension did aggravate conflicts arising from different causes. In the late 1570s, the Earl of Leicester used his position as Ranger of Snowdon Forest to extend Crown rights throughout Gwynedd, a campaign that met vigorous opposition from many local gentry like the Bulkeleys and Bodvels. It was alleged that Catholics were exploiting the opposition for sinister ends, and indeed the Llŷn squires were often connected to the Plas Du family. Families like the Bodvels were either recusants themselves, or had treasonous connections. At the same time, the west Wales opposition to the royal servant Sir John Perrott was led by a number of alleged Catholics, including Willliam Philipps of Picton.

THE LIMITS OF CATHOLIC LOYALTY

In light of all this, it is worth stressing that available measures of active Catholic loyalty do not bear out charges that Wales in general had strong recusant sympathies, at least in comparison with much of England. (It is a different question whether strong Protestant beliefs had made any notable headway before the civil war.) In 1603, 800 active recusants were recorded in the whole of Wales: 32 in Bangor, 250 in St Asaph, 145 in St Davids, 381 in Llandaff. This suggests a total of perhaps a quarter of one per cent of the population.

Alternatively, let us consider martyrdoms for the Catholic faith. The execution of laymen like Richard Gwyn (1584) or priests like John Roberts (1610) are frequently described in histories of the period, and there is little doubt that public sympathy in Wales was strongly on the side of the martyrs. On the other hand, the incidents must be placed in context. In the years of harshest persecution, between 1577 and 1618, there were ten known Welsh martyrs, out of a total for England and Wales of 209. This supposed 'heartland' therefore contributed barely five per cent of the martyrs, at a time when the Welsh represented six to eight per cent of the population of the kingdom.

Now, there might have been special circumstances here militating against persecution. There were few Justices or deputy-lieutenants who could be described as whole-hearted Protestants, and the gentry who did serve were often of moderate religious outlook. In consequence, they had a relaxed attitude to the Catholic sympathies of their neighbours, except at times of real political danger like the mid-1580s. But it is interesting that the government did not attempt to cow Catholic sympathies by staging executions locally, in sharp contrast to what happened in the North of England. In the era of persecution under Elizabeth and James, there were only two martyrdoms in Wales itself (respectively, at Wrexham and Beaumaris), compared to 42 in York, and many others in local centres like Lancaster and Durham. And while the Council in Wales was normally headed by relatively tolerant men like Sir Henry Sydney, there were also years when its activities were directed by more militant figures, like Bishop Whitgift. There were periods like the late 1570s when the Council became extremely active in seeking out whatever religious dissidence might exist. Threats of invasion aggravated matters: in 1584, four recusants were presented at Glamorgan Great Sessions; by 1587, the number was 77.

Again, we can assess Catholic loyalties by ordinations into the post-Reformation priesthood. By this criterion, then Welshmen made up only about four per cent of English and Welsh priests between 1559 and 1800. There were only 202 priests from Wales compared to 459 from Middlesex, 494 from Yorkshire and 876 from Lancashire. Insofar as it is possible to assess actual numbers of Catholics at any specific time, the figures are disappointing. The total at any given point in the seventeenth century is unlikely to have exceeded one per cent of the population, and was probably less. Under Charles II, there may have been at most 2000 Catholics in Wales, so they were a rare and somewhat exotic breed in much of the country. By 1767, 926 were recorded in a nationwide 'Return of Papists'.

MONMOUTHSHIRE CATHOLICS

But once again, regionalism came into play. Wales as a whole was not particularly Catholic in its sentiments; yet the country had local pockets which compensated for their size by their intense activism. One was in the north-east: in 1767, almost a quarter of Welsh Catholics were to be found in just two Flintshire parishes, of Holywell and Llanasa. The other such exceptional area was to be found on the Monmouthshire-Herefordshire border, where there appears to have existed a 'Welsh Lancashire', with a political importance far beyond what the rather limited numbers would suggest.

Of the 2000 or so Welsh Catholics in the 1670s, perhaps 900 were concentrated in Monmouthshire, in hundreds like Raglan and Abergavenny. Between Monmouth and Abergavenny, the Catholic population may have reached six per cent or more of the total, with a genuine popular base among farmers, labourers and craftsmen. In the towns, Catholics held many public offices, and worshipped with considerable freedom. In Abergavenny, Sunday attendance at the Jesuit church was sometimes greater than that in the Anglican parish church. Moreover, the power of this localised dissidence actually spilled over into national politics, and Welsh circumstances were pivotal in the Popish plot years.

Once again, ordinations provide a useful index to loyalties, and they suggest that the Counter-Reformation came late to Monmouthshire. No man from the county is known to have become a Catholic priest until 1578, and only ten more followed his example in the next

40 years. At that point, we can clearly see the impact of the new generation of Catholic peers and gentry in the county, as well as the new militancy of the Jesuits. One George Morgan became the first Monmouthshire Jesuit in 1600, and he became the founder of a local tradition. It is likely that the strength of Monmouthshire recusancy owed much to influences from Herefordshire and the English border shires, where there were many Catholic gentry. In 1605, the 'Whitsun Riot' in this country had appeared to be the first stage in a serious regional insurrection. Catholic influences made themselves felt through normal social and family ties. In addition, the Monmouthshire-Herefordshire border was a jurisdictional nightmare, with complex county and episcopal divisions that poorly reflected geographical realities. It was therefore a natural refuge in time of crisis.

Two families were central to the new Catholic strength in the area. The fourth Earl of Worcester was a faithful servant of the Crown, active in suppressing Catholic plots; but his family had a strong Catholic ambience, and his son the first Marquess was a militant believer. The fourth Earl's daughter Frances married Thomas Morgan of Llantarnam, from a house that had established itself on an old monastic estate. She was an enthusiastic convert, who was the chief patron of Father Robert Jones: 'Jones the Jesuit, the firebrand of all'. From the first decade of the century, Morgan and Somerset influence combined to create a real power-base on the borders.

In the 1620s, the two families founded an influential Jesuit mission at the Cwm, on the border between the two shires. By the 1660s, there may have been as many as 14 priests serving the area. Over a quarter of all Monmouthshire priests were members of the Society of Jesus, which is striking because the Welsh Catholics had a traditional aversion to the Jesuits, and were normally associated with other orders like the Benedictines. Between 1621 and 1700, 49 Monmouthshire men were ordained as priests, with the largest number choosing this course in the 1650s and 1660s. By this criterion, local Catholic sympathies grew steadily under the Stuarts and peaked under Charles II, at a time when Catholicism was fading rapidly elsewhere in Wales. During the seventeenth century, Monmouthshire accounted for almost half of all Welsh ordinations.

THE POPISH PLOT

The evidence of martyrdoms is also instructive. The persecutions of the Popish Plot years in Wales were much more damaging and more intense than the events of a century earlier, as they were concentrated in a shorter space of time and a narrower geographical compass. Of 24 known martyrdoms between 1678 and 1680, seven occurred in Wales or on the southern borders, at Hereford and Worcester; and that does not count several other deaths directly related to persecution. In the summer of 1679 alone, Fathers Philip Evans and John Lloyd were executed at Cardiff, Father David Lewis at Usk, and Charles Meehan at Ruthin; while William Lloyd died in prison at Brecon. Evans and Lloyd were members of the Jesuit mission, as was Walter Price who had been hunted to his death by his pursuers earlier in the year.

It was once thought that this savage persecution marked the end of Welsh Catholicism as a political force, but this would be a great exaggeration. Local Catholicism was not destroyed: ordinations of Monmouthshire men continued at the same impressive rate until almost 1700, and only thereafter did they slow somewhat. Welsh Catholicism did indeed decay during the eighteenth century, but only gradually after 1710. By the mid-eighteenth century, there were certainly under a thousand survivors in the whole of Wales, with an important contingent of middling gentry. By the early twentieth century, old recusant families like the Mostyns and Vaughans had survived to provide leading members of the new Catholic hierarchy.

But the Popish Plot crisis deserves further attention because of its extreme intensity, and what it suggests about the nature of confessional politics in the Stuart era. Why was the persecution so savage here, and so out of keeping with local traditions? One central reason was the very success of Catholicism in achieving conversions, and expanding their already strong base on the Welsh border. Catholicism in Monmouthshire after 1660 was stronger and more self-confident than it had ever been in Wales since the Reformation. Given the lack of reliable statistics, it is easy to see how contemporaries might have believed that the county was already half Catholic.

In addition, the frequency of conversions (in both directions) meant that families at all levels of society were divided between adherents of radically different religions. In fact, Catholics often had close relatives who were not merely Protestants but extreme Puritans and anti-Papists. In the struggles of the 1670s, the most violent anti-

Papists and priest hunters almost without exception came from families that had only recently abjured Catholicism. The priest-hunter who pursued Walter Price to his death was Charles Price, a squire who was also a close relative. The Popish Plot conflict was in a sense a family struggle, arising from the rapidly changing religious boundaries within this exceptional area.

CATHOLICISM AND POLITICS

But it is also possible to see these events in mainly secular terms, as the culmination of political conflicts that had already endured for several decades. Since the early seventeenth century, there had been a number of important conversions among the leading Welsh aristo-crats; and in turn, these Catholic peers were able to promote the faith among their clients, relations and neighbours. Among the most prominent of these lords were the Somersets of Raglan and the Herbert Earls of Powis. Both families enjoyed immense secular power, despite their exclusion from official positions; and both were naturally opposed by rival gentry factions in their respective counties. However, this opposition differed from the normal early modern battles between political 'ins' and 'outs' because it was complicated by religious rivalries.

The Herbert family were a wealthy house firmly established in the Welsh borderland, and they were ennobled as barons Powis in 1629. William, the first lord, was probably a discreet Catholic throughout the first half of the century, though the family's public commitment grew after the civil wars. The third baron married a daughter of the (Catholic) first marquess of Worcester, and emerged as a well-known Catholic leader, enough to attract allegations of treacherous plotting in the Titus Oates era. Until 1745, Powis Castle was the seat of peers who were either marquesses or dukes, depending on how much store one placed in the last minute creations of James II.

But it was the Somersets who attracted the most controversy, with their power located so perilously close to Bristol as well as the Irish sea-routes, and they were powerful in half a dozen border shires. Before the civil wars, Raglan was the greatest aristocratic seat in Wales; and for a century afterwards, many Welsh squires and magnates would regularly be found in the Somersets' English mansion at Badminton. From the 1590s, the family was also overtly Catholic. Although the family appeared to have been broken by the civil wars, the Restoration brought troubling changes. Even after the political disasters, the second Marquess was thought to be 'the greatest money'd man in the kingdom'. From 1667, the Somersets were headed by a new (third) Marquess who retained all his traditional links with the local Catholic gentry, and who naturally opposed attempts to combat Catholic expansionism locally. At a national level, he was also related to several of the greatest Catholic and (later) Jacobite peers. However, he had accepted the Anglican religion, and was therefore qualified to hold all the offices appropriate to his incredible wealth and landed power.

This now presented a critical dilemma for the government. From a Welsh perspective, the most serious danger arose from local Catholics and the threat of Irish invasion, and Worcester should have been treated with great caution. For the Court, however, Catholicism was at best a minor peril: the Somersets were seen rather as arch-loyalists, who would serve as a firm bastion against Puritan or Roundhead plots in Wales and the south-west. Therefore, the government of Charles II allowed the Marquess of Worcester to become President of the Council in 1672, and even placed him in charge of the castle and garrison of Chepstow, which gave him military dominance of the region. For local Protestants, this seemed to represent government connivance with the local Catholic faction.

During the 1670s, the struggle between Worcester and his political opponents proceeded on every front. There were direct battles between the Marquess and his enemies over a variety of issues, largely focusing on office-holding. Worcester's allies and clients included Justices like Henry Milborne, who flagrantly refused to enforce anti-Catholic laws, and who punished subordinates who attempted to do so. Worcester supported and defended him, while attempting to purge from the Monmouthshire Bench of Justices strong Protestants and anti-Papists like Sir Trevor Williams and John Arnold. Such political appointments became the source of bitter conflicts, accentuated by economic disputes. By 1678, Worcester had succeeded in purging from the Bench not just his Monmouthshire opponents, but also their allies in neighbouring counties. It is worth noting that these neighbours – powerful squires like Sir Edward Mansell of Glamorgan – had not hitherto been opponents of the Court, or indeed as implacably Protestant as Williams or Arnold; but they were now driven into opposition politics by Worcester's high-handed policies.

Worcester's power was immense, but his Catholic links made him vulnerable. Throughout the decade, leaders like Arnold and Williams allied with other border gentry like the Harleys and the Herberts of Cherbury in attacking the growth of 'Popery' in the area. The struggle even drew in strong Protestants whose royalism was otherwise impeccable, like the Trevors of Brynkynallt. They proceeded through parliamentary committees and investigations, where they presented a picture of a county sliding inexorably away from Protestantism. From 1678, the Titus Oates plot opened wonderful new opportunities, and local informers soon arose to prove how the conspirators would secure a base in south Wales. All the traditional elements of conflict were present in the new charges – the Marquess of Worcester and the Earl of Powis; the castles of Powis and Raglan; the Chepstow garrison; the threat to Bristol; the network of crypto-Catholic gentry and justices; and the Jesuit headquarters at Cwm. As the plot years progressed, these Welsh elements became central to the grand concoction of the Whig myth; and Worcester became a figure almost as controversial as the Duke of York himself.

Wales may not have been the recusant heartland of historical myth, but Catholicism did play a vital political role, if only in providing a common enemy for opposition politics. Much more substantial in nature – and of enduring significance for Welsh history – was another form of religious dissidence that emerged in the seventeenth century.

EARLY PURITANISM

The origins of Welsh Puritanism have naturally attracted great interest in light of the later triumphs of Welsh nonconformity; but it must be said that the picture before 1640 is rather bleak. Later Welsh nonconformists hunted assiduously for early predecessors, but they could find few convincing candidates. One distinguished exception was John Penry of Breconshire, executed in 1593 for his role in writing the Marprelate Tracts, but his influence in Wales is difficult to discern.

The continuous tradition of Welsh Puritanism can be clearly traced to a small group of ordained clergy, active in the southern and eastern fringes of the country in the 1620s and 1630s; and chiefly to three men associated with the southern parishes of Glamorgan and Monmouthshire: William Wroth, William Erbery and Walter Cradoc. Until well into the eighteenth century, Welsh Puritanism had many contacts with the dissent of Bristol, and these pioneers benefited from the extensive contacts between the regional metropolis and Welsh towns like Cardiff and Swansea. However, the early geography of Puritanism owed as much to the sympathies of gentry like the Lewis family of Fan in Glamorgan, one of the wealthiest Welsh houses.

About 1600, Wroth became a servitor to Sir Edward Lewis at Oxford, and thereafter the progressive clergy received rich livings from both Sir Edward and his brothers. Sir Edward's widow also made Wroth her chaplain, effectively removing him from ecclesiastical retaliation. This allowed the increasingly 'precise' group around Wroth to establish Puritan traditions in parishes around Cardiff and Newport. Wroth's own parish of Llanfaches became known as an 'Antioch', a missionary centre in the 'Gentile country' that was Wales. A list of his pupils and disciples reads like a Puritan hagiography, featuring such luminaries as Henry Walter of Newport or Morgan Llwyd of Wrexham. This circle enjoyed an influence out of all proportion to their numbers, because they were the Welsh leaders to whom radical English governments turned during and after the civil wars. By 1634, the Bishop of Llandaff attempted to take disciplinary measures against the three leaders, the first time since the Reformation that the established Church in Wales perceived that organised opposition might be expected from radical Protestants no less than Catholics. In Monmouthshire, new centres of activity now appear at Piercefield and Abergavenny.

In mid-Wales too, there were gentry as sympathetic as the Lewises, like the Harleys, who exercised great influence in Radnorshire and Herefordshire. All the early Puritan leaders can be associated either with the followers of the Lewises, Herberts and Harleys, and the parishes they dominated; but persecution served to disperse the new ideas across a much wider geographical region. Cradoc served Erbery as a curate in Cardiff, before moving in 1634 to Wrexham, where he played a decisive role in the conversion of Morgan Llwyd. Ejected from this town, Cradoc began several successful years travelling and preaching through the Marches. His converts included Vavasor Powell, who would become one of the most feared radical republican leaders. After spending some time with the Harleys, Cradoc returned in 1639 to Llanfaches, where Wroth had finally decided to establish a separatist church in the 'New England Way'. By this time, in the last years of peace, a Baptist presence also began to make itself felt, originally from a stronghold in southern Herefordshire.

121

By the outbreak of war, Welsh puritanism was a new but rapidly evolving movement. There were strong regional bases in trading towns connected with Bristol and Chester; and these congregations in turn influenced upland areas that served as the hinterlands of the urban centres. It was naturally enough on the southern coast where the first Baptist congregations appeared in the late 1640s, with their base at Ilston in Gower, though they soon spread into the western hills. Even before the war, radical religious ideas were said to be spreading in the uplands of the south-east as quickly as 'fire in the thatch', through the preaching tours of Wroth and Cradoc. These decentralised pastoral areas often proved congenial to religious dissent; and they often formed part of parishes in the gift of the Lewis family. (Incidentally, this is yet another topic where Iolo Morganwg's inventions have made it difficult to separate truth and fiction: Iolo wished that Puritanism should have had its origins in the Glamorgan *Blaenau*, and he invented stories accordingly.) In 1641, a pamphlet purporting to describe an eccentric 'Brownist' sect located the story in the Ebbw valley, in the western *Blaenau* of Monmouthshire.[6]

In intellectual terms, too, the movement had developed swiftly. In the 1620s, Wroth probably differed from his more conventional neighbours chiefly in his greater emphasis on moral reformism, and the role of the state in enforcing morality and discipline. It was the opposition to the Book of Sports which first mobilised the puritanically-inclined clergy to active opposition; and it was shortly after this that we find full-blown challenges to the organisation, discipline and hierarchy of the Church.

And although Wales was by no means a Puritan centre, it is notable how consistently the early Welsh leaders moved over the next few years to the most radical positions of the day. Erbery became a Seeker; Vavasor Powell was a Fifth Monarchy activist; Morgan Llwyd was a mystic who introduced Boehme's ideas to Wales. The followers of all three would generally by the 1660s have moved on to Quakerism: in Erbery's case, his family included disciples of the extremist James Naylor. It would be wrong to seek any one cause for these developments, and of course the Welsh Puritans lacked the strong Presbyterian framework that defended Puritan orthodoxy in areas of England; but it makes one curious about the exact content of the message delivered by Wroth, the

6. Edward Harris, *A true relation of a company of Brownists, separatists and nonconformists in Monmouthshire in Wales* (London 1641).

spiritual father of these early Puritans. Straightforward Calvinism it was not.[7]

In the early 1640s, religious dissidents were believed to pose an immense threat to the security of the established order in Wales, but the charges concerned the Catholics rather than the Puritans. In 1641, fears that Raglan would be the base for a Papist coup energised the Parliamentarian cause throughout England. Catholic fears did much to shape the course of the ensuing wars; but the real beneficiaries of the crisis were the Puritans. In 1640, the movement was at best marginal. By the 1660s, Protestant dissent had become an ineradicable part of Welsh religion and culture.

7. 'An account of the life of the Rev Mr Wroth, the first reformer in Wales in the seventeenth century', NLW Sir John Williams Add.MS 128C.

CHAPTER SEVEN

The Seventeenth Century Crisis

> The Law was ever above kings
> And Christ above the Law
> Unhappy Charles provoked the Lamb
> To dust he must withdraw
>
> Look not too much on few late things
> View all from first to last
> Since James the First's days and wonder not
> That such a sentence passed
>
> Morgan Llwyd, NLW 11434B

In 1642, there were few overt supporters of the Parliamentary cause in Wales. This apparent Royalist unanimity would have far-reaching effects, as the Parliamentary regime would need to rule Wales by means of individuals and groups far removed from the traditional elites. The 1640s and 1650s were therefore a time of real political turbulence in Wales, far more so than for most regions of England. We will often note the continuing importance of civil war references and issues in political debate over the next two centuries and more. For Wales, the mid-seventeenth century emerges as a true heroic age, a time of heroes and villains, and above all, of martyrs who would long be commemorated by their respective followers. These years established the vocabulary of Welsh politics for centuries to come.

THE OUTBREAK OF WAR

It is possible to find several strands of Parliamentarian sentiment in Wales in the early 1640s. Bristol had a strong influence in the south-east. North Wales had links with the metropolis through the cattle trade, and the Denbighshire Myddeltons had become wealthy London merchants under Elizabeth. Sir Thomas Myddelton was a prominent opposition politician, who attempted to raise the county against the King in 1642. There were also rumblings of opposition from various squires who questioned royal policies over religious or international policies, or who had grievances over patronage. In 1640 and 1641, there were orders to arrest several as suspicious characters. Most important in the long term, there were significant Parliamentary supporters in the Pembrokeshire boroughs and among the gentry, including two of the county's three MPs: Pembroke, Haverfordwest and Tenby were fortified for Parliament.

In reality, few of these stirrings disturbed the solid Royalist response: even Myddelton was forced out of his Chirk estate. Outside Pembrokeshire, Wales was a bastion for the King, a prolific source of money and manpower. Yet having said this, the enthusiasm for Charles I was by no means as solid as might have appeared at the time. In Caernarvonshire, for instance, there were no active Parliamentarians; but of seven commissioners of array, only one (John Griffiths of Cefnamwlch) can be described as active. In addition, we know that the Royalist diehards found themselves increasingly isolated as the war turned against the Crown. In 1645, the King's party began to fall apart, and mass defections were led by former Royalists like Sir Trevor Williams of Monmouthshire. Williams and his like sporadically supported interregnum governments, and then emerged as firm supporters of the Restoration. How are we to interpret this? Were the defectors simply turncoats motivated by fear and self-interest? Or were they perhaps responding to the threat of mass social unrest in south Wales and the borders, so recently the scene of Clubman demonstrations against the Royalists?

Both motives would be quite comprehensible to modern eyes, but there are other factors at work that are less immediately apparent. One might think of the defectors as cynics and turncoats, as firmer Royalists undoubtedly did, but it is also possible to see them as more principled and consistent believers in moderation and firm government. Both were equally threatened by Stuart flirtations with the Catholics as by Puritan or Millenarian extremism. Moderates therefore clung to whatever force offered security against such a threat: the King in 1642, Cromwell a decade later. This was the course taken by many gentry in the south, including the Earl of Carbery, and Sir Trevor Williams himself.

Also, political and religious issues might be less important in

125

shaping behaviour than the long-established power of clientage to great aristocratic families. The fervent response of Wales to the Royalist call in 1642 owed much to the passionate pro-Stuart enthusiasm of the Earls of Worcester. But there were other less visible forces to be reckoned with, as the Parliamentary leadership included aristocrats like the Earls of Pembroke, Essex and Leicester. None was a resident Welsh peer, but all had some Welsh estates or connections, and all had some political 'interest' there; on a vast scale in the cases of Pembroke and Essex. Their Welsh followers were in a minority in 1642, and had to join the apparent Royalist consensus; but when this facade fragmented, they were able to resume their natural loyalty to the families they had long followed.

Some contemporaries interpreted the crisis not in terms of social struggle or even of religious discontent, but of aristocratic insurrection plain and simple. In 1642, the Royalist soldier Sir John Owen of Clenennau wrote of 'all the passages that will happen between the King and the traitor Essex'.[1] In south Wales, the most prominent Parliamentarian commander was Rowland Laugharne, from a family long connected with the Essex family. As late as the 1790s, the nonconformist historian David Williams characterised the Parliamentary supporters in the region simply as 'the friends of the Earl of Pembroke'.

Clientage to a family like the Herberts could profoundly influence behaviour, and over lengthy periods. In Glamorgan and Monmouthshire, we can see a group of gentry families linked to the Earls of Pembroke who acted as a fairly coherent political faction from the 1630s into at least the 1680s, and whose politics fit neatly into neither 'Royalism' nor 'parliamentarian' loyalties. They acted together to defend certain central ideas and beliefs, but central to all was resistance to the Catholic tendencies of the Somersets. As the King came to rely increasingly on Worcester and the hope of Irish aid, so the King's Protestant support would tend to resume its natural loyalties.

WALES AND THE WAR

The course of the war for Wales was shaped by the King's need for money and manpower. Charles received vast quantities of money

1. NLW Brogyntyn/Clenennau MS 1019.

from the Earl of Worcester, commonly regarded as the wealthiest subject in the kingdom: after the Restoration, the Somersets plausibly claimed to have spent several hundred thousand pounds in the King's service. This generosity was essential in 1642, when Charles would have found it difficult to go to war without Somerset backing. In return, the Earl of Worcester became a Marquess, and was promised the Earl of Pembroke's lands in Monmouthshire.

Soldiers were also forthcoming. In the early stages of the war, the Royalists hoped to draw on Welsh levies to win the war, and the King's first headquarters was logically placed at Shrewsbury. In the autumn of 1642, there was a strong Welsh contingent in the 12,000 strong army that Charles marched to Edgehill and thence to the fringes of London. Meanwhile, there were continuing efforts to raise further forces in Wales. In November of 1642, the Marquess of Hertford and Lord Herbert of Raglan (son of the Earl of Worcester) had gathered another 7000 soldiers, whom they led to bloody defeats in Gloucestershire. Lord Herbert now devoted much of his vast wealth to raising yet another army, this time of 500 horse and 1500 foot; which was in turn squandered at Highnam in March 1643. The Court noted grimly that the money thus wasted by Herbert might have been enough to win the war for the King.

Even given the low quality of these troops (and many footsoldiers would have been armed with only farm implements) the numbers are striking. Later in the war, a trained army of three or four thousand men would be a formidable force. However, this waste of manpower did not exhaust the vital importance of Wales for the King. Welsh forces played a major role in actions like the siege of Gloucester and the capture of Bristol, and indeed in most of the fighting up to and including Naseby.

Wales was also vital because of the region's ports and its proximity to Ireland. If peace could be made with the Catholic Confederates, then there was the dazzling prospect of importing armies from Ireland. Their potential was shown by events in November 1643. Parliamentary forces under Sir Thomas Myddelton, Thomas Mytton and Sir William Brereton launched a sudden invasion of north Wales, and they rapidly overran Denbighshire and Flintshire. This was a potential catastrophe, as the region's defences had been denuded to supply what the Royalist leaders regarded as the 'front' in the English midlands. At this point, soldiers began arriving from the Duke of Ormonde's Irish forces: 4000 in Chester, others at Mostyn and in Anglesey. By January 1644, the Royalists had cleared north Wales, and were themselves besieging the Parliamentary base at Nantwich.

In fact, the Irish could not in themselves save the King, and Nantwich turned into a Parliamentary victory; but the crisis showed the usefulness of overseas links and the great harbours. In south-west Wales, the war was initially shaped by the struggle for ports like Milford Haven, which was ideal for the landing of forces from the west. However, Pembroke, Tenby and Haverfordwest had to be dealt with first. Because of the lack of energy of the Royalist commander, the Earl of Carbery, no attempt was made to take them until the summer of 1643. He enjoyed much initial success, taking Tenby and Haverfordwest. Only Pembroke held out under its mayor, John Poyer. He was joined by the Parliamentary forces commanded by Rowland Laugharne. In February 1644, the fortuitous arrival of a Parliamentary fleet immeasurably strengthened the Pembroke garrison, and permitted them to retake much of the shire by mid-March. The disaster forced Carbery into virtual retirement.

This ended one possible route for Irish aid, but Irish assistance became more ardently sought as the war progressed. It was allegedly in April that Charles gave Lord Herbert a commission to make peace with the Irish rebels, and to bring in several armies: two from Ireland, of 10,000 each; one from the Continent, of 6000. The exact nature of this commission has long been disputed, as have Charles' intentions, but Herbert (later Earl of Glamorgan) did indeed undertake negotiations. After the battle of Naseby, in June 1645, the discovery of papers in the King's baggage exposed the Irish dealings, and this may have done much to discredit the royal cause in south Wales.

The course of the civil war sharply highlights the regional divisions of Wales, and it is virtually impossible to provide a chronological narrative of the war in the country as a whole. There was a war in the north and another in the south, each with its own distinctive personalities, its own rhythms and patterns. Second, there was scarcely a 'Welsh civil war'. In Caernarvonshire or Anglesey, there were Parliamentarian supporters, but virtually nobody attempted resistance against the royal regime until Roundhead armies were conveniently close and assured of victory. Even those accused and arrested for sedition in 1641 or 1642 appear on royal commissions of array a few months later. For much of Wales, the years before mid-1645 were characterised by a unified response to defeat or resist forces from England. Only in south-west Wales was there truly a civil war throughout these years, in which Welsh people fought on both sides.

This theatre remained active through 1644. Carbery was now

replaced by Charles Gerard, an efficient professional soldier, who drove Laugharne from Carmarthen and recaptured Cardiganshire. By midsummer 1644, the Parliamentary territory in west Wales was confined to the old core of three boroughs. National events soon made their impact, as Gerard was called to help bolster the royal cause after the defeat at Marston Moor. Given this opportunity, Laugharne once more advanced, and took Cardigan by the end of the year. Gerard returned in the spring of 1645, defeating Laugharne near Newcastle Emlyn, and proceeding to retake his conquests. This time, the Parliamentary core was reduced to only Pembroke and Tenby; but Gerard was recalled yet again, as a consequence of the defeat at Naseby. In August, Laugharne won a major victory over the Royalists at Colby Moor. By the autumn of 1645, Laugharne was not only master of Pembrokeshire, he had launched invasions of Carmarthenshire and Breconshire. His victories were aided immeasurably by the growth of neutralist and pro-peace sentiment there.

North Wales suffered from the assumption that it was a land of irreproachable Royalism. As a result, it could be mulcted for funds, but there seemed little need to fortify it, while its soldiers could be sent to battlefields in the English midlands or north-west. This policy had a sound basis. If Chester and Shrewsbury were safe, the war was won; while if they were lost, nothing could save Royalist Wales. But there were also difficulties. The Welsh coast was vulnerable to maritime attack, and it was the merest good fortune that a handful of Royalist ships kept the coasts safe until well into 1645. Also, an essentially undefended countryside could easily fall prey to sudden attacks or raids, as occurred in late 1643. The royal cause in north Wales was initially dominated by John Williams, Archbishop of York, who wisely attempted to bring the fortifications of Conway Castle up to contemporary standards. Before the Irish landings in November 1643, it seemed that only Conway stood between Myddelton and an early Parliamentary occupation of most of north Wales.

From 1643, Myddelton allied with the Parliamentarian commanders in Cheshire and Shropshire, and most of the key battles occurred on the Marches. Oswestry fell to them in June 1644, Welshpool in August; and in September, there occurred at Montgomery the first major pitched battle in Wales to date. The Parliamentary victory here threatened the strongholds of Chester, Shrewsbury and Ludlow, and opened northern Powys to invasion. It also made it apparent that the next phase of the war would involve fighting in Wales itself, and the Welsh castles now gained great strategic significance. Only Chirk and Ruthin Castles held Myddelton back from complete victory in the north-east. Meanwhile, the war in the region became focused on the increasingly desperate attempts to relieve Chester from the Parliamentarian siege. The Royalist failure at Rowton Heath (September 1645) made the city's fall inevitable, though it survived until February the following year.

After Naseby, it is easy to see the rest of the first civil war as almost a mopping up operation, in which distant outposts like Caernarvon or Harlech could easily be taken in due time. However, this would be to misunderstand the concerns and hopes of both sides. By the summer of 1645, it was known that the King urgently wanted to bring in Irish soldiers, and his increasing desperation might lead him to make even rasher agreements in order to get them. In this context, the firm Royalist hold on western castles and ports was a matter of major concern. The Parliamentary forces could not relax their vigilance until the last of these awe-inspiring fortresses had fallen.

But even as Wales became the main scene of the war, so local politics were sharply changing in character. There were many reasons why it would be unrealistic to expect the whole of Wales to put up a fanatical resistance to Parliament, although there were some who wanted to do exactly this. In July and September of 1645, the King travelled to Wales to mobilise resistance, but he encountered instead a frank statement of grievances. Taxes and financial exactions were denounced, and there was concern in south Wales about the increasing role of Catholics in the King's forces. For Parliament, Catholic tyranny was a distant and rhetorical prospect. From the point of view of south-east Wales, it was an immediate threat.

There was also the dilemma of choosing commanders who were efficient but who lacked community sympathy and support. It seemed that one could either choose a Carbery or a Gerard. Although his relations with local society were excellent, the Earl of Carbery was a disaster as a commander. Gerard, by contrast, was an excellent officer, who unfortunately tyrannised over the gentry and allowed his men to plunder and abuse the local farmers. In north Wales, the two types were represented by the diplomatic John Williams, and the martial John Owen. Owen was a brilliant officer of absolute loyalty, but he brooked no civilian rivalry to his authority. By May 1645, he was charging Williams with treason, and had plundered his belongings. This was the most open expression of a long and savage rivalry that culminated the following year with the

Archbishop's defection to Parliament.

In addition, the people were naturally concerned about the fate of those towns on which Welsh regions depended for their prosperity. Welsh Royalism was in practice doomed by the fall to Parliament of Shrewsbury and Bristol (February and September 1645) and of Chester (February 1646). In the summer of 1645, the gentry of Glamorgan and Monmouthshire had grown progressively more unhappy with the exactions of Prince Rupert's officers and the armies they commanded. Concessions had been exacted, and the gentry had been given more power over local garrisons. In effect, this also gave local communities the ability to opt out of the war when the need arose. Bristol fell on September 10; within ten days, Cardiff and Swansea Castles had both passed to local Parliamentarians, while the Puritan-inclined squire Bussy Mansell took control of Glamorgan's military forces. By the end of October, Breconshire and Carmarthenshire had both made peace with Laugharne and Parliament, in an upsurge that united the gentry with the common people. Without either Bristol or Gloucester, the economic survival of south Wales was at issue.

By the autumn of 1645, the royal position in Wales was crumbling rapidly, and whole counties were defecting to Parliament. 1646 was characterised by gradual siege warfare against the castles of mid and north Wales. Though King Charles fell prisoner to the Scots army in April 1646, his castles in Wales endured long after this apparently fatal blow. Raglan fell on August 19, a day which marked an epoch in the history of the south. On the other hand, the major castles in the north and west did not begin to fall to Parliament until 1646: Chirk and Ruthin in the spring, Caernarvon, Beaumaris and Rhuddlan in June. At this point, north Wales experienced the sort of mass defections that the south had witnessed the previous year. Denbigh and Conway fell in the autumn, the former only after the castellan had received permission to capitulate directly from the King. Holt surrendered in January 1647; Harlech not until March.

THE SECOND CIVIL WAR

Even after such stubborn resistance, there were still Royalists willing to fight on, men like Sir Nicholas Kemys, Judge David Jenkins or Sir John Owen, all of whom well fitted the traditional myth of the Welsh squire as a pro-Stuart fanatic. In 1648, their continuing conspiracies bore fruit when the Royalists were joined by discontented Parliamentarians like Laugharne and Poyer. Their motives for rebellion were various, and included concerns about the religious policies of Parliament, as well as basic issues like the payment of soldiers; but the effects were dangerous. Poyer and Laugharne rebelled in Pembrokeshire, while more traditional royalists attempted to raise other regions in support. In March, Byron renewed John Owen's commission, whereupon he attempted to raise Merionethshire; Sir Trevor Williams and Sir Charles Kemys seized Chepstow. South Wales was restored to Parliamentary authority in May, after the battle of St Fagan's, and the capture of Tenby and Chepstow. Pembroke fell in July, which seemed to end the affair; but at this point, Byron launched a new rising in Anglesey. Not until October did Mytton's army secure the north after the battle of Red Hill.

THE INTERREGNUM

The second civil war was important less for its military events than for its impact on national politics. The frustration and anger of the Parliamentarian leadership justified radical policies, and a thorough purge of local government. This would have special significance for Wales, because it resulted in the implementation of a wholly new form of government, not merely a change of personnel. From 1649, the goals of administration were fundamentally redirected towards the conversion of Wales to radical Puritanism.

From Elizabethan times, radical Protestants had wanted intensive efforts to evangelise the 'dark corners of the land', those areas of indifference or Papist survival, among which Wales was invariably counted. The call for domestic evangelism gained a new urgency in the war years. In 1642, and above all in 1648, the King had easily raised forces in Wales for his 'malignant' cause, confirming yet again that the ordinary people had neither love nor respect for the gospel. (The possibility that the king's followers might be making a rational or informed choice was rarely considered, or at least admitted.) Evangelism would not only serve a religious goal, it would also buttress the Protestant and Parliamentarian cause in a region that would otherwise have to be garrisoned indefinitely. A converted people was a loyal people.

The Parliamentary victory opened the way for a series of experiments aimed at planting the seed of the gospel in Wales. All were controversial, and it is probably impossible to arrive at an objective account of the real goals and methods of the reformers. But there is little doubt that these efforts at propagating the gospel in Wales marked a radical social experiment, a sweeping attempt to build a wholly new social order on the ruins of a traditional establishment. At least in the propaganda of the time, the Welsh encounter with 'Propagation' was seen as a blueprint by extreme radicals like Hugh Peters and Major-General Harrison for the future theocratic governance of the whole realm. Earlier radicals had sought a purified nation in a colonial 'New England', but now it appeared possible that a 'New Wales' could be created at home; and many of the Puritan activists of the period had strong American ties.

Although there had been puritanically-inclined gentry in Wales in the 1640s, there were not enough to provide an alternative government to the traditional order, that was strongly Royalist. Ruling Wales therefore meant depending on trustworthy petty gentry, as well as the dynamic Puritan clergy from the old Wroth circle. Most of these had spent the war either in London, or serving as chaplains with the Parliamentary army. From 1646, they began returning to conquered Wales under the auspices of Parliament, and with funds supplied from confiscated tithes or sequestered estates. After the execution of the King, the radicals found themselves supreme both in London and the regions, and ambitious experiments became possible. In 1650, Parliament passed an 'Act for the Better Propagation of the Gospel in Wales'. Evangelism would be organised by a body of 71 Commissioners, divided between northern and southern groups. In both, a core of five or six men emerged to dominate the region.

The religious aspect of the scheme was dominated by a body of 25 salaried Approvers, who were to choose the clergy for the new Wales. The Approvers included most of the Puritan pioneers that had emerged in Wales before the war, such as Llwyd, Powell, Cradoc, Walter and Ambrose Mostyn. At first, the scheme was to select settled Puritan clergy assisted by itinerant preachers, but it soon became apparent that it would be difficult to supply the parishes with adequate men. On the other hand, ejection proved easy. By 1653 278 Anglican clergy had been dispossessed of their livings, most of the purge occurring during 1650. There was the prospect that Wales might find itself in an even worse spiritual state than under the maligned Bishops; and the propagation attempted to make up the deficiency with greater use of itinerants. There were probably 90 of these in Wales at the height of the scheme. In addition, the Propagation attempted to expand religious education, and some 60 schools were created in Wales during the decade. Their impact was limited by their use of English alone.

It was this gap between promise and achievement which opened the Propagation to controversy. Firstly, the Puritans had sought a godly learned ministry, but what they were supplying was unlearned hedge-preachers of questionable theology; and even the later nonconformist martyrologists found little good to say of many of the men now appointed. Worse was the question of how this system had been funded. The Commission was handling large sums from tithes and livings, perhaps £40,000 a year for the whole of Wales, but the money clearly was not going where it should. This raised the suspicion of corruption, and by the end of the decade there were specific charges that the Commissioners had misappropriated some £150,000. This sort of charge is difficult for the historian to evaluate, because so much depends on highly partisan testimony, and by definition, corrupt officials tend not to leave accurate records. In the case of Philip Jones, however, the evidence is so overwhelming as to be thoroughly convincing. Even the republican John Jones wrote an oblique letter to the Colonel, warning him of those who were tempted by 'riches, splendour and all other carnal and worldly honour and content, if you will but fall down to worship their prince'. The great estate that he accumulated around Fonmon Castle in the Vale of Glamorgan may well be one of the greatest monuments in Britain to unabashed public criminality.

Throughout the early 1650s, the Propagation was subject to intense public opposition, and the Act was allowed to lapse in 1653. In 1654, the whole system of approving ministers was placed under a centralised national system of Ejectors and Triers. However, the fate of Propagation finances continued to be a central issue in south Wales politics throughout the decade, with vigorous partisan divisions demonstrated by frequent purges of the committees which ruled the counties. The Propagation completed the alienation of many moderates already disgusted by the execution of the King. With the desertion of substantial figures like Sir Thomas Myddelton, Parliamentary rule was inevitably left in the hands of the sectaries.

PURITAN DIVISIONS

Before 1648, the Puritans were united by the common menace of the royal and episcopal regime, and found little time to address the questions that would arise from power. As late as 1653, the regicide John Jones of Merionethshire could write that 'If the government be so established as may produce the fruits of righteousness, peace and love to the saints I am not solicitous what form or shape it hath. When the Righteous are in authority the people rejoice, but when the wicked beareth rule, the people mourn'.[2] But in practice, the godly in power were increasingly divided over both political and theological issues, above all the question of continuity from the Stuart regime and earlier. How much of the old order could be used in a sanctified form by the new republican regime? Most, for instance, found no difficulty in using tithes, provided they were applied to proper uses; but William Erbery was one of several whose qualms about the whole system led him to refuse stipends he was owed.

For Wales, this became a vital issue after Cromwell assumed the quasi-royal title of Lord Protector, as the Puritan leaders split over the issue of republicanism. Vavasor Powell and many Welsh Puritans argued that earthly monarchy was a symbol of the rags of Antichrist, and that Cromwell was effectively a new Charles Stuart. Wales became a stronghold of the Fifth Monarchy party, which elsewhere in Britain tended to be an urban faction. In 1654, Powell organised a republican petition called *A word for God . . . against wickedness in high places* which attracted some 350 signatures, mainly from north and west Wales. This was answered the following year by a petition in favour of the Protectorate, the *Humble representation and advice*, orchestrated by southern leaders such as Walter Cradoc. The split was bitter and lasting. From the point of view of Cromwell's government, it was also deeply dangerous, as the controversy divided what should have been the regime's loyal support in Wales. And it drove into opposition some of the most valuable old Parliamentarians: when a Royalist rising occurred in 1655, the leading activist in suppressing it was Vavasor Powell.

The *Word for God* controversy is important because it allows us to identify in Wales what we can only describe as a political party, and one based on a degree of zeal and military expertise that could only be envied by later Welsh radicals. Vavasor's party included many

2. NLW Add., MS 11440d fo 171.

old Parliamentarian veterans, and through the 1650s they occupied strategic positions in Welsh garrisons and castles. This was obvious in 1659, when the Commonwealth turned once more to the radicals, and conservatives or moderates were ejected from county committees and the militia.

In much of Wales, this left political and military power firmly in the hands of extreme radicals and Millenarians, the followers of Vavasor, who now found themselves in control of the seven castles which dominated the north and west. We find William Wynne at Denbigh Castle, Hugh Price at Powis Castle, Lewis Price at Caernarvon and Hugh Prichard at Conway. These were signatories to the *Word for God*; but there were others less stringently opposed to Cromwell who nevertheless found themselves allied to the extremists as the Restoration became increasingly likely. Morgan Llwyd had not signed in 1655, but most of his immediate circle had, and the Llwydians found themselves acting in close alliance with the Vavasorians by the end of the decade. By 1659, Beaumaris Castle was originally entrusted to John Jones, the Cromwellian peer, but Irish commitments led him to place it under his kinsman, Robert Owen.

Just as the political consensus of the radicals was being rent by the debate over the *Word for God*, so there appeared a new movement that seemed to justify every warning ever made by high Anglicans that Puritanism was the gateway to anarchy. Most of the older Puritan leaders had seen the new churches as incorporating traditional ideas of ministerial authority, order and decency; but as the decade progressed, the godly found themselves increasingly challenged by the very different vision of the Quakers. In 1653, Morgan Llwyd dispatched a follower named John ap John to make contact with Fox and his followers. John returned a Quaker himself, and began to evangelize. From 1655, Quaker preachers were active throughout Wales. They stood and preached during the services in churches (or 'steeple houses'); they refused to pay tithes; they declined the traditional signs of social respect, and addressed superiors as 'thou'; and they asserted the superiority of the inner Spirit to the Scriptures themselves. And some of those who performed these rebellious acts were women.[3]

Not coincidentally, all the recorded centres of Quaker activity in south Wales were exactly the oldest Puritan congregations, where

3. Francis Gawler, *Record of some persecutions inflicted upon some of the servants of the Lord in south Wales* (London 1659).

136

members had had longest to consider and debate ideas like Liberty and the Spirit: Cardiff and Swansea were such centers, as was Llanfaches itself. This was partly a generational issue: people born in the mid-1630s had lived through a political and intellectual tumult when anything seemed possible, and it is scarcely surprising that bold speculations now became possible. Richard Davies of Welshpool (born 1635) describes the prolonged spiritual crisis in which he lived from 1647 until 1656, when he frequented all manner of congregations, including those of Vavasor. He finally found peace in Quakerism.[4]

The Quakers were both loyal Puritans, and old republican soldiers. The early martyrologies in Wales are littered with descriptions of the sufferers as 'a commission officer', 'a faithful soldier to the commonwealth', 'in actual arms for the commonwealth'. The Quakers made considerable inroads into the garrisons of the republic raising the spectre that the adherents of these frightening radical ideas were well-armed veterans. In 1660, the forces of the restored monarchy usually saw the Quakers as the most serious and direct challenge to the new order, and carried out mass arrests.

Under the Republic too, the more respectable and traditional Puritans were horrified by the new movement, and many of the best-known Puritan leaders were listed by the Quaker martyrologists as the worst persecutors, including former Approvers and Triers. But once again, attitudes were far from united. Even before the Restoration, some followers of Erbery and Llwyd found themselves drawn to Quaker ideas. In the persecutions of the 1660s, many old Puritan congregations of north and west Wales experienced a 'great convincement' to Quakerism. In Merionethshire and Montgomeryshire, Richard Davies dated this phenomenon precisely to 1662, the point at which it became clear that armed resistance to the new order was futile.

THE RESTORATION

With such ideas spreading, it is not surprising that there was increasing panic among the old elites by the late 1650s; and they were

4. *An account of the convincement . . . of that ancient servant in God, Richard Davies* (London 1710).

joined in this concern by many mainstream Presbyterians and Independents. When the monarchy was restored in 1660, the new regime was anxious about the possibility of resistance, and entrusted sweeping powers to local Justices and deputy-lieutenants, who were drawn both from the old Cavaliers and from moderates of the interregnum years. At least for the first two years, their rule was often draconian, with old Quakers and Millenarians as their special target. By the end of 1660, the Welsh castles contained several hundred Quaker prisoners. This new consensus was threatened only in 1662, when it became clear that the Church establishment was not to incorporate the moderate Puritans. Presbyterian and Independent clergy were gradually ejected from the livings they had held in the fifties, and the final confrontation came in August 1662, 'Black Bartholomew', with the removal of clergy who would not accept the Anglican settlement. The moderate Puritans, many of whom supported the Restoration, now found themselves in active dissent.

This might be taken as a convenient point to mark the end of the civil war crisis, but this would be misleading. Obviously, the revolutionary generation did not immediately pass away in 1660. Men who served the Commonwealth in arms often survived until the end of the century, and their children carried their memories well into the next century: Richard Davies the Quaker lived from 1635 until 1708. This chronology is important because the 80 years after 1660 often appear to be a rather dull hiatus separating the ages of Vavasor Powell and Howell Harris: two remarkably similar, and equally controversial, individuals.

Also, the civil war years and their aftermath had caused the emergence of a wave of radical leaders who were now deprived of their secular power, but could scarcely be expected to return without further comment to the humble drudgery of their farms or trades. For several decades, such men would represent an opposition to the traditional order in Church and State different from anything seen hitherto in the history of Wales. The hatred and fear they inspired is indicated by the frequency with which they are mentioned in the rumoured plots and risings so often discussed in post-Restoration Wales: Richard Edwards in Caernarvonshire, Vavasor and his followers in Montgomeryshire, William Wynne in Denbighshire. Undoubtedly, such plots were often bogus acts of provocation invented by Royalist rivals; but it would be equally unwise to assume that the radicals after 1660 were the passively non-resisting nonconformists presented so carefully by generations of dissenting historians.

THE CONSPIRACIES OF THE 1660S

Unrest in the 1660s was as frequent, serious and overtly political as anything that would be encountered before the 1830s. Plots by radicals and dissenters were rumoured in 1660 and 1661 in Caernarvonshire and Montgomeryshire, with the latter being feared as a Vavasorian stronghold. In 1661, popular hopes and fears are indicated by the widespread reports that a ghostly Roundhead army was seen marching towards Montgomery Castle to free the prisoners there. After a lull, plot fears resumed in full force in 1663 and 1664, and there were even charges that a national rising was planned to coincide with the movement in northern England. In 1665, Richard Edwards was alleged to be a leading conspirator in a scheme based yet again in Caernarvonshire and Montgomeryshire. To give a flavour of the time, we might quote extracts of a letter allegedly written in March 1664 by the Quaker Robert Owen, an associate of the regicide John Jones:

> our time grows short and . . . it stands in us all to hasten our work which we are ordained and called to by the Lord, to pluck down the whore of Babylon and the maintainers thereof, before the meeting of that Idol which our enemies call their parliament, for assure yourself that if we do not strike a stroke before that time we shall be cut off by piecemeal as many of our dear brethren have been already to our sad discomfort, witness our late brethren murdered in the north. . . .

> Colonel Philip Jones . . . hath prepared Fonmon to our great encouragement . . . Jones and Gunter have undertaken the east part of that country, Evan Lewis and John Griffith with their interest in Neath and Swansea the western part likewise. Carmarthen and Pembroke we are assured of at your pleasure and sight of your commission.[5]

If the letter is not authentic, then it certainly uses the correct forms and language. More to the point, it gives a perfect idea of the fears of the ruling elite in the years following the Restoration. There remained a profound danger, and it came from certain well-known sources: the towns, the radical army veterans and the dissenting congregations. Couple this with the danger of Dutch invasion (Fonmon stood near the port of Aberthaw) and Wales might be set ablaze. Another concern was the extent of correspondence (presumed to be seditious) between local radicals and their metropolitan counterparts. Here, as in so many other ways, the Restoration years prefigure the crises of the early nineteenth century and the Chartist era.

5. NLW Brogyntyn/Clenennau MS 1955.

No area or individual can be seen as wholly typical, but the fate of the Puritan leadership is suggested by the case of Henry Williams (*c.* 1620–1690) of Merthyr Tydfil. Williams (Harry William Thomas) represented a new type in the political history of Stuart Wales, in that he exercised great power on a basis quite different from that of the traditional landowners. The son of a plebeian hill farmer (a yeoman, not even marginally a 'gentleman') he was the first in his family to adopt a surname instead of a patronymic, and he may have been a monoglot Welsh speaker. In the wars, he joined the Baptist-congregation- cum- army-company of Jenkin Jones of Llanddetty, a prominent Breconshire radical. Williams became rich in the late 1640s by land acquisitions from the diocese of Llandaff, and by his ability to use armed force to settle land disputes in his favour. He became a Justice in 1649, and in the next decade became a major political figure in south Wales as a Vavasorian radical. Apart from his military strength, he owed his power to the large Baptist church which he led in the Glamorgan uplands. At Merthyr, his followers seized the church and persecuted the established minister, who was himself a conformist Puritan.

After the Restoration, the military power was gone, but the congregation remained, and this was estimated at several hundred strong in the later 1660s. When Williams entertained Vavasor at Merthyr in 1668, the ensuing meeting so terrified the Glamorgan Justices that they all (even former Cromwellians) concurred in mobilising the county militia to suppress it. Presumably, they saw the event less as a religious revival than as the beginning of an armed uprising, a thousand strong. One can only sympathise with their view, given the distinguished military records of many of the 'captains' and 'colonels' present in the crowd. Williams was involved in another alleged rising in 1683. He was also one of the Dissenters added to the county Bench by James II in 1687, when the King was seeking the support of the Dissenters. The return to power of Williams and his like goes far to explaining why most Stuart loyalists so welcomed the Revolution of 1688.

Williams thus represents a continuity from the civil wars to the 1690s, but the Roundhead tradition he established endured long after his death, through his congregation. Merthyr Tydfil established one of the first permanent meeting-houses in Glamorgan in the 1690s. By 1763, three-quarters of the area's inhabitants were Dissenters and from distinctly unorthodox congregations:

> presbyterians professing themselves for the most part arminians, with a few calvinists and fewer anabaptists, and among all these I am afraid are too many deists.

The rector had no doubt of the cause of this:

> Before the Grand Rebellion (they) were not so many but in those
> unhappy times of usurpation multiplied apace, took firm footing, and
> overspread this part of the country every way.

Later incumbents would suggest that nearly all the inhabitants were
Dissenters.

Under Charles II, the established authorities saw Dissent not just
as an offence against the Church, but as a political and above all, a
military danger. There were hundreds like Henry Williams. In the
1670s most Dissenting congregations in Wales bore a very military
aspect, with 'captains' common among the leadership. West
Glamorgan even offered a church dominated by a Major-General,
Rowland Dawkins of Gower. One church in Monmouthshire was
headed in 1675 by Captain Robert Jones and Major Blethin, both
well-known committee men from the 1650s. In Merionethshire and
Montgomeryshire, the extremists of the 1650s remained firmly in
control of the Baptist and Quaker congregations into the 1680s,
when their members led the Welsh emigration to Pennsylvania. The
scale of this movement appears quite sweeping. Between 1682 and
1700, some 900 Merionethshire people joined the 2000 Quaker
emigrants to Pennsylvania; and this at a time when the population of
the whole county was barely 20,000. The geography of Welsh
Quakerism is still recollected by a series of communities west of
Philadelphia: Radnor, Merion and Montgomery; Narberth,
St David's and Haverford.

The old radicals not only survived 1660, they had evolved an
institutional framework to maintain and preserve their views:
through the dissenting congregations, but above all, through the
boroughs and towns.

DISSENT AND THE TOWNS

St Paul had once exhorted the Christians of Corinth to 'Purge out,
therefore, the old leaven', a phrase much quoted by post-Restoration
Royalists. As they correctly observed, the 'old leaven' of radicals and
Puritans had secured a firm hold on many political offices
throughout Wales, especially in the boroughs, which became centres
of radical religion and politics into the 1680s. Throughout the reign
of Charles II, Anglican leaders often denounced the tolerance granted
to nonconformists, and they were generally referring to conditions in

towns, especially those within the orbit of Bristol. In 1672, Bishop Lacy of St Davids complained of the dissenting schools freely permitted in Swansea, Carmarthen, Brecon, Cardigan and Haverfordwest. We have already seen the allegation made in 1664 that the Puritan conspirators were assured of suppport in Swansea, Neath, Pembroke and Carmarthen, orchestrated through dissenting communities headed by their respective 'captains'. Swansea was a hotbed of tolerance, but there were many other examples, both from the large chartered towns, and the smaller places like Narberth or Newcastle Emlyn.

Haverfordwest was typical in the continuity of urban office-holding from the interregnum to the Restoration; but as a Parliamentary borough, it was able to express this dissidence in more visible form. In 1679, its MP was Thomas Owen, a Dissenter. The magistrates of the town tolerated Quakerism, while the elders of the Independent congregation included, naturally enough, a 'Captain Longman'. The mayor himself had been a strong Parliamentary supporter. Here, as at Carmarthen, the community was strongly Whiggish in tone well into the 1680s, and mob action thwarted attempts to enforce Anglican orthodoxy.

Dissent survived as more than just a plebeian movement. Throughout Wales, there were 'moderate' gentry who continued to favour Puritan causes like the evangelisation of the poor, and the adoption of militantly anti-Catholic policies. Ideally, such families would have favoured broad policies of toleration that would include within the Church all sound Protestants who rejected political radicalism. The ejections of 1662 removed the moderate clergy, who now found themselves the leaders of dissenting congregations, usually Presbyterian, but sometimes Independent. For many influential gentry, such an exclusion was not only barbarous, but politically divisive in the face of the Catholic menace in areas like Monmouthshire and Flintshire. The political elite was thus split for decades over the issue of toleration, and the Dissenters were able to use their influence with certain great squires to defend themselves from the worst excesses of other Anglican leaders.

There were violent persecutors among the clergy and gentry, and Merionethshire in 1677 had the distinction of being the last place in the British Isles where it was seriously proposed to burn heretics at the stake, with Quakers as the intended victims. But some of the greatest families simply refused to enforce the repressive laws. In west Glamorgan, the Mansells of Margam and Briton Ferry not only patronised the dissenting clergy and their congregations, they used ejected ministers to tutor their sons. Sir Edward Mansell even contrived to act with moderation towards Vavasor Powell. In the Wrexham area, political tensions ran high because this had been a stronghold of the Puritan extremists; but Lady Eyton protected the Dissenters after 1660, and employed the Dissenting pastor John Evans to tutor her children. And she was only one of the patricians whose houses were open to the nonconformists for their meetings.

Between 1662 and 1689, Welsh politics were shaped by attitudes to Dissent, and the related question of tolerating Catholicism. Those who became Whigs saw Catholics as the greater danger, and emerged as a united party in the campaigns against the Marquess of Worcester in the 1670s. They also formed a tactical alliance with the Dissenting leadership, with the schools of the 'Welsh Trust' as their particular cause. Those who feared Dissent were Worcester's allies, and they opposed each new measure of toleration: the Indulgence of 1672–1675, and the subsequent liberalisation after 1689. From the 1640s to the 1690s, political conflict in Wales follows a broad continuity, with Puritanism in its various forms as a central issue. It was this schism within the ruling elite that permitted the Dissenting sects to survive what could easily have been a terminal crisis in the 1660s.

CONCLUSION

The mid-century crisis is important because of its influence on later religious loyalties; but there are still stronger reasons for studying these years. For the first time in Welsh history, written records now give us the opportunity to hear the political thoughts and ideas of people far removed from the ruling elites; and often, those ideas run violently contrary to the assumptions of the traditional rulers. It is possible to debate how far the events of the civil war years can be described as truly revolutionary, especially in the original intentions of the activists, who can often be seen as the true conservatives, opposed to Court innovations. But having said this, the mid-century in Wales was a time of far-reaching social change, which often promised to go much further.

The war years had broken so many of the familiar moulds that formed everyday life. For a society rarely accustomed to a stage as broad as the shire, the mid-century had offered the spectacle of Baptist congregations spanning several counties. In a social order that accepted the dominance of the Church and the landowner, there were fresh memories of having plundered the manor house and the vicarage, of seeing the gentleman and the parson abase themselves to Parliamentary committees to regain a subsistence. In Anne's reign, Glamorgan Tories bitterly recalled their misdeeds; how, for example, in the heart of the Vale,

> Hugh Jones . . . was the sequestrator and usurper. This Jones was the greatest tyrant of our county, and if Colonel Jones had sought out all over the kingdom, he could hardly have met with one that would have come nigh to an equal pitch of barbarity, and oppression. For he did what he pleased and would drive a whole herd of cattle at a time from their proprietors if they were once made delinquents, insomuch that no man of a cavalier, whether la˙ man or priest, would call anything he had his own, that lived near him.[6]

Whereas the parish had once seemed a sacred and indispensable part of life, religious matters had passed into the hands of humble itinerant preachers. And everyone recalled a Wales in which such religious radicals exercised what can only be described as raw military domination. There had been a day when the castles had all been in the hands of men who loathed the characteristic ideas and beliefs of the gentry and the clergy; and they had armed strength to assert their opinions. These were images that could scarcely be forgotten overnight. In the following century, Protestant Dissent would be such a lively issue precisely because it evoked these images.

6. Quoted in Philip Jenkins ed., 'The sufferings of the clergy', *Journal of Welsh ecclesiastical history*, (1987), iv, 32.

CHAPTER EIGHT
Religion and Revivalism 1680–1780

EIGHTEENTH CENTURY DISSENT

Nonconformists of the eighteenth and nineteenth centuries retained a strong inheritance from the years of war and revolution; but this tradition was not passed on in a pure and unchanged form. Eighteenth century Dissent experienced vigorous controversies in which the substance of belief was changed into something far removed from what the earlier Puritans would have accepted as orthodox, or even Christian. This religious radicalism was also confined in its geographical scope, largely limited to the old centres of Stuart times; and it is unlikely that the civilised rationalism of the Old Dissent could ever have swept Wales to have become a national religion. The invincible Dissent of the nineteenth century therefore had a dual origin, owing something to the older Puritanism, but more to evangelical and educational traditions that originated within the established Church. It is the interplay between these different movements that makes the eighteenth century so crucial for later religious developments.

THE STRENGTH OF DISSENT

We can form a picture of the numerical strengths and weaknesses of Dissent about 1715 from the estimates collected by Dr John Evans. The material has to be used with care, and it may well be that figures for some congregations are 'suspiciously high'; but the list offers some important clues.[1]

1. Adapted from Michael Watts, *The Dissenters* (Oxford 1978) i.

Table 8:1 Dissenting Congregations in 1715 (The number of congregations for each county is followed by the supposed membership)

County	Presbyterian	Independent	Baptist	Quaker	Total
Ang/Caerns	—	2/250	–/–	–/–	2/250
Merioneth	—	1/150	—	3/?	4/300?
Denbigh	2/285	–/–	1/150	1/2	4/450
Flint	1/25	–/–	–/–	–/–	1/25
Brecon	1/150	4/1200	1/400	1/?	7/1800?
Radnor	—	3/850	2/1000	2/40	7/1900
Montgomery	1/120	3/300	—	6/?	10/?
Cardigan	1/250	2/1000	1/?	1/?	5/?
Carmarthen	17/4750	2/1350	3/900	4/?	26/7200?
Pembroke	1/500	3/480	1/?	4/70	9/1500?
Glamorgan	1/?	6/2060	5/1600	2/?	14/4500?
Monmouth	—	9/1180	7/2080	4/90	20/3350
Totals	25/7000	35/8800	21/6300	28/750?	109/22,850

Wales and Monmouthshire seem to have had over 100 congregations with about 23,000 members and 'hearers'. Independents were the strongest sect, followed closely by Presbyterians and particular Baptists. By far the weakest grouping was the Quakers, depleted by emigration and now reduced to only a few hundred supporters.

Wales in general was by no means the Dissenting heartland that it would later become. Dissenters may have represented about five or six per cent of the Welsh population; but this was far lower than the ten per cent frequently found in English shires of the West Country or the midlands. In addition, there were substantial local variations. Welsh Dissent was strictly a southern phenomenon, strongest in the prosperous areas most dependent on Bristol, and with closest ties to Somerset and Devonshire. Two-thirds of Welsh Dissenters lived in the three southern shires of Monmouth, Glamorgan and Carmarthen. In these counties, Dissenters comprised about one-eighth of the population. Naturally enough, it is in these parts that we find major institutions like the academies.

By contrast, the northern regions of Gwynedd and Clwyd appear as bastions of the establishment, where fewer than one per cent of the people could be claimed as nonconformists. There may have been as few as 1000 Dissenters in the five shires combined. At the end of the century, Thomas Charles of Bala would stress the lack of evangelical teaching in the north:

True religion had forsaken the country. There was nothing like the semblance of it in the Church, nor was there much of it among the few dissenters that were very thinly scattered here and there. . . . The Bible was almost an unknown book, seldom to be met with, especially in the houses of the poor.

In 1672, 136 southern congregations took out licences, compared to 49 in the north; and in 1810, there were still two chapels in the south for every one in the north.

There were also enormous variations within counties, as dissent was generally strongest in the sprawling parishes of the hills, where settlement was scattered and parochial control was weak. There were also footholds in the towns: Swansea retained a strongly Dissenting character, and there were congregations in most of the larger towns into the early eighteenth century. However, there were no local fortresses of Dissent to parallel the role played by Bristol or Norwich in England.

Welsh nonconformity in the eighteenth century was chiefly southern, rural and upland. Often, these churches were survivors from the time of Vavasor and his allies, but there was also new growth. Although not strong numerically, the Dissenters did continue their missionary endeavours throughout the difficult century after 1660, when some heroic ministers kept up the tradition of itinerant evangelism. Even in the worst years, there were figures like Stephen Hughes in Carmarthenshire, or Henry Maurice in Breconshire. William Jones was received by the old-established Baptist community in the Olchon valley, and then set out to evangelise south-west Wales. Based at Rhydwilym, this church drew its membership from almost 40 parishes and three counties. There were 33 members in 1669, 220 by 1723.

The older churches also continued to expand by a process akin to cell division. In Glamorgan, the historic church of Cadoxton in the Neath Valley spawned several offspring in the western uplands, at Gellionnen, Blaengwrach, Mynydd Bach and others; and these emerged as independent congregations by the early eighteenth century. These 'cells' were further strengthened by itinerancy. From Blaengwrach, the minister Henry Davies evangelized the hill areas from the 1720s to the 1760s, even penetrating into the Rhondda valleys, then one of the most remote areas of southern Wales.

In the south-east, little active Dissent survived in the lowland parishes after 1710. The strongholds of Nonconformity were rather to be found in hill parishes like Llangyfelach, Merthyr Tydfil and Gelligaer in Glamorgan, Mynyddislwyn, Aberystruth and Bedwellty

147

in Monmouthshire. Ironically, the persecutors of Dissent were quite unwittingly forcing their enemies into precisely those regions that would be of the greatest economic significance in years to come, especially after 1780. At the time, however, the hill parishes seemed more like an isolated refuge, where intellectual life pursued an essentially interregnum character through the early Georgian period. The Dissenting clergy and the better educated laity still treasured the classics of the writers of the radical years, while the congregations debated passionately over issues like infant baptism and Arminianism.

THE DISSENTING ACADEMIES

Persecuted and deprived of official position, the Dissenters could only look towards a better time in the future; but until relief came, it was essential to preserve their beliefs by evangelism and education. Through the eighteenth century, the Dissenters maintained a series of academies that offered an education comparable to anything offered in Anglican institutions like the grammar schools or colleges, and the survival of these bodies was a particular offence to Tory politicians for most of the period. Often, the academies were connected to a particular individual, like Philip Henry in Flintshire; or they were attached to a denomination. The Baptists established an institution at Trosnant (Monmouthshire) in 1732, the Independents at Abergavenny in 1757, the newer Methodists at Trefecca in 1768.

By far the most important was the Carmarthen academy, the closest parallel to a local university in eighteenth century Wales. The academy arose in an ad hoc way, as a school kept by the ejected Glamorgan clergyman, Samuel Jones, at his house at Brynllywarch. In the 1690s, there were probably about five pupils, though this number rose to 20 in the 1740s. From about 1698, the academy began a series of moves – none, incidentally, occasioned by outright persecution. The school sought a home at Abergavenny, Bridgend, and later (by 1710) in Carmarthen. This was not a permanent location, and the academy went through another series of migrations in mid-century.

Students took a four year course of studies, and the school fulfilled the best stereotype of the Georgian dissenting academy. Carmarthen enjoyed an excellent reputation for Classical scholarship and theology, but subjects offered included languages, mathematics, astronomy and other sciences. The school offered what can be described as a liberal education, and this tolerant attitude extended to matters of theology. Writers studied by the 1740s included deists and radicals like Locke, Woolaston and Samuel Clarke; so it is not surprising that the academy became a centre for Arminian and Arian thought. It was in the 1720s that Thomas Perrot apparently established this tradition, which grew stronger by mid-century under teachers like Samuel Thomas. From Carmarthen, pupils went out to radicalise congregations throughout south Wales, where the progress of Arminian and Arian ideas after 1750 can be traced through the appointment of a series of Carmarthen graduates as ministers. A few alumni made national reputations, including the political radicals Richard Price and David Williams, and the Methodist pioneers Howell Harris and William Williams of Pantycelyn.

THE GROWTH OF RELIGIOUS RADICALISM

Carmarthen academy was by no means the only factor in spreading religious heterodoxy among the congregations, as Dissent was by nature fissiparous. The lack of central structures to enforce discipline or orthodoxy – or the remoteness of such structures as did exist – meant that factions within congregations were likely to evolve distinctive religious ideas. Every individual was expected to read and interpret the Bible, and varying interpretations inevitably arose. Once these views were formed, it was an easy step to an overt split, and a new chapel would be erected by the 'heretics'. Welsh Dissent was thus inherently likely to give rise to frequent schisms, with new groups splitting off from the original.

There were two areas above all – respectively the Trinity, and the orthodox Calvinist view of election and predestination – where tensions were likely to lead to schism. Both topics had been the focus of lengthy intellectual debate; but there was also a temptation for what might be described as 'common-sense' interpretations, seeking a more rational and comprehensible account of these fundamental mysteries. In the case of the Trinity, orthodoxy was undermined by the constant use of the psalms in worship, and the frequent reiteration of their aggressive monotheism. This led some to Arianism, and a view of Christ as somehow subordinate to the Father; while there was little to prevent the next (Unitarian) step, of according divinity to the Father alone. By the early eighteenth century, disturbing theological questions were beginning to arise in the livelier and more intellectual congregations.

There is no necessary connection between Arminianism and Trinitarian heresies; but in the context of the time, these fundamental shifts were often linked in practice as part of a common tradition of inquiring 'liberalism'. It was natural that Arminian and Unitarian heresies would frequently arise, but both were ideas that were completely repellent to the orthodox. Denying the divinity of Christ seemed barely removed from outright atheism; while Arminians appeared little short of Roman sympathisers. It is also likely that some went still further in their speculations, towards deism and outright atheism. In the 1780s, the dissenting minister of Aberystruth was Edmund Jones, who wrote a comprehensively credulous treatise on Welsh ghosts and apparitions. In the tradition of Joseph Glanville, this was designed to counter what he viewed as the widespread sins of scepticism and materialism.

Between 1725 and 1730, the sects were in conflict over infant baptism, with great public debates in Merthyr Tydfil and Aberystruth. This contest was soon overshadowed by the Arminian challenge, which divided both Independents and Baptists in the next three decades. In Glamorgan the important Baptist congregation at Hengoed suffered a controversy that endured from 1729 until 1750, when the Arminian dissidents were finally expelled, only to found a new church at Craigyfargoed. The Independents were also rent, with the traditional Calvinists placing most of the blame on the heterodox pupils of the Carmarthen academy. In the 1750s, orthodox discontent reached such heights that the Independents withdrew their support from Carmarthen, and set up a rival academy at Abergavenny.

Arminianism became commonplace between 1730 and 1760, to be followed shortly thereafter by Arianism. From the 1780s, the chief menace was the adoption of Unitarian views. In Glamorgan, this was the course pursued by most of the oldest and most prestigious congregations, as at Swansea and Gellionnen. The case of Cwm-y-Glo (Merthyr Tydfil) is instructive. This was a remnant of the church established over several counties by Henry Maurice in the 1670s. In the 1720s, it had two ministers, one Arminian and one Calvinist (a common compromise). In 1732, conflict intensified when a new minister named Richard Rees arrived from the Carmarthen academy. In 1747, Rees and the Arminians led a secession church that established itself at Cefn Coed y Cymer; and this was a Unitarian congregation by the end of the century. The orthodox wing was Calvinist; but the minister here was succeeded by his son, who was yet another Arminian.

After 1780, the expansion of industry created a populous new Wales in precisely such parishes as Merthyr and Aberystruth, which became centres of Jacobin and Chartist thought. While such ideas appear novel and revolutionary, it can be argued that they really rest on much older traditions of religious radicalism.

LANDSCAPES

But continuity of this sort was not confined to the areas of later industrialisation. Throughout Wales, there were buildings, communities, even whole landscapes, which bore the unmistakable signs of a long radical and 'enthusiastic' continuity. Of course, the mere fact that a series of events occurred in a particular area over a period of time does not mean that they were connected, still less that landscape somehow shapes human thought or behaviour. But certain regions, certain towns or landscapes, seem inevitably to associate themselves with a particular set of beliefs or ideologies. Consider for example the Upper Wye country on the Breconshire/Radnorshire border, just west of Hay-on-Wye. This part of Wales includes the oldest standing nonconformist chapel in Wales, at Maes-yr-Onnen (1696), as well as fragmentary remains of another meeting house at Penyrwrlodd (1707); and a group of buildings associated with Methodist history over the border at Trefecca. What was the nature of the continuity in this region?

This was a dissenting stronghold at least from the 1640s, and nonconformists might well have been tempted to settle here in eras of persecution because of the area's location on the frontier between different counties and dioceses. Confused jurisdictions made it more difficult to organise efficient legal sanctions. Hay and Llanigon were probably Puritan centres before 1640, and were the bases for a Baptist church that ultimately spread its influence over much of west Wales. One associate was William Watkins of Penyrwrlodd, who served as sheriff of Breconshire in the radical year of 1649. There was a strong Independent church here in the 1670s, headed by a group of men whose signatures appeared in the *Word for God*. Like the Baptist congregation, this Vavasorian church had connections far afield, and in 1683 a millenarian plot in south-east Wales was said to involve this group and the old Roundheads of Merthyr Tydfil. There is also some evidence of Quakers at Glasbury and Talgarth; so this corner of Wales provided a great deal of business for the Bishops'

Consistory Court throughout the Restoration years. In Radnorshire, few gentlemen were prepared to serve the radical regimes of the interregnum, especially in the immediate aftermath of the act of regicide; but the government did find one such extremist house, in the Williams family of Caebalfa, in the nearby parish of Clyro.

In 1696, the Independent church built a chapel at Maes-yr-Onnen, for a membership estimated in 1715 at 250. From 1700 to 1742, the minister was one David Price, who kept a school at Llwyn Llwyd in the parish of Llanigon. Price carried the tradition of religious dissent on to a new generation, as his pupils included Howell Harris, from nearby Trefecca (he attended the school from 1728 to 1730). It was at Talgarth in 1735 that Harris experienced conversion. The revival that began in this old homeland of enthusiasm was carried to the whole of Wales by Harris and other early Methodists like William Williams, then a pupil at Llwyn Llwyd. In 1735, this venerable school became for a few years the home of the 'Carmarthen' academy, under Vavasor Griffiths – we note the name with interest. The old Dissenters raised in the traditions of the interregnum were thus a link to the newer and still more troubling radicalism of the next century.

And this area continued to play a central role in the history of Dissent. Howell Harris built at Trefecca the amazing 'castellated monastery' that would house the followers who had joined his revolutionary religious community, 150 strong by 1756. Harris had fallen out with most of his former Methodist allies over doctrinal and personal issues, which were complicated by his inability to take advice or criticism; and in 1755, he retired to lead this remarkable community. Trefecca served as an outlet for Harris's manifold interests: it became celebrated for its contribution to progressive agriculture; and it had a pioneering printing press.

Also at Trefecca stood a seminary (1768) for the ministers of the Countess of Huntingdon's Connection. From 1842 to 1910, the house built for Harris's community would become a training college for Calvinistic Methodist clergy. In 1858, this 'school for prophets' became one of the first centres of the great revival that ultimately swept the whole of Wales. In 1858 – as in 1735, or 1650 – the area was famous for its evangelical 'saints', who held lengthy and profoundly emotional prayer meetings in which they 'made prayers with long pauses and groans'. From this sanctified land, each respective movement would overrun Wales like a 'fire in the thatch'.

EDUCATION AND REFORM

Several regions could serve as well as the Trefecca area as visual reminders of the long continuity of traditions in Wales. Merthyr Tydfil would be one appropriate choice, as would the countryside between Narberth and St Clears, on the county boundary between Carmarthen and Pembroke. In such areas, we find the enduring vigour of themes which survive through what appear to be the longest and most barren periods of stagnation – political, religious or intellectual. Particularly notable is the continuity in the years between 1660 and 1735, traditionally regarded as a period of 'sleep' or worse. Continuity can be most clearly observed in the history of education, where old Dissent and new enthusiasm would each play their part.

The religious content and political control of education would remain an enduring concern in Welsh political life from the time of Vavasor Powell to the age of Nye Bevan, and beyond. In the 1650s, the Puritan reformers had placed a high priority on education and literacy as a means of propagating the gospel in Wales. Few of their schools survived the Restoration, but the idea of popular evangelism through education remained strong throughout the next century.

In the time of Charles II, the evangelistic impulse was particularly associated with Puritans and Dissenters like Stephen Hughes, Thomas Gouge and Charles Edwards (the last a former itinerant from the time of Propagation). Hughes spent three decades attempting to produce popular Welsh editions of books that would best promote literacy and godliness: the verses of Vicar Prichard, together with a New Testament and Psalms (1672), *Pilgrim's Progress* (1688) and the largest and cheapest edition yet produced of the whole Welsh Bible (1677). In collecting and editing the work of Prichard, he also gave it a name – 'The Welshman's Candle', *Canwyll y Cymry* – and helped create one of the most popular Welsh classics.

In the 1670s, Hughes, Gouge and their circle created an institutional framework for the work of evangelism. A Welsh Trust was established to found and organise schools throughout the principality, and this obtained support from a remarkable group of leading Churchmen and Dissenters, including Anglican bishops as well as Presbyterians like Richard Baxter and Thomas Firmin. This eirenic character was reproduced at local level, where the scheme was supported by the Bishop of St Davids, no less than by Dissenters like Hughes. The Welsh Trust therefore had a political purpose in addition to its educational role, in that it provided the basis for a

153

working alliance between moderate Anglicans and Dissenters. Lay support was essential to the scheme, and the squires who gave this represent a fascinating rollcall of the opposition politicians of the decade: old Puritans like the sons of Colonel Philip Jones, together with Anglican Whigs like Sir Trevor Williams. The Welsh Trust included virtually all the leading opponents of the high Tory Marquess of Worcester; and it is not surprising that the movement faded rapidly during the political crisis of the Exclusion years.

The Welsh Trust was a short-lived experiment, but it was a manifestation of a much older and stronger impulse. In the late 1690s, there was yet another attempt to achieve the moral and educational reforms associated with the interregnum, though without the politically radical connotations. In 1699, five men formed a new Society for the Propagation of Christian Knowledge, the SPCK. In its origin, it was not intended to concentrate on Welsh endeavours, but all the founders had either Welsh or border connections, and a renewed effort to found Welsh schools was perhaps inevitable. One of the original five supporters was Sir Humphrey Mackworth, who held a great estate at Neath; while Sergeant Hook had been Justice of Caernarvon.

The SPCK obtained support from Anglicans of all shades of opinion, including Jacobites and high flyers; though this traditional Puritan scheme naturally attracted families that had followed the reforming schemes of the Commonwealth. Mackworth himself was the son of a Cromwellian soldier. The ongoing feud between High and Low Church opinions may well have led to controversy within the movement, and Mary Clement notes that the SPCK rapidly lost support in Wales after the Jacobite rising of 1715. For whatever reason, the SPCK quickly seemed to be going the way of the Welsh Trust, as an ephemeral movement that soon lost its early vogue. Of 96 SPCK schools founded in Wales between 1699 and 1740, 79 were founded between 1705 and 1718.

Also, the SPCK schools were strictly limited in their geographical extent, much like the Welsh Trust earlier. In the 1670s, the vast majority of the schools were to be found in the four counties of the south Wales coast. Under the SPCK, almost a third of the schools (31) were established in Pembrokeshire alone, and 60 per cent of the total were founded in just the three shires of Pembroke, Carmarthen and Glamorgan. For all the society's occasional correspondents, the charity school movement needed the constant and dedicated support of a group of powerful lay patrons; and this it only found in the far south-west. The charity school movement in this area received important support from a group of gentry who – like the Mackworths – had shown Parliamentary and Puritanical sympathies in the 1640s, and who maintained their commitment to popular evangelism long after the Restoration. Much the most important was the Pembrokeshire gentry family of Philipps of Picton. Sir Richard Philipps had fought for Parliament in the first civil war, and his son served as a member of Cromwell's parliaments, and a militia commissioner for the Republic. He died in 1697, and was succeeded by Sir John Philipps, who was one of the greatest supporters of the charity school movement.

Sir John Philipps was close to Griffith Jones, who would establish the charity school idea on a new and more permanent basis. In 1716, Philipps presented him to the living of Llanddowror, near St Clear's; and Jones married his sister. As so often in Welsh history, the leadership of a social movement was closely intertwined by ties of marriage and kinship. Another of the baronet's sisters married John Vaughan of Derllys, who was (with Philipps) one of the most loyal lay patrons of the schools. Vaughan's daughter in turn was Madam Bridget Bevan, who became the main patron of the Welsh Circulating Schools established by Jones in the 1730s. Madam Bevan effectively ran the whole system after Jones' death in 1761.

Griffith Jones was important not only for restoring the charity school idea, but for pioneering many aspects of the religious revival of the 1730s. In educational terms, his circulating schools appear to have been a dramatic success. Jones's schools used ideas that were not wholly new, but they were now successfully applied to the society of rural Wales. Schoolmasters were itinerant. Their schools were held for three-monthly periods, at times of the year when demand for labour was slack, and adult attendance was expected; while night schools were also offered. The Bible and Church catechism formed the main substance of teaching.

Instruction was in the Welsh language, a decision based on pragmatism rather than principle. As Jones explained rather defensively in the 1740 *Welch Piety*:[2]

> Welsh is still the vulgar tongue, and not English. The English charity schools which have been tried, produced no better effect in country places; all that the children could do in three or four or five years amounted commonly to no more than to learn very imperfectly to read some easy parts of the Bible, without knowing the Welsh of it, nor the meaning of what they said when they repeated their catechism.

2. Quoted from T. Herbert and G.E. Jones, *The remaking of Wales in the eighteenth century* (Cardiff: University of Wales 1988), 65.

Welsh might endure for centuries yet; and meanwhile,

> What myriads of poor ignorant souls must launch forth into the dreadful
> abyss of eternity, and perish for want of knowledge?

By 1761, it was claimed that Jones' schools had taught 158,000
pupils. We may doubt the exact scale, but the endeavour lasted far
longer than either the Welsh Trust or the SPCK schools. In 1740,
there were 150 'Welsh schools' in Wales and Monmouthshire, with
almost 9000 pupils. This was numerically more impressive than
earlier efforts, though as with all these predecessors, there were
geographical limitations, and growth was slow. In 1740, the schools
were heavily concentrated in the south and west: half were in the
shires of Glamorgan, Carmarthen and Cardigan. The six counties of
north Wales could show only four schools between them. By 1746,
there were major advances into mid-Wales, and much of north and
west Wales had been reached by 1756. Progress was strong in
Anglesey and Llŷn. By the 1770s, schools were sparser in absolute
numbers, but they were spread over all parts of the country.

Though a clergyman of the established church, Griffith Jones
seemed to resemble both the itinerant preachers of the 1650s and the
Methodists of a later generation. As early as 1714, he was travelling
on lengthy preaching tours to the areas around his parish. Not
surprisingly, Jones was attacked in print in the 1740s as the spiritual
father of the enthusiasts. His attitude to the reformers was at best
cautious, but his career crossed theirs at so many points. Daniel
Rowland was first converted through his ministry, about 1735.
When Howell Harris converted Howel Davies, Harris sent him to
study at Llanddowror, where he later became a curate under Jones.
Davies later became known as the Methodist 'Apostle of Pembrokeshire'. Thomas Charles, a Methodist leader of a later generation, was
educated at Llanddowror school about 1760.

The Welsh circulating schools grew at precisely the time that the
religious revival was gaining steam, and it was often noted that a
revival was manifested by both increased church attendance and the
emergence of a Griffith Jones school. It may be coincidence, but the
areas in which the Methodist societies had established themselves by
about 1740 were exactly those regions of the south where the schools
were being founded. As in the 1650s, popular religious schooling
expanded alongside the work of itinerant evangelists.

THE GREAT REVIVAL

The Welsh revival had its origins within the established Church, among those clergy and pious laymen who wished to evangelise what they saw as the impious and ill-educated population of Wales. Griffith Jones was by no means the only evangelical within the established Church; it was the Anglican vicar of Talgarth whose preaching so stirred Howell Harris in 1735. The revival soon affected William Williams, who came from a dissenting family; but both Harris and Williams responded to the new spirit by attempting to take orders in the established Church. Daniel Rowland, the third of the revivalist leaders, was himself an Anglican cleric at the beginning of the movement.

The events of 1735 did not mark the creation of a distinct sect or even organisation. Methodism was firmly planted in the Anglican Church, from which it was only separated gradually and reluctantly; and this posed a real dilemma. Most of the Methodist leaders wished to remain within the Church, and they had a high view of the value of communion. However, mainstream clergy grew ever more hostile to this apparently subversive organisation within the Church, and remaining Methodist clergy were increasingly driven into the wilderness. But still, there was a reluctance to take the natural step, and to secede as a separate denomination. The decisive break did not come until 1811.

These Anglican roots must be stressed because Welsh Methodism is so commonly seen in the context of the dissenting tradition. There would always be clear connections between Methodism and the nonconformist sects, and our account of the Radnorshire border country has emphasised the elements of overlap and continuity. However, this might disguise the real novelty and independence of Methodism in its first century, when the movement differed sharply from the old Dissent in terms of politics, rhetoric and culture. In turn, Dissenters found new material for controversy in their attitudes to the revival.

From the late 1730s, the Methodist movement made enormous strides within the Church in Wales, especially in the south. In parts, Methodism followed the leadership of the Wesleys. However, there were also distinctive forms of Methodism that were to be far more important in Wales itself, above all that based on Calvinistic theology. In Welsh usage, it is customary to distinguish between 'Methodists' and 'Wesleyans'. The modern Presbyterian Church of Wales derives not from the Presbyterianism of Stuart times, but from the Welsh Methodism of the great revival. Calvinistic Methodism would be important for the nineteenth century history of Wales, as the movement that finally penetrated (and overwhelmed) the Welsh-speaking areas of the north and west. It also remains the only church of distinctively Welsh origins; and it is worth noting that although the Methodist revival was a national phenomenon in Britain, the Welsh aspect was a distinctive movement based firmly on local roots.

The revival placed its emphasis on dramatic inner conversion, and on passionate enthusiasm far removed from the normal practice of either the Church or the (allegedly) dry preaching of the old Dissent. Each of the major leaders had his following, organised into religious societies: the *seiat*, which was to become so fundamental an institution in much of Wales. By 1737, the three had combined forces to create a real national movement, which became a major sect within the larger Church. In the words of Howell Harris, 'There appeared now a general reformation in several counties – public diversions became unfashionable, and religion became the common talk'. In consequence, there was an explosive growth of societies and schools, while churches became crowded.[3] The revival offered a tremendous sense of excitement and emotional involvement, and it spread like wildfire in counties like Cardigan and Carmarthen. It is difficult to avoid the impression that the reformers were supplying a need that had gone unsatisfied for many years. The movement appears to have had a special appeal to the young: Harris, Williams and Rowland were all between 19 and 22 years of age at the beginning of the 'Great Awakening'. There was also a clear appeal to women, who made up 50 to 60 per cent of most of the early societies of which we have record.

From the viewpoint of a secular age, there is much about the Methodist message that requires explanation, in terms of its most basic assumptions about life, death and the nature of salvation. This can be illustrated by considering one early preacher, who was by no means a national figure. Thomas Olivers was born in Montgomery-shire in 1725, and was converted by hearing Whitefield preach at Bristol in 1748.[4] Prior to this, he reports that he had been a grave sinner, being particularly prone to 'swearing and horrid blas-phemies'. As in almost every case of such a spiritual autobiography, the convert attempts to depict his past in the blackest possible terms.

3. Howell Harris, *Brief account of the life of Howell Harris esq.* (Trefecca 1791) 25.
4. John Telford, ed., *Wesley's veterans* (London: Robert Culley, n.d.) i., 197–251.

To modern eyes, he fails to suggest that Georgian Wales was rife with many acts that would count as sinful except to the most dogmatic Puritan. To a later generation, most of his worst sins would appear to be, at worst, pranks.

Olivers, like so many contemporaries, believed that his sins were an expression of his fallen humanity, which had consigned him en route to eternal fire and damnation. In hearing Whitefield, he came to appreciate not only the depth of the danger in which he stood, but that he had been rescued from this precipice by a God who had given his son to be brutally tortured to death for one wholly undeserving of any assistance, let alone such a total gift. Whitefield's text, 'Is this not a brand plucked out of the fire?', perfectly encapsulates the drama of sin and rescue fundamental to the evangelical message.

In the immediate thrill of conversion, the appropriate response was usually wild enthusiasm far removed from concepts of rational religion, but familiar from accounts of ecstatic religion in all parts of the world. Typical behaviour included repeated shouts, ejaculations or rhythmic chants of prayers, coupled with groaning or weeping. Through the late eighteenth century, Welsh revivals were often characterised by 'jumping'.

> In the course of a few years, the advocates of groaning and loud talking, as well as of loud singing, repeating the same line or stanza over and over thirty or forty times, became more numerous, and were found among some of the other denominations in the principality, and continue to this day.

> Several of the most zealous itinerant preachers in Wales recommend the people to cry out *Gogoniant* (the Welsh word for Glory), Amen, etc etc to put themselves in violent agitations; and finally to jump until they were quite exhausted, so as often to be obliged to fall down. . . .[5]

Once the realisation of salvation came, in a moment of horror and relief, the only response was to forswear previous evils, and to live a new life based on personal godliness, coupled with missionary endeavour towards the still unconverted. Models for the new life were amply provided by the Bible, especially by the Book of Acts, with its vivid picture of Christians as small dispersed groups united by love, and set apart from a hostile pagan society. The true Church was an organism built from these cells, united by the visits and letters of its holy leaders.

Olivers' account is also representative in other ways. For example,

5. John Evans, *A sketch of the denominations of the Christian world*. . . (London 1804).

he depicts a long period of internal struggle before finally succumbing to this total conversion, in which religious moods alternated with periods of riotous living and sin. Commonly, these autobiographies depict one overwhelming conversion experience, but obviously we may ask whether many were 'finally' converted on numerous occasions over the years. John Prickard, a minister of Pembrokeshire origins, reports that at various times he had been profoundly affected by the preaching of Harris, Whitefield, John Wesley and Howell Davies, before finally succumbing. The spiritual wanderings of Prickard and Olivers were reflected by many physical changes of location, both in Wales and along the borders. Ideas were thus spread easily from Bristol or Chester to every corner of the principality. There was a lively marketplace of ideas, in which potential converts had numerous options about the exact form in which they could express their beliefs. Olivers – like most of his contemporaries – found no difficulty in beginning his new life with a cathedral Te Deum , to which he reacted with 'joy . . . rapture . . . awe, and reverence'. The evangelical movement was still firmly within the Church.

Welsh Methodism also placed immense significance in the revival or regeneration of the individual, demonstrated through a highly emotional and all-encompassing conversion experience. As Howell Harris wrote,

> We preach primarily to the heart and the spirit of man . . . faith in the heart rather than reason in the brain . . . we agitate the soul to its very foundations by plumbing it to its depths with conviction

Conversion was the theme of the *Theomemphus* of William Williams, one of the masterpieces of the revival. When in 1773 Thomas Charles heard Daniel Rowland preach at Llangeitho, he described his experience in this way:

> The change a blind man who receives his sight experiences doth not exceed the change I at that time experienced in my mind . . . I had such a view of Christ as our high priest, of his love, compassion, power, and all-sufficiency as filled my mind with astonishment – with joy unspeakable and full of glory.

Like many thousands of others over the next century and a half, Charles was given a standard by which he felt able to judge every aspect of his own conduct, and that of the society around him. When either individual or society fell short of this ideal, there was a divine imperative that it must be changed.

In the first century of Welsh Methodism, the movement

demonstrated certain themes that would remain powerful into the present century. One was the stirring power of revivalist religion, which has been as crucial in Welsh history as any electoral revolution or technological breakthrough. Revivals might occur in other sects, like the Baptists, but it was the revival of the 1730s that provided such a mighty precedent for all similar events up to the last convulsion of 1904–5; and it supplied a set of expectations by which later events could be judged. In itself, the great awakening fostered belief in the continual divine intervention in the hearts of believers.

A further movement in 1762 was centred in Daniel Rowlands' Llangeitho, which now became the 'Methodist Mecca', to which thousands flocked to hear sermons and to receive communion from the great man. Other revivals on this scale occurred roughly once in a generation – in 1790, 1817, and so on. And of course, national revivals were only the more spectacular side of the story: other movements were strictly localised, to a county or a region. Tracing the impact of such movements is complicated by the tendency of all reformers to overrate the apathy and corruption that preceded their activities. In Wales, this is a common theme, and spiritual life often appears to have consisted of a grand cycle of troughs of apathy, interspersed with revivals of flaming passion. It is a view that would find wide currency in the understanding of secular history and politics.

The appeal of the reformers was enormous, in that they were adding a new excitement and substance to refresh already well-known ideas; but they also owed much of their success to their dramatic new approach to evangelism. They took every opportunity to reach the unconverted wherever they might be found: in markets, streets or fields. This was an effective strategy for a decentralised society such as Wales, but it also offered disturbing historical parallels. This in itself made the Methodist assertions of loyal churchmanship seem specious, and goes far to explaining the violent hostility by most landlords and squires, and by many clergy.

Also, the Methodists attracted suspicion by their organisational structure. From the first, they were grouped into societies, with regional leadership being provided by 'Associations', *y sasiwn*. Between 1737 and 1750, 428 'societies' were founded, of which 346 were in south Wales. There were 51 more in the counties of Montgomery and Radnor, and 31 in the whole of north Wales. The southern groups were also concentrated in a few areas: around Llanddowror, between Llangeitho and Tregaron, near Trefecca and in the Vale of Glamorgan. It was perhaps inevitable that these local movements would tend to develop links, to act in unison. As in other areas, Welsh practice here preceded the English Methodists: the first Welsh Association met in 1743, over a year before Wesley's first. This was an admirably flexible and effective system of federal government; but societies and associations appeared to critics to represent a subversive parallel government, a cancer within the Church. Once again, a structure designed for effectiveness also served to conjure up images of conventicles and Puritan anarchy. In the strictest sense, was it not a Presbyterian church in form many decades before it took the title? From 1747, Welsh Methodists began erecting their own meeting houses.

Most Methodists made no attempts to be conciliatory. At Monmouth in 1740, Howell Harris attempted to address the assembled lords and squires of the county on the subject of their 'balls, assemblies, horseraces, whoredom and drunkenness'. The occasion he chose was Monmouth races, an event that was near-sacred to landed county society, but which also drew together all social classes. A riot inevitably ensued. For Harris in particular, persecution was not only common, it was a logical fate for the Christian in a pagan society. (Once again, the Book of Acts was a model, with the experiences of Paul at Ephesus.) In Montgomeryshire in 1739, Harris records forcible attempts to stop his preaching by a knight, an Anglican cleric and two Justices, all backed by a mob. At Machynlleth, the opposition was led by a gentleman, a cleric and an attorney. This gave a foretaste of regular 'persecutions' over the next few years, at Monmouth, Bala, Carmarthen, Newport, and many other places. Harris was the most contentious of the leaders, but most itinerants experienced something like this. When Thomas Olivers returned to his Montgomeryshire home in the 1760s, he was strenuously warned away from preaching both by the parson and by squire Blayney.

Resemblances to the old Puritans were enhanced from 1742, when methodism throughout Britain was divided between the Arminian views of John Wesley, and the strict Calvinism of George Whitefield. The Welsh largely sided with Whitefield, and Calvinism thereafter became the major tradition within the new Methodist societies. To some extent, the Methodists were tainted by their friends. Among the few gentry to lend support to the movement were some 'serious' Anglican families, whose predecessors had often been militant Presbyterians or Puritans in the 1650s. Wesley found his warmest supporters in Wales at Fonmon, among the descendants of Colonel Philip Jones.

Also, Methodism recalled the interregnum in that some plebeian supporters tended to drift into eccentric religious views reminiscent of the most extreme Quakers and ranters of the previous century. Few such opinions are recorded in print; but the diarist William Thomas portrays a thriving if little understood religious underworld on the fringes of the new enthusiasm.

The revivalists also attracted hatred from mainstream Anglicans for their alleged resemblances to Catholics. This is ironic, as Howell Harris was so traditional an anti-Papist that he saw the Seven Years War as a religious struggle, and actually joined the armed forces. But enthusiasm smacked of Jesuit mysticism, the excesses of friars and flagellants, and Harris himself contributed to this suspicion by his 'monastic' experiment at Trefecca. In 1752, Theophilus Evans published a devastating attack on the whole movement in *The history of modern enthusiasm*.

By the mid-eighteenth century, Methodism had become a profoundly controversial topic, but it is necessary to place the movement in context. Above all, it was still a regional phenomenon, and the emergence of Methodism as a national movement would have to wait a little longer. Also, despite the fears of conservative Anglicans, mainstream Methodism never acquired radical political or theological overtones; but the movement did indeed pose dangers. Just when it seemed that Dissent had been successfully contained, many of the most threatening manifestations of enthusiasm were again rampant, and this time within the Church itself. This was both an opportunity and a peril, and it is possible to imagine a world where the movement could have been channelled into the established order, and even be used to reclaim Dissenters for the national Church. But in the conservative atmosphere of the early nineteenth century, it became apparent that compromise was impossible.

CHAPTER NINE
Welsh Politics in the Eighteenth Century

POLITICAL REALIGNMENT 1688–1714

For Wales, the 'revolution' of 1688 marked a real transition, which we might even describe as the end of civil war politics. For half a century, the common division between Royalist Tories and Parliamentarian Whigs had not been possible in Wales. Both these traditions were represented, but there was also a sizeable moderate faction who distrusted the Stuarts and their Somerset allies little less than they feared the radicals and Roundheads. James II seemed to fulfil all their worst apprehensions, as the King had not only favoured Catholics and high Tories like Powis and Beaufort, he even turned to the Dissenters. There were few active supporters of James in 1688, though many would regard his actual deposition as illegal and sinful, and a number of clergy suffered as nonjurors. But the outcome of the insurrection was that the old nightmares from mid-century were eventually quelled. The Tory and Catholic peers were definitively excluded from power, and King William's Irish victories ended the danger from that quarter.

In the 1690s, Welsh politics reformed around new issues, and new factions. This thorough realignment involved some surprising outcomes, as the old moderates fragmented. Some, like the Morgans of Tredegar, joined the new Whig cause. Others, however, became 'country' opponents of the Williamite court, and gradually drifted towards the new Tory party under Anne. Ironically, this brought families like the Harleys and Mansells under the same political roof as their ancient enemy, the Dukes of Beaufort.

But religious issues continued to dominate the new politics, at least for another half a century. The Dissenters obtained toleration in

1689, and the Tories saw themselves increasingly as defenders of an embattled Church. The dissenting academies were a particular source of offence, and there were repeated demands for a 'Schism Act' to stamp out such blatant violations of traditional law. Toleration of Dissenters and the growth of low Church views suggested that the Church was simply not safe under its Whig protectors. From 1704, high Church politics became central to the Tory cause.

In 1709, the Church gained a near-martyr when the government attempted to prosecute Dr Sacheverell for his attacks on the 'false brethren' who betrayed the establishment. Sacheverell gained enormous support, especially in north Wales. When he was acquitted in March 1710, 'a great rabble' in Wrexham 'went with a drum before them to several of the dissenters' houses and broke their windows, and also those of the meeting house'.[1] By chance, this was the time at which the assizes were gathering in various parts of the country, and throughout Wales, the assize sermons of 1710 were extreme in their pro-Church militancy. In Welshpool, the parson orginally chosen for the honour was forced to stand down by popular pressure, only to be replaced by a true firebrand whose words were openly seditious. When Sacheverell visited the midlands and north Wales later in the year, his reception in towns like Wrexham was more fitting for a reigning monarch.

High Tory politics were increasingly popular in Wales, often in the towns which had once been so hostile to Church interests. This is best understood if we appreciate that the target of rage was less Dissent itself than the policies which it symbolised. It was a symbol of many miscellaneous grievances, of the conduct of the wars and their attendant taxation. As we will see in Chapter Eleven, the Welsh economy was intimately linked with the fate of trading towns like Liverpool and Bristol, and therefore questions of war, peace and colonial trade were fundamental to prosperity. In practice, Wales' economic interests were best expressed by Tory policies. By 1710, frustration with Whig policies had become intense, and the Dissenters suffered accordingly.

There were Welsh Whigs, but the overwhelming tone was Tory. In fact, the chief political division in Wales was within the Tory cause, between those who favoured the restoration of the Stuart Pretender, and the Hanoverians who supported the accession of George I. Ironically, the high Church successes tended to encourage the Jacobites, who were ultimately risking their lives and fortunes for

1. Geoffrey Holmes, *The trial of Dr Sacheverell* (London: Eyre Methuen 1973).

the enthronement of a Catholic King. Technically, Jacobitism was a well-justified cause, in that the deposition of the Stuart dynasty might have been illegal and unconstitutional. In addition, most Jacobite politics were largely rhetorical, offering the thrill of conspiracy without the danger of serious consequences. In Aberystwyth in 1710, several of the leading gentry of west Wales were said to have toasted the Pretender on their knees.

On the other hand, more moderate views also had their supporters. Sir Thomas Hanmer of Flintshire was Speaker during the critical last months of Anne's reign, and is widely credited with helping to secure the succession for George. In addition, Robert Harley's widespread Welsh network tended to oppose the Pretender, a decision that would be decisive for the cause of 'moderation' in the south-east. Sometimes, families were split by this issue. In Glamorgan, the moderate Lord Mansell of Margam was at odds with his Jacobite son.

Between about 1704 and 1720, politics in Wales became bitterly divided over issues like the Church and the succession, and party loyalties came to have serious consequences in everyday life. As parties succeeded each other at Westminster, they increasingly used the patronage available to them to reward their followers and penalise their enemies. A victorious party could reward its friends with one of the many new jobs opening up in the military or the colonies, the bureaucracy or the diplomatic service. When Thomas (later Lord) Mansell entered the ministry in 1710, his correspondence was filled by petitions from those seeking favours. Conversely, enemies would be removed from office, even those positions like Justice which were regarded as a fundamental part of the perquisites of a gentleman. Purges of the Commission of the Peace became regular, and harrowing: in Glamorgan, six Whigs were ejected in 1712 to make way for ten Tories, who included five clergymen. Seven Tories fell between 1714 and 1717 to be replaced by ten Whigs. Also damaging, even ruinous, was the high cost of elections. New parliaments were summoned every three years between 1689 and 1715, and elections were increasingly likely to be contested. This vastly increased the expenses incurred by gentry estates already suffering from taxation and economic crises.

THE WHIG ESTABLISHMENT

In 1714, the accession of George I marked the beginning of a long period of Whig domination. The failure of Jacobite plots in 1715 and 1722 made it obvious that the new regime was stable, and the Welsh Tories now faced the dilemma of how to deal with a government with so much power to harm its enemies. Exclusion from office might be tolerated for a few years; but what if it were to last a generation? The regime made full use of its powers of patronage, dispensed through a series of local Whig magnates who acted almost as regional governors in the cause. In each area, the Tory leaders were to be balanced by Whig competitors. In the south-east, the Somersets would be challenged by Morgans of Tredegar; Lord Lisburne would uphold the cause among the Tory gentry of Cardiganshire; the Harley and Powis influence on the borders would be countered by Lords Herbert and Coningsby. The Marquess of Winchester ruled Carmarthenshire in the Whig interest.

In Gwynedd, the dominant family at the turn of the century was the Bulkeleys of Baron Hill, strong Tories and (at least rhetorically) Jacobites. From 1707, a Whig faction here emerged under the Wynns of Boduan and Glynllifon. Through their influence in the boroughs of Nefyn and Pwllheli, the Wynns began the mass creation of loyal burgesses who were able to swamp the Tories in the election of 1713. From 1713 to 1790, successive Wynns effectively dominated the borough, and they even maintained a presence in the county representation in this strongly Tory area. They received rich rewards from the government, including offices worth some £1300 a year. The office of Constable of Caernarvon Castle (1714) was no mere sinecure, as it gave the power to admit even more burgesses if need arose. The Wynns were baronets by 1742, Lords Newborough by 1776. Conversely, the Bulkeleys were resolutely excluded from the proud offices they had once held, such as chamberlain or Vice-Admiral of north Wales. Families like the Wynns or the Morgans were a minority among the landed community, but their patronage power was immense. They could regulate the Bench and the lieutenancy, and choose the sheriffs who played such a role at election time. The local Whigs would be strengthened over coming decades as government servants gained wealth through service in law or the military, and settled as Welsh landowners. In Glamorgan, the Whig cause in the 1730s was dominated by Admiral Thomas Matthews, and Charles Talbot, the Lord Chancellor.

THE ELECTORAL CHALLENGE

In addition, the local Whigs had the immeasurable assistance of the government at election time, which could give victory against apparently overwhelming odds. They were helped in this by the curious nature of the franchise in Wales. Most Welsh counties had a single borough seat, chosen by groups of contributory boroughs. In practice, this meant that the borough franchise was malleable. For instance, the member for Monmouth borough was chosen by the freemen of:

1661, 1679 – Monmouth alone
1681 – Monmouth, Newport, Chepstow, Usk, Abergavenny
1685 – Monmouth, Newport, Chepstow, Usk
1689 – Monmouth, Newport, Usk

This system proved vulnerable to legal challenges, when a defeated candidate might charge that the right to elect should rest only with certain boroughs as opposed to others. Such challenges were frequently made, and they were decided by partisan parliamentary committees.

The long Whig dominance was a great advantage to local candidates. The government appointed sheriffs, who enjoyed great latitude in permitting or disallowing votes. In the Glamorgan election of 1745, the Tory candidate Sir Charles Kemys Tynte probably out-voted the Whig Admiral Matthews by some 200 votes; but the sheriff's decisions changed this into a Whig victory. (And the Tory leaders were lucky to get away with expenses of only £2500.) Contested elections often resulted in petitions to Parliament, where they were decided on partisan lines. In the 1720s and 1730s, there was a series of controversial decisions which not only swung contests to ministerial supporters, but also changed the franchise for the long term benefit of Whig families. Usually, these revisions served to reduce still further the borough franchise. In Montgomery, the borough member was elected by the burgesses of Llanidloes, Welshpool and Llanfyllin as well as Montgomery proper; and in 1679, 500 voted here. In 1728, however, the 'out-boroughs' were excluded from the franchise, creating in effect a pocket borough for the Whig Lords Powis. Under George III, there were only 80 electors. Similar changes were feared in Glamorgan in the early 1730s.

FLINTSHIRE AND DENBIGHSHIRE

The full potential of government interference in an election was demonstrated in Georgian Flintshire. The county gentry were solidly Tory, with the major divisions lying between Hanoverians like the Hanmers and Jacobites like the Eytons. However, between 1727 and 1742, a determined ministry assault almost overturned the Tory control of the area. Their main agent in this was George Wynne of Leeswood, a petty squire who had become rich through the discovery of lead on his estate. In the late 1720s, Wynne began to cultivate Walpole, and he secured many rewards including a baronetcy. More useful for political purposes, he also became Constable of Flint Castle with all that implied for the ability to qualify voters. In addition, the Lord-Lieutenant was Lord Cholmondeley, Walpole's son-in law.

In 1734, Wynne faced the high Tory Sir Stephen Glynne in the borough seat, and won decisively. This intervention not only secured one more seat for the ministry, it also intimidated Tory opponents by threatening defeat and financial disaster. Glynne had lost £4000 in his endeavour, and his experience deterred the county member, Thomas Mostyn, from seeking re-election in 1741. In this contest, however, the Flintshire Tories were able to mount a major assault on the Whigs and the ministry in both the county and borough seats. The county fell easily. In the borough, however, Sir George Wynne was elected once again, only to find that matters had changed at Westminster, and he was ejected on petition. The Tory squires had won; but it is remarkable that they had been forced to put so much effort and expense into retaining such a natural heartland as Flintshire.

Even where government was not quite so intimately involved, eighteenth century politics could be so lethally expensive as to force the protagonists to seek an accommodation. Denbighshire provides an excellent illustration. Politically, the county was dominated by the landed gentry of the wealthy area to the east of the shire, between Wrexham and Llangollen, in the hundreds of Bromfield and Chirk. There were 1800 county electors in the 1680s, while the borough member was jointly chosen by the resident freemen of Denbigh, Holt and Ruthin: 1400 voted in this constituency in 1715. This was a large electorate, but a long tradition of dominance by the Myddelton family of Chirk had made the seat relatively cheap to fight. Costs for a typical election under Charles II ran at only thirty or forty pounds. In the next century, however, this relatively cosy arrangement was destabilised by the rise of the Williams-Wynn family of Wynnstay, the beneficiaries of an impressive series of inheritances.

This family was founded by Sir William Williams, who served as Speaker of the House of Commons in 1681, and who bought an estate near Oswestry. His son married the heiress of another Denbighshire estate, which passed to the family in 1719. At this point also, the family acquired their seat at Wynnstay, and the estate began a long history of absorbing the remnants of other once-great properties that were now ruined by debt or family extinction. Sir William's grandson was Sir Watkin Williams-Wynn (died 1749), who was one of the leading members of the Tory party under the first two Georges. His landed wealth and influence were such that he played a major role in the politics of perhaps ten counties: most of north and mid-Wales, as well as the northern Border shires.

This new landed power could not but affect the hold which the Myddeltons were acquiring over Denbighshire: Sir Watkin was a Tory extremist (a Jacobite, at least by popular reputation) while the Myddeltons were more moderate Tories. Sir Watkin held the county seat from 1716 until his death, with a brief hiatus in 1741; while the Myddeltons found themselves confined to the borough. Electoral combat now became intense, with bitter contests in 1716 and 1722.

However, it was the 1741 election that became one of the great set-piece battles of eighteenth century Wales. Typically, each side began many months in advance by the mass creation of leaseholders, who would be entitled to cast votes in the forthcoming contest. Money was poured into the respective campaigns, with Myddelton being wholeheartedly backed by the Walpole administration. When the votes were counted, Williams-Wynn had won by 1352 votes to 933; though the sheriff promptly invalidated 600 of his supporters, and declared Myddelton elected. This was flagrant even by the standards of the time. It also coincided with the crisis in Walpole's power, so Myddelton was displaced, and even jailed for a time. Williams-Wynn eventually regained his seat; but it had cost him a rumoured £20,000. On the positive side, Wynnstay dominated the county representation until 1885. Richard Myddelton held the borough from 1747 to 1788. By the 1780s, the 'most perfect cordiality' existed between the families of Myddelton and Williams-Wynn.[2]

The Denbighshire contest also serves to remind us of the importance of parliamentary politics in eighteenth century Wales. In

2. T.H.B. Oldfield, *History of the boroughs. . . .* (London 1792) iii 1–47.

retrospect, it is easy to see election contests as the games of a narrow ruling elite, with little impact on the wider community. In reality, political conflict opened the door to the expression of real popular issues: another reason why the continuing party struggles were potentially dangerous for the Tory landed community. From the early eighteenth century, the Wrexham area was dominated by the Williams-Wynn estate, and his politics did much to colour political manifestations in the town. In 1715, rioting among local colliers developed a Jacobite hue, and one of the leaders left the area to offer his support to the invading Stuart armies. Political conflict was expressed in adherence to the rival factions associated with Wynnstay or Chirk. In the 1720s, each side had its own tavern, respectively the Eagle and the Lion; and at election time, each was the scene of vast banquets and political celebration.

Electoral conflict was an expensive business for the gentry, but it also offered real opportunities for others in the society. Professionals. like lawyers benefited because their expertise was called into service; all voters could ask a heavy price for their support, while the extension of the franchise might involve major changes in the economic arrangements of the estates. And for both voters and non-voters, the candidates had a duty to reward support by patronage. Chirk or Wynnstay might in effect have been buying votes by their lavish entertainments and expenditure, but they were also hostages to the electorates they bought thereby. In 1740, severe food rioting in Flintshire and Wrexham led to petitions to Sir Watkin that he find a way to relieve shortages. When he could not, the rioters cheered for the Myddelton faction. Popular disturbances were relatively commonplace in Georgian Wales, and they provided a perilous background for an election contest.

The same comments would apply to all parts of Wales. In Carmarthen borough, for example, it was political instability which gave the town its endemic tradition of riot – a term quite inadequate for the incipient civil war of late 1755. In November, a Whig attorney recorded that:

> There are five hundred desperate fellows come to town from
> Pembrokeshire and other places armed with firearms and quarter pieces,
> and I am told ship guns, with a great number of gentlemen . . . all the
> shops are shut up.

The Tories responded that their invasion had only been to counter Whig aggression:

> the town mob had for a long time with impunity maimed several

persons, beat out the brains of the barber at the (Tory) Red Lion . . . so that it was necessary to send for guards; and . . . a strong party arrived from Pembrokeshire, who were quartered at the Red Lion and elsewhere; upon this, the mob reinforced themselves with men from the country and having fortified the castle and upper house, made port-holes, etc, and supplied themselves with great guns and small arms. The upper gate is fortified by the Red Lion people and called Newgate, where the prisoners taken by the sheriffs on one side are put . . in short, the town is full of fire, smoke and tumult . . by an advertisement published in the papers, the true cause of all this is the violence of party, and a dislike to the Jacobites.[3]

TORIES AND JACOBITES 1714–1760

The power of the Whig government seemed beyond challenge, and the number of ministerial supporters elected in Wales rose from eight in 1715 to 14 in 1734. It was only natural that some old Tories should make their accommodation, as did the Myddeltons. Others, however, chose to resist even in the face of such odds: they adopted extremist tactics and affected Jacobite opinions. They expressed their collective rage and frustration by provoking riots or by persecuting local Whigs; by operating an entire clandestine network for nonjuror clergy and army deserters. This opposition culture had the support of some of the greatest magnates in Wales – the Duke of Beaufort and Sir Charles Kemys in the south-east; William Powell and Lewis Pryse in Cardiganshire; Lord Bulkeley and Sir Watkin Williams Wynn in the north. In the mid-1720s, high Tory sentiment was institutionalised through societies like the 'Sea Sergeants' in south-west Wales, or the 'Cycle' in the north. Many gentry houses would certainly have owned the trappings of sedition: a portrait of the Pretender, or an ornate glass with which to drink his health. Many a collection of family manuscripts contains verses and songs that could in theory have got their writer hanged. Some corresponded with the exiled Court in frankly treasonous terms; others visited to pay their respects.

The ostentatiously anti-government views of such men encouraged wild optimism in the Jacobite Court in exile, and for three decades, we regularly find Wales listed as a likely base from which to launch

3. T. Herbert and G.E. Jones, *The remaking of Wales in the eighteenth century* (Cardiff: University of Wales 1988), 29; David W. Howell, *Patriarchs and parasites* (Cardiff: University of Wales 1986), 134–135.

insurrection. About 1721, Jacobite spies had compiled a list of likely supporters, that included virtually every Tory leader. Pembrokeshire was extremely 'loyal' to the Pretender. Monmouthshire was ruled by peers like Windsor and Beaufort; Montgomeryshire was solid under Lord Hereford and Mr Pugh of Mathafarn. Only Carmarthenshire, tragically infected by the Whig Marquess of Winchester, offered little hope.

Of course, Wales did not rise – in 1722, or in 1745. In the latter year, there was overt support for the Young Pretender only from a handful of Welsh supporters, one of whom – David Morgan – became a martyr to his cause. Two others, from the Catholic Vaughan family of Courtfield in Monmouthshire, fled into Spanish exile. There is abundant evidence that the great majority of 'Jacobite' squires were striking a pose, or rather, hedging their bets. This should be stressed, as there is a Welsh historical tradition which sees the eighteenth century gentry as dedicated Jacobite fanatics, perpetually waiting for the opportunity to rise. This view is represented by the romantic novel, *The white rose of Arno*, by Owen Rhoscomyl (1897), which portrays the Welsh gentry of 1745 as virtually indistinguishable from the Jacobite chieftains of the Scottish Highlands.

Yet minimising the Jacobite tradition is not to understate the real significance and continuity of Tory party organisation in Wales in the difficult years between 1714 and the 1750s. Conspirators or not, the Tory gentry did evolve a sophisticated opposition culture, based on party clubs, on attendance at certain taverns and sporting events, on support for particular clergy and writers. Nationally, the Tories gathered at the mansions of magnates like the Duke of Beaufort, at London coffee houses like the Cocoa Tree, or at the great events of Oxford University. Locally, party organisation served to mobilise support at parliamentary elections, or in the contests for control of boroughs. In Carmarthen, the Sea Sergeants were fundamental to Tory organisation from the late 1720s. In addition to the Jacobite clubs, the Tories dominated the new masonic lodges which emerged at this time, as at Carmarthen in 1726, or Haverfordwest in 1741. A new Carmarthen lodge in 1753 was based at the Red Lion inn, the Tory headquarters in the riots of these years. The success of such clubs is indicated by their emulation by Whigs. In the 1760s, the Wynns of Caernarvonshire created the 'Garrison of Fort Williamsburg', a political club notionally based at a model fortress named after King William III.

Also, the Tories had hopes of power without needing to invoke foreign invasion. From the mid-1730s, there was increasing dissension within the Whig party, with a growing opposition that included such figures as the Duke of Bolton (the earlier Marquess of Winchester). It was natural to hope that the Tories might ally with such opposition Whigs against Walpole, as occurred in the early 1740s. Later, Tory hopes centred on participation in a coalition ('Broad-Bottom') government, a prospect that seemed all the more likely if George II were to be succeeded by his son, the Prince of Wales. The premature death of the latter in 1751 proved a tragic disappointment to the opposition, who found themselves excluded for another decade.

In all these manoeuvrings, the Welsh Tory leadership played a large role. Apart from the Duke of Beaufort and Sir Watkin Williams-Wynn, this included Sir John Philipps of Picton in Pembrokeshire, long a mainstay of the 'Sea Sergeants' and allegedly a Jacobite. Philipps was one of the most powerful Tory leaders in west Wales with a strong interest in the critical boroughs of Haverfordwest and Carmarthen; but he was also a figure in national controversy, as 'Sir John Broad-Bottom'.

THE NEW POLITICS 1760–1790

In 1760, the accession of George III fulfilled many of the hopes of the old Tories. Sir John Philipps entered the administration, and the Seven Years War (1756–1763) had been fought on precisely the lines that the Tories had long advocated: a 'blue-water' naval and colonial struggle, without excessive involvement in land warfare. The following decade was marked by a process of political realignment similar to that of the 1690s, with new parties and issues emerging.

However, there was one essential difference from that earlier period. As the substance of political conflict changed, so did the structure of parliamentary representation, a fundamental change that affected Welsh politics for a century. Partly in consequence of the gerrymandering under Walpole, electoral conflict declined during the century after 1730. Contested elections were disasters to be avoided at all costs, and thus magnates attempted to form consensus with little regard for ideological issues. Party managers like George Rice of Dynevor brought competing sides together and tried to distribute offices and constituencies with as little ill-feeling as possible. In 1761, for example, the two Radnorshire seats were sought by three individuals: the Marquis of Carnarvon, Howell Gwynne, and Thomas Lewis of Harpton. Negotiations were successful:

> If Mr Gwynne can be brought into Parliament without expense at some other place, and my Lord Carnarvon and his friends will give no opposition to Mr Lewis for the town of Radnor, and the lieutenancy and Custos Rotulorum shall remain in Mr Gwynne's hands; and Mr Lewis continues steward of the king's courts, Mr Gwynne is ready (with the approbation of his friends which is not at all doubted) to desist for this election and give his interest and that of his friends to the Marquis of Carnarvon: by which his lordship will come in for the county of Radnor without any opposition.[4]

The pact was ratified in a formal treaty, which even included a secret protocol.

When Thomas Oldfield surveyed the constituencies in the 1790s, he found Wales a tranquil setting of general harmony between the magnates.[5] There had been a bitter contest in Anglesey in 1784 between the interests of the Earl of Uxbridge and Lord Bulkeley; but all had now been happily resolved by a simple partition, whereby Bulkeley held Caernarvonshire, and Anglesey fell to the Earl of Uxbridge. Myddeltons and Williams–Wynns ruled Denbighshire, and respectively controlled the borough and the county. The Wynnstay estate also dominated Flint borough, and had an important interest in the county seats of Merionethshire and Montgomeryshire. The Welsh boroughs were even less representative. In Anglesey (Beaumaris), the right of election was in the 24 members of the corporation. Brecon had 300 burgesses; but they were wholly dominated by the Morgans of Tredegar. Lord Milford ruled Haverfordwest, Lord Powis Montgomery; the Stuarts had Cardiff in their pockets, although they needed to consult with three other families. This was to be the structure of Welsh parliamentary politics up to 1832, and long afterwards in some areas.

On the other hand, the decline of parliamentary conflict did not mean the end of politics. Far from it, wholly new issues and rhetoric now entered political life, and the new campaigns were able to utilise the party structures evolved earlier in the century. Between 1760 and 1780, there emerged a generation of radical leaders, often from industrial families or progressive gentry, who sought to create new coalitions: with professional and commercial groups, but also with

---

4. Sir Lewis Namier, *The structure of politics at the accession of George III* (second ed., London: Macmillan, 1973), 271.

5. T.H.B. Oldfield, *History of the boroughs* . . . (London 1792).

Dissenters. The new politics of the 1760s often foreshadows nineteenth century radicalism.

Among the most important leaders were Robert Morris and Sir Watkin Lewes, both from West Glamorgan industrial families. They attempted to drum up support for a Wilkite petition in south-west Wales, and they supported the opposition on issues like American and Irish rights. Their allies included industrialists like the northern ironmaster John Wilkinson; and squires like John Pugh Pryse in Merionethshire, Robert Jones and Sir John Aubrey in Glamorgan. Often, political radicalism was accompanied by ostentatious scorn for conventional morality, and some members of this circle were associated with the legendary Hellfire Club.

The new radicals were organised in part through the masonic lodges, which now became common in south and west Wales. Usually, the lodges had originated as Tory bodies, often connected to the Sea Sergeants. When the Tory leadership entered government after 1760, their followers were often left in a familiar quandary. Toryism had for so long been the major strand of opposition that it was difficult to come to terms with being a party of government. This was especially true when the political controversies of the day so directly affected towns like Swansea, Haverfordwest and the other satellites of Bristol. Any colonial problem was a direct challenge to the economic health of southern Wales. Increasingly, therefore, the lodges came to express radical views, and they proliferated. There were perhaps ten lodges by the early 1770s, based chiefly in the market towns of south Wales: Swansea, Carmarthen, Haverford-west, Cowbridge, Bridgend, Brecon and Cardiff.

There were many contacts between these secular radicals and the Welsh Dissenters from the more theologically liberal congregations, who had embraced Arian and Unitarian views. When a new masonic lodge was formed at Bridgend in 1777, its Master was Richard Price (1723–1791). He came from an old family of Glamorgan Dissenters, and was educated at Llwyn Llwyd. From 1772, he became close to the reformist group associated with the Unitarian-inclined Earl of Shelburne. This also included the Glamorgan squire Sir John Aubrey, and the Dissenting minister David Williams of Monmouth-shire (1738–1816). This group supported the rights of Dissenters, and favoured religious 'liberalization': that is, a movement away from Calvinist or Trinitarian orthodoxies. Price was an Arian; Williams' widely praised proposal for reforming the Creed was 'I believe in God. Amen'. This liberalism made it easy for them to sympathise with freemasonry, the movement that best expressed enlightenment ideas of deism, rationalism and benevolence.

Price and Williams favoured economic reform, and the rights of the American colonies and Ireland. From 1776, they attained a national and European reputation, and Williams was a friend of Benjamin Franklin. This was the year of Price's *Observations on the nature of civil liberty*, which sought to transform the specific grievances of the colonies into universal statements of rights. In 1782, Williams' *Letters on political liberty* presented truly radical demands, including manhood suffrage and complete toleration. Also relevant to Wales was the case of the Dean of St Asaph, tried for publishing the allegedly seditious *Principles of government* in 1782. His acquittal was greeted with widespread demonstrations of support in the Wrexham and Ruabon area. Popular disaffection was sharpened by the economic crisis of these years, a downturn suggested by the increase in poor relief payments between 1776 and 1783.

In 1778, the relative tranquillity of north Wales was interrupted when a new surveyor of Crown lands was appointed, with the express aim of checking and reversing gentry incursions. The landed community was suitably outraged, and promised to fight. This was a return to a familiar Elizabethan theme; but what was new was the radical rhetoric, the language of rights and resistance, espoused by gentry like Sir Watkin Williams-Wynn (he had recently sponsored a new masonic lodge at Wynnstay). In 1781 and 1782, several Welsh counties followed the English model and formed Associations to demand parliamentary and financial reforms. They threatened to withhold supply for the Crown if demands were not met.

In electoral terms, the new radicalism had a more limited effect, inevitably in view of the electoral structure. But there was an impact, chiefly in the south. Oldfield remarked on the frequency of 'independency' and electoral insurgency in the region in the 1780s. There had been no less than three elections where magnate cliques had been overturned by Independent groups, respectively in Glamorgan, Pembrokeshire and Carmarthen. Now, this must be placed in context, as the reformers were neither revolutionary nor plebeian. In Glamorgan in 1789, the wealthy squire Thomas Wyndham had led a gentry movement to overcome an alliance between the aristocratic houses of Bute, Plymouth and Beaufort. In Pembrokeshire in 1780, an insurgency had defeated an attempt by Lords Milford and Kensington to control the county representation; but the victor was Sir Hugh Owen of Orielton, from one of the shire's most distinguished families. In Carmarthen, there was an added complication in that the insurgents were attacking the Bishop of St Davids in addition to secular magnates. Even in the north, there was a taste of the new politics in 1796, when a contentious election in Caernarvonshire was enlivened by the pamphleteering of 'Shôn Gwialan': a radical activist, believed to be David Williams. As in Carmarthenshire, a major target was the local Bishop – in this case, Warren of Bangor.

But all these campaigns involved a fascinating use of populist rhetoric and intense propaganda, aimed at portraying the dominant aristocratic political factions as arbitrary, repressive and hostile to religious freedom. In addition, all made heavy use of lengthy historical precedent dating back to the mid-seventeenth century. The Owens of Orielton were known for their 'invariable attachment to the cause of liberty'; while the Carmarthen affair was marked by anticlericalism. The bard of the Glamorgan reformers was none other than Iolo Morganwg, who composed election songs and verses; and there were active attempts to woo Dissenters for the opposition cause of the 'Patriots' or 'Independents'. These elections – together with the Monmouthshire contest of 1772 – demonstrate a new dimension of political propaganda in Wales, as well as the influence of new issues, new concepts of rights, and new democratic sentiments.

DEMOCRATS AND JACOBINS 1790–1800

The French Revolution had an immense influence on the Welsh radicals. In November 1789, Richard Price preached a sermon in support of the Revolution, *On the love of country*. On the first anniversary of the storming of the Bastille, his presentation to a reform meeting at the Crown and Anchor tavern was so enthusiastic that it was read before the National Assembly in Paris. Apart from stirring the reformers, it was Price's work which stimulated Burke to produce his jeremiad against revolutionary France. David Williams too saw France as the best hope of humanity, and took French citizenship in 1792. However, his political connections were Girondin, and he returned to England in 1793 in some danger.

Williams and Price might have been considered distant and rather abstract thinkers. In the 1790s, however, radicalism that found its model in the French republic was widespread in Wales, among social classes well below these respectable intellectuals. In addition, this was a time of social crisis, which will be discussed in greater detail below (see chapter thirteen). There were frequent food-riots in many Welsh towns between 1793 and 1801, with some of the most serious disturbances occurring in 1795 (notably at Denbigh) and in 1800–1801. The spectre of Jacobin activists capitalising on this unrest was terrifying for the government, and the rioters themselves perhaps realised the power of this menace. At Swansea in 1793, a series of pamphlets denounced specific local grievances that led to dearth, but in each case, the refrain is the same: 'Look at France . . . .France is a warning.' There were Jacobin traditions in several Welsh market towns, at Swansea and Haverfordwest, Bala and Dolgellau.

Enthusiasm for the revolutionary cause came in part from the radical Dissenting congregations, many of whom were re-exploring their Puritan roots: in the last quarter of the century, there was a revival of interest in the life and work of such predecessors as Llwyd, Erbery and Vavasor Powell. The political outlook of at least some Dissenters is exemplified by the career of Morgan John Rhys (1760–1804). He joined the liberal Baptist congregation at Hengoed in Glamorgan, and became a minister at Pontypool, but in 1791, he realised that his true purpose was linked to the cause of France. The Revolution ushered in the last days before the coming of Christ, and it was his role to ensure that the Revolution took a radically Christian direction. Armed with Bibles, he set off to convert the country. Back in Wales in 1793, he lived in the Trefecca community, and used its printing press to produce the *Cylchgrawn Cymraeg* (Welsh Journal), a pioneering radical paper that attacked slavery, taxation and the Church establishment, demanded educational reform, and generally supported the cause of the new France. Rhys also reprinted Volney's *Ruins*, a major influence on British Jacobinism. (In 1796, a successor journal produced by an Independent minister published a Welsh translation of the *Marseillaise*.)

In 1794, fearing arrest, Rhys fled to America where he attempted to establish a Welsh community in the land of 'Beulah': now the less than idyllic Cambria County, in Pennsylvania. Transatlantic solutions were perhaps natural in view of the strong Welsh element in the American Baptists, represented by national leaders like Morgan Edwards and Dr Samuel Jones. For three decades, the American denomination had experienced both radicalisation and rapid growth, and there was a long tradition of cross-pollination with the Welsh homeland.

A History of Modern Wales 1536–1990

The radical component within Welsh Dissent was strengthened in the 1790s by the growth of Unitarian ideas. This coincided with the rise of politically radical views, but it did not necessarily stem from secular thought. We have already seen that the older Dissenting sects had for many years been split by tendencies to theological liberalism and rationalism, with the Carmarthen academy as a major source. In the last quarter of the century, these tendencies found their natural culmination in Unitarian thought, which took the dramatic step of denying the divinity of Christ. The ferment of ideas was the subject of many comments, mostly appalled reaction by the orthodox. It was the Methodist Williams of Pantycelyn who wrote to Thomas Charles in May 1790 of the 'palpable and dreadful errors' now common in much of south Wales. This involved 'Denying the doctrine of the Trinity, which is the foundation of Christianity'. Among the Baptists in particular, it was common to deny Jesus both divinity and Sonship.

> They cannot bear the word divine blood; they preach that his blood – by which we understand his sufferings and death as a satisfaction for sin – is no better than the blood of a common man, which is horrible to think of. . . .Believe me, dear Charles, the antitrinitarian, the socinian and arian doctrines gain ground daily[6]

The following year, the Methodists fired a warning shot against the radicals by excommunicating one of their own clergy, Peter Williams, for the rather technical trinitarian heresy of Sabellianism.

In 1794, the ordination of Thomas Evans (*Tomos Glyn Cothi*: 1764–1833) marked the emergence of the first officially Unitarian congregation in Wales. Like many of the Welsh radicals, he was influenced by the pioneering London congregation at Essex Street, under its minister Theophilus Lindsey. Tomos Glyn Cothi was one of many Unitarians in the 1790s who supported the ideas of Liberty emanating from France. In 1795, he published a journal called *Y drysorfa gymysgedig* (The miscellaneous treasury), a successor to the work of Morgan John Rhys. But it was apparently a rendition of his 'Song of Liberty' which earned his imprisonment in Carmarthen jail in 1803. One verse ran,

---

6. Sir Thomas Phillips, *Wales, the language, social condition, moral character and religious opinions of the people* . . . (London 1849), 136.

180

> And when upon the British shore
> The thundering guns of France shall roar,
> Vile George shall trembling stand,
> Or flee his native land,
> With terror and appal;
> Dance Carmagnol, dance Carmagnol.

Another reformer was David Jones (1765–1816), Priestley's successor at his Birmingham meeting house. Under the pseudonym of the 'Welsh Freeholder', Jones engaged in a pamphlet war with Bishop Horsley of St David's between 1791 and 1794.

The religious movement spread rapidly through schisms and conflicts within existing congregations, especially those of the Arminian Baptists. Elsewhere, existing congregations joined the movement *en masse*, as in the case of older chapels in the Glamorgan uplands. About 1800, a series of prominent ministers emerged as the leaders of a new Unitarian sect: William Thomas, Benjamin Phillips and David Phillips in Carmarthenshire, Josiah Rees in Glamorgan. A South Wales Unitarian Association was formed in 1802, and the following year, the body held its first public assembly at Cefn Coed y Cymer in Merthyr Tydfil, a chapel with roots in the earliest days of Dissent.

Religion provided one focus of unity for the radical movement. Since the 1760s, the reformers had also been united through their activities among the London Welsh societies that had proliferated during the century. Watkin Lewes himself was the treasurer of the Society of Ancient Britons. In 1770, the Gwyneddigion society was formed; in 1792, the Cymreigyddion. It was these cultural societies which served to draw together the diverse strands of Welsh radicalism in the late eighteenth century, in the aftermath of the enthralling events in France. Democratic radicalism thus combined with radical religion and cultural nationalism: an intoxicating mixture. In the last 15 years, the movement has also provided the basis for some of the best historical writing on modern Wales, notably by Gwyn A. Williams and Prys Morgan.

Rationalism and religious liberalism were both authentic popular movements with ancient roots in Wales; but so was their apparent antithesis, the popular veneration for prophecy and archaic Welsh tradition. The two strands achieved an unlikely synthesis in the druidism concocted by Iolo Morganwg in the 1780s. We have already seen that Iolo was a career forger, who used his wide contacts with the true bards and poets of Glamorgan to create spectacular though plausible 'finds'. These were published in a series of works between 1789 and 1807. Central to his system was the revival of druidism, which he regarded in best eighteenth century style as a deist cult that truly reflected the spirit of Nature. Druids were a kind of proto-Masons, who would not have been wildly out of place in *The Magic Flute*, and whose religion was eminently rational. In 1792, Iolo held a midsummer meeting of his druidic gorsedd, in Primrose Hill, London; and the originally separate worlds of bards and druids became connected in the minds of many.

This cultural 'revival' also had a strong radical bent. The 1792 gorsedd was attended by declamations to the goddess Liberty, 'rous'd on Gallia's injured plain'. The following year, Iolo composed his 'Song on the Rights of Man'; and he remained a strong Jacobin and radical through the early 1790s. He was in contact with Tomos Glyn Cothi, who attended a midsummer gorsedd in 1797; in 1802, Iolo himself would be one of the founders of the South Wales Unitarian Association. The Gwyneddigion, too, drifted to the political left, and Owain Myfyr was a strong democrat. In 1790, their eisteddfod offered its chief prize for an essay on Liberty. About this time, the society was influenced by John Jones, *Jac Glan-y-Gors* (1766–1821), a Welsh exile who kept a Southwark inn. In 1796 and 1797, Jac published two of the more extreme statements of Welsh Jacobinism, *Seren tan gwmwl* (The Star behind a Cloud) and *Toriad y dydd* (Daybreak). Both relied heavily on the work of Tom Paine, and both were deeply controversial, forcing the author to flee London. Another member of the Gwyneddigion, and president in 1800, was Thomas Roberts (1766–1841). In 1798, he published *Cwyn yn erbyn gorthrymder* (A protest against oppression), which denounced tyranny in Church and State with a particular emphasis on the evils of tithes.

Cultural and radical enthusiasm also focused the legend of the 'Welsh Indians'. There was a steadily growing myth about the medieval Prince Madoc who was said to have discovered America, and left a Welsh colony there. This led to an intensive search among the Indian tribes for linguistic traces of that settlement, and in 1791, the discovery of an allegedly Welsh tribe (the Mandans) was announced at the Llanrwst eisteddfod by William Jones of Llangadfan (1726–1795). He was one of the more remarkable figures of a remarkable age, a Voltairean radical who was one of the first openly to espouse Welsh political nationalism. The Welsh Indians were not only noble savages, they had retained much of the early law and religion of nature; and they provided a precedent for Welsh settlement in the new republic. The Welsh radicals of the 1790s had strong transatlantic links, and migration was commonplace. Rhys'

'Beulah' was only one of several schemes to create a democratic Welsh homeland in America. William Jones sought the aid of the British and American governments for his planned settlement in Kentucky; but most of the movement lacked a grand plan. In the 1790s, as in the 1680s, burgeoning radical movements in Merioneth and Montgomeryshire were decimated by the flight to the freer shores of Pennsylvania.

In 1797, the French landing at Fishguard caused real panic among the authorities about the danger of fifth column activity among Welsh nonconformists. Local ministers and their congregations were harassed – as at Felinganol and Llanglofan – and some spent lengthy terms in jail while evidence was sought. In fact, the fears were illusory, and the exact location of the landing had been fortuitous. The government was also paying too much of a compliment to the endurance and consistency of the Welsh radicals. By this time, many were disenchanted by the bloodshed in France, together with the rise of Napoleon, while the repression in Britain naturally had its effects. Political radicalism was increasingly channelled into religious and cultural outlets. The Welsh Jacobins ultimately proved as ineffective as the Jacobite plotters of mid-century.

THE LEGACY

Yet there was an aftermath. Many of the radicals who flourished in the 1790s were fairly young men, commonly born about 1764 or 1765, and they often survived into the 1820s or beyond, to carry these powerful memories to a new generation. There were 30 Unitarian chapels by the 1840s, all but one in the counties of Glamorgan, Carmarthen and Cardigan, and these local centres had a quite disproportionate impact on Welsh political history. The movement was strong in Merthyr Tydfil and the new industrial communities, where clergy like David John carried the older traditions into the Chartist era. Tomos Glyn Cothi served a Unitarian meeting house in Aberdare from 1811 until 1833. Freemasonry also flourished: between 1800 and 1830, there is evidence of lodges in 20 centres, and all the large and middling towns of Wales were represented. This was a rather different movement from the heroic days of the American war, and while there were certainly radical masons and lodges, masonry in general had begun its transition to respectability.

Again, the ideas that sprang from the fertile mind of Iolo Morganwg enjoyed a long influence in the industrial areas, and Iolo's son Taliesin lived in Merthyr until his death in 1847. Taliesin and fellow druids like Thomas Williams (*Gwilym Morganwg*) kept alive the 'druidic' tradition, supplying a religious, cultural and nationalist context to the political radicalism that re-emerged in the 1820s. These were the areas in which the eisteddfod became a radical and 'patriot' phenomenon, tied in to the plebeian culture of alehouses and popular sports. American links and sympathies also remained strong; and the cult of the 'Welsh Indians' no doubt assisted the reception of Mormon ideas in the 1840s. Merthyr Tydfil was a major centre, the home of the paper *Udgorn Seion* (Zion's Trumpet). There were six Mormon chapels by 1851, almost as many as the established church. The *Book of Mormon* was translated into Welsh by the Rev. John Davies, (1784–1864), who had been initiated into the gorsedd by Iolo personally in 1818.

Iolo's ideas reached a climax of a sort in the career of Dr William Price (1800–1893), a druidical enthusiast who traced the roots of Greek civilisation to the Pontypridd area, and who earned national notoriety by the 1884 cremation of his son 'Jesus Christ' Price. When not worshipping the sun or parading in druidical robes, Price was a convinced political radical, the Chartist leader in the Pontypridd area, and a pioneer of the miners' organisation and the cooperative movement. But this bizarre career conceals the extent to which Iolo's ideas had joined the mainstream. At Carmarthen in 1819, the gorsedd became an integral part of the eisteddfod; and from 1858, a politically defanged (though druid-run) eisteddfod began its career as the definitive national gathering of Wales. In the 1860s, eisteddfod competitions often focused on the contributions made by the Ancient Britons and their Welsh scions to the ascendancy and glory of the 'British' imperial system. In 1820, a new and staunchly respectable Cymmrodorion Society would be refounded by none other than *Jac Glan y Gors.*

We should also emphasise the reaction to the Jacobin upsurge. While the reformers have received much attention, it is less commonly noted that this decade was critical in the formation of a conservative tradition in Wales. In the 1770s, the old high Church tradition had revived in opposition to attempts to undermine trinitarian orthodoxy. It was a client of the Duke of Beaufort's, Thomas Nowell of Cardiff, who preached an incendiary sermon, by which he no doubt hoped to emulate Sacheverell. He was in a minority, but the crisis of the 1790s effectively forced both the

Church and the propertied laity to decide how far they could safely flirt with reform. In the nineteenth century, conservatives looked to the 1790s as much as the interregnum to justify their strict refusal to countenance change.

Religious liberalism was associated with the political radicals, and the early nineteenth century church reacted by becoming a much more orthodox and conservative body. Relations with the Dissenters suffered especially. It was an evangelical churchman of the 1790s who invoked yet again the shades of the interregnum:

> When they (the dissenters) had the reins of government in their hands in former times, what havoc and devastation, what sacrilege and cruelty etc were committed throughout the land! And who knows but the same restless factious spirit still lurks in the dark, and only waits a fit opportunity of breaking out, with redoubled force unto all manner of outrage and rebellion from which, Good Lord deliver us![7]

A withdrawal from exposed positions was also apparent in the case of the more orthodox Dissenters, who placed a new emphasis on Calvinist and trinitarian doctrines: in 1799, the west Wales Baptists suffered a general schism following the purge of heterodox congregations. The Methodists, meanwhile, adopted very conservative political positions in order to differentiate themselves from the like of David Williams. In 1802, Methodist leaders engaged in a vigorous pamphlet war to rebut allegations of Jacobinism. They showed their orthodoxy by rejecting efforts at worldly reform, together with condemning radicals in terms more suited to the highest churchmen. As we will see, the ensuing conflicts did much to weaken the political potential of the new Dissent for decades to come.

7. Quoted in T. Herbert and G.E. Jones, *The remaking of Wales in the eighteenth century* (Cardiff: University of Wales 1988), 24.

PART THREE

Industry and Nonconformity

CHAPTER TEN
The Nonconformist Triumph 1780–1914

REES HOWELLS

Rees Howells was the son of a poor coal-mining family. After a brief stay in Pennsylvania, he returned to a mining job in the Brynamman area, but he had been transformed by a revival currently sweeping Wales. This gave him a profound sense of being predestinated, justified, and glorified before God, so that he enjoyed frequent mystical experiences and was constantly advised by the Holy Spirit. He became not just a preacher, but a famous intercessor, who could (it was believed) use prayer to achieve real change in everyday life: to heal sickness, resolve disputes, convert sinners. He could even alter the course of worldly politics; to make Parliament draw back from passing Popish laws, to halt the careers of anti-Christian European despots. Under divine orders, Howells raised the funds to buy a number of landed estates in west Glamorgan: some became the sites for religious colleges, others were used for pious land speculation. His achievements here were all the sweeter because they were gained at the expense of Catholic rivals, whom Howells hated for the millions of souls their church held in bondage throughout the world. In one such confrontation, he was immeasurably strengthened by a chance encounter with a relic of the Scottish covenanters.[1]

He could easily have been a contemporary of Vavasor Powell or Williams, Pantycelyn, but he was not. He lived from 1879 to 1950, he was converted in the revival of 1904, and his most successful intercession was said to have come in affecting the politics of the Munich crisis (the prayer in question was a simple but heartfelt

1. Norman Grubb, *Rees Howells intercessor* (Christian Literature Crusade, 1987).

'Lord, bend Hitler'). Howells' career epitomises many of the themes that recur through the history of Dissent from the seventeenth century onwards: the belief in an immediate divine role in worldly affairs, and the necessity for community righteousness; belief in providentialism, in evangelical revivalism; the inseparable nature of secular politics and affairs of the spirit; and a hope for the mystical vision of the Glory of God as the highest aim in human existence. It is these religious themes that provide much of the continuity of modern Welsh history.

THE TRIUMPH OF DISSENT

Beliefs like those of Howells also came to influence a large proportion of the Welsh population. This was not achieved overnight: in the seventeenth and eighteenth centuries, the common historical emphasis on the careers of the evangelical leaders often exaggerates their real influence. Evangelicals and Methodists were definitely in a minority in 1750, but they formed a substantial majority of the population a century later. By the 1850s, Dissenters may have outnumbered Anglicans by four or five to one, and the evangelical zeal of Dissent seemed to increase with each new revival. This is one of the great transitions in Welsh history, one that had a profound influence on most aspects of politics, society, culture and everyday life.

There were many contemporary attempts to explain the explosive growth in Welsh Dissent. Commonly, the critics blamed long-standing problems and abuses within the Church, even when the writers were faithful Anglicans like Arthur J. Johnes or Sir Thomas Phillips. Both stressed the ancient history of plunder and neglect by lay authorities; the abundance of poor livings, of absentee pluralist clergy, and the linguistic and cultural divisions between pastors and their flocks. Johnes specifically mentioned the Church's 'want of sympathy with the feelings and tastes of the people', as well as the 'progressive spoliation by the English government of the religious and literary endowments of Wales.' He also explored a nationalist critique, comparing the 'Welsh period' of the Church under the early Stuarts, when preferments generally went to local men, with the 'English period' from 1760 to 1800.

The four dioceses were poor and remote. Phillips offered this table to illustrate exactly how parlous the economic condition was about 1830:

Diocese	Llandaff	St Davids	St Asaph	Bangor	Total
Benefices worth:					
£50–75 pa	35	86	5	7	133
£100–150	65	200	35	44	344
£200 or more	92	121	92	72	377
Totals	192	407	132	123	854

Almost a sixth of Welsh livings were worth £75 or less, at a time when even £150 was scarcely a respectable income. While few of the clergy were as well-off as their English counterparts, those of the south were uniquely badly placed. The average net income of a Llandaff clergyman was barely two-thirds that of his counterpart in north Wales. In the two northern dioceses, there were 109 livings (43 per cent) where the tithes belonged to someone other than the parochial clergyman. In Llandaff and St Davids, however, the figure was 53 per cent.

Perhaps most significant, the parochial structures reflected the geography of the pre-industrial world. Parishes were small and compact in the lowlands and the anglicised areas, vast and poor in the uplands. In the years of industrialisation, there is a neat inverse relationship between areas with strong parochial structure and those that experienced the sharpest population growth. And the poorest livings also included many of the parishes most likely to experience industrialisation. Increasingly, the Church in Wales was not where the people were to be found, and vice versa. The Dissenters, on the other hand, were strong in precisely the areas of weak Church control. In 1811, Merthyr Tydfil had a population of 11,000, and seating for perhaps 400 Anglican worshippers; but the number of communicants was only 40. In the four key industrial parishes of Merthyr, Aberdare, Bedwellty and Aberystruth, there were 21 churches by 1857, a figure that represented a real growth in building and the provision of seating; but at the same time, there were 137 nonconformist chapels.

If not inevitable, then the Dissenting victory was at least predictable. Less so was the thorough triumph enjoyed by Dissent in all parts of Wales, as the south was traditionally more sympathetic to Dissent than the north. The older congregations survived and flourished in south Wales, above all the Baptist and Independents, who suffered little from the growth of newer movements. By 1861, 61 per cent of the Baptist chapels in Wales were to be found in the four counties of the southern littoral. The Baptists and Independents both grew in numbers in consequence of the repeated revivals: there were 86 Baptist congregations in 1798, 379 by 1847. It was chiefly the Independents who colonised the new industrial settlements, overwhelming the older groups who had moved to Unitarianism.

THE METHODISTS

But in terms of numbers, the Methodists were the real winners of the nineteenth century boom. They were already the leading sect by the 1850s, and they maintained a steady 35 per cent or so of the Dissenting population until 1905. However, they were mostly to be found outside the areas of cities and industry, in the regions where Dissent had traditionally been weakest. This meant that the Methodists were building on fresh ground in the north and west, which they soon dominated. By 1905, the rural Welsh-speaking core of Dissent was also the heartland of Welsh Methodism.

This explosive growth had begun in the 1780s, when some ministers from the south-western counties began the systematic evangelisation of 'dark corners' like Gwynedd. One of the most successful was Evan Richardson (1759–1824) from north Cardiganshire, who in 1781 established a school on the Griffith Jones model at Brynengan in western Caernarvonshire. At the time, the evangelical cause was extremely weak in the region, but Richardson promoted a Methodist revival centred in Eifionydd. His school moved its location on several occasions, arriving by 1787 in Caernarvon town, where there was a Methodist chapel by 1793.

The Methodists had set a precedent that was soon eagerly followed by the old Dissent, who also sent missionaries from the south-western congregations. Leaders like Christmas Evans, Henry Davies of Llangloffan (Baptist) and George Lewis (Independent) all travelled north in the late 1780s, and enjoyed much success in areas hitherto regarded as almost hopeless for Dissent, in Llŷn and Anglesey, Trawsfynydd and Llanuwchllyn: places that would be regarded as nonconformist bastions throughout the next century. In turn, they converted and trained a new generation of leaders from the north itself.

The 'conquest' of Gwynedd in these years was at least as significant in the long term as the contemporary upsurge in radical thought and protest which has enjoyed so much attention in recent historical writing. Meanwhile, William Williams o'r Wern and John Roberts of Llanbrynmair presided over an expansion of the Independent cause in Denbighshire and Montgomeryshire respectively; and the Independent academy even came to be based in the north, at Wrexham. All the sects enjoyed surges in membership following revivals like the one which began at Beddgelert in 1817, but the Methodists achieved the greatest gains, and by 1820, there were 60 societies in Caernarvonshire alone.

One of the southern immigrants became the charismatic leader of the Methodist movement in Wales. This was Thomas Charles, a former Anglican curate, whose personal circumstances led him to settle at Bala in 1784. He pioneered a number of innovations that were designed both to spread Methodist influence, and to make individual congregations more resilient. He is best known for his development of the older idea of Sunday Schools, organised by groups of readers who would visit an area for some months to teach both reading and basic religious knowledge. This elementary piety would be nourished by abundant supplies of cheap Bibles and other texts, naturally in Welsh. And adult attendance was demanded, a feature that the Welsh institutions maintained into the present century. Charles' work was epitomised by the oft-told legend of Mary Jones, the ordinary girl who walked 50 miles barefoot to receive from him the ultimate treasure that the world could offer: a Bible.

In addition, Thomas Charles began *Y drysorfa ysbrydol* (The spiritual treasury), one of the first of the many sectarian journals that would be so vital a force in nineteenth century Welsh culture. In ecclesiastical matters, Charles encouraged local Methodist societies to select their own leaders, thus increasing the parallels between Methodism and the existing dissenting sects. In 1791, the excommunication of Peter Williams for heresy showed that a supposedly non-existent church was now acting like a fully-fledged autonomous sect. Also in the 1790s, preachers were increasingly likely to seek the protection of the Toleration Acts by registering their meeting-houses as places of 'Protestant dissent'.

Matters came to a head in 1811, when the north Wales Methodists finally ordained a group of eight ministers, including John Elias and Evan Richardson. By the end of the year, there had been 21 ordinations, at Bala and Llandeilo. The schism was not as total as later events made it, and there would long remain a sense of common purpose between Church and Methodism. As Elias wrote,

> there is no methodist in the country opposed to paying tithes or any such impost; and no true, sincere methodist can be opposed to the established Church.[2]

2. Sir Thomas Phillips, *Wales, the language, social condition, moral character and religious opinions of the people* . . . (London 1849), 161.

As late as 1834, Elias could still assert his loyalty to the 39 articles at the Bala *sasiwn*: for all its difficulties, the establishment was better than popery. Also, there would for another half-century be Anglicans, both clergy and laymen, who were Methodists within the Church of England – men like Richard Bassett in Glamorgan – but they were increasingly seen as isolated and even eccentric figures.

THE AGE OF JOHN ELIAS

The new Methodist church was thus forced to define itself in terms of a dissenting sect. The precise form of organisation was shaped by a small group of clergy; above all, by John Elias, who was a dominant figure from 1810 until his death in 1841. Elias, a pupil of Evan Richardson, won his prestige in large part through his legendary skill as a preacher. In what is often known as the golden age of the Welsh sermon, he was regarded as one of the 'holy three' master preachers, and the greatest among the Methodists. Elias had a major influence in ensuring that the new Methodist church would be essentially Presbyterian in tone, and thoroughly Calvinist in theology. In 1823, the church acquired a Confession of Faith (*Cyffes Ffydd*) on the model of the Westminster Confession; and in 1826, a Constitutional Deed incorporated the property of the denomination in the connection as a whole. In theology, Elias believed in what has been described as hyper-Calvinism: unquestioning acceptance of the ideas of total depravity; unconditional election; limited atonement; irresistible grace; and the perseverance of the saints.

Elias, the 'Pope of Anglesey', was also determined that the new church would not share the common trend of Welsh dissent to produce theological liberals and political radicals. Of course he was not unique in his conservatism, but he did much to ensure that the Methodist church and its journal, *Y drysorfa*, rigidly opposed every major movement of political reform. This included Catholic emancipation, the 1832 Reform Bill, and (naturally) radical movements like Rebecca and the Chartists. Welsh Methodists in London who favoured Catholic rights were excommunicated, and in 1839 the Llandovery *sasiwn* prohibited any of the faithful from becoming a Chartist. Elias and his contemporaries had a traditionally puritan emphasis on the evil nature of the unregenerate mass of the population, and a corresponding belief that their abuses should be suppressed, by law if necessary. This was an absolute imperative where the Sabbath was concerned.

In retrospect, it is difficult to feel much sympathy for Elias and his contemporaries in the Methodist leadership, who (from a modern liberal view) appear to have been on the wrong side of every conceivable issue. Also, Elias in his last years was seen as excessively reactionary by members of his own church. From 1828, a more liberal strand of Methodist opinion was led by ministers like John Jones of Tal-y-Sarn and Robert Roberts of Rhos. In 1841, Elias was succeeded by the much more liberal Henry Rees, brother of the political reformer, Gwilym Hiraethog.

Even so, liberalisation did not extend to the war being waged by the Methodists on every aspect of the traditional popular culture of Wales, including Sunday fairs, mapsants, mumming, seasonal customs, and most games and sports. The campaign against popular amusements extended to vernacular drama, and even to harping and songs, to the horror of both political radicals and cultural patriots. Ministers boasted that such secular manifestations were heard no more in converted areas, and the only surviving harps were those popularly attributed to the angels. William Jones of Llangadfan remarked in 1789 that 'the enthusiasm of the Methodists' helped to 'spread an universal gloom over the country'. In 1802, the harpist Edward Jones blamed 'the sudden decline in the national minstrelsy and customs of Wales' on 'the fanatic impostors, or illiterate plebeian preachers'.

THE CULTURE OF DISSENT

Methodism was like all the nonconformist sects in being a religion of the word, whether spoken or written; so adherents of the movement attached a high premium to literacy, to the skills of rhetoric, and the capacity to make a public presentation. Many radicals would find lay preaching an ideal training for political oratory. Of course, the vast majority of Dissenters were not political radicals. For them the greatest part of this cult of the word was the immense value attached to the sermon as a staple of intellectual life and (though many would have resented the term) as an art-form. But the evangelical impulse which motivated many to criticise and change conditions also provided the verbal tools with which to achieve this.

The relationship between Dissent and social radicalism was complex, and Welsh Dissent was anything but monolithic. John

Elias was as conservative as one could imagine; but there were also middle class agitators like David Rees of Llanelli. In the early nineteenth century, the Unitarians were well to the Left of the spectrum, with Unitarian ministers prominent among the leaders and supporters of both Chartism and the Rebecca protests. Meanwhile, the Independents were active in agitation over more moderate issues like education and the Corn Laws. The Baptists were more conservative, but many celebrities, like Christmas Evans, shared the strong respect for authority that characterised Elias. Pauline doctrines on submission had had a real impact. Only from the 1840s were all the sects active in campaigns for civil and religious liberty.

The evangelical movement had a huge influence on Welsh culture through the glorification of oratory and rhetoric. It also popularised the hymn as a tool of instruction and an expression of communal solidarity. Williams of Pantycelyn made his greatest contribution to the revival as a writer of hymns, while others who wrote hymns or set them to music have become known as leading contributors to the Welsh cultural tradition. Great nineteenth century figures included Thomas William (1761–1844) and Ieuan Gwyllt (1822–1877). As we will see, the love of choral music was well on its way to becoming a vital distinguishing feature of Welsh life; and by no means only for nonconformists.

THE 'POPES'

There is so much that divides us from the social and intellectual life of the eighteenth or early nineteenth centuries, so many fundamental assumptions that we cannot share; but the religious gulf is perhaps the hardest to surmount. It is natural to write of Wales between, say, 1810 and 1840 in terms of breakneck industrialisation, or of emerging class politics. For many Welsh people living in those years, however, the most important changes were occurring elsewhere, and they could never be measured or catalogued in government investigations or statistical reports. We have already seen that this was above all the golden age of Welsh preaching, the era of the 'holy three': John Elias and Christmas Evans of Anglesey, and William Williams o'r Wern (in Denbighshire). Respectively, the group included a Methodist, a Baptist and an Independent, but all owed at least some of their inspiration to the enthusiasm of the evangelical revival.

In its origins, Puritanism had been strongly anticlerical, but the new generation of nonconformist clergy and preachers enjoyed a personal prestige that often verged on idolatry. Opponents were not slow to point out the paradox, especially when the Methodists seemed to espouse an irrational enthusiasm that was felt to resemble Catholic practice. We hear of many Methodist leaders receiving the derogatory name of 'Pope' (Christmas Evans was merely the 'Bishop of Anglesey'). Throughout the nineteenth century, great ministers like Herber Evans or Evan Jones of Caernarvon were seen as true spokesmen for the nation no less than for godliness. Charges of theocratic ambitions seemed particularly justified in 1912 when the Rev. Josiah Towyn Jones was elected to Parliament for East Carmarthenshire. However, the chapels had mobilised Liberal support throughout the party's years of glory in the previous half-century.

Leaders of presence, with celebrated skills in the pulpit or the press, might enjoy an extravagant cult and a vast personal following, both within their lifetime and afterwards. This was reinforced by an industry selling their books and sermons, and offering prints, paintings and busts of the great preachers and revivalists. A leader like John Elias or Nathaniel Rowland might rule a particular denomination in a county for decades. In addition, Welsh nonconformity showed a rather dynastic nature. William Williams, Daniel Rowland, John Elias – all left sons or grandsons who enjoyed great prestige in Methodism, and who continued to work in the home territories of their ancestors.

Perhaps the greatest example of such a nonconformist dynasty was to be found among the descendants of Thomas Charles, as illustrated by this genealogy:

The Charles Family

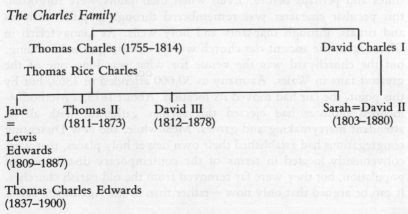

Thomas Charles (1755–1814)   David Charles I

Thomas Rice Charles

Jane   Thomas II   David III   Sarah=David II
=   (1811–1873)   (1812–1878)   (1803–1880)
Lewis
Edwards
(1809–1887)

Thomas Charles Edwards
(1837–1900)

Most of the men in this table were Methodist clergy. David
Charles I was one of the first ordained ministers in the Methodist
communion. His son was a hymn-writer and the Moderator of the
south Wales Association (Thomas Charles Edwards held the latter
position in the 1880s). For much of the nineteenth century, the
family dominated the training and educational institutions of the
Methodist connection. In 1837, David III and Lewis Edwards
founded at Bala what became the preparatory academy for the
Methodist ministers of north Wales. Edwards headed this institution
for half a century, in which time Bala trained many of the leading
figures of the denomination. He was succeeded as principal by his
son. By 1842 the south Wales Methodists had followed suit with
their own academy, at Trefecca (this moved to Aberystwyth in
1906). David Charles II was secretary of the southern institution, and
David III was principal from 1842 to 1862. The family was also
crucial in secular causes. David III and Thomas II were both leading
activists in the campaign to establish a national University College of
Wales: of which the first principal was their brother in law, Thomas
Charles Edwards. All were part of a new nonconformist clerisy.

A NEW GEOGRAPHY

In exploring the impact of the new evangelical movements, we are
also struck by the novelty of the emerging religious geography of
Wales. The old parish churches rapidly declined as centres of
community life. They may have been small and poor, but the
churches marked sites that had been sacred since early Christian
times and perhaps before. Even when their saints were forgotten,
this peculiar character was remembered through popular customs
and rituals, through mapsants and holy wells. At Llangyfelach in
Glamorgan, the ancient *clas* church was an undistinguished building,
but the churchyard was the venue for what was long one of the
greatest fairs in Wales. As many as 30,000 attended in 1869, but by
this point, the fair had moved its location. About 1815, a Methodist-
inclined minister had ejected this secular gathering with all its
attendant merrymaking and games. Meanwhile, the new Dissenting
congregations had established their own newer holy places, that were
conveniently located in terms of the contemporary distribution of
population; but they were far removed from the old parish churches.
It can be argued that only now – rather than in the Age of the Saints

or the Reformation – does the pre-Christian map of holy places in Wales change decisively.

In terms of secular political economy, 'Wales' by the 1830s was defined by the vast economic enterprises of the southern and border shires, while the towns and villages of the north and west faded into insignificance. In religious terms, however, some of these heartland communities were acquiring a reputation for dynamic and vibrant spirituality. The eighteenth century revival had been centred in rural west Wales, and Methodism would always be more powerful in the north and west than in the industrial south. It was thus based on the smaller urban centres of Wales, far removed from the areas of rapid growth. In the mid-eighteenth century, Llangeitho or Llanddowror were the centres of religious Wales, as surely as Swansea and Carmarthen were its commercial hubs. Later nonconformists commemorated early centres like Llangeitho or Ilston with all the enthusiasm that their worldly counterparts built statues to generals or admirals.

The clearest illustration would be Bala in Merionethshire, a town that barely existed from the statistical viewpoint of a Gradgrind: it was at best a minor regional centre, that was not even served by a rail route until the mid-1860s. Yet it was a key road junction, and an important market centre, that acted as the focus for a sizeable hinterland. In religious terms, its importance cannot be overstated, and Thomas Charles made this the base for his evangelical work throughout north Wales. In 1790, the town was the setting for one of the greatest revival meetings so far seen in Welsh history; and there were 20,000 present for a meeting in 1814. The Charles and Edwards families created and maintained here the Methodist academy for north Wales. In 1842, Bala also acquired the major seminary for Independent ministers, where in 1853 Michael Daniel Jones became Principal in succession to his father. Through clergy and educational leaders like the Jones's and Edwards's, Bala gained a significance in Wales totally disproportionate to its economic importance. Lewis Edwards and Michael D. Jones would also become national leaders of radical Liberal causes in Wales.

The importance of clerical 'dynasties' and of ecclesiastical centres like Bala indicates that the sects were evolving towards more stable ecclesiastical structures. This was apparent in the case of Methodism after the age of John Elias. The church had thoroughly emancipated itself from its Anglican origins by 1830, but it was long debated whether the organisation should have an educated ministry, or whether godly enthusiasm was enough. Not until 1833 did a

Methodist minister become an MA, when Lewis Edwards took this degree at Edinburgh. In the next decades, the new seminaries of Trefecca and Bala foreshadowed a new degree of status and professional expertise for the clergy. In 1840, the Methodists also developed their own missionary society, directed at the evangelisation of India and Brittany. Edwards and his opinions came to dominate the church as thoroughly as Elias' ultra-reactionary views had once done. The Methodists began within the church, and had become a sect; it was Lewis Edwards who more than anyone else made the movement once more into a conventional church, with a definite Presbyterian structure and a general assembly. He provided that church with a sense of continuity and stability that would be essential to Methodism during its age of triumph after 1840.

REVIVALISM

In the century after 1740, Methodism had played a leading role in the growth of dissent. It might be expected that the new emphasis on ecclesiastical structures and a professional clergy or ministry might tend to slow or even reverse that expansion; but that would be to ignore the way in which the sects had institutionalised revivalistic enthusiasm. In the late nineteenth century, clergy from all the major sects promoted revivalist missions: the Methodists sponsored the Forward Movement, Church evangelicals organised the Keswick conventions. In addition, there were new groups like the Salvation Army. Most originated outside Wales, but all had an impact there. In fact, the 1904 revival can be seen as an outgrowth of the Keswick movement.

Revivals, 'great' or merely local, were frequent events, and they played a vital role in the growth of congregations in the nineteenth century. In part, the movements owed their success to their apparent relevance to everyday life. Sudden and dramatic expansions, crises or collapses were familiar events in the social and economic history of the time, especially in the industrial areas; and so were extreme and incomprehensible scourges like epidemics. It was natural that people should turn to religious interpretations which fitted these patterns. Sometimes, revivals can be closely associated with specific secular events, like the cholera epidemics of 1831–32 and 1849. Crisis, redemption, revival: these were far from being abstract or distant concepts in nineteenth century Wales.

The numerical impact of religious revivals might be immense. In 1840, a Merionethshire revival was said to have added 2000 to the Methodist denomination in that county alone. Anglesey and Caernarvonshire were the setting for spiritual expansion at the end of the decade. However, it was the Great Revival of 1858–9 which became one of the most celebrated of these events.[3] It apparently developed in response to the American revival of 1857, and stirrings can be observed in several parts of Wales in the following year: in Caernarvonshire, in northern Cardiganshire, and at the Methodist seminary of Trefecca, the 'school of the prophets'. One of the leading preachers in Cardiganshire was Humphrey Jones, a Wesleyan minister newly returned from America. Throughout the country, the common text for the revival, almost a slogan, came from Amos's warning, 'Woe to them that are at ease in Zion'. It was taken as a threat of imminent judgement.

By 1859, we hear of enormous victories for the evangelicals in every county, both in rural and industrial areas. In the north, 'The chief work . . . is in the vast slate quarries, amongst the thousands who toil in the great excavations and caverns made by their own hard hands and strong arms'. In Cardiganshire, virtually all the 200 employees of the Frongoch lead mines were affected, transforming work-breaks into prayer meetings. 'There is hardly a house in the whole neighbourhood without a family altar'. The iron areas of the south were equally enthusiastic; and one consequence of the revival was an upsurge in church membership. We hear that the Methodists acquired 400 new members in Aberystwyth, 3000 in Carmarthenshire, and new building activity followed: even the established Church gained in membership. One much-cited measure of success was the allegedly widespread closure of public houses.

The vigour of revivalism is not in doubt. However, one of the most important signs of the movement's importance comes paradoxically from the lack of its obvious impact in everyday life. The revivalist writers naturally wished to show the great impact they had caused on the community, and this they did with tales of converted individuals or towns. But in almost all cases, the sins recounted are strictly limited in nature: overwhelmingly, drunkenness and blasphemy are mentioned, with a few examples of sabbath breaking (chiefly from the industrial south). At Aberaeron, the minister notes that the external observances of religion had always been thoroughly satisfactory, but that the revival might have affected internal values.

3. Thomas Phillips, *The Welsh revival* (Edinburgh: Banner of Truth Trust 1989).

Near Llandovery, a minister noted that 'there are only half a dozen persons in this valley who do not make a profession of religion'. The Vale of Glamorgan was known as a 'dark corner' of Wales only because 'the inhabitants were most absorbed in worldly cares'.

A real shortage of egregious sinners was becoming apparent, a problem resolved by creating new and stricter standards for what constituted 'temperance'. From the 1830s, the nonconformists moved towards teetotalism (*dirwest*) rather than mere moderation in alcoholic consumption. By the 1870s, this new movement had become a social and political force of amazing dimensions, with the Blue Ribbon society attracting a mass membership, far more than most secular political movements in the century. At least by the standards of the time, it seems that even the pre-revival Wales of the 1850s conformed in large measure to the moral vision of the evangelicals. Temperance, originally an outgrowth of Dissenting strength, helped achieve a still more thorough harmonisation of values.

Dissent permeated daily life, but the faithful adherent received much in exchange for this subjection. In the industrial areas, the chapels established their social and cultural hegemony by providing a comprehensible form of community in these radically new societies. It was here that the uprooted found mutual support and encouragement, socialisation and education, social services, political organisation, culture and recreation. In the 1890s, one large Rhondda chapel offered at least one function every day except Fridays and Saturdays.[4] Monday night was the prayer meeting, followed by the students' circle; Tuesday was the Band of Hope, and the Young People's Society; Wednesday the Prayer Meeting and 'Spiritual Class'; Thursday the 'Religious Class'. On Sundays, the spiritual extravaganza included the young people's devotional meeting, the regular service, sermon and children's worship, the children's singing school and the Sunday School gatherings. The day concluded with evening worship and congregational singing practice. This routine did not include extraordinary events of thanksgiving, temperance meetings, or the *gymanfa ganu*.

4. E.D. Lewis and I.G. Jones, 'Capel y Cymer' *Morgannwg* 25 (1981) 137–164.

NUMBERS

For most observers of nineteenth century Wales, the growth of nonconformist sentiment was a fact quite as obvious and significant as the process of industrialisation itself. In political terms, the growth of Dissent was for many years a more central question than anything arising from the new industrial society. However, attempts at quantifying the change were less successful: tons of coal or pig–iron were far easier to count than souls. From the 1880s, there was much pressure for a religious census in Wales, though this was opposed by those who stood to lose from its findings. Initially, this meant the Anglicans, who feared that matters might be even worse than 1851; but soon the nonconformists themselves feared that their predominance might not be quite as overwhelming as they hoped. Moreover, the problems of methodology were immense. What exactly was a 'member' of a congregation, or an 'adherent', or a 'hearer'? Should children be counted as sharing the loyalties of their parents? Might the established Church claim as its followers everyone not clearly attached to some other body? The many different attempts at quantification approached these problems with various degrees of care.

With these caveats in mind, it is possible to sketch the rise of nonconformist Wales in numerical terms. As material things, chapels are easier to count than congregations. In 1810, there were about 829 Anglican churches in Wales, compared with 430 chapels; though the latter figure does not include another 525 Methodist institutions, which were still notionally part of the Church. By 1832, the number of chapels (Dissenting and Methodist combined) was 1420; estimates suggest about 1700 in 1845. Growth followed the mid–century revivals, and by 1905 there were 4526 chapels compared with 1546 buildings connected with the establishment. Glamorgan was an extreme case, but it suggests the level of growth. In 1800, there was a total of perhaps 200 places of worship in the county, two–thirds of which belonged to the established Church. By 1906, the number of churches and chapels had increased to almost 1500, 80 per cent of which represented some shade of Protestant dissent. In south Cardiganshire in 1901, there was one place of worship for every 186 people.

Estimates of actual numbers are more questionable, especially before the 1840s, but tentative figures can be given. The 1851 religious census had shown that Dissenters had about 80 per cent of worshippers; though the survey also suggested that almost half the population was not attached to either church or chapel. In 1861, there were 263,000 dissenters in the four main denominations; there were 352,000 by 1882. The difficulty of dealing with such statistics results partly from the dramatic fluctuations that were possible in religious loyalties. If we believe the best estimates, Wales had 465,000 nonconformists in 1903, but 549,000 by 1905. In the aftermath of the great revival, chapel membership had apparently swelled by 18 per cent in two years. This may have been technically correct, but it suggests a very fluid situation. By 1913, membership stood at around 523,000.

The 1905 census found the sects at their high noon. By that date, this was the distribution of denominational loyalty among the Protestant churches:

Table 10:1 Religious Affiliations in Wales 1905–6

Group	Communicants (thousands)	Percentage of Total
Anglican	193	26
Methodist	189	26
Independent	175	24
Baptist	143	19
Wesleyan	41	5
Total	741	100

(There were also some 65,000 Catholics)

The Dissenters had 1,538,000 'sittings' compared with only 459,000 for the established Church. Anglicans could take some consolation: they were still the largest denomination in the country, and although nonconformists outnumbered them by perhaps three to one, this was a major improvement from the mid-century figure of four or five to one. The figures could thus be read in various ways, but it could not be denied that nonconformist worshippers continued to outnumber Anglicans. By 1905, Dissenters probably formed 40 per cent or more of overall population in five Welsh counties, which were also the areas with the highest proportion of Welsh speakers: Anglesey, Caernarvon, Merioneth, Carmarthen and Cardigan. Conversely, Dissent was weakest in border shires such as Flint and Monmouth, where under 20 per cent were nonconformists. However, these figures only speak of overall population. In terms of the worshipping population, nonconformists were a large majority in all parts of Wales.

The numbers are impressive, but they scarcely convey the impact of nonconformity on a specific area. To do this, let us consider the area now covered by the Pontardawe rural district, in the uplands of west Glamorgan. This administrative area (of some 55 square miles) includes the town of Pontardawe, as well as several older communities, such as Clydach, Brynamman, Ystalafera and Llangiwg. The population grew from perhaps two or three thousand in 1801 to about 30,000 in 1911.[5]

About 1810, there were probably six or seven places of worship in the area, the uncertainty arising from the question of when a certain Independent church split into two, a common event in nonconformist history. Two of the churches were Anglican, probably three Independent, one Baptist, and one Unitarian. Nonconformist expansion was strongest in the years between about 1844 and 1870, when some 20 new places of worship were built. This chronology also suggests that the 1851 census understates the parlous state of the established Church in Wales. Although the census shows that Anglicans formed only a minority of religious adherents in Wales, it fails to show how rapidly the Dissenters were outbuilding them at precisely this time. In 1851, there were four Anglican churches compared to 15 nonconformist chapels. By 1870, five churches confronted 29 chapels. In 1910, there were over 50 places of worship, only nine of which were Anglican. Being Glamorgan, and an area with an ancient dissenting tradition, the new chapels were over-whelmingly Independent and Baptist: only three of the nineteenth century chapels were Methodist.

The mid-century building boom had a formative influence on the townscapes of Wales, establishing as it did the nonconformist chapel as an almost ubiquitous presence. It was also around this time that chapels came to bear their distinctive Biblical names. Some of these, like *Calfaria* (Calvary), were chosen for obvious reasons, but others have lost the resonance they possessed in an age of common Bible-reading. In the 1820s, Clydach had a 'Hebron', named after a dwelling-place of Abraham and a seat of King David. From the 1840s, the great majority of chapels bore some such name, usually from the Old Testament, and reflecting certain common themes. Popular in these decades were names like 'Zion', 'Jerusalem', or 'Tabernacle', indicating that this was a centre where the congregation united with God in a place of peculiar sanctity. It also fitted the extensive use of the psalms in worship, stressing to the congregation

5. Compiled from John H. Davies, *History of Pontardawe and district* (Swansea: Christopher Davies, 1967).

that they were a chosen people with a holy mission arising from a
covenant with God – this was the idea recalled in names like 'Shiloh'.
The whole Bible, Old and New Testament, applied literally to
everyday experience.

Another important theme was suggested by the popular 'Goshen'
or 'Zoar', respectively a land and a city which God set apart for his
chosen to rescue them from the horrors which he would visit on
pagans and sinners. The names stressed the believer's call to
'nonconformity' with worldly ways. 'Bethesda', or 'house of
mercy', similarly indicated this sense of election, separation, rescue,
and direct divine intervention. 'Ebenezer' illustrates the common
idea that the holy people were in combat with a hostile or godless
world (1 Sam: 7: 5–14). By the 1870s, therefore, Wales had acquired
not only a host of new public buildings, but a whole theological
landscape for those trained to understand; and the flourishing Welsh
Sunday Schools ensured that these lessons were driven home. By
1906, Glamorgan alone had 290,000 pupils enrolled in Sunday
Schools.

The character of the grandiose new chapels built between 1850
and the 1880s can only be described as triumphalist, to use a term
usually applied in a Catholic context. One of the finest was the
Morriston Tabernacle, opened in 1873, and seating 1450. It was
termed a 'Cathedral' by the *Cambrian*:[6]

> The chapel seems to stand out as one great redeeming feature in the
> whole of that huge manufacturing district – it is an oasis in a desert, an
> object worthy of admiration in the midst of unsightly works and
> manufactories of every size and description.

Tabernacle was Gothic, but the buildings were often strictly Classical
to stress the distinctions with high Church excesses. 'Classical', of
course, did not necessarily mean restrained: witness the magnificent
Corinthian porticoes found on chapels like Bethesda at Mold (1863).
Zion at Llanrwst (1881–1883) has been described as of 'exceptional
size and grandeur'.

Equally typical were grand and pretentious works like Bethania at
Cardigan, Zion at Llanelli and Mount Pleasant, Swansea. Chapels
were magnificent in the great and prosperous centres of Dissent: the
'Meccas' like Swansea or Caernarvon. In booming industrial areas
like the Rhondda, the buildings often offered accommodation for
1000 or 1200 worshippers. This enormous construction activity
naturally ran the congregations into considerable debt that was often

6. Quoted in Norman L. Thomas, *Swansea's districts and villages* (Neath, n.d.), 201.

not cleared for years – Morriston Tabernacle was finally paid off in 1914. But the mere fact of indulging in such extravagance suggests the unbounded confidence with which the sects faced the new century.

TENSIONS IN ZION

It is possible to portray the rise of nonconformity as a series of almost inevitable victories and gains, parallel to the growth of industrial production and prosperity. But as with Welsh economic progress in the nineteenth century, the nonconformist triumphs were perhaps more ephemeral than they appeared. This is suggested by the history of the revivals, those culminations of the nonconformist religious experience. Although revivals were in many ways triumphant occasions, they also serve to illustrate real strains and contradictions within dissent.

The rhetoric of political nonconformity drew heavily on ideas of democracy, equality, civil rights and individual choice; but there were in reality several serpents in the puritan Eden. The evangelical impulse to transform the world was of its nature majoritarian rather than democratic, in its (remarkably successful) attempt to impose puritan standards on the unregenerate mass. It would have been an enormous task to explain to a contemporary nonconformist why a later generation might consider such an activity morally suspect. On the other hand, there were other issues where nonconformists were vulnerable by contemporary standards, and some at least were aware of this weakness.

Nonconformist congregations, even those of radical political bent, were usually organised in hierarchies dependent on wealth, age, and gender. One newspaper account of 1892 characterised the diaconate as the 'big nobs',

> shipowners, builders, shopkeepers, lawyers etc who can out of their surplus well afford to contribute liberally to the church collection, at the same time screwing the wages of their poor workmen down to a minimum.[7]

Another journalist in the same year suggested that 'very few, if any churches would now ever dream of electing a son of toil to be a

7. Trevor Herbert and Gareth E. Jones, ed., *People and protest: Wales 1815–1880* (Cardiff 1988), 101, 104–105.

deacon'. Biblical injunctions at least condemned the respect paid to the richer members of the group, but the exclusion from power and spiritual status of younger men and all women long seemed too natural to be worth comment or dispute. That this was a muted or potential source of grievance is suggested by the explosions that occurred during revivals that offered a democratic access to grace, a chance that was seized above all by women and the young.

The appeal of revivalism to women and (to use an anachronism) teenagers was remarked on by observers of all revivals, notably the well-documented events of 1859. But the clearest illustration occurred in October 1904, when a revival began in Newquay, Cardiganshire. By November, the movement had overwhelmed south-west Wales and penetrated the southern coalfields; and the spiritual fires burned until the following summer. (The leader was Evan Roberts, of whom the much abused word 'charismatic' can be used with absolute correctness.) The incredible intensity and geographical range of the revival suggests that it was able to offer solutions to deeply felt conflicts and problems. One was political: the movement occurred at a time when chapels throughout Wales were divided over the proper response to unionisation and political movements other than political Liberalism. But paramount were the needs of women and the young, who were the leading champions of this new reformation.

As in the 1640s or 1730s, the message was that any individual could find the Holy Spirit without (or despite) the aid of hierarchical structures. Trance-like prayer, ecstatic singing and shouting, were symbolic statements of the immediacy of Grace. At Bethesda in Caernarvonshire, a town just recovering from a catastrophic lockout in the slate quarries, we hear of 500 women meeting daily in prayer. In the south, 'the insolence of the young men' was a salient feature of the new piety: often the same young men who would shortly attempt to displace the older and more conciliatory leaders from their union positions. In south Cardiganshire,

> We have had some incomparable meetings . . . the old people as if thrust aside, and the young people taking complete control of our prayer meetings, men and women; the young women taking a public part in our prayer meetings[8] . .
>
> The young people, the young women, and the older women have received bountifully of the fire . . . it is the young women who first break out in praise and prayer

8. David Jenkins, *The agricultural community in south west Wales at the turn of the twentieth century* (University of Wales 1971).

Revivals also challenged the hard-won status of the clergy, especially among the Methodists, leading to forceful controversy between defenders of a learned ministry and exponents of untaught faith. 'Anticlerical' sentiments came both from converted laymen and from pastors within newer sects like the Forward Movement. The Salvation Army was said to owe its appeal to its willingness to allow the socially humble to 'rise in the ranks'.

The element of conflict is neatly illustrated by a *cause célèbre* of 1915, when Caradoc Evans published an unflattering portrait of rural nonconformist Cardiganshire in the stories collected as *My people*. The book was violently denounced by Liberals as highly placed as Lloyd George, and by broad sections of dissenting opinion. There were strenuous attempts to have the 'renegade's' work banned. Evans' sin was not merely to have depicted Welsh country people as mean, crabbed and lascivious, but he had suggested that such a community was not the harmonious *gwerin* of radical myth. Instead, it was a highly stratified society dominated by the wealthy farmers and church elders, the 'Fathers in Sion', at once rulers and judges over the labourers, oppressors of their wives and families. For the nonconformist leadership, this suggestion of class conflict was worse than any heresy. The horror was magnified by the political circumstances of the early twentieth century, when Liberal and nonconformist rule was increasingly challenged by ideologies of socialism and syndicalism. The crisis in nonconformity reflected the decay of social consensus, no less than the emergence of long-suppressed internal tensions.

CONCLUSION

But this is perhaps to look too far ahead. As we will see, nonconformity enjoyed enormous success in shaping the Welsh political agenda throughout the nineteenth century. The Liberal Party, which based itself in Dissenting interests, experienced a virtual one-party hegemony from 1880 to 1918. This emerging and largely nonconformist nation also possessed an economic base and a consequent political importance that would have been inconceivable a century before. Industry, like nonconformity, was a familiar theme in Wales: both predated the civil war. But it is only in the later eighteenth century that the two phenomena began the triumphant progress which permitted them to shape and dominate subsequent national development. From nonconformity, it is therefore natural to turn to the other great force which shaped Welsh life after 1760: the industries of coal, copper and iron.

CHAPTER ELEVEN

The Coming of Industry

In recent years, it has been common to attack the idea of the Industrial Revolution as a sudden or overnight event. In the words of Dr J.C.D. Clark, the transitions to industrial society were 'slow, partial, belated, complex and irregular', occurring gradually between about 1760 and 1840. In the case of Wales, there may indeed have been a takeoff about 1790, but the revisionists are correct to see the process of industrialisation as long, slow and complex. 'Belated', however, it emphatically was not. The growth of industry in Wales began remarkably early, certainly by the end of the seventeenth century. Industrialisation was thus an internal development, the logical consequence of consistent processes; it was by no means the deus ex machina it sometimes appears to be, an alien and externally imposed phenomenon. 'Pre-industrial' Wales was much more open to growth and development than it is often given credit for.

This chapter will trace the development of the 'powerhouse' Wales of the 1790s onwards, emphasising the importance both of local roots and of influences from the wider national and imperial worlds.

INDUSTRY AND THE GENTRY: 1660–1740

One of the great myths of the Industrial Revolution in Wales concerns the foundation of the Dowlais iron works in 1759, when a group of nine partners took a 99-year lease on mineral rights from Lady Windsor. The rent was £31, with no provision for royalties. This was to be incredibly advantageous for the partners, only one of whom was a local squire. (The most important of the group was Isaac Wilkinson, a Shropshire ironmaster.) Dowlais flourished, and the Windsor estate saw next to nothing of the vast profits. Here, surely, we see the Welsh landowners at their worst: feckless absentees, ignorant or contemptuous of commerce or industry, owning priceless properties that were just waiting for able English entrepreneurs to see their full potential. As we will see, the Dowlais story (though true) is ultimately misleading. The Windsor estate in the 1750s was one of the worst administered in Wales, at a time when most landowners were vigorously active in the assertion and aggrandisement of their rights with the specific aim of enhancing industrial growth. And this process had been under way since at least 1690.

If we return to the Restoration years, we find that Wales had numerous wealthy families who possessed abundant capital and a strong commercial outlook. It also had great mineral wealth, much of it easily accessible in terms of the technology and the communication networks of the day. Where the different elements came together – accessible minerals, good sea communications, local capital – industry thrived. When the Duke of Beaufort visited Flintshire in 1684, the chief spectacle for this distinguished tourist was 'the lands and various works and machines of the lead and coal mines belonging to Sir Roger Mostyn'. The Duke himself had recently been involved in a savage political and tenurial struggle with the commoners of Wentwood Chase in Monmouthshire. The battle assumed archaic legal forms, but the real prize was the timber which the Duke sought for his ironworks. It was a contest that would be repeated many times throughout Wales over the next century.

Between 1660 and 1690, small industrial enterprises proliferated on landed estates throughout Wales. This was nothing radically new – indeed, the origins of the south Wales coal trade must be sought in the activities of the monasteries. But about 1690, economic growth reached a new and much more intense stage. In 1693, new companies began to exploit the lead and copper resources of west Wales, which had previously been a Crown monopoly. Soon, the crucial figure in Welsh industry was Sir Humphrey Mackworth, a Shropshire squire who acquired the Glamorgan estate of Gnoll by marriage, and began a massive expansion of iron and coal enterprises in the Neath area.

It was apparently Mackworth who conceived the notion of a widespread and interdependent economic region, shipping lead or copper ores from west Wales or Ireland to Neath, where they would be smelted, thereby expanding the market for local coal. His works could further branch out into processing by-products like silver and litharge. By 1700, his vision had been brought into existence. Mackworth's coal enterprises were innovative in technological terms, as they used steam engines, deeper shafts, and even tramways. His economic tribulations after 1710 had no adverse impact on the region's flourishing industries, which were bolstered in the next two decades by several new metallurgical enterprises.

By 1730, Swansea had become the metallurgical centre that it would remain for two centuries. Coal, meanwhile, had become a major item for export, to France and Ireland no less than the West Country. For 20 miles around, the production of coal for sale had become a vital aspect of the wealth of most of the great estates in the region. 'Corn, coal and cattle' were the products of a typical estate. Further afield, these changes had other impacts, notably in the ore-producing areas of Cardiganshire and the neighbouring seaports. Outside the areas directly affected by Mackworth's dream, the Hanbury family created at Pontypool a revolutionary industry of tinplate and japanning. Already by the 1730s, Wales was providing perhaps one-sixth of British pig-iron.

The generation after 1690 was crucial in the establishment of industrial traditions in much of Wales. In Cardiganshire, squires had been feuding over the possession of lead mines at least from the 1630s; but in the 1690s, this area emerged as the 'Welsh Indies', the 'Welsh Potosí'. There were soon 'lead-rushes' (to coin a phrase) in Flintshire, Carmarthenshire, and on the Powis estates in Montgomeryshire. As in the case of the Mackworth operations, the first quarter of the century saw intensive technological development, and the improvement of communications. The early enterprises were small in terms of numbers employed, but they had set a precedent. Between 1730 and 1790, industry grew steadily as men and money from existing enterprises branched out to create new ventures.

INDUSTRY AND THE COMMUNITY

Early industry had an impact on the local community and its political structures far out of proportion to the strictly economic influence of the new mines and factories. Industrial development went far towards influencing political attitudes, particularly over matters like peace and war. Tory sympathies were enhanced by the geographical accident that placed the most promising areas of industrial development in lordships held by the Tory Dukes of Beaufort. Naturally, they granted lands and rights to those they found politically sympathetic.

In local affairs, industry placed a high premium on what had previously been desirable practices and policies. Every manorial right now had to be enforced vigorously, if not violently, and there was a spate of battles on such apparently ancient feudal topics throughout the century. Also vital was control of boroughs, for burgesses often had trading rights. This was a delicate matter. A squire might attempt to subject a borough to his influence for reasons connected with party politics, or even family prestige; but in so doing, he was attacking his neighbours both politically and economically. Underlying economic agendas gave a new virulence to the borough feuds of eighteenth century Wales.

Industry might not have been the economic mainstay of a majority of landed estates, even in the most 'progressive' areas of west Glamorgan or south Carmarthenshire; but the squires often acted as if this was in fact the case. The new arrangements made it imperative to control nominations to the Bench, for reasons far removed from the persistent conflict between Whig and Tory. In 1705 and 1706, the power of Mackworth's opponents on the Bench permitted their victory in an industrial war for control of mines and copper works. When all else failed, rival justices conscripted Mackworth's workers into the military, or led mob attacks against them. In Cardiganshire in the 1750s, Crown agent Lewis Morris was jailed by hostile gentry who resented his attempts to prevent their encroachments on newly discovered lead mines. Controlling local office was necessary for prosperity and industrial survival.

Finally, the economic conflicts which now got under way did much for the status and wealth of the stewards and attorneys, those key individuals who alone stood a chance of asserting an estate's manorial rights to timber or minerals, or who could settle a feud over a disputed borough charter. Legal expertise was at a premium; and from mid-century, stewards and solicitors began regularly to take their place among the elite of Georgian Wales. Often the major figures had established themselves by their valour in industrial combat: men like Thomas Williams of Anglesey, attorney and copper pioneer; or the three generations of Gabriel Powells in Gower and Swansea, who fought encroachments on the Beaufort lordship for over 70 years.

Industry and mineral exploitation tended to promote instability, by providing sudden accumulations of wealth for people who had hitherto been nonentities in the county community. The resulting fortune might for a few years make a petty landowner into a magnate. In Flintshire, the delicately balanced parliamentary politics of the 1720s were destabilised by the wealth flowing from the lead mines on the estate of Sir George Wynne of Leeswood (worth perhaps £22,000 a year). On the other hand, not even this cornucopia could survive the legendary cost of northern elections, and the Wynnes were ruined by the 1750s. In the south, industry laid the foundation for the electoral successes of great families like the Mackworths and Hanburys. There were repeated dramatic finds through the century – at Halkyn, Esgair-Hir, Esgair-Mwyn, Parys Mountain – and each was regarded as an El Dorado of the day, albeit in base metal. Parys (1762) produced some 20,000 tons of copper a year, and led to an industry employing 1000 people. It also stimulated the growth of a new town, at Amlwch.

WAR AND COLONIAL COMMERCE 1740–1790

Industry did much to determine the political alignments of Georgian Wales. It is not a new observation, but Welsh industrialisation owed a great deal to successive French governments. It was in the war years of 1689–1714 that we see the innovations associated with Thomas Newcomen, Abraham Darby and Humphrey Mackworth. Darby's use of coke for iron-smelting in particular opened the possibility for the virtually limitless production of good quality iron; and the use of steam meant that drainage would be available to dig the required coal. The foundations were laid, ready for further building between 1742 and 1815, an era of persistent warfare. Each new spurt of enterprise thereafter coincided with fair accuracy to the demands of war. The navy in particular consumed as much iron, brass and copper as Welsh plants could produce. As one stimulus receded and the industries were consolidating, just then another international crisis set off a renewed need for ships and weaponry. Purely military demand, however, was only a part of the story. The nature of these wars was deeply important for Wales, the economy of which was becoming ever more imperial in terms of markets and raw materials. Wales supplied copper for slavers' currency, and cheap textiles to clothe the plantation populations of the western hemisphere.

Also, Welsh industrial growth was unusual in the revolutionary years in the extent to which it was based on mercantile capital. Generally, the prosperity of Welsh regions was intimately connected with their neighbouring cities. English financiers and entrepreneurs were the making of the Welsh industrial boom after 1780. This may suggest a backwardness in Welsh society, but it would be more appropriate to explain it in terms of the metropolitan role that English cities had long played for Welsh regions. Glamorgan and Monmouthshire were chiefly developed by finance from 'their' metropolis of Bristol, just as Liverpool or Whitehaven money financed the industries of north-west England.

Bristol and Liverpool tied the Welsh economy to the fate of the colonies. Bristol flourished on the profits of the middle passage, the trade that took slaves from Africa to America or the West Indies, and then returned to Britain with sugar or tobacco for consumption or re-export. The towns of south Wales depended for their prosperity on Bristol; and they too came to share in this Atlantic trading activity. This did much to shape political loyalties. Bristol's trade would grow and prosper in the event of wars, if those wars were victorious naval affairs dedicated to the expansion of empire and of colonial commerce. For Bristol – as for its satellites, like Carmarthen, Swansea, Cardiff, or Newport – Toryism was thus a form of enlightened self-interest. The industrialists of west Glamorgan were closely tied into the middle passage and the concept of empire: they bought ores from America or Ireland; they provided iron and copper to fit out the warships that defended English commerce. War was the making of the port of Swansea: annual tonnage of shipping using the port rose five-fold between 1768 and 1800, and by 1790, an observer claimed that the port was twice as active as Bristol itself.

From the mid-eighteenth century, we hear regularly of members of southern urban families having relatives in Jamaica, Antigua or Barbados, or else actively participating in slave-raids in Africa. Others still joined Bristol privateering ventures, and money from this source appears in an impressive number of contexts in Welsh industry. The 'privateering men from Bristol' invested heavily in the Cardiganshire copper mines in the 1750s. More directly, a good naval war in the English Channel made it difficult for Newcastle firms to sell coal in the West Country, which thus became a captive market for the counties of south-east Wales.

In the north, Liverpool played a similar role, and the naval wars created a boom in the copper mines. The slate industry owed its prosperity after 1780 to the activities of the Pennant family, classic Jamaica *nouveaux riches*. Richard Pennant, Baron Penrhyn, revolutionised the slate industry; while as MP for Liverpool, he campaigned to defend the slave trade.

Generally, war and colonial commerce were good for the Welsh elites, though of course there were exceptions. From the 1760s, entrepreneurs from Chester and Liverpool had outflanked the Shrewsbury drapers by exporting cloth direct from Welsh ports like Barmouth and Aberdyfi, to destinations in the Americas or the Caribbean. This was ingenious, but it was perilous in that the Welsh hinterland came to depend on these distant markets, and thus to the vagaries of imperial politics. The American and French wars were as bad for communities like Barmouth, Bala and Dolgellau as they were stimulating for Swansea or Aberystwyth.

This background helps to explain the proliferation of industrial plants from about 1740, and the concentration of activity in war years (1756–63, 1775–83, 1793–1815). Between 1749 and 1756, we hear of new tinplate works in Caerleon, and increased copper smelting at Neath abbey. The 1740s and 1750s were also the height of the lead-mining industry in Cardiganshire and Carmarthenshire. Between 1759 and 1765, a number of famous names appeared in the iron industry (Dowlais, Plymouth, Tredegar, Cyfarthfa). The annual rent specified in the leases of ironworks rose elevenfold between 1756 and 1764 alone, suggesting that this was a highly profitable enterprise.

The importance of war emerges in any number of case-studies of leading entrepreneurs, but the 1740s and 1750s are particularly rich in this way. In Carmarthenshire, Robert Morgan was an ironmaster who owned a rolling mill at Kidwelly, as well as several forges. From 1758 to 1763, his works were chiefly involved in casting guns, and the Board of Ordnance accepted 739 of these, eight per cent of the total they accepted in these profitable years. Morgan also cast guns for the merchant ships and privateers of Bristol and Liverpool. Weaponry apart, he sold iron and tinplate to shipbuilders and naval dockyards. He presided over a substantial expansion of the west Wales metal industries under the stimulus of the French wars.

Representative in another way was Anthony Bacon, the real founder of ironmaking at Merthyr Tydfil. Bacon was originally a merchant active in the Maryland trade, who settled in England in the 1740s. He entered the African trade in guns and slaves, and won a government contract in 1758 for victualling troops in West Africa. At the same time, he was beginning the creation of 'Bacon's mineral kingdom' in Glamorgan. Until 1782, when an Act prohibited MPs from holding government contracts, the great majority of his industrial activity was directed to the production of cannon, guns and ammunition.

Bacon's career parallels at several points that of Chauncy Townsend, whose fortune derived from contracts granted in 1744 to provision British forces and settlements in Nova Scotia. Like Bacon, he entered Parliament, and in the 1750s he showed interest in the burgeoning industries of south Wales. He invested in new coal mines, transportation from which would be improved by an innovative wagonway. He became a substantial coal-owner in the Duke of Beaufort's lordship around Swansea, and he developed a copperworks (1755). In 1757, he went into the lead and spelter trade. The Townsend enterprises remained a major industrial force until well into the next century.

In north-east Wales, too, the importance of military contracts is apparent, though they did not all have to stem from the British government. In 1753, the Wilkinson family took over the forge of Bersham, converting it to the use of coke for smelting. From 1768, John Wilkinson held armaments contracts from the Russians and Turks, and in 1774 he began supplying the French armed forces. Allegedly, the family assisted the French out of radical and pro-American sentiments. Whatever the reason, Wilkinson cannon were manufactured by the new technique of precision boring that the family had developed for the purpose. This skill proved to be vital in the evolution of the finely fitted cylinders required for Boulton and Watt steam engines. In 1792, Wilkinson established a new forge at Brymbo, near Wrexham.

The stories of Morgan, Bacon, Wilkinson and Townsend could all be repeated many times, but the major themes would recur: war provided government contracts, markets and (ideally) new colonies. Appropriately, the next boom for Welsh industry began in 1777, with the coming of a zinc works at Swansea, and a new textile plant on the Lancashire model at Holywell. Between 1778 and 1784, four of the major iron works were built (Sirhowy, Ebbw Vale, Beaufort, Penydarren). As one boom faded, so another one would soon be getting under way, with a further expansion of metallurgical enterprise coinciding with the long French wars between 1793 and 1815.

Obviously, it would be unwise to note the coincidence of war and industrial expansion, and simply claim *post hoc, ergo propter hoc*. More generally, it can be said that the political and international environment of these years thoroughly favoured industrial expansion. On the other hand, this is not to underestimate the significance of technological change. The use of coke for smelting became widespread from the 1750s, and this lessened dependence on timber. It also tended to concentrate the iron industry in the areas of the south where coal and iron ore were to be found in convenient proximity. In the 1780s, the Welsh ironmasters applied the Cort process of puddling iron. At the end of the century, we seem therefore to have a real industrial revolution, rather than merely the cumulative growth of individual enterprises. The effects would soon be observed in production increases of Stakhanovite proportions. A Welsh iron furnace in the 1780s produced perhaps 20 tons a week, a figure that increased by a figure of four or five by 1810. In 1790, total British iron production was 90,000 tons; by 1830, south Wales alone was making 278,000 tons.

TAKE-OFF: IRON 1790–1840

By the 1790s, we seem to have something like the classical notion of an industrial take-off, with an enormous expansion of iron and copper production. Throughout the Welsh economy, economic trends between 1790 and 1815 can only be described by such hackneyed terms as 'explosive', or simply, 'revolutionary'.

This is best illustrated by the case of the iron industry. By about 1780, Anthony Bacon dominated production in the Merthyr area, and his activities had attracted a number of others as managers or partners, men like Thomas Guest, Francis Homfray and Richard Hill. All the great ironworks were in operation by the time of his death in 1786: Dowlais, Cyfarthfa/Hirwaun, Plymouth and Peny-darren (the 'big four'). It is a fascinating speculation how this power could have been used if he had been succeeded by an heir of comparable vision or ability. In fact, his inheritance was divided and ultimately sold to ironmasters already active in the area. By 1794, Richard Crawshay was sole proprietor of Cyfarthfa; by 1800, Richard Hill had secured control of the Plymouth works; and the Guests held Dowlais itself. Others moved slightly further afield: it was Jeremiah Homfray who established the Ebbw Vale works in 1789.

Though often in competition, the masters could cooperate on schemes like the Glamorganshire Canal of 1794, sponsored by Richard Crawshay and Samuel Homfray. In 1804, the two were at odds over a momentous bet, when Homfray proved that a locomotive could move a load of iron ten miles along a railway from Penydarren to Abercynon. The feat was achieved by Richard Trevithick, utilising his improved version of the Watt engine. The contest won Homfray a thousand guineas, and suggested a whole new direction for the economic history of the region. The ironmasters were thus being forced by the exigencies of one dynamic industry to transform other parts of the infrastructure. Moreover, the coal industry was carried along on the coat-tails of iron: as iron production soared, so did extraction of the coal on which smelting depended. More coal meant access to deeper seams, which could only be obtained with adequate drainage; and that, in turn, needed better steam engines. Steampower had been known in Wales since the days of Mackworth, but now we find the efficient Watt engines: there were eight in Wales by the 1790s.

Between 1790 and 1820, a number of new figures appeared in the industry. Josiah John Guest established himself as the sole ruler and sovereign of the Dowlais works by 1815. The success of Richard Crawshay at Cyfarthfa and Hirwaun attracted two of his Yorkshire nephews, Joseph and Crawshay Bailey. After Richard Crawshay's death, he was ultimately succeeded as sole master by his son William. This generation, of Crawshays, Baileys and Guests, witnessed the great age of the iron industry. Production expanded enormously at the older plants, while at the same time furnaces were being erected at a dozen new locations.

Among newer works, the Homfrays had already shown the potential of the heads of the Monmouthshire valleys with the enterprises at Ebbw Vale and Sirhowy. Samuel Homfray married the daughter of the Morgan family of Tredegar, and gave the name of this house to his new works of 1800. By 1809, the Monmouthshire canal carried over 9000 tons of Homfray iron. The Baileys also played a key role in the further expansion into Monmouthshire from 1810, with the creation of Nantyglo and Beaufort. By the 1830s, the list included names like Abersychan, Beaufort, Blaina, Varteg and Clydach. West of Merthyr, iron had expanded into the Aberdare region at Abernant and Llwydcoed. There were about 50 works in the whole territory. Between 1750 and 1796, the number of iron furnaces in south Wales rose from nine to 26. By 1830, there were 113 furnaces; by 1848, there were almost 200 furnaces producing 631,000 tons. The figure of a million tons was approached in the 1850s.

The 'revolution' can be witnessed in progress at any one of the great plants. At the Dowlais iron works, annual production was 1000 tons in 1763, 2000 tons by 1790; over 15,000 tons by 1815. In 1806, production at the Plymouth works was 4000 tons; by 1815, the figure was nearly 8000, and by 1846, it was 35,000. By 1826, the number eight furnace here was said to be the largest in the world. In 1820, a total of 49,000 tons of iron was being shipped down the Glamorganshire canal by just the four great firms of the Merthyr area. The canal carried 133,000 tons by 1839. The Monmouthshire canal and associated tramroads carried 34,000 tons in 1810, 176,000 by 1839.

As a proportion of total British production, south Wales gained its greatest importance in the 1820s and 1830s:[1]

Table 11:1   The Iron Production of South Wales 1720–1880

Year	Pig Iron Production in South Wales(thousand tons)	Per cent of Britsh Total
1720	5	19.4
1796	34	27
1823	182	40
1840	525	36
1860	969	25
1880	890	12

The Merthyr-Dowlais area alone had 44 furnaces by the 1840s. Dowlais, with its 7000 employees, really looked like the sort of place Marx had in mind when he described the Victorian capitalists having put to shame all the pyramids and temples of the ancients. It would be difficult to claim this for the 30- or 40-man works of the previous century. By 1840, there were probably 150,000 people directly dependent on the works at the heads of the valleys, not counting the commercial towns of Monmouthshire and east Glamorgan: probably another 40,000 or more people. In this new society, almost 200,000 depended on the monstrous iron furnaces and the hellish pits.

The Welsh iron industry was at its height in the first two decades of the Victorian era, and the traditional names continued to dominate. They survived technological changes, and even led the way. The hot blast process pioneered at the Ynyscedwyn works allowed the use of anthracite coal, with which south Wales was so abundant. In the 1860s, the Siemens brothers of Swansea developed

1. Philip Riden, 'The output of the British iron industry before 1870', *Economic history review* 30 (1977): 442–459.

open hearth techniques. At the same time, the railway boom that was spreading around the whole world created an insatiable demand for Welsh iron, and the potential spoils seemed enough to accommodate a whole new generation of entrepreneurs. The Fothergill family were the most exciting of the new generation in Glamorgan. Like the Baileys, they had migrated from the north in the 1790s to take advantage of the abundance of new opportunities: Richard Fothergill (1822–1903) controlled ironmaking around Aberdare, and acquired both the Plymouth and Penydarren works in the 1860s. This put him at least on a par with the Guests and Crawshays, while he served as MP for the Merthyr-Aberdare constituency in 1868. In Monmouthshire, the Ebbw Vale iron and coal company had absorbed many of the older concerns.

By the 1860s, however, there had been troubling changes in the industry. Perhaps the earliest crisis was essentially historical: just as the industry was celebrating its centennial, a series of 99-year leases fell in, only to be renewed at much less favourable terms. The crises of the 1870s were still more serious, marking the beginning of the end of what was already the 'old' industrial world. Economic crisis now combined with coal strikes to weaken the iron industry. The Fothergill enterprises largely failed by 1880, and the Plymouth works closed (though its coal enterprises continued to be productive). Even more lethal was the technological revolution associated with the Bessemer process, and the transition from iron to steel. This had been introduced at Dowlais as early as 1856, but only some of the works had the will and capacity to invest and compete: Tredegar and Cyfarthfa lived on in the iron age until the installation of Bessemer converters as late as 1882 and 1884. By 1885, Wales was producing a combined total of 570,000 tons of Bessemer and Siemens steel, but from fewer centres than were to be found in the old iron country.

Even when the ironworks repaired their fortunes in subsequent years, the revival was deceptive. The industry had been located where it was because of the excellent supplies of coal and iron ore. However, it was rapidly becoming cheaper to import iron ore, and thus to locate iron and steel plants close to dock facilities. Rail transport then allowed the coal to be brought to the site of the furnace. Between 1869 and 1900, there had been a shift of the iron and steel industry to the coast, around ports like Swansea, Newport and Cardiff. In 1891, a new 'Dowlais Works' opened at East Moors, Cardiff. By 1900, there were 17 plants near the coast compared to 11 inland, and the process continued apace. Unfortunately, this made large industrial areas effectively obsolete, a fact that would become disastrously apparent in the new century. It was symbolic that when Sir Josiah Guest's grandson entered Parliament in 1906, he represented not historic Merthyr, but the still brasher boom city of Cardiff.

COAL

Of course, there was always more to industrial expansion than iron and steel; and of all the success stories of nineteenth century Wales, none could really compare with the dramatic expansion of coal. This was an ancient trade in many parts of Wales, though coal could only be mined commercially when seams lay near easy routes of communication. The most valuable eighteenth century seams were those within a few miles of the ports of Swansea and Neath. Other deposits were known, but these were regarded as so difficult to mine and transport that they were only for the use of people in the immediate vicinity. About 1700, the whole of Wales was producing perhaps 200,000 tons a year, with the north considerably in advance of the south. Matters might improve, for instance with the use of superior technology, but production seemed unlikely to rise significantly. At Cardiff in 1782, the customs report could state that 'we have no coal exported from this port, nor ever shall, as it would be too expensive to bring it down here from the internal part of the country'.

These prophecies were less than accurate. By 1870, the south Wales field produced 13.6 million tons of coal. At the height of the industry, in 1913, south Wales had increased its production to almost 57 million tons, a fifth of British production. Of this 70 per cent was exported (a much larger proportion than for other fields); and the coal industry directly employed perhaps a third of the male labour force of Wales. The figures are impressive, even in an age of dramatic growth, but even so they scarcely convey the extent to which Wales had come to be built on coal, in economic terms no less than geological South Wales in particular had become a society inextricably bound at every point to the mining, sale and shipping of coal. Wales also became increasingly important in total British production:[2]

2. Sidney Pollard, 'A new estimate of British coal production' *Economic history review* 33 (2), 1980.

A History of Modern Wales 1536–1990

Table 11:2   Welsh Coal Production 1750–1850

Date	Average annual coal production (million tons)		South Wales production as per cent of British total(approx)
	South Wales	North Wales	
1750–5	0.08	0.1	1.8
1781–5	0.5	0.2	6.2
1801–5	1.2	0.35	8.6
1821–5	2.5	0.45	11
1831–5	4	0.65	12.4
1841–5	5	1	12
1846–50	6.5	1.2	12.8

MARKETS

The Welsh coal industry was fortunate in the variety of its production. Initially, it offered the type of coal needed for coking to supply the early iron furnaces. This was what provided the impetus for the rapid growth of south Wales production after 1760, and the ironworks provided between a third and a half of the market for coal well into the mid-nineteenth century. When steamships came into their own from the 1830s, Welsh coal proved ideal for this purpose too and the maritime age of steam precisely coincided with the days of glory of Welsh coal. Steamship companies, navies and railway companies all provided essential markets. Other areas of Wales offered house-coal cleaner and less smoky than the traditional wares of northern England. When the iron and steel industry developed the hot blast process, the anthracite which this required was to be found abundantly in the western coalfields.

In other words, once the coal was made available for sale, the potential markets seemed limitless. In the 1830s and 1840s, the coal entrepreneurs succeeded in forging a direct link with the vital market of London, which had previously been the preserve of the Newcastle men. In 1828, Robert Thomas opened at Abercanaid (near Merthyr) the first pit aimed explicitly at this market, and his widow Lucy Thomas pioneered sales in London. In 1840, John Nixon secured the coal contract for the French navy. Cardiff was soon exporting to a major French market, re-establishing a connection at least as old as the days of Queen Anne. Coal exports tripled between 1828 and 1834.

224

TRANSPORTATION

But before coal could be raised or sold, there had to be an assurance that it could be transported to a place where it was in demand. Since the early years of the century, the coming of canals served to make coal-ports of Newport and Cardiff. Until 1834, further development was thwarted by the export duties levied on coal shipped from all ports except Newport. By this time, south Wales was exporting perhaps a million tons each year, overwhelmingly for sale for domestic heating. But to meet the needs of the new markets opened by Nixon and the rest, much more capacity was required, and this was provided by the expansion of the port of Cardiff. In 1839, the Marquess of Bute promoted the building here of the Bute West Dock, which seemed at the time a speculative venture. Its cost – £350,000 – seemed an incredible figure, but it was quite in keeping with the spirit of the time and the buccaneering history of the Bute family. And the gamble paid off magnificently, as prosperity was assured by the opening of the Taff Vale Railway (TVR) of 1841. This proved to be the crucial and long-sought link between Cardiff and Merthyr Tydfil. By 1845, Aberdare was added to the network, and by 1856 Cardiff became part of a network linking south Wales to southern England. From 1854, the Rhymney railway permitted the Monmouthshire coalfields to help feed the growing demand.

The port and railways opened the coal valleys to the markets of Europe and the world. In 1841, the TVR carried 41,000 tons of coal; the figure grew to 594,000 tons by 1850, 2.13 million by 1860. Cardiff's success seemed assured, inevitable, perhaps eternal. In the decade after 1856, the flow of coal from the uplands had become so substantial that no less than three new dock developments were opened: the Bute East, Roath Basin and Penarth, all linked to the Taff Vale line. It was in 1870 that Cardiff's population finally overtook that of Merthyr Tydfil, that once startling product of what already seemed a rather primitive age of industrialisation. By 1907, there was a further dock named after Queen Alexandra, in what was now the city of Cardiff.

By this stage, even upstart Cardiff had been challenged for supremacy in the coal trade by the still less probable boom-town of Barry. From 1884, a group of coal owners and shipping magnates led by John Cory and David Davies of Llandinam sought to free themselves of the Bute family stranglehold on the coal trade. This insurrection resulted in the creation of new docks at Barry (1889), linked to the mining areas by new railways. As a coal-port, Barry had actually overtaken Cardiff by 1913. Together, the three ports of Cardiff, Barry and Penarth were then handling an outgoing tonnage equal to that of either London or Liverpool.

The booming market for Welsh coal led to the exploitation of new geographical areas, initially at Aberdare and the Cynon valley, and later in the Rhondda valleys. In the mid–1830s, Crawshay Bailey had bought up land in the valleys south and west of Merthyr, including property in the Rhondda as well as the Aberaman estate at Aberdare. With Sir Josiah Guest, he was a prime sponsor of the rail link to the TVR. Together with the new technologies that permitted the sinking of ever deeper pits, the railway made Aberdare yet another Welsh boom town.

It was natural that Aberdare should experience early exploitation. Lying immediately west of Merthyr Tydfil, its resources were detected early, and the lands purchased by men who often had links with Merthyr and its iron industry. Matthew Wayne had served Richard Crawshay as manager, and had been a partner in the Nantyglo enterprise. In 1827, he developed an iron works at Aberdare, for which he used the canal link to Cardiff. In 1837, Matthew and his son Thomas reached the 'four foot seam' of coal here, and they began the 'Merthyr-Aberdare Steam Coal Co.' By 1846, the company raised some 48,000 tons.

Also from the Merthyr middle class was Samuel Thomas, a shopkeeper who began prospecting for coal in 1842. By 1849, he was a partner in the Ysgubor Wen pit; and his enterprises so prospered that they became the core of the legendary Cambrian Combine, which would dominate the industry at the turn of the century. His son, David A. Thomas, was a millionaire who entered the peerage in 1915 as Lord Rhondda. Perhaps the most successful of the new men was Thomas Powell, who began operating in the Gelligaer area in 1829. From 1840, he moved the centre of his activities to Aberdare, where the Duffryn colliery was in operation by 1844. By the time of his death in 1863, he owned 16 collieries. In 1864, Sir George Elliot built these enterprises into the Powell Duffryn Company, which came to dominate the Aberdare valley.

THE RHONDDA

The potential of the Rhondda had long been realised, but transportation difficulties made it uncertain when (if ever) the region might be exploited. In 1800, this was the parish of Ystradyfodwg, a classically remote Welsh area, largely free of the influence of squires and parsons. In the heart of the region, the traveller Benjamin Malkin was lyrical in his description of Llwyn-y-Pia, with its 'pure transparent stream . . . stately and aspiring cliffs':

> Hereabouts, and for some miles to come, there is a degree of luxuriance in the valley, infinitely beyond what my entrance on this district led me to expect. The contrast of the meadows, rich and verdant, with mountains the most wild and romantic, surrounding them on every side, is in the highest degree picturesque.

But already, there were portents of the transformation made famous in popular culture by Richard Llewellyn's novel *How green was my valley*. In 1807, Walter Coffin sank a pit at Dinas Rhondda, and used the canal to market his production. His operations expanded greatly after 1832, with the opening of the new markets for Welsh coal. By the early 1850s, there were new collieries around Treherbert; and a rail link followed in 1856. However, the real expansion began in the 1860s, with the worldwide demand for steam coal. In 1860, Archibald Hood sank pits at Gilfach Goch in the Ely Valley, and at Llwyn-y-Pia itself, laying the foundation for the later Glamorgan Coal Company. There would be 30 pits in the valleys by 1870.

In 1864, David Davies leased large areas of the Rhondda, and opened coal works at Parc and Maendy. These marked a breakthrough because Rhondda coal was deeper than was customary for the mining technology of the day. The collieries here penetrated ever further underground. Whereas pits 100 yards deep had once been noteworthy, 200 yards was achieved by 1876, 500 by 1913. Between 1868 and 1885, Davies initiated some of the best known Rhondda collieries, which became part of the Ocean Coal Company (1887), with capital of £800,000. D.A. Thomas was also active in the 1870s, founding the Clydach Vale colliery; and in 1874 he struck the six-foot seam.

Other pioneers here included William T. Lewis, who had married the granddaughter of Lucy Thomas. In the 1870s, Lewis opened the 'Lewis Merthyr' pits in the lower Rhondda, and his combination of business drive and political skill made him the effective chieftain of the coal owners for decades. He also acted as the agent and representative of the Bute estate. Like the Thomases at Cambrian, he too gained a peerage: in this case, as Lord Merthyr (1911).

Several of the Rhondda pits were acquired after 1868 by the Cory brothers, powerful Cardiff ship owners, as part of their scheme to establish a worldwide network of coal depots and agencies: there were 80 bunkers by the time of John Cory's death in 1910. Thus the affairs of Cardiff and Pentre were ultimately shaped by the events in the imperial sphere; in this case, the opening of the Suez Canal. By 1869, south Wales was exporting some two million tons a year to France and the Mediterranean lands; plus over a million tons to destinations as far afield as Africa, the Americas and the Far East. In 1911, the leading recipients of Welsh coal exports were France, Italy, Egypt, Argentina and Brazil. At this point, south Wales was the source of roughly a third of the world's coal trade.

The exploitation of the Welsh coalfields is symbolised by the successive emergence of several great ports, each acting as an outlet for the mineral-rich hinterland. Swansea occupied this role in the eighteenth century, and was followed by Newport, Cardiff and (to a lesser extent) Barry. In the later nineteenth century, the emergence of the Rhondda was paralleled by the growth of mining in eastern Carmarthenshire, the Aman and Gwendraeth valleys, which found their outlet to the sea at Swansea and Llanelli. These coalfields had been known and exploited in the eighteenth century, but the new hunger of industry for anthracite stimulated demand enormously. By 1913, Welsh anthracite production approached five million tons. As the western collieries developed, so did the new towns and villages of the area, like Ammanford, Pontardawe and Gowerton.

The expansion of coal mining after 1840 transformed a Welsh economy still barely accustomed to the growth of iron. The Rhondda surpassed previous achievements, producing two million tons of coal by 1876, but 9.6 million by 1913. The coalfields in Glamorgan alone employed 38,000 men in 1861; 117,000 in 1891; and a remarkable 220,000 by 1911. The 'Welsh Miner' had become an inevitable stereotype. Welsh business and labour, transport and towns, banks and retailing – all had come to depend to some extent on coal.

THE SOUTH WALES METAL INDUSTRIES

The industrial complex of south Wales was not confined to iron and coal. As we have seen, the west Glamorgan industries had been based on copper and non-ferrous metals from the early eighteenth century. Businesses were drawn here by the easy access to coal near the coast, in an area of relatively cheap labour. Swansea was a metal town into the twentieth century, and west Glamorgan industries including the smelting of copper, lead, zinc; and a brass foundry. Less commonplace materials included cobalt and arsenic. By the mid-nineteenth century, the Swansea copper industry had become a major producer of sulphuric acid, which in turn attracted other industries. In 1902, this was the key factor in Ludwig Mond's decision to establish a nickel works at Clydach; by 1914, the plant employed some 850 workers.

Non-ferrous ores initially came from the British Isles, from Cornwall, Cardiganshire or Ireland; but from the 1820s, Swansea was increasingly the centre of a world empire, receiving shipments from many countries, from Chile, Africa and Australia. As Cornish miners reached new destinations around the world, the ores they found followed the historic route to Swansea. The industry reached its height in the 1880s, when 60 per cent of copper ores bought to Great Britain came to Swansea. This was perhaps the worst of the industrial areas in terms of social impact, as non-ferrous smelting produced a great deal of smoke and pollutants, leaving a heritage that was only starting to be cleared in the mid-twentieth century; but the trade employed 3000 or so hands at any given time. It also permitted Swansea port to enjoy some glorious decades.

Also vital for south Wales was the tinplate industry. In the early eighteenth century, the trade had had its capital at Pontypool. Even by the 1750s, there were only four tinplate works – two each in the counties of Monmouth and Carmarthen – and the industry long continued to be a south Wales speciality. Production rose in the same dizzying spirals we have come to expect from the examples of iron and coal. In 1805 4000 tons were produced by south Wales, 37,000 tons by 1850, and 68 per cent of the latter was exported. Most of this was destined for the canning industry of the United States.

An already vigorous industry was revolutionised (that word again) by the discovery in 1866 of a new technique for rolling plates, and the use of steel rather than charcoal bar iron. In 1875 the Siemens works of Landore near Swansea found that its open-hearth steel was perfect for the new type of tinplate, and this marked a new stage in the concentration of the industry in west Glamorgan. Access to Siemens steel also stimulated the growth of tinplate works in the area. By 1875, 57 of 77 tinplate works in Great Britain were to be found in south Wales; by 1891, the figure was 86 out of 98.

In 1882, the export trade in tinplate was the main incentive for the new Prince of Wales dock in Swansea. In 1889, 430,000 tons of Welsh tinplate were exported, 77 per cent of it to the United States.

Unfortunately, this reliance on overseas markets made the industry vulnerable to international politics. In 1890, the McKinley Tariff effectively closed the American door to British tinplate. This achieved a political victory by simultaneously wrecking the prosperity of the Welsh industry, and forcing Welsh workers to migrate to the new plants being established in the United States. A severe depression followed, but matters improved after 1901. By the outbreak of war in 1914, Welsh production stood at 848,000 tons. The tinplate boom contributed both to the realignment in the steel industry, and the new emphasis on coastal sites near ports.

THE NEW CORPORATIONS

The industrial might of south Wales created the opportunity for a new kind of commercial and political power quite different from the personal autocracy exercised by a William Crawshay. In iron and steel, the latter part of the century was marked by the growth of corporate giants marked by vertical integration: the Ebbw Vale Steel, Iron and Coal Co; Baldwins; and Guest Keen. This last emerged from the old Guest enterprise, now directed by Lord Wimborne. Guest Keen merged with Nettlefolds in 1903; and the new giant GKN controlled not only Dowlais but the troubled Cyfarthfa works. The conglomerate had an issued capital in excess of £4.5 million. In tinplate, the greatest of the Victorian entrepreneurs was Richard Thomas, a classic self-made man of enormous drive and independence; but shortly after his death in 1916, 'Richard Thomas and Sons' became a public company.

Equally symbolic in their way were the Mond family, originally German Jewish immigrants. Ludwig Mond founded the corporations Mond Nickel and Brunner, Mond (chemicals), which were both massively expanded by his son Sir Alfred (from 1928, Lord Melchett). Sir Alfred Mond's Amalgamated Anthracite dominated the western coalfields in the early twentieth century, and the family had interests in gas. This economic power had political manifestations, as Sir Alfred was Liberal MP for Swansea from 1910 to 1923, and Carmarthenshire 1924–1928. In 1926, Brunner, Mond became the core of the new cartel, Imperial Chemical Industries, in which Mond served as first chairman.

The coal industry had long been ruled by powerful individuals like W. T. Lewis, perhaps the closest that Victorian Wales came to producing a robber baron in the American mould. The turn of the century boom was directed by a large number of colliery companies, with 214 owning Glamorgan mines in 1913; but the vast majority of the wealth was in the hands of a few giant corporations, like Powell Duffryn, Ocean, Lewis Merthyr, the Cambrian, GKN and Cory Brothers. In 1913, the ten largest Glamorgan corporations controlled 75 collieries with half the county's coal production, and employed almost 80,000 men. D.A. Thomas had for several years followed a deliberate plan of forming a multi-million pound coal combine to parallel the various cartels emerging in the contemporary United States. Between 1906 and 1910, he acquired the Glamorgan Coal Company, the Naval pits and the Britannic Merthyr. Under various names, the Lewis, Thomas and Davies enterprises controlled the Rhondda into the 1930s and beyond.

These new trusts confirmed the contemporary view of the region as 'American Wales'. The new goliaths could also take unpopular decisions affecting communities, an important ability at a time when so many concerns were relocating. In political terms, the growth of impersonal corporations tended to undermine the traditions of class collaboration that were so strong in the years of Liberal political domination.

OTHER REGIONS

The economy of nineteenth century Wales may have been based on iron and coal, but there was much other activity. The traditional lead industry flourished in north Cardiganshire in the mid-nineteenth century, and there was a mid-century boom with the working of the Frongoch mine. In the century after 1760, the ports of west Wales flourished on the strength of a diverse trade in textiles, slate, lead and copper. The Pembrokeshire coalfields were at their height in the mid-nineteenth century, with a thriving export trade from the new port of Saundersfoot.

This passage – from a government report at the end of the century – suggests the diversity of the economy about 1832[3]

Most of the chief towns of Wales had some special industry of their own that gave employment to a large proportion of their inhabitants. Thus,

3. Quoted in Trevor Herbert and Gareth E. Jones, *Wales 1880–1914* (Cardiff 1988), 33.

hats were largely made at Carmarthen and Monmouth, boots at Narberth, Haverfordwest and Lampeter, and stockings, knitted gloves and caps (called Welsh wigs) at Bala. Amlwch had its tobacco manufactories and Llanerchymedd was famous for snuff and boots. Most famous of all was Swansea for its porcelain and china, an industry which was also carried on at Nantgarw in another part of the county of Glamorgan. The town of Holywell was remarkable for activity in various manufactures, there being in 1831, 256 males, upwards of twenty years of age, employed in the manufacture of silk and cotton goods, in making paper, and manufacturing iron, copper, brass and lead. Mold, at the same time, had 230 men employed in the cotton manufacture.

The emphasis on textiles is important. New technological advances were influential in this area, including the use of water power, canals, and devices such as the spinning jenny. Dolgellau became the home of several mills; while the flannel manufacture of Newtown made it 'the Leeds of Wales'. Limestone was quarried in various regions, especially in the north-east. The mid-century rail boom also provided many construction jobs in the vast building site that was Wales. The railways themselves employed 20,000 workers by 1901.

However, it was this very transportation boom that tended to undermine industries in much of Wales, by providing highly efficient competition, for textiles in particular. From the 1860s, the profitable flannel trade moved its centre of activity to Teifiside, where it remained until the 1920s. After 1870, there was also a steep decline in the lead and silver enterprises of mid-Wales, and the copper of Anglesey. The success of rail virtually destroyed coastal shipping operations on which so many local enterprises had depended. Many older industries faded in the latter part of the century.

THE NORTH-EAST

It was in the north-east that there developed a heavy industrial zone most comparable to Glamorgan or Monmouth, with well-developed coal and iron enterprises in existence by the seventeenth century. And although the region was already dwarfed by the expansion of Aberdare, the northern coalfields around Wrexham were producing in excess of a million tons a year by the 1840s; a figure rising to three million tons by the end of the century. In 1848, Flint had 'extensive collieries' employing 8000 men.[4] The Mostyn/Mostyn Quay area

4. *Parry's railway companion from Chester to Holyhead* (reprinted by E. and W. Books, 1970), 39–53.

had several pits, producing some 70,000 tons of coal a year. There were important iron and steel undertakings, such as the iron empire of the Wilkinson family at Bersham. In the 1880s, it was at Brymbo (and not in the south) where there was erected the first furnace in Wales to apply the new basic open hearth technology. Other ironworks stood at Cefn Mawr and Acrefair.

Industry led to urbanisation. Involvement in iron and coal made Wrexham a real industrial centre, which also carried on trades like brewing and (from the 1870s) brickmaking. The canalisation of the Dee led to the growth of Connah's Quay at the expense of older river ports, and to the ultimate emergence of a series of industrial communities around the new centre: Shotton, Hawarden Bridge, Queensferry and others. In 1896, the opening of John Summers' Iron Works appeared to secure the continued industrialisation of Middle Deeside.

Flintshire possessed an admirably diversified economy. Textile mills were in existence at Holywell and Greenfield by the 1780s. Earthenware, tiles and firebricks were made at Buckley and exported through Connah's Quay: in fact, the towns were linked by a horse-drawn railway as early as 1790. Non-ferrous industries were crucial to the local economy. Halkyn mountain had been a prime source of the Grosvenor family fortune since Stuart times, and at Mold, we hear in 1848 that 'the lead mines in this locality have been exceedingly prolific'. The Milwr mine near Holywell was equally valuable. The industry here (which employed several thousands) bore many resemblances to conditions in and around Swansea. At Bagillt, there were 'very extensive' collieries and lead works by the 1840s, and this became a smelting centre for ore from Ireland, the Isle of Man and much of Wales. The Flintshire smelters made perhaps a quarter of all British lead. In the 1840s, the lead-ore markets both at Flint and Holywell were the most important of their kind in Britain. Only after 1880 did the area encounter difficulty, with the continued growth of Swansea and the influx of cheap overseas ores. As in the south, non-ferrous industries diversified to include copper, zinc and brass. They also led to chemical enterprises such as the making of vitriol at Holywell and Flint. This was the basis for the later production of synthetics, and Courtaulds were manufacturing rayon at Flint by 1917.

SLATE

The production of slate well deserves the title of 'revolutionary' industrial activity. Slate had long been worked in the counties of Caernarvon and Merioneth, but on a small scale and localised basis. From the 1780s, Richard Pennant transformed the industry by imposing his personal direction. Leases of slate-rich land were called in, and the quarries were worked directly. By the end of the century, 12,000 tons a year were being exported through the port of Bangor. Apart from roofing, Welsh slate was also used for writing materials in schools. Pennant's success stimulated other entrepreneurs: also in the 1780s, the Assheton Smith family developed the Dinorwic quarries, while a host of smaller adventurers reorganised Merioneth-shire quarries like Ffestiniog and Nantlle.

The mid-century expansion of rail and port facilities permitted an export orientation comparable to that of south Wales coal. At the height of production, in 1898, the north Wales quarries were producing half a million tons annually. A series of bitter strikes and lockouts at the turn of the century paralysed the industry, and production by 1914 was only half this. However, the industry was vital for Gwynedd. About 1870, slate accounted for perhaps a quarter of the total value of property and profits in the region; and the industry employed up to 14,000 men. The profits of families like the Pennants and the Assheton Smiths made them industrial magnates on a par with southerners like Lords Rhondda or Merthyr.

A WELSH DIMENSION?

A number of reasons can be suggested for the importance of Welsh industries: abundant mineral resources located near good ports; the financial facilities offered by Bristol, Chester and Liverpool; accessibility of skilled labour in Cornwall and Shropshire; wealthy landowners with a highly entrepreneurial outlook. Overall, geo-graphical determinism seems crucial. Given the new technology of smelting iron by means of coke, the valleys of the eastern coalfield were a natural enough setting for future concentrations of industrial plants. Population and communications followed that imperative. From the mid-eighteenth century, two key elements were added: new patterns of demand (from war) and sources of mercantile capital from Bristol and Liverpool. Thereafter, there was rapid movement

234

towards takeoff.

But there is still one piece of the explanation that appears to be missing, and which requires explanation or at least comment. Briefly, was there really no 'Welsh dimension' to these events? Apart from the question of geographical accident, there would appear to be none. Nothing in Welsh society predisposed the local community to favour industry, except in that upland Wales had a 'pastoral-industrial' society common to much of northern and western Britain. Nothing about Welsh social structure made local elites particularly enthusiastic or reluctant to develop their estates, or to cooperate with progressive outsiders. It is true that cultural changes during the eighteenth century had tended to separate the upper classes from their inferiors in terms of language, religion and economic outlook; but it remains to be seen whether the gulf between classes in Wales was any wider than that which separated rich and poor in Hampshire or Lancashire.

The process of early industrialisation in Wales suggests a society essentially homogeneous to that of England, remarkably so when we consider the linguistic barrier. Wales was not an early pioneer of industry because it was Welsh; but it became far more Welsh in consequence of these changes, above all, because of the emergence of Welsh urban centres.

CHAPTER TWELVE
Consequences

The growth of industry radically changed Welsh society, and not merely in the regions that now came to rely directly on the world of iron, coal and steam. Demographic change provides the most obvious index of this transformation. Between 1801 and 1851, the population of Wales rose from 587,000 to 1.16 million, with a further increase to 2.66 million by 1921. The growth in the first half of the nineteenth century represented an average rate of almost 15 per cent per decade. In the following 70 years, the rate of increase fell somewhat, but to a still impressive 12.5 per cent. The largest per centage increase throughout the period occurred with the coal boom between 1901 and 1911, when population growth exceeded 20 per cent. The number of individuals added in this decade alone was roughly equivalent to what the total population had been in 1700. To give some idea of the rate of expansion, let us imagine that the nineteenth century rate had continued unchecked after 1921. Wales today would have some 6.4 million people, instead of the three million of reality. Only the economic disasters of the 1920s and 1930s stopped this miraculous increase.

By far the greatest part of the increase was in the two most heavily industrialised counties Glamorgan and Monmouthshire. These together had 116,000 people in 1801, 389,000 in 1851, 1.52 million in 1911 – respectively 20, 33 and 63 per cent of the total Welsh population. This growth was impressive even by the standards of the Industrial Revolution. Monmouthshire, with an average decennial increase of 28 per cent in the first half of the century, achieved the notable feat of approaching the rates of the contemporary United States. Glamorgan's days of glory arrived slightly later. The county had half a million people by 1881, and exceeded 1.1 million by 1911: almost half the population of Wales.

But growth was not confined to the south-east. Between 1670 and 1801, early industrialisation actually had its sharpest impact in the north and west, on mineral-rich counties like Cardiganshire and Anglesey, both of which more than doubled their numbers. Carmarthen and Flint followed closely; while the rate of increase in Glamorgan and Monmouth was barely up to the overall average for the whole country. Between 1801 and 1851, Glamorgan and Monmouth showed much the most impressive performance, but all regions recorded substantial population growth: between 40 and 80 per cent in ten counties, and almost 30 per cent even in Radnorshire. Breconshire's rate of increase was a striking 90 per cent. Moreover, this growth coincided with substantial emigration before 1860, the United States being the favoured destination.

Matters changed after 1850, with the ascendancy of coal. In the second half of the century, the growth of Welsh population was equally impressive, but it was much more localized. At the summit, again, were Glamorgan and Monmouth. Below them came a second tier of counties with substantial industrial and population growth: Carmarthen, Denbigh, Flint and Caernarvon. Between 1851 and 1911, each of these recorded a population increase between 30 and 55 per cent. Finally, there were the remaining seven counties, predominantly rural, which experienced no growth. Six had a net population loss between these dates, and in three cases (Anglesey, Cardigan and Montgomery) the loss was severe, of the order of 10 or 20 per cent.

Many thousands migrated from the farms to the industrial valleys and towns: perhaps half a million left for Glamorgan and Monmouthshire between 1850 and 1911. It was after 1851 that the enormous disparities between the industrial and rural regions became most apparent, with all that implied for cultural divergence. And although counties have been used as the unit of analysis here, growth was usually concentrated in particular areas of a shire. In Carmarthenshire, the highly industrial south-east of the county was linked to a rural upland core.

The attraction of the south meant that Wales did not experience a net loss through migration. In fact, this was the only area of the British Isles to experience net immigration between 1860 and 1914. Welsh emigration, similarly, was of a very different character from that of other regions of Britain or Ireland. Much of it occurred within Britain, often to London and Liverpool. Also, the technical skills of the industrial workers made them a highly prized commodity, who were actively sought in regions seeking to create new manufactures, as in Teesside and in the north-eastern USA. By 1891, there were at least 228,000 Welsh people in England; another 100,000 in the United States.

URBANISATION

By the early nineteenth century, we can even perceive true urban growth, a real novelty for Wales. Even at the end of the eighteenth century, no Welsh town had more than 10,000 people, and the largest communities were 12 centres with between two and eight thousand.[1] In 1801, the four towns of Cardiff, Swansea, Merthyr and Newport had only 18,000 between them; by 1921, the combined total was 530,000. Growth was dramatic in the earlier part of the century: Swansea had almost 7000 people in 1801, 34,000 by 1861; Newport had 1400 people in 1801, 25,000 by 1861.

The earliest changes affected the area where the uplands of Glamorgan and Monmouthshire met, in the four historic parishes of Merthyr Tydfil, Aberdare, Bedwellty and Aberystruth. The last two had 2200 people in 1801, 34,000 by 1841. There were towns in the area, around iron centres like Tredegar, Ebbw Vale, Beaufort, Nantyglo and Blaina; but the Monmouthshire hills did not evolve an entirely new city. Glamorgan, on the other hand, experienced the rapid growth of a real town at Merthyr Tydfil. This developed a flourishing popular culture, and a class structure far removed from that of traditional society.

Merthyr had a dramatic impact on the wider community, as a magnet for immigrants, a hub of communications, and a market for agricultural produce. Merthyr and Dowlais combined had 7700 people by 1801, 46,000 by 1851: an average growth rate of over 43 per cent per decade. By 1913, Merthyr had 84,000 people. It was only one of a series of new Welsh cities, but it attracted most attention because it was the first to develop outside a corporate or manorial framework of the sort we find at Newport or Swansea. It was thus something new, though it was soon followed by a series of other upstart towns, like Aberdare after 1840 or Barry after 1890.

---

1. In 1801, the largest towns in Wales were Swansea, Carmarthen, Wrexham and Merthyr Tydfil. In the second rank, we find Brecon, Haverfordwest, Caernarvon, Denbigh, Aberystwyth, Dolgellau, Welshpool and Holywell.

During the 1840s alone, Aberdare's population grew by 132 per cent, to reach 15,000.

At a lower level, it would scarcely be possible to list the many southern communities that merely doubled their population in the first half of the century. Below the triumphs of Merthyr and Swansea, there were many lesser success stories, at Pontypool, Neath, Llanelli, Pontypridd, Caerphilly and so on. Even smaller towns might have a quite disproportionate influence on a historically rural area. In Gwynedd, the slate communities of Bethesda and the Ffestiniog area were puny by southern standards, but they represented urban growth on a scale that was startling for the pastoral north.

Today, there are 19 Welsh towns with populations in excess of 25,000. Of these, 16 are located in Glamorgan or Gwent, with one (Llanelli) a few miles over the Dyfed border; and Wrexham and Colwyn Bay representing the north. This was a geography that would have been utterly foreign to an observer from 1800, but quite familiar to his successor in 1890. By the end of the nineteenth century, Wales had achieved something very like its modern urban structure.

COAL AND URBANISATION

From the 1840s, the rapid urbanisation of south Wales was predominantly a response to the soaring fortunes of the coal industry. In 1801, Cardiff had scarcely 2000 people, while there were perhaps 1000 more in the rural communities of Barry and Ystradyfodwg (essentially the Rhondda valley). By 1901, the three communities had a combined population well in excess of 300,000; and there seemed no likelihood that these intoxicating trends would slow in the foreseeable future. In 1841, Cardiff had 10,000 people, but it was the rail link and the new dock which launched it to even greater heights than Merthyr had ever known. The population grew as follows:

$$1861 - 33,000$$
$$1881 - 83,000$$
$$1901 - 164,000$$
$$1921 - 200,000$$

Urban growth at this rate had an economic impact of its own, in terms of employment in construction, and demand for materials like bricks, slate and lead, all obtainable from Welsh industries. In addition to its housing needs, Cardiff was also the first Welsh town to erect public buildings appropriate for the major city it proposed to become, with the splendid complex at Cathay's Park. By 1905, Cardiff was declared a city, at a time when even Merthyr was struggling for borough status.

The population of Rhondda had grown even more rapidly than Cardiff's. There were under 1000 people in the Rhondda in 1851; 17,000 by 1870; 114,000 by 1901. By 1911, the population had swollen to 153,000. If Rhondda had been a true city, it would soon have been challenging Cardiff for pre-eminence in Wales. The country would then have been dominated by two mushrooming communities both utterly dependent on coal; and in their ways, both as much frontier boom towns as San Francisco or Melbourne. But the wider impact of the new Rhondda was strictly circumscribed by geography. Even at its height, this area was in reality a maze of overgrown villages, like Treorchi, Ystrad, Tonypandy, Ferndale, Tylorstown, Maerdy and the rest.

The Rhondda demonstrates, albeit to an extreme degree, the nature of the new urban expansion. It was a society of migrants, often far removed from their geographical roots: in 1911, only 58 per cent of the Rhondda's people had been born in Glamorgan. The rest of Wales supplied 19 per cent, England 7 per cent. A sixth of the population was drawn from 'elsewhere', from Ireland and Scotland, but also Spain, Italy and other lands. The community was disproportionately young and male. Between 1880 and 1914, males generally comprised at least 55 per cent of the population, the level that had also prevailed in the iron districts of the 1830s. As befitted a young society, the new communities had extremely high birth rates. In 1840, it had been claimed that Tredegar was a town of 7000 people, 1500 of whom were under seven years of age. The Rhondda's birth rate in 1911 was nearly 36 per thousand. This was equivalent to the rates once common in mid-century Britain, but long since declined in other regions. The Rhondda, like Aberdare or Merthyr before it, bore all the signs of a frontier community.

THE NEW SOCIETY

Such a picture suggests that the new Wales was a relatively simple society based entirely on the stratification of heavy industry. There were indeed areas where masters, iron-workers and miners comprised a large proportion of the population, and the middle classes were chiefly noticeable by their absence. This was often remarked in the social surveys following the political turbulence of the 1830s, which was in part blamed on the lack of subtler social gradations. But the new towns soon evolved the complex structures appropriate to a more advanced economy. This is suggested by the distribution of employment in Glamorgan in 1901:[2]

Table 12:1 The Distribution of Employment in Glamorgan in 1901

Type of work	Number employed (thousands)	Per cent of total labour force
Group A		
Mines and quarries	108	31
Conveyance of men, goods and messages	39	11
Metals, machines, implements and conveyances	38	11
Building and construction	21	6
Other, general and undefined workers	21	6
Subtotal	227	65%
Group B		
Domestic offices or servants	32	9
Food, tobacco, drink and lodging	21	6
Dress	20	6
Professional occupations	14	4
Commercial occupations	12	3.4
Agricultural	10	3
Textile fabrics	4.4	1.2
General or local government	3.6	1
Subtotal	117	33.6%

Of 353,000 employed, 64 per cent can be categorised in one of the group A occupations, which includes those working in industries like mining; iron, tinplate and non-ferrous metals; docks and railways; or building (the 'general' category must include many in these sectors). This emphasis is exactly what we might expect given the time and place, as is the limited importance of agriculture; but

2. A.H. John ed., *Glamorgan county history* (Cardiff 1980) v, 358.

more surprising is the strength of services and retailing, and of newer industries. The occupations listed in Group B accounted for a third of employment in Glamorgan (as well as 93 per cent of the 63,000 female workers). Domestic servants accounted for the fourth largest work category. Some certainly worked for landowners and squires, but there were only 60 or so of these families in the county at this time. The existence of this army of domestics therefore suggests the existence of a middle class with the means and will to employ them.

The professional and commercial classes were chiefly concentrated in the newer urban centres. Middle class communities established themselves as the economic booms began to consolidate the prosperity of the successive 'frontier' towns. The 'shopocracy' was a potent force in Merthyr by the 1830s, when they were the particular beneficiaries of the 1832 parliamentary reform. At this time, there were perhaps 16 towns in Wales with at least a core (15 or more individuals) active in law or medicine: ten of these were to be found south of Brecon, where Swansea and Carmarthen were the most important centres. By 1881, civilisation had gone so far in Merthyr as to offer

> some regular, well-built streets, a court-house, a market house, several elegant private residences, a large number of respectable shops, four churches, and not fewer than 36 dissenting chapels.[3]

Welsh banks began to emerge from about 1770, initially in the traditional service centres like Brecon and Cowbridge, but increasingly in the expanding towns like Cardiff, Merthyr, Newport and Swansea. In north Wales, the link to industry was quite clear. The 'Chester and North Wales Bank' was the creation of the Williams family, the Parys Mountain tycoons, together with the Holywell smelters. The scale of early enterprises, north or south, is hard to gauge. According to census data, there were only 11 individuals in the banking profession in Glamorgan by 1861, but this soon changed. Including brokers and insurance agents, the financial professions employed over 740 individuals in the county by 1911.

The shift to a coal-based economy also placed a new emphasis on commerce and export, and on the professional elites of trading towns like Cardiff, Barry and Swansea. In 1908, a *Contemporary Biography* listed 400 or so of the leading figures in south Wales. About 140 of these were nobles, gentry or magistrates. Almost 60 of the remainder were lawyers, the largest group of whom (14) came from Cardiff

3. T. Herbert and G.E. Jones, *People and protest: Wales 1815–1880* (Cardiff 1988), 28.

and Barry. The distinguished professionals also included a large contingent of doctors, as well as mining engineers and accountants. They were heavily concentrated in the great towns of Glamorgan and (to a lesser extent) Monmouthshire; and they increasingly filled the public offices that once characterised the landed gentry. The emergence of a substantial middle class is suggested by the spread of wealthy suburbs around towns like Swansea and Cardiff, and the creation of new communities like Penarth. There was also a strong middle class in the resort and retirement communities; and minor clusters in the new university centres.

Throughout Wales, the professional class swelled in numbers during the century, often as a result of the expansion of local trade and industry. Dr Merfyn Jones has remarked on the limited impact of slate production in developing an indigenous middle class in Caernarvonshire; but even here, there were in 1891 no less than 360 doctors, lawyers and accountants, as well as 1500 teachers and 381 nonconformist clergy. In the south, with its more diverse economy and larger towns, the middle class was accordingly stronger.

TRANSPORTATION

Welsh urbanisation marked a sharp departure from older traditions; equally revolutionary was the development of new forms of transportation in the industrial era. Wales has always been characterised by difficult internal communications and dispersed settlement – in fact, the country owed its survival as a distinct entity to this very inaccessibility. Between 1790 and 1870, changes in transportation laid the foundations for a thorough realignment of Welsh society; for new relationships with England, and perhaps for greater unity within the land of Wales itself.

Road improvements began in the 1750s, with connections spreading out from Shrewsbury to the leading towns of mid- and north Wales, such as Wrexham, Welshpool and Mold, and the emergence of turnpikes in the south. The scale of activity is suggested by the work of William Edwards, a Dissenting minister and bridge builder, whose single arch span at Pontypridd attained European celebrity. He continued in employment across south Wales through the latter half of the century. Between 1815 and 1826, Telford rebuilt the turnpike road from Shrewsbury to Bangor and Holyhead, via Chirk, Corwen and Bettws-y-Coed. This involved some impressive engineering achievements, such as the Conway suspension bridge of 1822–26. Between 1819 and 1826, the Menai bridge was spanned by the first large scale iron suspension bridge.

Sometimes, the incentive for improvement can be seen as a near-desperate response by industrialists anxious to link remote eyries in the Welsh uplands with markets and with raw materials. In 1767, it was Anthony Bacon who sponsored the development of a new road from Cardiff to Merthyr Tydfil. Canals promised a much more effective solution to the dilemma of transporting heavy cargoes. In 1766, the first Welsh canal was built at Kidwelly, though there was then a lengthy delay before a building boom got under way. Between 1789 and 1794, eight separate canals were projected and built, with a total length of 128 miles. Naturally enough, all were located in the powerhouse region of the south-east, roughly between Swansea, Brecon and Newport. Crucial to industrial development were the Monmouthshire and Glamorganshire canals, as well as the routes along the Swansea and Neath valleys. Between 1810 and 1820, mid-Wales and the north east were the centres of activity, with the creation of the Brecon and Abergavenny (1811), the Montgomeryshire (1819) and the Ellesmere canal (1819).

But it was the railways that had the most striking effect on Welsh society. Three main phases can be traced. In the first, the key areas of the Welsh economy developed local lines, chiefly in response to urgent industrial demand. As early as 1829, there had been schemes to build rail links to the mineral resources of the Bute estate, and the expansion of the sale-coal trade brought pressure from entrepreneurs like Thomas Powell. After many abortive schemes and false starts, rail-building began in earnest between 1838 to 1848. Cardiff was linked to Merthyr by the Taff Vale line, subsequently extended to Aberdare. Swansea was connected to Pontardulais; and there was building in the Llanelli area. In the north east, Ruabon was linked to Shrewsbury and Chester; and a local line connected the Ffestiniog slate quarries to the sea at Portmadoc.

The second phase, between 1849 and 1856, was marked by the completion of the east-west routes. In 1847, the South Wales Railroad Company was formed (it became part of the Great Western in 1863). The southern line from Newport to Cardiff and Swansea was completed by 1850, and subsequently extended to Carmarthen (1852), Haverfordwest (1853) and Milford Haven (1856). By 1853, the Vale of Neath Railway linked Merthyr and Aberdare to Neath and (later) Swansea.

In the north, the Chester-Holyhead route was built between 1844 and 1850, a £3.5 million project that involved two celebrated 'monster tubular bridges' across the Conway and the Menai Strait. The scale of this route is explained by the imperial, even grandiose ambitions of the builders to make not only a route to Ireland, but to create a centre of world importance. 'Holyhead', it was said in 1848, 'will be very soon looked upon as the principal key to the Atlantic'. As the heir to Bristol and even Liverpool, it would control 'a large portion of the West India and American trade'.[4] The hope may have been disappointed, but the route was crucial for north Wales. By 1852, the line was linked to Bangor and Caernarvon. Between 1848 and 1852, rail links permitted the emergence of the great slate ports of the north, Port Dinorwic, Port Penrhyn and Caernarvon.

Finally, between 1857 and 1869, came the most difficult phase, that was in a sense the most revolutionary: the completion of the internal network that brought remote communities of inland Wales into contact with a wider Britain. Building a route from (say) Cardiff to Merthyr meant following and improving well-known lines of communication; but the inland extensions meant a real reorientation, the joining together of areas that hitherto had had only the most tenuous connections. This phase also involved some of the most difficult and ambitious engineering achievements, and it was appropriate that the key entrepreneur in mid-and west-Wales was David Davies, whose mining activities in the Rhondda were undertaken against equally formidable natural obstacles.

From Llanelli, a line was constructed to Llandeilo (1857) and Llandovery (1858). By 1868, this was extended to Shrewsbury, via Llandrindod Wells. By 1863, branch lines served Tenby and Pembroke. In the mid-1860s, Carmarthen was connected to Llandeilo and Pencader. From Pencader, the line was now extended to Aberystwyth by the 'Manchester to Milford' line. Aberystwyth was soon connected to Pwllheli and the north-west; and between 1859 and 1866, the mid-Wales line linked Aberystwyth to Shrewsbury. In 1869, the mid-Wales line was joined to the routes of the north-east by a route that ran from Dolgellau to Bala and Ruabon. In the south-east, Brecon was connected to Merthyr, Newport to Shrewsbury and Hereford. Further branch lines were created to penetrate the various 'island' communities of Wales – to Llantrisant and the Vale of Glamorgan; and into the Gwendraeth and Rhymni Valleys. In 1886, the Severn tunnel improved the link between south Wales and southern England, to the benefit of the coal trade.

4. *Parry's railway companion* . . .

A History of Modern Wales 1536–1990

We will often have cause to note the effects of this new rail network on every aspect of Welsh society. One change was the further decline of north Wales in relation to the south, with its elaborate infrastructure. Only in the slate areas had the inland routes penetrated as far as their southern counterparts, so northern regions remained more isolated. This would naturally have its impact on many aspects of life: on politics and the distribution of news; on the impact of new forms of mass culture; on the links between farmers and the regional market; and perhaps above all, on the survival of Welsh language and culture.

But there were many other kinds of impact on individual communities. New rail connections assisted the growth of Aberystwyth as a regional centre – in 1872, it became the seat of a Welsh University College – but they also reinforced the role of Shrewsbury as the effective hub of mid-Wales. Another consequence was the emergence of minor towns as regional or even national centers, which benefited from the development of tourist and leisure industries. New resorts grew to serve the needs of urban and industrial populations in both Wales and England. In fact, the promoters of the Aberystwyth line foresaw the creation of a tourist complex here, and planned luxury hotels at Aberystwyth, Aberdyfi and Borth. In the north, Rhyl preceded the rail boom, but it also benefited from it. The new pier dated from 1866. Llandudno enjoyed spectacular growth, with accommodation for some 8000 visitors by the 1870s. These developments would ultimately transform the whole coast from Conway to Prestatyn. Builth and Llanwrtyd Wells grew in mid-Wales.

Leisure and resort business assisted the growth of new urban centres, often with substantial English populations. This tended to strengthen the Church and Conservative causes in areas where they had been weak; but it also reduced the proportion of Welsh speakers. And for the first time, Wales had rudimentary national centres where it was reasonable to expect visitors from both north and south. Llandrindod Wells is an excellent example here. Though an old resort, it gained a new stimulus from the rail connection. By the end of the century, it was often chosen as the base for national events such as evangelical revivals; and for Liberal Party conferences, where delegates from both north and south, Cardiff or Caernarvon, would be on ground that was Welsh but neutral.

THE IMPACT ON THE COUNTRYSIDE

The new forms of communication further spread the influence of urban and industrial Wales. At first sight, there appeared to be little real impact on the farmers of Radnorshire or Anglesey. Agriculture continued to be a major employer and source of wealth throughout the nineteenth century, with the familiar and inevitable distinctions shaped by Welsh geography. The north-western counties fattened livestock, while the more fertile north-east concentrated on making butter and cheese. South Wales was characterised by dairy production. Drovers continued to supply English markets, and substantial ports exported corn, oats, barley and dairy produce: in the south, Carmarthen and Solva, Haverfordwest and Aberthaw; in the north, Pwllheli, Beaumaris and Amlwch. Many of the older market towns appear to have continued essentially untouched by current events. Carmarthen achieved a population of 10,000 by 1831; and then remained at almost exactly this level for the next century.[5]

But industry had had an impact far greater than this initial impression might suggest. Agriculture declined both in absolute and relative importance, and this changed the nature of traditional rural society. In 1851, the proportion of the working population of Wales still dependent on agriculture was only 30 per cent; by 1911, that figure had fallen still more sharply, to perhaps 10 per cent. In the latter year, there were only six counties where the agricultural population represented over a quarter of the work force (Anglesey, Cardigan, Merioneth, Montgomery, Pembroke and Radnor). These were the areas that suffered the most dramatic population losses.

The industrial regions exerted a tremendous pull on the labour forces of surrounding shires, contributing to labour shortages in the farming areas. This is obvious in later Victorian times, but the pattern can be traced at least from the 1790s. This in turn helped keep wages high, though few employers could compete with the wages offered in the Rhymni or Rhondda valleys; and farmers were encouraged to turn to activities that required less labour. In addition, agricultural areas far removed from the industrial country were directly affected by its cycles of prosperity and slump which affected the demand for labour. We will see that the interchange of people between the different regions might have helped spread radical ideas and tactics, especially during the Rebecca years.

More important, the industrialising regions acted as an enormous

5. David Howell, *Land and people in nineteenth century Wales* (London: Croom Helm, 1978).

market for produce of all kinds: for butter and cheese, for wool and flannel shirts, potatoes and slate, and above all for meat. The old trade in Welsh ponies now became a major enterprise in the counties of Carmarthen and Cardigan, in order to satisfy the limitless demand for pit-ponies. Glamorgan, long one of the most productive farming regions in Wales, probably became a net food importer by the opening years of the century. Before the 1840s, southern farmers often sold their goods in the great markets of Bristol, where they were bought by Glamorgan middlemen. With the coming of the railways, the iron and coal country became a local market for the whole of south and mid-Wales, a process reflected by the growing harmonisation of price levels across the region.

Changes in labour supply and market demand caused a shift towards pastoral farming: between 1870 and 1913, the proportion of cultivated land under permanent grass rose from 57 to 75 per cent. New demand encouraged expansion of cultivation. Between 1840 and 1870, there were over 100 enclosure Bills relating to Wales, affecting 128,000 acres: a figure almost as large as the wartime boom from 1797 to 1817. Enclosures were often followed by greater sophistication in agricultural techniques.

Finally, and less tangibly, the attitudes associated with industry may have affected the rural population because of the impact on landowners, who were often entrepreneurs themselves. They became more aware of commercial considerations, and the possibility of deriving profit from their estates. Others might eschew industry themselves, but (from the 1790s) they sought to transform their own rural environments at least as thoroughly as anything being done by the Guests or Pennants. Some – like Thomas Johnes of Hafod or Thomas Mansell-Talbot of Penrice – spent vast sums in building projects intended to create perfect domestic settings surrounded by glorious gardens and forests.

Others, like William Maddocks, had at least a pretence to utility in their vast projects. In the first quarter of the century, he undertook the drainage of the Traeth Mawr, the treacherous sands where Merioneth met Caernarvonshire. On the new land, he built a model town, complete with public buildings, theatres and a race-course. This was to be a junction on the road to Ireland, and communication improvements naturally followed. Tremadoc was one of several such planned communities from this era, of which only Morriston was wholly oriented to the new industries. The Grevilles' new town at Milford Haven was designed to exploit the Irish trade, but with American commerce another tempting prize.

SOCIAL CONSEQUENCES

The new economic and technological arrangements thus affected the whole of Wales. Of course, the changes were most dramatic in the south-eastern counties, where the social problems were immense. They would probably have overwhelmed the wisest and most benevolent dictatorship ever achieved or imagined; and nineteenth century Wales possessed an administrative structure far removed from this. The process of industrialisation had been under way for over 50 years by the time that new structures emerged to deal with the social issues raised. In the 1840s and 1850s, observers frequently remarked on the disastrous public health situation in Welsh towns like Merthyr or Aberdare, and modern historians have drawn freely on such accounts to depict the negative consequences of the Industrial Revolution.

Such contemporary accounts can rarely be faulted on grounds of factual accuracy, but it is important to put them in perspective. As Professor Gwyn Williams notes, conditions in the towns and industrial villages were not necessarily worse than those in the countryside. Poverty was a common occurrence for workers in iron or copper or coal, but it was likely to be sporadic, interspersed with good times and high wages. The earnings of skilled industrial workers were Olympian by the standards of contemporary rural Wales. In the best years of the 1820s and 1830s, labourers drew in 15 or 18 shillings a week, but there were many earning over a pound. Furnacemen earned up to 30 shillings, puddlers 35, and the most skilled up to two or three pounds. With several members working, it was quite possible for a family to have an income of three pounds. The observers who so frequently denounced urban ills were as likely to attack the sins of excess as the problems of hygiene. Luxury, ostentatious furnishings, sumptuous Bibles, and wasteful cookery were sins as apparent as drink or brutality. Real, enduring, biting poverty was far more likely to be found among the hills of Cardiganshire or Montgomeryshire, from which so many thousands fled south and east.

Yet having said this, the new urban conglomerations had much to criticise. They had grown with scarcely a thought for providing the necessities required for simple survival, let alone what later generations might consider an adequate standard of living. The industrial centres attracted a large labour force, but housing was provided on an utterly unsystematic basis. There were exceptions to this, such as the revolutionary tenement housing developed by the

Morrises at Morriston; but they were few. The new towns were therefore overcrowded, ill-built, and lacked basic sanitary provision. Merthyr in the 1840s was of special concern, the town

> having sprung up rapidly from a village to a town without any precautions being taken for the removal of the increased masses of filth necessarily produced by an increased population, not even for the escape of surface water . . .
> A rural spot of considerable beauty has been transformed into a crowded and filthy manufacturing town, with an amount of mortality higher than any other commercial or manufacturing town in the kingdom.

That was in 1849, when 'the crowning evil . . . was the utter want of provision for the supply of water', and this in an area of high rainfall.[6]

Any of the growing towns could produce similar stories, as of course could stagnant communities like Carmarthen. At Swansea, the worst poverty was to be found in the Irish section, of Greenhill. In 1853, a survey here found it common for six or more to sleep in a room, with no chance of moving people away in time of epidemic:[7]

> The character of these houses and the premises on which they stand is in every way bad, no cleanliness within, and no drainage without: stagnant water soaking through the walls, with no place to discharge itself, or having its usual vent choked up – the floors in many cases of the houses unbricked and in wet weather becoming a mass of mud – the garden in almost every case heaped with ashes, and in many cases stored with pig-dung . . .
> The privies attached to these houses are in many cases dilapidated, open to the air, and emitting most foul smells, and their approaches covered with ordure. Where these have been recently emptied it has been but to create a fresh nuisance, by making an underground pit with the walls unprotected, through which constantly percolates into the adjoining houses the fluid contents. To this circumstance, in my opinion, is to be attributed the great mortality of these houses and streets where the levels much vary.

There is no suggestion here that Greenhill was presenting any new problems: all that was novel was that by 1853 there was a Medical Officer of Health sufficiently concerned to point them out.

Water supply and sewerage became controversial because of the epidemics that became commonplace from the 1820s. Wales experienced four great cholera epidemics between 1832 and 1866, with the experience of 1849 being much the most lethal: almost 400

6. Joseph Gross, 'Water-supply and sewerage', *Merthyr historian* ii (1978) 67–78.
7. Quoted in Thomas, *Swansea's districts and villages*, 121–2.

died in Cardiff alone. But the worst afflictions occurred in Merthyr Tydfil. 160 died here in 1832, nearly 1700 in 1849, and 400 more in 1854. Even this understates the magnitude of the crisis in the town. Between 1851 and 1865, there was only one year (1860) when there was no epidemic. Cholera was only one problem, coexisting as it did with typhus, smallpox, scarlet fever and measles. In the dreadful years of 1864 and 1865, all four of these diseases hit together; in 1866, cholera returned. These diseases all affected different regions of Wales, though on a strictly local basis. For instance, the cholera of 1849 had little impact on the north; which was much harder hit by the outbreak of 1865–1866. Bangor had a typhoid epidemic in 1882; and Caernarvonshire experienced widespread smallpox in 1871.

The appalling sanitary conditions naturally contributed to high death rates. The Welsh rate was 20.2 per thousand in 1841, 22 in 1848, 25.8 during the cholera year of 1849. Not until the 1890s did the figure fall below 20. Infant mortality ran at 125.5 per thousand live births in 1839, and improvement was slow. The figure was at or over 120 until the 1880s, and fell below 100 only after 1910. The situation was also much worse in particular locations. In Cardiff, the death rate between 1842 and 1848 was 30 per thousand; and within such high-risk towns, there were still more unhealthy pockets. In Cardiff, this meant the Irish sections like Stanley Street and Love Lane. Merthyr recorded an overall rate of 30.2 per thousand in 1853, but this was far exceeded in sections like 'China' or Tydfil's Well. Infant mortality in Merthyr was rarely below 190 per thousand in the 1820s or 1830s, if we take only children dying before their first birthday. However, the first five years were an exceedingly dangerous period. In the very worst years – such as 1823 – burials of children under five were 713 for every thousand baptisms, 40 per cent above the normally dreadful rates.[8] Adults faced a high risk of death or mutilation by industrial accident.

For the normal and healthy adult, the most pressing need was economic subsistence. The iron and non-ferrous industries were all subject to cycles of boom and slump, chiefly because of the dependence on armaments and exports. Labour disputes might also shut down a works, though most commonly such conflicts only came when depression from other causes was already likely. This meant reliance on savings and the assistance of friendly societies; but most would soon be forced to return to the welfare system provided by the Poor Law. Before 1834, this assumed the obligation of each

8. Gwyn A Williams, *The Merthyr rising* (London: Croom Helm, 1978), 50.

parish towards its own, and removed paupers to their place of settlement. Such an assumption had arguably been appropriate for the 1660s, but it was wholly inadequate for the diverse immigrant communities assembled in the industrial districts.

Soaring poor rates in the early nineteenth century were accompanied by a series of efforts to reform the law. Some required a labour test, others paid a supplement to the low wages of the employed pauper; but all these reforms were based on the wage labour that characterised the English farm, rather than the new relationships prevailing in Welsh heavy industry. The Poor Law system was one of the first administrative structures of the old world to approach collapse under the strains of the new environment.

There was also a perception that the industrial areas were characterised by lawlessness and violence, far beyond what could be dealt with by the traditional structure of Justices and constables. These comments were naturally encouraged by the endemic labour violence and political protest of the 1830s and 1840s (see Chapter Thirteen). Normal criminal activity was also associated with 'rookery' areas, like Merthyr's 'China'; while Cardiff's Bute Street claimed the position of the vice capital of Victorian Wales. It would be useful to know more about criminality, and important work has been done by scholars like Dr D.J.V. Jones. On the other hand, crime rates inevitably depend on bureaucratic priorities and official perceptions, and our knowledge of illegality is strictly limited by the lack of formal policing before the 1840s. Long after that date, the official records provide an account that is so partial as to be almost worthless. In 1846, only 500 convictions were recorded for the million people of Wales, and only 30 of these involved offences against the person.

THE AGE OF REFORM 1848–1870

Before the 1840s, the towns lacked the simplest amenities; a situation that changed only with the mid-century perception of a thorough national crisis in public health and civil order. Between about 1850 and 1880, there were a series of reforms as far-reaching in their way as the industrial developments of the time. Legislation at national level spurred local reforms, though parliamentary measures were only really effective when they were seen as relevant to local problems and conditions. One of the first of the great reforms was in the realm of poor relief, with the Poor Law Amendment Act of 1834. This aimed to end outdoor relief and the paying of wage supplements, with the reduction of the rate burden as a primary goal. In order to administer the new system, areas were grouped into Unions, with a thorough disregard of traditional boundaries of parish and county. Caernarvonshire included the total area of two Unions and parts of three others. Most of southern Anglesey was included in the Unions based in Caernarvon and Bangor-Beaumaris. Pwllheli Union included 32 parishes; Caernarvon 17. Merthyr Tydfil found itself the centre of a populous Union encompassing eight parishes.

Ideally, each Union would erect a workhouse, and progressively end outdoor relief. In reality, this was a difficult goal. There were objections on the grounds of the expense of the new system, but also because of the barbarous nature of the workhouse. Carmarthen built a workhouse, a 'Bastille', which was duly stormed by the Rebecca rioters in 1843. Other towns were much more circumspect. Merthyr did not build until 1853, in part because there were sufficient fears of public disorder without adding new grievances. In 1837 10,000 Merthyr residents petitioned against the new system; and by 1871, the Merthyr Union had eight 'outdoor' paupers for every one receiving indoor relief. There was violent resistance to the new law in Montgomeryshire, which in turn led north Wales Unions to be cautious about its adoption. Bangor-Beaumaris erected a workhouse in 1845, but it held only a tiny proportion of the area's paupers. Conway built a workhouse in the 1860s. Outdoor relief continued to operate throughout the century.

The experience of Poor Law reform suggests the limitations of central intervention; but the Union system would help shape social policy in the following decades. Union districts were often used as convenient administrative units; and the Boards of Guardians provided a model for other local structures. Public health reform is a case in point. This also derived from parliamentary legislation, but national decisions here had a much greater impact on local events. In 1848, the Public Health Act created a General Board of Health, and authorised the creation of local Boards. In the first few years 17 communities adopted the measure; 70 by 1870. In 1858, the Local Government Act authorised local bodies to undertake general sanitary reform, together with the provision of cleaning and lighting.

Merthyr was an early subscriber to the Public Health act, choosing a local Board in 1850; and this marked the beginning of a major era of reform. The town was fortunate in the activism of the engineer, G.T. Clark, one of the Dowlais trustees. Largely through his urging, the town began the creation of a modern water system between 1857 and 1861. By 1862, several thousand houses in Merthyr had running water. Apart from the obvious hygienic advantages, this also permitted the development of a firefighting service from 1861. From 1865, Clark was the major figure in promoting the development of a sewerage system; though it was 1875 before houses were connected to the system in significant numbers. At the time of the 1848 Act, Merthyr had no hospital. It was only in 1849 that 'houses of refuge' began to be set aside on an emergency basis, to accommodate healthy members of families suffering from epidemic diseases. The local workhouses at Merthyr and Aberdare developed infirmary facilities, and there were fever hospitals from 1866. Voluntary hospitals emerged from 1860, with G.T. Clark's wife as primary sponsor. Not until 1888 did the town get a General Hospital.

Merthyr was unusual in the scale of its problems, and in the comprehensive vision of Clark and his like. Most social and medical services depended ultimately on private charity, and throughout Wales there were some magnificent donors, like the industrialist Richard Thomas, or the Cory family; but reforms came in a piecemeal manner, even within the same town. At Swansea, the ancient core suffered terribly from cholera in 1831–2, but not at all in 1849, because the more prosperous citizens had secured the services of a modern water company for their section of town. Greenhill had not been so lucky.

The mid-century Acts permitted local authorities to build a variety of new types of institution. Physical health was clearly the most pressing need, but counties and towns soon turned their attention to other social problems. Glamorgan, for example, built a new county asylum in 1864, and a juvenile reformatory in 1874. In architecture, as well as discipline, these often owed a great deal to the precedent of the workhouse and the prison: common manifestations of what American historian David Rothman terms the 'age of the asylum'.

POLICING

It was also in the early Victorian era that Welsh communities first developed professional police forces, in response to the public order problems posed by industrialisation. Specifically, the civilian force allowed the possibility of controlling riots or strikes without recourse to the extreme solution of military involvement that had been so commonly invoked between 1793 and 1839. There had been local forces in this era, either developed from parish constables or (as at Tredegar) controlled by the ironmasters. Merthyr already had some 40 officers by 1842, rising to 165 by 1872. It was in 1839, the year of the Chartist rising at Newport, that Glamorgan took advantage of the new Act permitting the creation of county police forces. The Rebecca movement helped spread the police idea to other counties, which had been besieging the Home Office for the dispatch of London constables. Carmarthenshire created a force in 1843, Cardiganshire the following year. The new forces were initially small, 20 or 30 officers per county, but they became an established part of the political landscape.

The police were anything but specialised crime-fighters. They possessed a wide range of social responsibilities, varying from place to place, but often including fire-fighting and the control of weights and measures. There was also the likelihood of dealing with political unrest. Many remote areas were reluctant to establish forces, deterred by the costs of a professional police; but the spread of the railway changed this. In Pwllheli, this was the factor that finally provoked compliance with the county system, but not until the 1870s.

As in poor law and health, local reform resulted in the growth of central coordination, channelled through the powerful figure of the Chief Constable. These were often figures of real prestige: in Glamorgan, only three men held the office between 1841 and 1936, and the third incumbent (Lionel Lindsay) was the son of the second. Lindsay, a former head of the gendarmerie in Egypt, also epitomises the military and colonial nature of the new structure. He was far from untypical in this background. When Caernarvonshire appointed a Chief Constable in 1856, one of the many military applicants for the post stressed the relevance of his experience gained in service 'against the hill tribes on the western frontiers under Sir Colin Campbell'. The urgent nature of the social problems in nineteenth century Wales resulted in the creation of administrative structures far removed from the local and personal power associated with the traditional landlord Justices.

In the 1840s, the 'Condition of Wales' formed the theme of many inquiries, both official and private, examining the glaring failures in the provision of education, public health and social welfare.

Looming over all, however, was the question of public order, whether or not this agenda was openly stated. The new industrial Wales appeared to be riotous and disorderly, with unrest reaching a crescendo between 1830 and 1844. A contemporary observer could well have been forgiven for seeing the industrial south as the likely core of radical revolution in wider Britain.

CHAPTER THIRTEEN
The Politics of Protest 1790–1860

There were particular tensions associated with the new societies and the industrial towns; but often, the disorder must be seen in the context of much older radical traditions.[1] We have already described the long influence of radical puritanism around Hay and the Upper Wye country. For a parallel in industrial Wales, we could choose no better example than Merthyr Tydfil, a place that authorities had associated with riot and dissent in the seventeenth and eighteenth centuries. The town was throughout the early nineteenth century a centre of major strikes, of riots and disorders. As we will see, there were violent outbreaks in 1800, in 1816, and above all, in 1831. This was the first Welsh seat to have a working-class parliamentary candidacy, in 1841. The suffrage at that date made this no more than a propaganda gesture, but in 1868, a newly expanded electorate gave the seat to another pioneer of Welsh politics: this was Henry Richard, a leader in the radical Welsh strain of nonconformist liberalism that would soon sweep the country. In 1900, the town chose Keir Hardie from the newly formed Labour Party. A later MP, S.O. Davies (1934–1972), was a left-winger as devout (and downright awkward) as any to be found in the Labour Party. It was said that Merthyr was one of the only constituencies to have an independent foreign policy, and one that was based on resolute opposition to NATO.

Throughout the nineteenth and early twentieth century, Merthyr was a centre for newspapers expressing the most radical views of the day: Chartist in the 1830s, Socialist after 1900. The town had a

1. This chapter is largely based on the classic work of scholars like David Williams, D.J.V. Jones and Gwyn A. Williams, in the books and articles described in more detail in Chapter Twenty.

tradition of community solidarity, and a long history of defending its values by riot if necessary. Both in the 1830s and 1930s, mass action effectively sabotaged local implementation of unpopular reforms in the poor law or welfare systems. In the 1970s, the town appeared to be a bellwether once again, by leading the defection of working-class industrial Wales from the Labour Party towards the nationalism of Plaid Cymru. Merthyr Tydfil was far from being the only centre of Welsh radicalism. Indeed, in the Chartist era the town was moderate compared to the physical-force militants of the Monmouthshire iron towns. In the present century, the 'Little Moscows' were customarily to be found further west, in the Rhondda valleys.

We have little difficulty in understanding the strength of radicalism in the new industrial communities. On the contrary, the real problem seems to lie in the relative infrequency of open insurrection. Why were events like the Merthyr Rising not regular, indeed annual, events? One essential issue was that of the solidarity of labour. It would have been an obvious tactic to spread disputes in, say a copper or iron works to the whole industry. This was critical when there was a threat of military intervention, as the authorities could have been prevented from concentrating their limited forces, and would have had to rely on the dubious aid of the militia. When strikes did spread, as in 1816, the authorities were panicked. The ironworkers and sale-coal miners could join in common action, and the whole coalfield was at a standstill in 1822, 1830 and 1832. The 'Scotch Cattle' movement demonstrated some degree of cooperation across the Monmouthshire iron country. A few years later, the chartists offered the best hope for unity, when leaders like Hugh Williams succeeded in drawing together a substantial regional coalition of local groups.

Coordinated action did occur, but it is possible to exaggerate it, and thus to distort the political significance of industrial outbreaks. It was more than mere chance that prevented these disorders from developing into general insurrection. Wales as a region was prone to riot and protest between 1790 and 1850; but there were a number of common themes that tended to reduce the potential of such outbreaks. Above all, geographical factors handicapped the wider organisation and unity of purpose that might have been expected across a whole region or even industry. Wales often seems like a federation of island communities, each with distinct traditions, its own aspirations and fears. One industrial valley saw little in common with the next, and early radical centres like Merthyr and Swansea might in practice have belonged to different worlds, rather than sharing the same county.

The workers of upland east Glamorgan were slow to develop the militancy that characterised their neighbours in west Monmouthshire, though the two groups were separated by only a few miles. Even in one town or district, the workforce at one plant might see little in common with those of another, who served a different master. In Merthyr, it was a rare achievement when the workers of Dowlais could find common cause with those of Cyfarthfa. When Merthyr collaborated with Tredegar and points east, it was an astonishing accomplishment.

This would seem to suggest strict limits on the early development of a sense of class consciousness even in south Wales, this vanguard of the industrial era. It also reflected the practical difficulty of influencing wider opinion by mass meetings. Strikes and protests rarely involved anything but the most rudimentary ad hoc leadership. In Glamorgan, it was the 1850s before workers generally elected strike committees to negotiate their grievances, three decades after Monmouthshire had pioneered these tactics. Without recognised leaders, communication with other districts was all but impossible.

When strikers or food rioters did succeed in spreading their cause, it was by the cumbersome means of literally thousands of protesters marching en masse to another works or district and collectively calling on the people there to join them. It could be done. Successful examples were the food riots in west Glamorgan in 1793, and the 1816 iron strike in Merthyr and western Monmouthshire, with the wandering crowd in the latter year possibly approaching 10,000 strong. But it limited the scope of action to at most a few miles. Failure to achieve widespread coordination was strategically disastrous. In 1839, the Glamorgan men failed to support the Monmouthshire-based attack on Newport. Three years later, the Monmouthshire Chartists declared that they would refuse to support industrial campaigns in Glamorgan. This decentralisation of activity explains the unique horror attached by respectable writers to the secret oath-bound networks of the 1830s.

Early riots and protests were usually strictly local in nature. With few exceptions, they were also limited and defensive affairs. A Dowlais strike in 1853 was one of the few actually to seek an improvement in wages and conditions. Much more common was the protest of communities on the edge of destitution, seeking to prevent further deterioration. It is the protests of the 1790s that are generally classified as food riots, while later conflicts can easily be seen as industrial disputes; but these later struggles too often resulted in part from soaring food prices. Violence most often grew from a threatened or actual change in the provision of the basic necessities of life: either a cut in wages or a rise in food prices. Even a straightforward wage-cut was less resented than the associated chicanery practised by most employers: failing to give the required notice of such a cut, or lengthy delays in paying wages. Also critical was the artificial inflation imposed by the 'truck' system. This involved the payment of wages in the form of paper that could only be used at the company's own shops. Truck proved one of the most fertile sources of workers' grievances in the first decades of industrialisation. Though prohibited by law in 1831, the system had a long afterlife: as late as the 1870s, in Maesteg or Pontypool.

1790–1830

Food riots had often been recorded in eighteenth century Wales, particularly in years of crisis like 1766. In the early years of industrialisation, these outbreaks became much more frequent. The cause was usually dearth arising from poor harvests, but violence was most likely when human activity might have contributed to natural problems. Corn-dealers and speculators were often accused of cynically permitting hunger by exporting produce in times of shortage. As in much of Europe, protesters who tried to interfere with such shipments usually saw themselves as enforcing natural justice and the popular moral economy. This was an attempt to enforce cherished community standards, by the action of crowds that virtually always included a large proportion of women. From the late eighteenth century, however, the development of industrial populations meant that there was an ever-growing number of people in Wales who could not supply their own food, but who served as a profitable market. There was thus an increased need to export food from the country, which increased the opportunity for potential conflicts and riots when harvests were bad.

Difficult years for crops might lead to disorder throughout the land. In early 1795, there were food riots in Caernarvon, Aberystwyth, Narberth, Bridgend and Carmarthen. Later in the same year, there were outbreaks in the north-east, at Mold, Denbigh, Abergele and Ruthin; Pembrokeshire and Monmouthshire followed in the summer, with Haverfordwest recording one of the

largest confrontations. 1800 and 1801 were also dreadful, with
responsible magistrates fearing that troubles in the industrial areas
would result in plunder and riot spreading along the whole south
Wales coast. Troops found themselves in frequent use in these years,
as the authorities attempted to thwart the general rising that (as far as
we can tell) no-one outside the Home Office ever contemplated. In
January 1801, soldiers were stationed in readiness at Holywell,
Denbigh and Caernarvon; ever-difficult Haverfordwest soon followed.

The nature of the protests was changed by the growth of
industrial communities. Workers in the copper and coal industries
took the lead in early food riots, and their particular grievances
increasingly became the major motivating force behind protests. In
the hunger year of 1795, Neath also experienced a copper strike. In
the next three decades, it was the iron industry that was generally at
the centre of conflict. The ironworks were highly dependent on the
arms trade, which made them vulnerable to fluctuations in the
international situation, and to sudden tragedies like the outbreak of
peace. Periods of slump and falling prices inevitably led to wage
cuts, which were commonly the occasion for collective bargaining
by mob action. In 1813, protests were led by the Cyfarthfa men,
whose employers feared 'Luddism'; and sabotage in such an
environment offered a potential of catastrophe far in excess of what
might be achieved with a power loom. This was the time that the
authorities built at Brecon a new barracks for regulars: close enough
to the iron country to be accessible, sufficiently removed to avoid
subversion of the troops.

After the end of the French wars, industrial Wales entered the first
of its general industrial crises, with falling demand for iron
coinciding with high wheat prices. The inevitable protests began in
the Merthyr area in the autumn of 1816, and a week-long strike
probably involved some 15,000 to 20,000 people. Most of the major
centres along the heads of the valley were affected, from Merthyr
east to Llanelly and Clydach, and unrest spread as far as Newport. In
the aftermath of the crisis, regular troops were stationed in the area,
and not merely in the usual garrison towns such as Brecon and
Abergavenny. Merthyr and Tredegar found themselves playing host
to the 25th Infantry.

Wage cuts frequently motivated strikes, though rarely on the
massive scale of 1816. In Monmouthshire 1822 saw a 13-week iron
strike that was joined by the colliers. There was mass resistance again
in 1827, in 1830 and 1840. The Monmouthshire iron country was the
most militant region in Wales at this time, and alongside the new

industrial society there evolved new tactics and forms of protest. Judging by the appalling memory they left in the historical record, they must have been most effective.

It was in the early 1820s that western Monmouthshire first heard the name of the 'Scotch Cattle', a movement that intimidated blacklegs and committed sabotage during times of industrial conflict. They threatened their targets with warning letters, and soon moved to the next stage of breaking their houses or persons. The 'Cattle' – possibly hundreds strong – signalled their approach with horns, guns and loud bull-like noises, sounds which often had the desired warning effect in themselves. The actual attackers were often drawn from another part of the county, which made identification nearly impossible. 'Scotch Cattle' activity was at its height in Monmouthshire in the conflicts between 1832 and 1834. The group faded from prominence thereafter, presumably as its membership became involved in Chartist activities. However, occasional outbreaks were recorded in Glamorgan as late as 1850.

'Scotch Cattle' was probably used in a generic way by any labour group employing extra-legal tactics. Like 'Black Hand' or the early Ku Klux Klan, it was a label of convenience rather than a hierarchical secret society. On the other hand, both the term and its associated mythology were useful: the 'Cattle' served the 'Scotch Bull' ruling the 'nine thousand faithful children' of his 'Black Domain'. These images gained force from their roots in the widely-known customs of pre-industrial Wales. The 'Cattle' attacks derived heavily from older rituals of public humiliation similar to the English Skimington Ride (the Welsh had stigmatised their targets by riding them on the wooden horse, the *ceffyl pren*).

THE CRISIS: 1830–1844

Between about 1830 and 1844, south Wales appeared to be one of the political storm centres of the British Isles. The new industrial societies of the south-east had long been regarded as potentially violent and insurrectionary, and they fully justified these expectations with the outbreaks of 1831 and 1839. More surprising at first sight was the emergence of large scale protests in agrarian west Wales from the late 1830s. This was alarming for the government: a general insurrection in the industrial valleys could barely be contained, but the additional menace of rural guerrilla warfare was appalling, raising as it did the spectre of a second and closer Ireland. There were some 400 regular soldiers in south Wales at the opening of 1839, and only 1000 by the end of the year. This was scarcely enough to hold an insurgent country. And there was evidence of cooperation and cross-pollination between the radicalism of the iron towns and the county towns, the decaying boroughs and the country villages, united by contacts with metropolitan agitators. These years mark a dramatic new phase of popular political organisation in Wales.

The campaign for parliamentary reform was vigorously supported in Wales, where Glamorgan and Monmouthshire contained some of the most glaring examples of the inequitable distribution of seats. In addition, the reform crisis between 1830 and 1832 coincided with industrial and other protests that gave a broad social dimension to the franchise demands. These three years were not only among the most disturbed in nineteenth century Wales, the conflicts also achieved a degree of overt politicisation rarely witnessed hitherto. It was a time of conflicts that have entered mythology: when Wales fought its Peterloo, its Eureka Stockade; and when it acquired one of the first of its many martyrs.

Between 1830 and 1832, labour conflict was rife in Wales, and union organisation on modern lines can be discerned. At Bagillt in Flintshire, 1830 marked the creation of a branch of the Friendly Associated Coal Miners' Union Society, which was affiliated to the National Association for the Protection of Labour. At the end of December, striking Flintshire miners attempted to spread the conflict throughout the north Wales coalfield. Militia cavalry under Sir Watkin Williams-Wynn engaged the miners in 'the battle of Gutter Hill'; but the strike ended in a substantial victory for the union. By the following autumn, the union had established lodges throughout Wales, north and south. This resulted in a lockout at the Merthyr ironworks, where the union was defeated and driven out by November. Other battles in collieries and copper works ended this ambitious attempt at unionisation by the end of 1831 (though clandestine labour activism was very much alive in Monmouthshire).

Meanwhile, the campaign for parliamentary reform was tumultuous. In 1831, there were election-related riots at Caernarvon, Montgomery, Llanidloes and Haverfordwest. The unrest at Newport involved leaders who would later earn celebrity from their role in Chartism: at the end of the year, it was John Frost who established a branch of the Political Union of the Working Classes. Perhaps 20,000 people paraded for reform at Swansea.

As so often in the history of Welsh mobs and protests, Carmarthen was in a category of its own. By 1831, the town had been deeply divided for almost a century, and the struggles had left a lively tradition of partisan activism, with a network of party clubs and taverns. Originally a Whig-Tory feud, the town's divisions eventually became the 'Red-Blue' conflict between rival aristocratic houses: Red for Tory Dynevor, Blue for Whiggish Golden Grove and Cwmgwili. By the 1820s, the Blue party had become a radical group with leaders like the Unitarian attorney George Thomas, and the later Chartist Hugh Williams. Even the Red candidate for Parliament, John Jones, was in practice an independent with a surprisingly un-Tory record. In radical Carmarthen, electoral reform was indissolubly linked to issues of religious liberty and economic grievances. The election of 1831 proved to be one of the most bitterly contested in recent Welsh history. The election began at the end of April, and riots and disturbances continued for several days; a pattern that recurred with the second contest of the year, in August.

But of all the conflicts of this year, it was the struggle at Merthyr Tydfil which stands out as the bitterest encounter between government and people. A movement originally intended to promote reform triggered one of the legendary insurrections in Welsh history, the Merthyr Rising of 1831. In early May – as Carmarthen was returning to what passed for order – there had been mob activity in support of reform candidates. The 'middling' and Unitarian radicals who had taken over the local administration were joined in their demands by William Crawshay II, an ironmaster with forceful radical convictions. At the end of the month, there was a new campaign for electoral changes, with political demands attached to issues of economic self-interest. On May 30, some 5000 people gathered at Waun Hill to press for a list of demands that included resistance to wage-cuts, and abolition of the Court of Requests. Central to the affair, this latter was a small claims court which permitted the recovery of minor debts, in a process that often involved distraint of property. In times of depression like 1829, the court often acted as a real provocation to an already suffering population.

By Wednesday, June 1, the crowd had moved to direct action, and the Court of Requests was destroyed. The local Justices Henry Bruce and Anthony Hill attempted to intervene, but they met defiance in a striking new guise. The crowd dipped a cloth in calf's blood to create a powerful symbol of the equality and common suffering of mankind: this was the red flag, that would so often reappear as a rallying point in Welsh history. Realising the scale of the protest, the Justices retired and sent for military assistance from Brecon: some 450 soldiers had arrived by the weekend. Soon, there was a local general strike, and all the ironworks were stopped.

By Friday 3rd, the action had shifted to the Castle Inn, where a crowd several thousand strong negotiated with the magistrates and employers. About noon, the crowd apparently tried to seize the weapons of the soldiers, who opened fire. In the ensuing battle, at least 20 rioters were killed, and possibly many more; but even this carnage seemed to be no more than a first step. The remaining protesters now set up camp at Cefncoed y Cymer, where they drilled under their new red flag; while the authorities established their base in Penydarren House. On Saturday 4th, a body of Swansea Cavalry arrived in the region, but they were stopped by rioters from Cefncoed. After handing over their weapons, the troopers were permitted to depart unharmed.

The Merthyr conflict was looking less like a riot than a minor civil war, while the authorities naturally feared a direct assault on Penydarren House. Their greatest worry was that the insurrection would spread, and it was an important achievement when the soldiers prevented a Monmouthshire contingent from joining the Merthyr crowd. On the Monday, there was a series of further meetings and confrontations, but the crowd was increasingly demonstrating real divisions of opinion. Only a few wished to proceed to full-scale insurrection, and the protesters began to split into two or more camps. A growing number heeded the appeals to disperse, and the rising was at an end by the Tuesday.

But the affair had its aftermath. Two men were sentenced to death as a result of the conflict. One was Lewis Lewis, *Lewsyn y Heliwr*, who had been such a visible and active leader that some have suggested him as a likely spy or provocateur. In fact, he was reprieved – unlike the other accused, Richard Lewis or *Dic Penderyn*, a young miner who was accused of wounding a soldier in a struggle. There were real doubts about the evidence in his case, leading to a movement for commutation; but Dic was executed in August 1831, becoming the protomartyr of the union and radical tradition in Wales.

Merthyr did not produce a revolution, but the rising opened a decade of rapid development for the radical movement in Wales. In the 1830s, the town became the centre of what was now a self-consciously working-class culture, with all its institutions. In 1831, Merthyr acquired a branch of the Lancashire-based National

A History of Modern Wales 1536–1990

Association for the Protection of Labour, and we have seen that the ironworks were the setting for a battle over the right to unionise. The strike that autumn led to fears of a new rising in the aftermath of the events at Bristol.

There was also a new radical press in Merthyr, which derived its inspiration from Unitarian clergy and activists. Central was the family of the pastor, David John, and his two sons David and Matthew (David senior had come from one of the radical west Wales congregations that had grown out of the Baptist schisms of the 1790s). Other Unitarian leaders included the weaver Morgan Williams, who wrote the English-language material for the new working-class paper, *Y Gweithiwr* (The Worker: 1834). In 1840, there appeared the *Merthyr Advocate and Free Press*, and *Udgorn Cymru* (Trumpet of Wales), both published by Morgan Williams and the younger David John. Willliams became one of the first working-class parliamentary candidates in Wales, when he ran for Merthyr in 1841. At the hustings, he received a large majority by show of hands; though of course the limited nature of the suffrage meant that his opponent Sir Josiah John Guest secured the election. (Also in 1841, a Chartist candidate ran for Monmouthshire but received no votes.)

By the late 1830s, the powerful radical movement in upland Glamorgan had become part of a national organization, which has over the years been the subject of some of the finest studies undertaken on Welsh history. The Chartists found many supporters in industrial south Wales. The great Chartist petition of 1839 included nearly 15,000 signatures from the Merthyr area, another 5000 from west Glamorgan; but the new agitation acted as a focus for deep-seated local grievances in a surprising variety of Welsh regions. The petition included 1100 signatures from Pembrokeshire, from Narberth, Templeton and Saundersfoot; Carmarthen town produced over 1000. There were also 1000 south Cardiganshire signatures, from the area between Llandyssul and Cribyn. This was the legendary 'Black Spot', an area that had become a centre of rural Unitarianism, due largely to the lack of resident gentry and clergy.

Chartism was not confined to one or two industrial centres, or even to the boisterous south-east. In fact, some contemporaries stressed factors altogether different from the wages and truck-shop issues of the iron districts. The *Cambrian* newspaper claimed that Chartism was basically an extension of three existing campaigns: against restrictions on Dissent; against the new Poor Law; and in favour of relieving agrarian discontent. In addition, an economic slump provided the immediate circumstances for the movement, especially in mid-Wales textile towns. The reformers received strong support from radical dissenters, from Unitarians and many Independents. In Aberdare, the Unitarian chapel was a focus of organisation, carrying on the tradition of Tomos Glyn Cothi. Chartism became a powerful movement, but it was also a label which could be generically applied to specific protests: to union activities, to attacks on the new workhouses, even to the destruction of tollgates.

Many major figures in Welsh Chartism were far removed from the plebeian radicals of the Merthyr outbreak, and local issues and grievances must be sought. At Carmarthen, the reformist leader was Hugh Williams, a respectable solicitor whose father had been involved in the Montgomeryshire lead industry. Williams also had connections with English middle-class radicals like John Bright and Richard Cobden – who married Williams' sister in 1840. The Williams circle also included Henry Hetherington. It was partly under these English influences that Williams became the sponsor of radical organisations in Wales, though he should also be seen in the line of continuity from the local 'Blue' party and their concerns. Williams was one of the first guardians of the poor elected for Carmarthen under the 1834 reform law; and he devoted his time in office to criticising and obstructing the system. In 1836, he sponsored a great radical gathering at Carmarthen, where a branch of the London based Working Men's Association was created in the following year.

As at Carmarthen, Newport Chartism grew out of local urban and elite politics. Eighteenth century Newport had chafed at the rule of its neighbours at Tredegar House, whose steward in the town possessed immense power. From 1822, the agent Thomas Prothero was regularly assailed by John Frost, who emerged as a local tribune. He served as Mayor of Newport in 1836. Like Hugh Williams, he had metropolitan radical connections, and demonstrated wide-ranging interests in the reform of the franchise and the boroughs. By 1838, he led a branch of the Working Men's Association that provided Williams with his local contacts.

The six points of the Charter were officially formulated in 1838: manhood suffrage; secret ballot; abolition of property qualifications; payment for MPs; annual parliaments; equal electoral districts. They were disseminated through the existing radical network, and Hugh Williams was soon sending emissaries throughout south Wales: to Pontypool, Merthyr, Swansea, Newport and Llanelli. At the national Convention of 1839, the Welsh delegates included Frost,

Williams and Charles Jones of Montgomeryshire. The movement made its presence felt with a series of mass meetings that regularly attracted 2000 or more hearers. The LWMA dispatched Henry Vincent to south Wales, with high hopes of achieving an alliance with dissenters and trade unionists (a foretaste of the triumphant coalition achieved by later Liberalism).

From the spring of 1839, it was clear that the year was unlikely to end without an outbreak of at least Merthyr proportions, though it was uncertain if the event could be contained to a local conflict. Particularly restive were mid-Wales woollen towns like Newtown, Llanidloes and Welshpool, all hard hit by a slump. The Lord-Lieutenant's request for aid was met by a less than overwhelming response of three officers from the Metropolitan police. A riotous crowd dominated Llanidloes for a week, until the dispatch of soldiers from Brecon. 32 Chartists were sentenced at the July Assizes of that year, despite Hugh Williams' legal efforts on their behalf.

Attention now turned to the industrial south, where the associations established in Newport and Merthyr had had extraordinary success over the winter of 1838–1839 in mobilising support in the coal and iron communities of the uplands. Apart from industrial workers, the Charter found enthusiastic supporters among shopkeepers and tradesmen. D.J.V. Jones has estimated that by 1839, there might have been as many as 25,000 Chartist members and sympathisers in the 50 associations of Glamorgan and Monmouthshire.[2] Newport was clearly a major organisational centre. There were at least 450 Chartist members here, and it was the base for Henry Vincent's *Western Vindicator*, his counterpart to the *Northern Star*. The town attracted government attention: Frost was purged from the county Bench in March, and in May Henry Vincent was arrested and jailed. Over the summer, the prospect of armed conflict grew steadily as Chartist membership increased; there was even a clandestine arms factory at Llangynidr.

In July, Parliament officially rejected the Chartist petition. It was probably in that October that the decision was made to launch an armed insurrection. Opinions differ about the exact motives of the scheme. With traditional paranoia, contemporary government supporters saw the Monmouthshire plan as a first step in a coordinated national rising: when Newport had fallen, the halt in the Welsh mail would give the signal for insurrection to the midland Chartists. Modern historians of leftist inclination feel some sympathy for this

2. D.J.V. Jones, *The last rising* (Oxford 1985).

conspiracy view, because it makes the actual rising a grander and more stirring lost cause than it often appears. Some see the action as a demonstration rather than a rising; while others stress the role of government provocateurs and manipulation. The best historian of the era, David Williams, was handicapped by his considerable distaste for industrial radicals, and tended to overstate their lack of clear thought and organisation. The best current opinion is probably that of D.J.V. Jones, who sees the 1839 scheme as a true revolutionary rising, directed towards a local insurrection.

On November 3, the Chartist forces began to gather in the Monmouthshire uplands. John Frost would lead the contingent from Blackwood and Argoed; Zephaniah Williams from Nantyglo and Ebbw Vale; William Jones from Pontypool. The three units would meet at Cefn, outside Newport, and would then advance into the town. The affair was blighted from its inception – by weather, by poor organisation, by lack of clear purpose. Ultimately, the Pontypool contingent failed to appear, but there were between five and eight thousand men in the group that marched into Newport on November 4. Here they were met by a small force of soldiers and special constables fortified in the Westgate Hotel. The government forces opened fire, probably killing 20 or so of the rebels. This broke the rising, and the Chartists dispersed. Three of the leaders, including Frost, were sentenced to be hanged and quartered for high treason, but the sentences were commuted to transportation to Australia. (All were ultimately pardoned, but only Frost chose to return, in 1856.)

Despite the relative ease of the victory, there was concern that the attack on Newport would not be an isolated incident, but instead (as all logic demanded) that the Monmouthshire attack would be part of a Welsh rising. Cardiff in particular was seen as a likely target for a rising based in Caerphilly and Pontypridd. Others suggested that victory at Newport might have signalled the Chartists of Merthyr and Aberdare to march on Cardiff – or, much more serious, on Brecon, with its garrison. We can only speculate what might have happened if the rising had been led by strategists with the intelligence and foresight for which they were given undue credit by the Home Office and the magistracy.

The repression that followed the Newport debacle effectively broke the Chartist movement. Not until 1842 were there signs of a Chartist revival, with mass meetings at the celebrated radical headquarters of Three Horseshoes, Merthyr. It was also at this point that trade unionism began to revive in the uplands of Monmouthshire and east Glamorgan.

REBECCA

It was in June 1839, at the height of the Chartist crisis, that there commenced the great rural protests, the 'Rebecca Riots'; and the chronology alone raises questions about possible links between rural and industrial radicalism. Also, such connections were a natural outcome of the cyclical and even seasonal nature of much of the employment in the industrial areas. The move from, say, Pembroke-shire to Merthyr was rarely a decisive single event: a worker might well return to his rural home in times of slump. In returning, he often brought with him the ideas and tactics that were currently in vogue further east. 'Mother Rebecca', symbolic leader of the tollgate protests, can be compared with Monmouthshire figures like the 'Scotch Bull', the patron of labour terrorism; or to earlier figures like Ned Ludd. More specifically, the authorities were intrigued by the presence of Hugh Williams in the heart of the disturbed area (at St Clears), and by his role in providing legal representation for indicted rioters. Chartist writers were quick to claim the Rebecca activists as part of their movement.

Yet Rebecca must be seen primarily as a local development, the most dramatic and successful of a series of protests in rural Wales over the previous half-century. Since the 1780s, Welsh communities had frequently experienced riots and disorders, often over the issue of food exports during time of dearth. These incidents occurred most commonly at ports and market towns serving a rural hinterland, as at Carmarthen in 1818. Enclosure was also an issue in parts of Wales. During the farming boom of the French war period, there had been enormous incentive to exploit and settle quite marginal land. This led to violent resistance in Caernarvonshire, Pembrokeshire and Cardiganshire, but it also left a legacy of many potential conflicts: enclosures from common land; large numbers of cottagers with dubious title to their holdings; and unrealistic rent levels. In the 1820s, there were arson attacks against the houses of people who had bought enclosed Cardiganshire lands, foreshadowing rural protest campaigns against outside 'intruders' in our own time.

Also, the farmers suffered from broader economic problems. Despite the development of drovers' banks at Brecon or Llandovery, credit and ready money were difficult to obtain. Farmers were thus vulnerable to financial panics like that of 1825–1826. In the next decade, government reforms of the tithe and the Poor Law created a new demand for payment in cash as opposed to goods, increasing the pressure still further. The Swing Riots of 1830 found local echoes in the sending of threatening letters in the south-east, while special constables were sworn in across the region. It was the more advanced regions that were more likely to employ day-labourers, who were badly hit by the crisis; and it is therefore in the southern and eastern fringe that we now find attempts to organise to press for higher wages.

Protest therefore needs little explanation, but the crisis of 1838–1844 included new elements, above all the state of the roads. Eighteenth century Wales had been notorious for its communications, and there had since the turn of the century been a movement to rebuild roads. This had meant the creation of turnpike trusts that theoretically undertook the work of improvement in exchange for the right to erect gates and charge tolls. In practice, the system worked badly in much of Wales. Improvements had often been slight, but tollgates had become a widespread phenomenon, even on country lanes. There were many overlapping jurisdictions on short stretches of road, so that multiple payments might be required for short journeys: 11 gates in 19 miles was a frequently recounted example. David Williams remarked that Swansea and Carmarthen in particular were so hemmed in by gates and guards that they resembled besieged cities. The impediments to travel were particularly resented in areas where farmers needed lime fertiliser for their fields, coal for their fires: things that could only be obtained by lengthy (and now expensive) travel. The system staggered along while collection and regulation were inefficient, and the gatekeepers allowed favours to friends and neighbours; but in the late 1830s, the trusts were increasingly farmed by newcomers like Thomas Bullin. These had a strong interest in efficiency and profit based on strict enforcement.

In 1839, that year of universal militancy, protests began against the gates. The first targets were the gates of the Whitland Trust, one of the more notorious organisations in terms of the state of its roads and the inflexibility of its 'farmer'. In June, the destruction of a gate at Efailwen in Carmarthenshire heralded the start of a mass movement. The rioters were a well-disciplined group hundreds strong. They usually warned of their intent by letter, and tried to avoid causing physical harm resulting from their well-planned rituals. Led by 'Mother Rebecca', the group would march along the road until they encountered the gate. Unable to proceed, Rebecca would appeal to her daughters for assistance in removing this obstacle, which they would usually do with great thoroughness and enthusiasm. As we might expect from a Biblically-obsessed culture,

Rebecca took her name from a Genesis passage about the woman of that name 'possessing the gates of those which hate them'.

The movement reached an early height in the summer of 1839, but then faded away until a dramatic revival throughout Pembrokeshire and Carmarthenshire from late 1842 into the spring of 1844. (This may reflect the influx of migrants returning home during the iron lay-offs of these years.) Protests also occurred in several neighbouring counties, as far away as Rhaiadr and west Glamorgan. As Rebecca spread, so did the scope of the grievances the 'rioters' were resisting. The New Poor Law was a major target: as early as January 1839, the Narberth workhouse had been burned down. In June 1843, a mass meeting in eastern Carmarthenshire drew up a list of demands that also included the abolition of the existing magistracy, who were attacked for their class bias and heavily partisan behaviour. A few days later, some 500 Rebecca supporters rode into Carmarthen where they attracted supporters possibly running into the thousands. Their banner read:

> *Cyfiawnder: A charwyr cyfiawnder ydym ni oll,*
> *Rhyddid a gwell lluniaeth, toll rydd a rhyddid.*

> 'Justice: We are all lovers of justice;
> liberty and better food, free tolls and liberty'.

The crowd attacked and occupied the workhouse before being driven off. For the authorities, this was a worrying challenge; and a fight at Pontardulais in September 1843 marked a new degree of armed conflict in the protest.

The movement also attempted to impose more widely its notions of social justice, for instance in the enforcement of rent levels. As one squire wrote in June 1843,

> The county of Carmarthen is being valued by the emissaries of these miscreants, and any farmer who pays more for his farm than their ideal standard will have the midnight incendiary to enlighten him of his error.[3]

Pressure grew for an army barracks to be erected at Carmarthen, which would thus become a 'second Brecon' to overawe the insurgent countryside (the new base would in fact be built rather later, and at Pembroke Dock).

Despite the growing parallels to Ireland, the Rebecca affair ended relatively happily. Under the influence of sympathetic coverage in *The Times*, the government appointed a Royal Commission that

3. T. Herbert and G.E. Jones, *People and protest: Wales 1815–1880* (Cardiff 1988), 131.

supported the movement's demands; and an Act of 1844 consolidated the trusts. Like the Anti-Corn Law League, and unlike the Chartists, this was a strictly limited movement demanding limited reforms within the existing social and political framework. Rebecca faded after 1844, though the name was often used for rural protests in Wales. 'Rebecca' led the protesters in the poaching wars on the Upper Wye and its tributaries, conflicts that continued sporadically in Radnorshire from 1856 to 1868, and which flared to new heights between 1877 and 1882. Between 1858 and 1869, 'Rebecca' destroyed fences used to enclose mountain land in Caernarvonshire. The name had become synonymous with successful rural protest.

Historically, too, Rebecca left a golden memory, as we would expect from a tradition that has always idealised the independent dissenting farmer or craftsman. The Rebeccas enjoyed the position of gallant resisters or Robin Hoods, above all to the Welsh historians who denounced the criminal brutality and drunken savagery of the Scotch Cattle and the Newport rebels. In 1866, the nonconformist Liberal Henry Richard stressed that the rural riots had been a desperate response to blatant injustice. Despite the attempts of 'a few evil-minded persons', Rebecca 'had no political significance whatsoever, and implied no dissatisfaction to the government'. This *Welsh* event stood in stark contrast to the nefarious Chartist outbreaks, which were 'of *English* inspiration', concentrated in 'the mixed and half-anglicized population of Monmouthshire and the other adjacent coal and iron districts'.[4]

But the contrast is too sharply drawn. While Rebecca did indeed draw little blood, we should stress the similarities with movements like the Cattle. Both were using ritualised mass action to enforce community standards and natural justice, and both were capable of bloodcurdling threats. Both, also, represented traditions with clear Welsh roots. And only by selective use of the evidence can overtly violent rural protests be distinguished from the noble good intentions of the 'original' Rebecca leaders.[5] The treatment of the rural and the industrial movements is only one illustration of a common theme that we find in nineteenth century Welsh politics, and in subsequent history. In both cases, the Liberal and nonconformist tradition found it difficult to come to terms with the realities of a mass industrial society.

4. Henry Richard, *Letters on the social and political condition of the principality of Wales* (London 1866), 71–75.
5. A point made strongly in David J.V. Jones, *Rebecca's Children: a study of rural society, crime and protest* (Oxford 1989).

THE ROOTS OF THE UNION TRADITION

This hostility would also be evident from the history of the trade union movement. The employers had a clear group self-interest in opposing unionisation, but we frequently find hostility to mass labour movements in Liberal and 'Radical' sections of Welsh opinion, and from sections of nonconformity. Activities like the union campaigns of 1830–1831 met violent resistance from quite progressive employers like Walter Coffin in the Rhondda; and the Methodist *sasiwn* issued a stern denunciation of unions in general and the National Association for the Protection of Labour in particular. In 1832, *Y drysorfa* plainly stated that industrial unions were 'contradictory to the word of God and to the laws of the country in which we live',[6] so membership involved excommunication. In 1836, a Methodist conference at Nantyglo received warm hospitality from the normally strictly Anglican Crawshay Bailey. But the future of radicalism in Wales lay with the labour organisations rather than rural protesters like the Rebecca rioters.

There is evidence of rudimentary union organisation in Wales from perhaps 1710, and there were early prosecutions in Swansea under the Combination Acts of 1799. Activity was intense and widespread, though often poorly recorded. In Caernarvonshire, there were constant labour conflicts in the great building work that created the new community of Tremadoc about 1812. This is so well known chiefly because local conservatives attributed the unrest to the notorious agitator Shelley, then in residence; and the poet's biographers have naturally investigated the affair.[7]

In the first decades of industrialisation, the cooperative impulse was expressed in two forms. First, there were overt organisations like friendly societies, which enjoyed a great vogue in the iron and coal country. Apart from widespread groups like the Oddfellows, there were also distinctively Welsh groups like the Ivorites, who took their name from the Welsh lord glorified in Iolo's pseudo-medieval effusions. On the other hand, there were clandestine movements, avowedly trade unions or else ritualistic groups like the Scotch Cattle. One would like to speculate that the overt groups acted as a cover for the illicit activities, a model found in other countries at different times; but there is not a shred of evidence for it.

6. T. Herbert and G.E. Jones, *People and protest: Wales 1815–1880* (Cardiff 1988), 91–93.
7. See for example Paul Foot, *Red Shelley* (London: Sidgwick and Jackson 1980); Richard Holmes, *Shelley: the pursuit* (London: Weidenfeld and Nicolson 1974).

In the militant centre of Aberdare, the friendly societies were strongly promoted by the Baptist minister, Thomas Price of Calfaria, as a counterweight to the organised union movement which he detested.

The Chartist years were accompanied by a real upsurge in industrial conflict that continued into the 1860s. In 1843, the west Glamorgan copper employers demanded wage cuts of 25 per cent, stringent even by the standards of the day; and a five week strike resulted in the defeat of the workers. The coalfields were also active between 1847 and 1853. Glamorgan experienced coal strikes in 1853, 1857 and 1867, prior to the great series of pit battles of the early 1870s. Despite the decline of political activism (or perhaps because of it) strikes were lengthy and often violent. In the Aberdare valley in 1850, a four month colliers' strike involved threats to sabotage the crucial rail lines. The homes of strikebreakers were attacked with guns and explosives, resulting in the offer of substantial rewards. Again in Aberdare, the 1857 strike may have involved four or five thousand workers. Militant traditions were also apparent in the lead and copper mines of north Wales. Holywell copper miners were on strike in 1850, while in 1856, troops were brought in against the lead miners of Talargoch in Flintshire. In 1869 a coal dispute at Mold led to the shooting deaths of four protesters.[8]

Some degree of union organisation can be traced in the events of mid-century. In 1844, the Chartists founded a Miners Association, but its impact in Wales was neither strong nor enduring. The great majority of industrial actions suggest that solidarity might be strong in a particular works or town, but wider affiliations were little in evidence. This picture of decentralised militancy provides a sharp contrast to the tight organisation that characterised the coalfields in particular at the end of the century. On the other hand, the lessons learned from the Chartist experience were by no means forgotten, and individual organisers lived on into the last years of the century. Professor I.G. Jones has suggested how Glamorgan industrial politics in the 1850s and 1860s were affected by loose coalitions of old Chartists, leaders of unions and friendly societies, and 'Liberationists', nonconformist opponents of the Church establishment.

Unionism was thus slow to develop in Wales. Even when a union movement did emerge, it was dominated by the issues of nonconformity and Liberalism, and independent Labour politics

8. T. Herbert and G.E. Jones, *People and protest: Wales 1815-1880* (Cardiff 1988), 170.

were still a long way off. In Glamorgan, the radical groups of the 1860s won their greatest victory in promoting the 1868 election of Henry Richard, as opposed to a specifically Labour candidate. Considering the extreme militancy of earlier years, this relative moderation is perhaps surprising; but at the end of the century, south Wales in particular would reclaim its place as an industrial storm-centre.

CHAPTER FOURTEEN
The Old Order

In the first half of the nineteenth century, Wales acquired a vanguard role in the British economy, in a process that resulted in new alignments and conflicts based on class and religion. But for all their impact, it would be misleading to concentrate entirely on the breakthroughs being accomplished in Tredegar or Swansea. Long after industrialisation was in full career, much of Wales appears little affected by the world of iron and steam, of slate and coal. In many areas, it would be difficult to discern immediate differences between the world of 1870 and that of 1720. In political structures, as much as in the shape of the landscape, it can seem as if the world of the Monmouthshire valleys belonged to a different country, another century.

Much of Wales continued to be ruled by essentially the same families and houses who had held power for centuries. They survived, and they had been buttressed rather than displaced by the new industrial wealth. This evidence comes above all from the survey of landownership undertaken at the behest of Parliament in 1872. Irritated by radical rhetoric about the grossly unjust distribution of land, Conservatives were delighted to support plans for a 'New Domesday Book', to survey patterns of landownership throughout Great Britain. The result, published the following year, was far from what they wished. The report showed that the concentration of land in the hands of the very rich was perhaps more extreme than most critics had suggested.

For the historian of Wales, the 1873 survey is a precious resource. Many caveats must be expressed about the definitions and the measurements used to assess individual landlords, but the general picture is not in doubt. Landownership was highly concentrated throughout the United Kingdom, but especially so in Wales. This table summarises the findings of the inquiry:[1]

Table 14:1   The Landowners of Wales in 1873

Category	Number	Acreage held	Per cent of Wales owned
Peers	31	557,000	13.5
Great landowners	148	1,263,100	30.6
Squires	392	672,300	16.3
Greater yeomen	1224	612,000	14.8
Lesser yeomen	2952	498,400	12.1
Small proprietors	17,289	431,800	10.5
Cottagers	35,592	7300	0.2
Public bodies	723	79,700	1.9
Total	58,351	4,121,600	99.9

There were 571 squires or great landowners in Wales in 1872, roughly one per cent of the total number of proprietors. This tiny group between them owned 60 per cent of the land. 4176 yeomen, with between a hundred and a thousand acres, held another 27 per cent.

The most powerful section of the landed community was the 180 or so peers and great landowners, each with at least 3000 acres of land, and a gross annual rental exceeding £3000 a year. They took in about a third of the total rental of the principality. The concentration of landownership in the hands of great proprietors varied according to region, and smaller landowners and owner-occupiers were most in evidence on the borders, in Radnorshire and Breconshire. In the three western counties of Anglesey, Caernarvon and Cardigan, great proprietors utterly dominated the landscape, with 60 or 70 per cent of the total acreage. Half the land area of Caernarvonshire was owned by just five families; three-quarters by 35 families. Four men alone – Lords Penrhyn, Newborough and Willoughby D'Eresby, and George Duff Assheton-Smith – owned 129,000 acres of the county, equivalent to some 200 square miles. In addition to landownership, two of these families also controlled the county's industrial wealth. Lord Penrhyn had a recorded gross rental of over £60,000 from Caernarvonshire alone; but his slate enterprises cleared an annual profit of at least another £100,000. Cardiganshire also

1. Howell, *Land and people* . . . 20–21; J. Bateman, *The great landowners of Great Britain and Ireland* (London 1878).

demonstrated extreme polarisation of landed wealth. Sir Pryse Pryse, the Earl of Lisburne and Colonel William Powell between them owned 93,000 acres. The county's social life inevitably revolved around their three seats, of Gogerddan, Crosswood and Nanteos, a reality that had changed little since the 1720s. In the whole county, only four other men fell into the category of 'great landowner'.

In terms of numbers, the largest concentrations of such land-owners were to be found in the southern coastal counties of Glamorgan (25 individuals), Carmarthen (13), Pembroke (15) and Monmouth (12). In the north, Denbighshire offered the most landed magnates, with 14. Many of the great estates were spread over several counties, quite possibly over two or more countries. If we count Welsh lands alone, then we can find about 20 individuals who each owned estates in excess of 20,000 acres. These empires customarily brought in rentals of ten or twenty thousand pounds. Many of these magnates were peers: the Duke of Beaufort, the Marquess of Bute, the Earls of Powis or Dunraven, Lords Windsor, Harlech and Dynevor, and so on. There were also commoners, like Christopher Rice Mansell-Talbot, with 34,000 acres worth £44,000. The commoner with twenty to thirty thousand acres of Welsh land was no rarity: men like Sir Richard Williams-Bulkeley of Baron Hill (Anglesey), or Charles Philipps of Picton Castle (Pembs).

It is debatable who was the greatest landowner in Wales. One of the largest in acreage was Earl Cawdor, with his seat at Stackpole. He had over 100,000 acres and a rental of £45,000. However, only half of this land was in south-west Wales, while the rest lay in northern Scotland. Similarly, Welsh estates represented only half of the 60,000 acres of the Earl of Powis. Close behind Cawdor came Sir Watkin Williams-Wynn with his 91,000 acres, and £47,000 rental. The overwhelming majority of these acres were indeed to be found in Wales; and for over a century, this landed power gave his family an enormous political role in the counties of Denbigh, Montgomery and Merioneth. In the 1870s, he was the 'King of Wales'. Lord Tredegar owned a mere 39,000 acres, all in Wales; but this estate produced an annual rental of £125,000. Also among the elite was Lord Penrhyn, with 50,000 acres worth £71,000.

Finally, and probably at the very peak, was the Marquess of Bute, with a total of 116,000 acres. Only an eighth of this was located in Wales; but this Glamorgan estate alone gave a rental of £180,000. It was this wealth, derived from the fantastic profits of coal and steam, that powered the Bute estate; and these very modern resources permitted the Marquesses to indulge their ultimate medieval fantasies, at Cardiff Castle and Castell Coch.

LAND AND INDUSTRY

In the nineteenth century, the Welsh ruling elite had been broadened considerably in consequence of the great fortunes built on the new industries. In the 1970s, Professor Rubinstein sought to counter what he believed to be myths about Victorian society. First, he argued that industrial wealth was not as significant as had been believed, in comparison with the fruits of financial or landed enterprise; and second, that industrial families were not really active in massive investment in land with the aim of building up great estates. South Wales, however, tends to reassert the familiar picture. Among the fabulously wealthy, Rubinstein listed men like Richard Crawshay and his grandson William, as well as several Welsh coal magnates like the third Marquess of Bute, or Lords Rhondda and Merthyr. And they did indeed move into land. When William Crawshay died in 1834, he left an estate estimated at £700,000. His son, another William (1788–1867), built the Gothic castle at Cyfarthfa, and also the country mansion at Caversham Park in Berkshire. He was clearly interested in moving from trade to land, and his estate was worth at least two million pounds.[2]

It was also about 1830 that Joseph Bailey withdrew from his industrial enterprises, and began a career of land purchases that would make his grandson one of the wealthiest landowners in Wales. John Homfray bought and redeveloped the ancient castle of Penllyn, and his descendants became country squires. The new families expressed their genteel aspirations by intermarrying with the landed elite. In Glamorgan, Crawshays intermarried with Franklens, Dillwyns with Llewellyns. Ironmaster Samuel Homfray married a daughter of Sir Charles Gould Morgan of Tredegar, one of the richest landed commoners in Britain.

In the 1750s, squires tended to withdraw from the direct administration of industrial enterprises, preferring to lease lands and mineral rights; though some remained involved into Victorian times. But this does not indicate any new contempt for 'trade', still less for the income it offered. It is remarkable to see how easily the new industrialists were absorbed into the existing social structure, encountering attitudes quite different from the snobbery that allegedly existed against early Victorian commercial men. As new entrepreneurs moved into Glamorgan or Monmouthshire, they were added fairly rapidly to the Bench of Justices: no doubt, largely

2. W.D. Rubinstein, *Men of Property* (London 1981).

because they were almost the only propertied men in these remote areas. Still, this was a quick path to social acceptance. In Glamorgan, new Justices appointed between 1782 and 1800 had included all the major ironmasters: Crawshays, Hills, Homfrays and others. The industrial elite was thus admitted to the Bench without an overt bourgeois revolution; and apparently, with little fuss or complaint.

Landed politics were sufficiently flexible to absorb the industrialists with minimal difficulty, and the first industrialist MPs and parliamentary candidates appeared in several Welsh counties between 1810 and 1820. From the 1830s, most of the leading industrialist families of south Wales entered Parliament. Some, like the Guests and Dillwyns, represented boroughs near the scene of their enterprises. Others chose county or border seats that would once have seemed appropriate only for the greatest landowners: various Baileys successively represented Newport, Breconshire, Herefordshire and Worcestershire.

By 1873, we can clearly discern the impact of new money on the landed community. Crawshay Bailey of Nantyglo had 14,000 acres, 12,000 of which were in Wales; Sir Joseph Russell Bailey of Glanusk had 28,000. The latter attended Harrow and Christ Church, and would enter the peerage as Lord Glanusk in 1899. H.A. Bruce had already become Lord Aberdare in 1873; the Vivians became Lords Swansea in 1893. In north Wales, the great Victorian mansion of Kinmel reflected the vast profits from the Anglesey copper mines, wealth which had propelled the Hughes family into the peerage as Lords Dinorben.

However, the greatest triumph was perhaps that of the Guests. Sir Josiah John Guest had withdrawn from direct involvement in his iron enterprises by the 1840s, and had taken up residence in Canford Manor, Wimborne. His son attended Harrow and Trinity, Cambridge, and entered the peerage as Lord Wimborne. Sir Josiah had also begun accumulating vast landholdings, apparently with a view to their prestige rather than the actual value. In 1872, Sir Ivor Bertie Guest owned a massive 53,000 acres: the Glamorgan tract of 6000 acres produced £28,000 a year; while his 34,000 acres in Ross-shire was a gigantic sheep-run producing only £1000 a year.

The importance of industry and mineral exploitation is also apparent from the number of estates where a smaller number of acres obviously produced a vast income. Normally, a purely landed estate of three or four thousand acres would produce a gross rental of an equivalent number of pounds. Lord Aberdare, on the other hand, derived £12,000 from an estate of less than 4000 acres. In Gwynedd too, landowners with slate holdings might find the value of their property greatly inflated. Proximity to one of the new rail routes tended to increase the value of an estate, and landowners often encouraged improved transportation for just this reason. Few could compete in this regard with C.R.M. Talbot, whose enormous property on his death in 1890 included some three million pounds worth of railway investments.

SQUIRES

Below the 20 or so leviathans were the families with rentals of (roughly) four and eight thousand pounds, and then the squires with two or three thousand. These 500 or so families represented the most visible faces of landed power for the majority of people in rural Wales. A respectable income could be produced either from vast and fairly barren lands in the north and west, or from quite compact and productive properties in the south. Where industrial opportunities were lacking, the landowners often found themselves nowhere nearly as wealthy as their large holdings might suggest. In Merionethshire, the landscape was dominated by five great estates, with their seats at Rûg, Ynysmaengwyn, Rhiwlas, Mawddwy and Nannau: a geography that would have been broadly familiar in Georgian times. Together with the Williams-Wynn estate in the county, these six together owned some 84,000 acres, but the total rental was a mere £42,000. Thomas Pryce Lloyd of Nannau owned 17,000 Merionethshire acres, which brought him a mere £4000 a year. Cardiganshire estates were almost as unproductive: the Crosswood estate of 43,000 acres brought in only £11,000 for the Earl of Lisburne. Disparities between north and south were aggravated by the nature of the emerging rail network. It was Lord Mostyn who promoted the line from Aberystwyth along the Merionethshire coast as a desperate attempt to increase the value of his properties in that county.

By contrast, southern estates might bring in six or eight times the rental per acre, even without mineral rights. Against the Merionethshire or Cardiganshire squires, we might set distinguished Glamorgan examples like John Whitlock Nicholl-Carne of St Donats Castle and Nash, worth £4500 from his 3200 acres; or Thomas Picton-Turberville of Ewenni, with £4800 from 3300 acres. This level of income and landownership might also be represented by Charles

Mansell-Lewis of Stradey (Carms), John Lort-Philipps of Lawrenny (Pembs); or dozens of other provincial magnates from throughout the south and the borderland.

'Squires' with between one and three thousand acres were common in the three south-western counties. Such families were generally commoners, often with prestigious ancient names, though the connection with their ancestors might be tenuous. The landed community maintained its identity through a variety of traditions and institutions: the militia and the Bench, through public service, and above all through the world of sport and hunting. The central institutions of upper-class life were perhaps the hunts: the Llangibby hounds, the Tenby and Pembrokeshire hunts, and so on. Cardigan-shire and Pembrokeshire were for many years ruled as much by the officers of the Tivyside Hunt as by their respective Quarter Sessions, the different groups being very similar in composition.

THE POWER OF THE LANDOWNERS

Old and new, great and merely middling, these landowners dominated Welsh justice and local government well into the mid-Victorian years. Their power cannot be assessed by simply discussing one family or house: the families were intimately bound together, especially by ties of kinship, which provided the cement of landed society, but which linked that community to other powerful groups – to industrialists, to town elites, to the clergy and to other professional classes. No one case is typical, but the family of C.R.M. Talbot provides a useful illustration. He was MP for a Glamorgan county constituency from 1830 to 1890. Between 1820 and 1840, four of his sisters married other local magnates: Richard Franklen of Clemenston, John Dillwyn-Llewellyn of Penllergaer, John Mont-gomery Traherne of Coedarhydyglyn and John Nicholl of Merthyr Mawr. In their origins, none of the four families represented ancient wealth or power. All were old lines, but they had customarily been petty gentlemen or professionals, who had only established them-selves in the county elite after the demographic crisis of the mid-eighteenth century.

Landed and industrial power were therefore in close alliance by the time that marriage with the Talbot sisters consecrated admission into the highest circles of the county community. All the families demonstrated considerable political power. Both John Dillwyn-

Llewellyn's brother and father served as MPs for Swansea constituencies; John Nicholl and his father held a variety of constituencies
between 1802 and 1852. Politically, the Nicholls were diehard
Tories, the Dillwyn-Llewellyns were radical Liberals, while Talbot
himself was a moderate Whig who looked increasingly out of place
in the Gladstonian Liberal Party as the decades progressed. However,
the circle owed its power less to ideology than to landed wealth.

Of course, men like John Nicholl and C.R.M. Talbot were MPs.
More striking is the breadth of their power in other institutions like
local government and the administration of justice, where gentry
power prevailed until the creation of county councils in 1889. Talbot
was Lord Lieutenant of Glamorgan from 1848 to 1890; two
successive Lords Ormathwaite held the post in Radnorshire from
1840 to 1895. The Bench had been considerably broadened in its
membership, but much power rested with the old gentry. The
Chairman of Merionethshire Quarter Sessions in the mid-Victorian
years was a Price of Rhiwlas; Glamorgan usually selected a Jones of
Fonmon. In Radnorshire, the incumbent for the first two decades of
Victoria's reign was the Rev. Richard Venables of Llysdinam, a
'squarson' who was also Archdeacon of Carmarthen. And while the
new county councils were often radical bodies, the gentry were far
from extinct. From 1889 to 1928, the Clerk of the Glamorgan
County Council was Sir Thomas Mansell-Franklen, a nephew of
C.R.M. Talbot and the former Clerk of the Peace under the old
regime.

In the Edwardian period, the Lords Lieutenant continued to be
aristocrats like Lord Tredegar or Earl Cawdor. The landed families
were powerful in the militia establishment, gathering as the officer
corps of the Carmarthen Royal Garrison Artillery, or the Imperial
Yeomanry forces of Pembrokeshire or Glamorgan. And they
continued as Justices, appointed following the recommendation of
the Lords-Lieutenant. After the Liberal triumphs of recent years, the
survival of the Tory magistracy was a real grievance in counties like
Merionethshire; and only now did Richard Davies become the first
dissenting Justice in Anglesey. In Caernarvonshire in 1889, the
county council had only nine Tory members, seven of whom were
magistrates; but of the 33 Liberals, a mere six held this rank. In times
of social and industrial conflict like the great slate lockouts, the
magistrates and police were accused of acting without restraint from
the more democratic police committees. Even in Cardiff, police
maltreatment of a Liberal election crowd in 1886 was viewed as
unjustified assault by all but the most committed Tory partisans.

THE GENTRY AND THE PROFESSIONAL CLASSES

The power of the landed elite in 1870 was remarkably similar to what it had been two centuries earlier. In both periods, all the major gentry families were closely linked to local professional and 'middling' houses. In the Talbot circle, we find the Trahernes active in local ecclesiastical affairs, especially in the diocese of Llandaff. With their in-laws from the families of Knight, Bruce and Edmondes, they held many of the choicest offices and livings in the diocese, naturally enough benefiting from the patronage of families like the Talbots and Nicholls.

Again as in 1670, the ties to professional families continued to reinforce landed power in much of Wales. Perhaps this also helps to explain the endurance of this authority in the face of so many apparent challenges. Many landowners had industrial interests, and drew lawyers and businessmen into their ambit as partners, agents or managers. This slowed the emergence of any *bourgeois* interest. The Talbot estate was faithfully served as stewards over several generations by the family of Llewellyn of Baglan (no relation to the Dillwyns). These Llewellyns, originally attorneys, also became landed gentry and magistrates. With the Talbots, they became indispensable to the Anglican cause in the western half of Glamorgan. Often of the highest architectural quality, 'Talbot' and 'Llewellyn' churches remain landmarks in many industrial communities.

Local professional dynasties like the Franklens, Trahernes and Edmondes exercised a long hegemony over the affairs of Welsh country towns like Cowbridge and Brecon. Bridgend was dominated by the Wyndhams, Swansea by the Dillwyn-Llewellyns. More spectacular was the position of aristocrats in some of the largest urban and industrial centres, above all the role of the Marquesses of Bute in developing Cardiff. The Talbots created Port Talbot, the Lords Penrhyn made Bangor. Urban politics often centred on the struggle against such a landed neighbour: of Newport against Tredegar, of Bala against Rhiwlas.

THE LAND QUESTION

At local level, the mansions of the landed elite dominated the surrounding countryside in terms far more than the merely visual.

Domestic service in such houses continued to provide a major source of employment until the end of the century. Above all, the squires were landlords over the tenants, with enormous power over matters like rent-levels and evictions, over farming practices and improvements. In 1887, 89 per cent of the cultivated land was occupied by tenants, leaving only ten or eleven per cent for owner-occupiers This gave the landowners great authority over daily life, and the exact nature of their rule became one of the vital political issues in the latter half of the nineteenth century.

As radical Liberalism increased its political hold after 1868, 'landlordism' became a fundamental cause, and the 'land question' was central to Welsh politics between 1886 and 1895. The stereotype was that of a courageous (and essentially homogeneous) peasantry, nonconformist and Welsh-speaking, who were exploited by a decadent anglicised squirearchy. This was the view presented from the 1880s by writers and orators like Tom Ellis or, T.J. Hughes (*Adfyfr*), and it became a commonplace of nonconformist Liberal papers like the *Baner*. Typical are these passages taken from the *Cenedl* in 1893.[3]

> Besides being useless and immoral, spending money on horses and harlots, they are merciless tyrants. They cruelly oppress those who work hard to keep them. This doubles and trebles their sin. Besides going to the workman's pocket to steal his money, they enter his head and heart to rule his religion and his politics. They say to their tenants you must believe the same things as we do in politics, and profess the same religion, and woe betide you if you don't do this. Have we not a bitter experience of this in Wales?

> . . . . We see that the land has been usurped through fraud, craftiness and oppression, by a handful of unprincipled people, and that those few people have not only stolen the land, but also oppress the people who cultivate it and live on it; that a vast portion of the gains of the land is grasped by those lords, and spent on frivolous and sinful pleasure, and that the country is thus greatly impoverished.

We will often encounter manifestations of this conflict: in debates over the nature of the magistracy and local government, tithes and sectarian education; but in essence, the debate concerned matters of landownership and estate administration. The landlords were accused of being absentees only interested in drawing the maximum rental from their estate, to the neglect of the interests of the tenantry, still less of thoughts of improvement. Callous disregard for an alien and

3. Quoted in H.M. Vaughan, *The Welsh squires* (Carmarthen: Golden Grove, 1988), 196–8.

subordinate people led to rack-renting and casual evictions (often for religious or political reasons). Meanwhile, the heavy concentration of property in a few hands led to a hunger for land among many thousands, who were driven to proletarianisation in the coal and iron areas. Overused land became exhausted and the countryside endured a vicious circle of poverty and exploitation.

The radicals were thus portraying Welsh landowners as parasites on the worst Irish pattern, and their rhetoric enjoyed immense success. When in 1926, Herbert M. Vaughan wrote an elegaic and favourable account of *The Welsh Squires*, he was defending the indefensible, struggling against a stereotype of enormous force. More recently, the work of David Howell has shown that Welsh landowners were more akin to their neighbours in England than in Ireland. Of course rural hierarchy was extreme and there were areas of conflict; but Welsh landlords often worked from the basis of a paternalistic ideology. Most were slow to evict, and the 'great evictions' of Liberal and nonconformist tenants were in reality small and strictly localised occasions. Despite the notionally arbitrary nature of landlords' power, tenants often succeeded their relatives in one holding over generations.

Also, the radical critique was based in part on regional prejudices, being far more relevant to those areas of the north and west with which they were most familiar. The countryside of Cardiganshire or Merionethshire did indeed suggest a spectacle of primitive farming, of rural poverty and decay. In fact, this does not reflect the nature of landed power so much as the slow spread of farming practices and building styles, which generally proceeds from the south and east, leaving 'Irish' patterns to linger in north and west.

Landlords as oriented to the market as most clearly were generally saw the virtues of improvement, and leases were used to enforce progressive and responsible farming techniques. From necessity rather than sentiment, landlords and agents often permitted their tenants to run up substantial arrears: after all, ruined or dissatisfied tenants and labourers always had the alternative of moving to the cities or industrial towns. Without romanticising the great estates or their owners, the squires and lords were not the stage villains they are sometimes portrayed as.

Only in one area did the landowners demonstrate real obduracy that did indeed provoke unnecessary conflict, and that was in the matter of the game laws and the attendant measures to suppress poaching. Into the present century, the gamekeeper may have done more to cause 'Irish' comparisons than either the squire or his steward. Only thus can we explain the long and bitter feuds over poaching and fishing in mid-Wales, which gave 'Rebecca' protests a 40-year afterlife. Not until the Ground Game Act of 1880 was one of the worst provocations removed, when farmers were at last permitted to destroy rabbits and vermin on their land.

The creation of the 'land question' is an instructive lesson in the development of political rhetoric in Wales. The areas most subject to English influence were also the parts controlled by great landlords, and furthermore they retained Conservative loyalties. It was a natural political device to assert that so alien a creation as Toryism could only come about through gentry intimidation: through the power of Lord Ormathwaite in Radnorshire, the Earls Cawdor in South Pembrokeshire, the Dukes of Beaufort and Marquesses of Bute in their respective fiefs. Lady Charlotte Guest, a strong Liberal partisan, wrote of the Glamorgan county election of 1837:

> The tory landlords brought their tenants up themselves like flocks of sheep and made them break their pledge words. They absolutely dragged them to the poll, threatening to turn them out of their farms unless they voted plumpers for Lord Adare. One man shed tears on being forced to this.[4]

Another possibility, of course, is that both landed power and Conservative loyalties were separate consequences of common economic and geographical factors. In the 1830s and 1840s, the more 'anglicised' arable areas had a real economic interest in the maintenance of the Corn Laws, and thus tended to vote for Conservative candidates who ran as the 'farmer's friend'. Conversely, the Liberal candidate in Glamorgan in 1837 had urged lower food prices, and issued handbills with the slogan 'Down with the farmers'. Intimidation was scarcely needed to organise farming interests behind the Tory candidate, who was generally a landowner.

We can also learn a great deal about the prejudices and assumptions of the opponents of the landed regime. The land reformers may have consciously distorted the reality of rural Wales; but they also demonstrated a real and quite sincere inability to comprehend the changes taking place in Wales: above all, that the decision to move to the industrial valleys could reflect anything other than desperation. In reality, even the harsh conditions of Aberdare or Tredegar offered economic and social opportunities far greater than the highly limited world of rural Wales, to say nothing of the very

4. Earl of Bessborough ed., *The journal of Lady Charlotte Guest* (London: John Murray, 1950), 53–55.

different but equally authentic communities being forged around the pits and furnaces. That this world could somehow exercise a positive influence on the 'true' Wales of the farming shires was near-heresy. Also, the radical portrait of rural life can be criticised for the absolute emphasis on the sturdy nonconformist peasant as the epitome of virtue and justice. In reality, rural society would have been sharply divided by class and economic interest, even if the landlords and their agents had all vanished overnight. The agricultural community was composed of diverse interests that could find at best a temporary unity in causes based on language and religion: rural society was composed of large farmers and small, of labourers and paupers.

THE END OF THE OLD WORLD

Gentry-ruled Wales perished neither in 1832, nor 1868. Politically, 1889 marks one convenient point of transition, with the passing of much power from the old Justices to the county councils. The Liberal victories of 1906 can be seen as another key change, with candidates from ancient families being defeated by radicals, noncon- formists, even representatives of the miners' union. In fact, there are simply too many symbolic dates that one could choose between 1880 and 1918. The propaganda against 'landlordism' had perhaps taken its toll in reducing the value attached to the status of landed gentry; while the First World War and its aftermath wrought further damage. H.M. Vaughan called the war the 'crowning catastrophe'. The officer class suffered casualties quite as appalling as their inferiors: both Nanteos and Penrhyn lost heirs in the fighting. In 1915, another young officer lost was Lord Ninian Crichton-Stuart, son of the Marquess of Bute, and the last of his house to represent the Cardiff constituency.

Meanwhile, the families at home were devastated by war taxes. Without attempting to trivialise the disasters of the war, it was one of the great symbolic tragedies of these years that even the Tivyside Hunt ceased to function. After 1918, the decline in domestic service made the great houses harder to operate. The estates were increasingly selling off lands by this time, permitting former tenants to begin a buying spree that dramatically increased the proportion of owner-occupiers. Between 1914 and 1922, virtually all the greatest estates sold off the bulk of their land, including such legendary names as Margam, Cefn Mabli, Baron Hill and Glynllifon.[5]

But the landed estate did not lose its value overnight. Well after the assault on landlordism had begun there were still *nouveaux-riches* who wished to establish themselves in a great mansion, either purchasing an existing house, or even building anew. It was in 1893, perhaps the low point of landed prestige in Wales, that the Cardiff shipowner John Cory built himself the splendid mansion at Dyffryn House. Coal wealth was the basis for a number of Edwardian country houses: Craig-y-Parc near Cardiff, or Morgan Williams' remodelling of St Donats Castle. Lord Rhondda established himself at Llanwern, David Davies at Llandinam; and in 1942, Margam itself passed to a wealthy brewer. Most spectacular among the new arrivals was William Randolph Hearst, who in 1925 purchased St Donats, which he proceeded to transform into a British equivalent of his Californian Xanadu. It was of course an epitome of snobbery and vulgarity, but it offered a social centre where medieval barons manqués could fulfil their fantasies. (Lloyd George, scourge of the gentry, was one of the more distinguished visitors.)

It was the Second World War which effectively ended the age of the gentry in Wales. Some old estates remain to this day, with ancient families at their traditional seats: Glamorgan offers Penrice or Fonmon castles, or Merthyr Mawr House. But such houses were mostly lost or transformed. In the 20 years after 1945, there was a massive destruction of historic properties: Hafod and Baglan, Llanwern and Stackpole, Dunraven, Harpton and Glanusk, and all too many others.

When they were not demolished, the great houses found a new role as public buildings. Many became educational institutions: St Donat's became the seat of Atlantic College, Llanarth is a Benedictine school, Dyffryn a sixth-form college. Others used the rural location of the houses to good advantage to promote centres of agricultural training, as at Gogerddan or Golden Grove. Cefn Mabli and Hensol were hospitals. Perhaps the best solution was restoration as part of the emerging 'heritage' industry which boomed from the 1970s. As stately homes or country parks, great houses began to bustle once again with more activity than they had perhaps known since Stuart times. Some became major attractions, and these were often the greatest houses: Margam Park, Powis Castle, Cardiff Castle, Nanteos, Erddig, Chirk, Penrhyn Castle, Tredegar and Plas Newydd. Perhaps most successful was St Fagans Castle, now the

---

5. John Davies, 'The end of the great estates', *Welsh history review* 7 (1974).

core of the Welsh Folk Museum, a magnificent example of the popular presentation of history.

Much therefore remains of historical and architectural interest; but of the power of the landed elites, there remains virtually nothing.

LAND AND CHURCH

Central to the social and political ideology of the traditional elites was the Church. For a nineteenth century Liberal, it would have been perfectly natural to follow an account of the landowning class with a discussion of *Eglwys Lloegr* – the Church of England in Wales. Just as the Welsh squire was cast as the grasping alien tyrant, so the Anglican clergy were portrayed as his lapdogs. The Church tended to be strongest where the gentry and landed elites possessed most power, while it scarcely existed in many pastoral and industrial areas. Throughout the country, clergy were most frequently chosen by powerful landowners, either local or absentee. Where livings were substantial, the incumbents were often gentry scions, like the Rev. Henry Glynne of Hawarden, whose brother, Sir Stephen, was Lord-Lieutenant of Flintshire.

Occasionally, this benevolent despotism of squire and parson was accepted and even popular. It is ironic that Wales should have been the setting for one of the best-known accounts of a docile gentry-ruled countryside where life revolved around the manor-house and vicarage, the paternalism of Squire Baskerville and Parson Venables. It is all the more remarkable that this account – Kilvert's *Diary* of life in Clyro (Radns) in the 1870s – should describe the Upper Wye country, an area with a tradition of religious radicalism as flamboyant as could be found anywhere in Wales.

But this was exceptional, as resistance to Anglican authority grew throughout rural Wales in the latter half of the century. This made for a powerful equation between nonconformity, democracy and patriotism; and for a linkage between Anglicanism, oligarchy and 'anglicisation'. The growth of nonconformity after 1800 contributed to the sense of crisis in the Church, a conflict that increased with every new Revival; while the rise of Methodism threw into question the loyalty of all rural areas. This undermined the whole nature of establishment. If the community at large was generally Anglican, then it was possible to justify the large proportion of clerical Justices, the payment of tithes and the enforcement of ecclesiastical law.

When the majority of the public belonged to competing sects, the situation became anomalous, and flagrantly unjust. The political campaign against the establishment began in earnest in the 1840s, though the Welsh Church retained its official position until 1920.

Having said this, the Welsh Church deserves some credit for its response to the nonconformist assault. From the 1830s, a wholesale Church revival had been the aim of a series of able bishops. Among the best were Alfred Ollivant at Llandaff (1849–1882), Connop Thirlwall at St Davids (1840–1875) and Vowler Short at St Asaph (1846–1870). Unlike so many of their predecessors, they were usually resident, and they took care to make or encourage appropriate appointments to livings. They were increasingly unwilling to tolerate the old compromise whereby a squire appointed an English incumbent, who then employed a Welsh-speaking curate to serve the parish. The new Bishops travelled to every one of their dispersed parishes – a mobility made possible by the railways – and they were great builders. Between them, Ollivant and Thirlwall restored or rebuilt some 350 churches, and hundreds of parsonage houses. They were often assisted by able deans and chancellors, like J.M. Traherne and William Bruce Knight in Llandaff.

From the 1840s, the episcopate responded to the Dissenting challenge with a series of measures that proved remarkably effective. For example, the institution of district chapelries permitted the expansion of Anglican services into the highly populated areas. The Bishops were so successful in sponsoring the creation of networks of Church-run schools that by the end of the century, these often provided the only form of education offered in many areas that were otherwise nonconformist. This paradox led to intense political conflict after 1900. The Church also developed institutions of higher learning: St Davids Lampeter was opened in 1827, and it became a centre of Welsh intellectual life. (Ollivant had been Vice-Principal here from 1827 to 1843.) Anglican teacher training colleges soon followed.

Men like Ollivant and Thirlwall were able to mobilise the activism and generosity of lay magnates to come to the material aid of the church. Some were lavish in their donations and their building activities: we have already noted the activity of the Talbots and Llewellyns in western Glamorgan. Equally dedicated was Lord Penrhyn in Caernarvonshire. Lay generosity was channelled through organisations like the Church Extension Societies, the membership of which often included the leading county landowners. At lower social levels, lay involvement was encouraged by the spread of

Church-related societies, and the introduction of the office of lay reader in the 1870s. In the diocese of Bangor, Dean Cotton attempted to promote lay involvement by extending the use of Welsh, and promoting communal activities like Welsh hymn-singing. From the 1870s, it became increasingly common to speak of a Church revival, a movement symbolised by the Rhyl congress of 1891, and by the lively debates in Church papers like *Yr haul* or *Y cyfaill eglwysig*.

The Church would also draw strength from the intellectual currents in the wider society. From the 1820s, Wales was profoundly affected by the Romantic interest in medieval history and anti-quarianism. This enthusiasm is suggested by the secular building activities of these years: the grand castles of Cyfarthfa and Penrhyn, of Margam and Halkyn, Talacre and Hawarden, Hensol and Gwrych, all substantially built or rebuilt in the 1820s and 1830s. It was at this time that restoration work at Powis Castle was specifically aimed at giving it a more appropriately ancient appearance.

Within the walls of such houses, a full-scale medieval revival was under way. Lady Charlotte Guest edited the translation of the Mabinogion (1838–1849); Maria Jane Williams of Aberpergwm collected Welsh airs and folk-songs. The amazing Lady Llanover transformed herself into 'Gwenynen Gwent', the patroness of all that was Welsh, bardic and antique. To the mingled awe and amusement of the neighbouring gentry, she transformed her household into a pastiche of a medieval hall of the *uchelwyr*. Generations of the Guests favoured the name 'Ivor', after the proverbially generous patron portrayed by Iolo Morganwg. We can only speculate if such a neo-medieval movement would have been so successful if there had not been so many new families in quest of the facade of antiquity.

THE ROMANTICS

But Romantic posturing was indissolubly married to real scholar-ship, and the noble ladies patronised able antiquaries and literary experts, encouraging a significant cultural revival. One beneficiary was Thomas Price (*Carnhuanawc*) who published a (Welsh-language) History of Wales to 1282 (1836–1842); and who developed links with the antiquaries of Celtic Brittany. In the 1820s, several of the leading scholars became engaged in a fierce controversy about the correct

293

spelling of Welsh. Authorities like John Jones (*Tegid*) advocated extensive 'reform', and others like William Bruce Knight indignantly attacked this as cultural vandalism. The battles may appear trivial in retrospect, but they do illustrate one point of real consequence: the new antiquarianism was firmly rooted in the established Church as much as the gentry, so that questions of culture and nationalism were by no means the preserve of the Dissenters. In the first half of the century, Anglican enthusiasm for the traditional culture stood in marked contrast to the indifference or active hostility expressed by many nonconformists, and especially of John Elias' Methodists.

Tegid, Carnhuanawc and Knight were all clerics: indeed, they are collectively known in Welsh history as *Yr hen bersoniaid llengar*, which Prys Morgan renders as the 'old clerical patriots'. The group also included clerical poets and literati of note, like John Blackwell, *Alun*, or *Ieuan Glan Geirionydd*. Some built on the Celtic theories originating with Iolo Morganwg; and Bishop Burgess of St Davids (begetter of Lampeter) was admitted to Iolo's Gorsedd. He even presided over the Carmarthen eisteddfod of 1819, one of the first to graft the new druidism on to a traditional cultural festival. There was a strong clerical element in the Cambrian Societies and the movements for provincial eisteddfodau, both of which developed after 1815. In 1832, the Beaumaris eisteddfod ('a splendid congress of bards') was patronised by Sir Richard Williams-Bulkeley, and attended by the Duchess of Kent and Princess Victoria.[6]

Medievalism also had its impact on religious affiliations, and prepared the ground for the Tractarian movement. Some of the most forceful early advocates of nationalism in Wales were Anglicans and clerics, especially Oxford movement sympathisers like Rice Rees, Richard Williams Morgan and John Williams (*ab Ithel*). This was also the mould from which came Morris Williams (*Nicander*), a Tractarian cleric who promoted Welsh culture and poetry in the diocese of Bangor. As in England, High Churchmanship was often accompanied by medieval sympathies – Ab Ithel published *The ecclesiastical antiquities of the Cymry* in 1844 – and this antiquarianism led to nationalistic views. In the 1840s, nationalistic sentiments were apparent in the resistance to the proposed merger of the dioceses of Bangor and St Asaph. Churchmen like Dean Cotton and Sir Thomas Philipps led the opposition to the Blue Books (see Chapter Fifteen).

This was also the time at which the pressure for the appointment of Welsh Bishops engendered much controversy. Both Ollivant and

6. *Parry's railway companion.*

Thirlwall encountered much opposition, not least from the husband of Lady Llanover. Both had to make gestures in the direction of learning or patronising the language, while Vowler Short pioneered techniques of bilingual education. For the activists, Welsh Anglicanism was no mere alien graft, but an authentically Welsh successor to earlier Celtic and medieval Christianity; and the episcopate had to reflect that fact. In a time when the establishment was increasingly under attack as alien or irrelevant, the new theories provided an ideology that shrewdly combined piety and patriotism.

RITUALISM

The Oxford movement did not immediately gain ascendancy in Wales. At least until 1870, the Evangelicals were clearly in the ascendant, and the modern emphasis on the high tradition owes much to the pattern of later developments. In 1859, there were Anglican clergy throughout Wales who rejoiced at the great revival and welcomed its converts into their churches. However, High Churchmanship had an early and stimulating impact on Wales. Isaac Williams of Aberystwyth was curate to Newman at Oxford, and himself became a Tractarian scholar. His brother erected at Llangorwen a church that introduced to the Wales of the 1840s many of the ritualist styles and theories. There was another centre in Breconshire, at Llangasty Talyllyn. In the see of Bangor, Bishop Christopher Bethell (1830–1859) established Tractarian centres in parishes like Llanllechid and Glanogwen (Bethesda). Such buildings could have been viewed as isolated eccentricities, but it was soon apparent that 'ritualism' had a genuine appeal within the Church, especially to the landowning classes who were so crucial through their control of patronage.

The gentry entered wholeheartedly into the movement. Theodore, son of C.R.M. Talbot, worked as a missioner in Holborn until his death in something approaching Anglo–Catholic sanctity in 1876. Other families sponsored ritualism in their localities; and most of the most notable Tractarian churches in Wales are to be found in the most gentrified and Anglicised areas, such as Gower and south Pembrokeshire. 'High' traditions were often established in a community almost by chance, and then flowered into an enduring tradition. Cardiff and Aberdare both became Anglo–Catholic centres, and Aberdare was the initial centre for the distinctly high theological college of St Michael and the Angels.

The High Church movement also had the controversial effect of drawing upper class men and women towards Catholic ideas and practices, and sometimes to full conversion. A cause célèbre occurred at Pantasaph, in Flintshire, where a new Anglican church was being built to commemorate the marriage of the landowners, the later Earl and Countess of Denbigh. In 1850, the church was redesigned to fit the new Catholic loyalties of the patrons, and a legal struggle failed to regain the building for the establishment. Pantasaph, meanwhile, acquired both a convent and Capuchin friary. By the third quarter of the century, Wales had a number of Catholic peers and squires, including some of powerful landlords like the Earls of Dunraven (1855) and Ashburnham (inherited 1878). By far the most important was the third Marquess of Bute, converted in 1869. By 1918, even a Crawshay died in the arms of the Catholic Church.

In 1848, the Jesuits founded a college of St Beuno at Tremeirchion, near St Asaph, and this soon became a haven for dozens of converts from Anglicanism. From the 1860s, the Catholic priesthood in Wales developed a cohort of Welsh-speakers of some academic quality, men like Hugh Jones of Caernarvon or William Williams of Aberystwyth. Also in the 1860s, there was a movement to revive the monastic tradition within the Church of England, with the eccentric community of Father Ignatius at Capel-y-Ffin. By 1913, the leading community, at Caldey Island made a wholesale transition to Rome.

By the 1860s, the Anglican Church in Wales had freed itself of most of the worst charges that could be made about alleged indifference or apathy among its clergy. Nonconformist propaganda now turned instead to the rival theme that the Anglicans were contaminated by ritualism and Romanism. The change in rhetoric indicates success of a kind. Also at this time, the Church began to develop an image more in keeping with the cultural nationalism of the time. In 1870, Gladstone appointed Joshua Hughes of Llandovery to the see of St Asaph, the first Welsh-speaking Welsh Bishop in the see since 1727. Thenceforward, it became politically essential to take account of such considerations, and the new Bishops were usually Welsh in language and culture. In fact, this new Welsh episcopate often bore a close resemblance to the nonconformist leadership, and Hughes was a strong evangelical. His son, Joshua Pritchard Hughes, held the see of Llandaff from 1905 to 1931: he was a strict sabbatarian and temperance advocate, an enemy of ritualism, and an advocate of

7. Robert Lucas, *A Gower family* (Lewes: Book Guild, 1986), 122.

Welsh culture. Accordingly, such men increasingly attracted widespread respect outside the Church proper. John Owen (Bishop of St Davids 1897–1926) receives the benediction of the *Dictionary of Welsh biography* as 'a thorough Welshman in language and sympathy'.

It is striking how well this particular part of the old regime recovered from the massive disadvantages it faced in mid-century. While the Welsh Church hardly enjoyed the apparent success of the lay aristocrats and squires, the Anglican tradition was far stronger by 1900 than could possibly have been foreseen in early Victorian times. They were after all the largest sect within the country, a position that would have seemed highly improbable in the 1840s. The body that was ultimately disestablished was in far sounder health than it had been a century before. And unlike the Welsh gentry class, the Church actually had a future in the coming century.

PART FOUR
Modern Wales

CHAPTER FIFTEEN

Inventing a Nation: Wales 1840–1880

The English know how to reconcile people of the most diverse races with their rule; the Welsh, who fought tenaciously for their language and culture, have become entirely reconciled with the British Empire. . . .

Friedrich Engels[1]

By about 1840, Wales was becoming what may well have been the most modern society in Europe; and the economic and technological arrangements of this new world opened the way for new forms of politics, propaganda and communication. From the 1830s, the Welsh were influenced by the most advanced intellectual currents of contemporary Europe – idealism, nationalism, liberalism – and these were disseminated by a vigorous new press. The new ideas found such a warm welcome because they represented the latest Continental mode, but they were also immediately relevant to local conflicts and alignments. In south Wales, the tripartite conflict between traditional aristocracy, industrial bourgeoisie, and proletariat was no mere intellectual formulation of German economists. It was the stuff of interest-group politics, the underlying structure and explanation of the lengthy battles over tariffs and cheap food.

Welsh radicals did not share the scepticism or materialism of their European counterparts, but they found much to appreciate in Continental struggles over free thought and ecclesiastical tyranny. And the Welsh agreed that a solution must be found in state secularism, opposed to sectarian oppression. The growing religious divide of the era also accentuated the challenge to the rule of the landed classes in the countryside. The religious basis to social conflict gave protesters both an ideology and a universally comprehended

1. Quoted by Robert Griffiths in Osmond ed., *The National Question Again*, 198.

language of opposition. By the 1840s, the political structures of Wales were dominated by an elite separated from the ruled by religion and language, no less than economic interest.

In addition, the modernisation of Wales posed the national question in uniquely acute form. Wales was fulfilling the Victorian dream of progress and internal development to an astonishing degree; but in all this, what became of traditional culture, values, society? What was the place of Wales and the Welsh in the new Britain? Was it enough to become another economic power-house like Lancashire, but with a memory of a Celtic identity as vague as that of Cornwall or Cumberland? This sort of question was first posed systematically in the mid-nineteenth century, and the issues have not been solved yet. However, issues of national identity emerged alongside other forces and movements, especially nonconformity and political Liberalism.

These different forces need not have merged as completely as they did in the mid-nineteenth century, and we could easily imagine other contexts in which radicalism might have found a leading foe in nonconformist theocracy. Alternatively, events of the 1830s made it quite likely that the older sects would be aligned against an axis of Methodism and the establishment. It was not inevitable that 'nonconformity' would emerge as the solid political bloc it sometimes appeared to be; or that it would include Methodism. Even stranger was the role of Welsh culture and nationalism, which had earlier seemed wedded to the world of druids, Unitarians and democrats. The progressives, in turn, denounced the aggressive philistinism of the evangelicals and 'fanatics', who were striving to annihilate traditional poetry and music. John Elias and William Price, the Methodist and the druid, appeared to occupy opposite ends of the cultural spectrum; and it took a real effort of imagination to conceive the late Victorian eisteddfod where respectable ministers play-acted as pagan priests.

But as we will see, the three forces of Liberalism, nonconformity and nationalism did effectively merge, to create a set of political assumptions and commonplaces that still remain widespread among the Welsh people.

THE NEW PRESS

Between 1830 and 1850, political controversies in Wales involved issues and forms of action that would have been inconceivable a generation earlier, and a profound political crisis most apparent in the violence of Merthyr and Newport. Among the nonconformists, there was also a sense that enormous opportunities had been presented and perhaps forfeited with the Reform Bill of 1832 and the Municipal Corporations act of 1835. In the 1840s, the passing of rigidly conservative leaders like John Elias now freed dissenters to participate in reform campaigns.

It is scarcely surprising that a wide range of journals and newspapers arose to meet the thirst for news, discussion and comment that could not be met by the older sectarian press. In turn the new media provided the platforms for a rising generation of political and cultural leaders. *Seren Gomer* had advocated parliamentary reform since 1814, but there now appeared a wave of reformist papers. In 1830, David Owen published *Yr efangylydd* (Owen, 'Brutus', later defected to the high Tory cause). In 1835, the Independent David Rees began *Y diwygiwr*, which he edited until 1865. This supported campaigns like the Corn Law agitation, but also favoured Chartist demands and the Rebecca movement. As so often in Welsh history, a religious subtext is apparent: the Welsh title might equally well be translated as 'the reformer' or 'the revivalist', and either title would be appropriate for the new leaders who at once challenged the political and religious Establishment. *Y diwygiwr* also attacked tithes, the church rates and the special status of the Anglican church. Also in 1835, there appeared the first issue of *Cronicl yr oes* (Chronicle of the age), a radical paper edited by the Methodist minister Roger Edwards in spite of Elias' thunderings.

The 1840s were a lively time for the new press. In 1843, at the height of the Rebecca crisis, there appeared the first numbers of two papers – *Y cronicl*, and *Yr amserau*, both manifestations of Independent radicalism. *Y cronicl* (a monthly) was edited by Samuel Roberts (1800–85), universally known as 'SR'. SR was an Independent minister from Llanbrynmair, Montgomeryshire (and the son of the Rev. John Roberts). He demonstrated a universal enthusiasm for causes, for righting the wrongs of society, and can be credited with converting the numerous grievances of traditional nonconformist activism into a systematic programme. Of course he opposed the injustice of the tollgates and the new Poor Law; he hated the petty oppressions of landlords and their stewards; he advocated temperance and popular education as a means to uplift the lower classes; he also supported woman suffrage. He combined his enthusiasm for local and immediate campaigns with issues of international and universal relevance, including pacifism and opposition to slavery (a cause he adopted as early as 1830). Unlike many other radicals, he even carried his pacifism to opposing apparently just wars like the struggle to liberate the American slaves.

What is perhaps most remarkable about SR was that his multi-faceted radical enthusiasm was so widely shared, as were his long struggles to pursue morally correct and consistent solutions. *Yr amserau* (The Times: a fortnightly) was published by another Independent minister, from rural Denbighshire. This was 'Gwilym Hiraethog', or William Rees (1802–83), the brother of that Henry Rees who headed the Welsh Methodist movement from 1841 to 1869. The newspaper was published after Gwilym took up a living at Liverpool – as so often in history, one of the leading Welsh cities. *Yr amserau* published his letters on every conceivable issue of the day, on tithes, education, disestablishment. As with SR, early opposition to the Corn Laws led to a more general attack on landlord power in Wales, particularly when the landed classes were also seen as the mainstay of the Church.

The Independents produced some of the most thoroughgoing and tireless radicals of Victorian Wales. Henry Richard (1812–1888) was an Independent minister who struggled for nonconformist rights, the defence of tenants, and non-denominational education. In addition, he carried the advocacy of pacifism to new heights, and in 1848 became secretary of the International Peace Society, which called for arbitration to replace warfare. In 1866, Richard also brought Welsh grievances before the wider British public in a series of articles in the *Morning Star* and *Evening Star*. The most influential reader was Gladstone, who began the long interest in the affairs of Wales that made him something like a popular idol there.

As a final case-study of this generation, we might take the Methodist, Thomas Gee (1815–1898), a Denbigh publisher. In 1845, he supported the publication of *Y traethodydd*, a Methodist cultural quarterly edited by Lewis Edwards of Bala and Roger Edwards of Mold. This aspired to be the first Welsh counterpart to English publications like *Blackwoods* or the *Quarterly*. Between 1856 and 1879, Gee produced in *Y gwyddionadur* a pioneering Welsh encyclo-paedia. In the aftermath of the repeal of the Stamp Act in 1855, a cheap press became possible in Wales no less than England, and in 1857 Gee published the weekly *Y faner* (The Banner). In 1859, *Y faner*

merged with *Yr amserau* to create *Baner ac amserau Cymru*, which
Gee's editorship made a crucial radical force in Welsh life and
politics. By the 1870s, its circulation was around 50,000.

For 50 years, Gee presented the radical agenda of disestablishment
and nonconformist rights, the rights of tenants, and free undenominational mass education. By the 1880s, the Welsh press had become a
lively field with a strong Liberal and nonconformist bias represented
by papers like the Methodist *Goleuad* or the Independent *Y tyst* (The
Witness). There was also *Y Cymro* (The Welshman); *Yr herald
Cymraeg*; *Y genedl* (The Nation); and the English-language *Cambrian
News*. There were dozens of periodicals, monthly, weekly and
quarterly; but Tory and Anglican platforms were notable mainly by
their scarcity.

THE NEW LIBERALISM

Gee, SR, Richard and Gwilym Hiraethog can be taken as
representative of a powerful and influential generation of radical
reformers, whose liberal and democratic faith was based on older
puritan impulses. Several major components can be identified, some
of which would be wholly shared by nonconformists anywhere in
Britain; though others were more distinctively Welsh. Pacifism
probably falls into the first category. Apart from religious qualms
about the morality of war and international politics, there was a
common middle-class hostility to the resolutely aristocratic ethos of
the armed forces, diplomacy and colonialism.

There were also distinctively Welsh interests at work. The more
people studied Welsh history, the more they could have noted that
the Victorian rhetoric of conquest and empire was the same
justification used for the annexation of Wales; and the more they
might identify with the victims of that empire. Clearly, this was not
true for all parts of Wales. The industrialised south-east did well
from empire throughout, and above all from the 1880s; while the
whole industrial economy depended more or less directly on war
from the 1730s to the 1930s. But in the more rural and
nonconformist areas, the benefits of empire might not have
outweighed the apparent moral cost. Pacifism remained a leading
force in Welsh nonconformity and radicalism well into the twentieth
century.

Pacifism was accompanied by a strong sense of internationalism, a concern for the rights of small oppressed nations and peoples. From the 1840s, the Poles, Italians and Hungarians were all idealised as noble sufferers in the cause of liberty, and Kossuth was venerated. The plight of American slaves was also deeply felt, in part because of the close Welsh links with America. There might have been 200,000 Welsh emigrants to the USA over the whole century, and many returned to tell of American movements and conditions. The 1859 Revival was heavily influenced by the American upsurge of 1857. Welsh Liberal nonconformists sympathised wholeheartedly with the slaves, the Republican Party, and the federal cause in the subsequent civil war. In 1853, Gwilym Hiraethog pioneered the genre of the Welsh novel with his *Aelwyd F'ewythr Robert*, a popular piece based on *Uncle Tom's Cabin*.

Within Wales, Liberal grievances involved an indissoluble mixture of causes that could all ultimately be traced back to the legal anomalies of nonconformity. Some issues were simple and obvious, like burial in parish churchyards or payment of church rates. Others, like the payment of tithes, were more complicated because they involved economic issues, and existing practices appeared to punish or restrict the rights of tenants and small farmers. Ameliorating these grievances produced some of the sharpest parliamentary conflicts of the 1860s and 1870s, but few were yet prepared to go as far as wholesale 'Liberation', the disestablishment of the Anglican Church.

THE IRISH DILEMMA

National, economic and ecclesiastical questions all had obvious Irish analogies, but this was one case of thwarted national aspirations that was too close for safety. Radicals like David Rees had admired Daniel O'Connell and Thomas Davis, but Irish methods and solutions were long seen as too radical for the Welsh situation. Not until the 1880s would the example of Michael Davitt's Irish Land League be seen as an appropriate solution for religious and social injustices in the Welsh countryside; and only then did any significant body of Welsh opinion seek to emulate Irish calls for home rule.

Religious issues were in the forefront here. Nineteenth century nonconformity was the direct heir of the long Puritan and Whig tradition of conspiracy politics, the Catholics and specifically the Irish being the most common villains. This tradition helped to divide Welsh Liberalism in the late nineteenth century, when many radicals saw the Irish nationalists as potential allies; yet there were still important nonconformist Liberals who saw the Catholic threat as paramount. This naturally drove a wedge between the Liberals of the rural and industrial areas, as Irish Catholics became an influential force in the politics of Cardiff or Merthyr, and their aspirations had to be accommodated.

During the general election campaign of 1886, Liberal election platforms in Cardiff were graced by Charles Parnell and John Dillon; yet at just this time, fears for Irish Protestantism ensured that Liberal Unionism enjoyed a brief vogue in Wales, attracting the sympathy of some of the most popular heroes of Dissent. Thomas Gee strongly opposed Home Rule, while David Davies of Llandinam narrowly failed in an attempt to defeat the official Liberal in Cardiganshire. Richard Davies, MP for Anglesey, was one of several prominent nonconformists driven into political retirement over this issue. As late as the 1920s and 1930s, nonconformist papers like *Y tyst* and *Seren Gomer* regularly expressed concern about renewed Popish plots between the Vatican and allies like Mussolini and (of course) independent Ireland. Republican Spain even attracted some Welsh support not because it was antifascist, but because it was anticlerical.

Within Wales, the anti-Popery tradition had its greatest importance as a political issue in the form of the attack of ritualism and high Church doctrine within the Church of England. From the 1840s, the spread of Puseyism helped to detach the Methodists from their nostalgia for the Anglican establishment. The influence of high Church doctrine among the gentry and aristocracy promoted the belief that the nonconformists were engaged less in a class struggle than in a latter-day version of Foxe's *Martyrs*, an image regularly expressed in *Yr amserau*. The Marquess of Bute and Earl of Dunraven were not only oppressive landlords, they were Catholics allied to Catholic and ritualist squires. Church control of education was wrong partly because of the insidious influence of ritualism on young minds; and so on.

THE EDUCATION CONFLICT

It was the issue of education which most firmly united the nonconformist cause with national and linguistic issues. As throughout the whole of Britain, religious control of education was a great controversy in mid-century. From about 1815, there were two major societies offering to support schools established by local voluntary endeavour, and these developed into distinct networks. 'National' schools looked to the established Church, while 'British' schools offered non-denominational education of a sort acceptable to the dissenters, who provided much of their support. However, it was the National schools that predominated in Wales, which gave the Church a dominant (and controversial) role in Welsh education at least until 1902.

The National schools succeeded because they effectively had a 30-year start on their rivals. In Caernarvonshire, the first schools of this type were almost as old as the society itself. There were nine National schools by 1833, mainly concentrated around the episcopal capital of Bangor. By 1847, there were 50 Church related schools in the county, either National or else supported by local efforts. Anglican landlords like the Penrhyn family were generous supporters, and local nonconformists were often sympathetic (at this point, many Methodists remained sympathetic to Church doctrines). British schools made hardly any impact until the 1840s. Also, the monitorial system of the National schools was familiar from the example of the Welsh Sunday Schools, which similarly relied on more advanced pupils helping others in the absence of the trained teacher.

In 1843, the denominational role in education became of immediate political concern when a Bill proposed the establishment of Church-controlled schools for children working in mines and factories. This led to much opposition, expressed for instance in the 'Letter to the Welsh People' of Hugh Owen (1804–1881). This reasserted the nonconformist position on denominational schools, and led directly to a major expansion of the British schools in Wales: as Owen had written, 'the plan adopted in British schools is entirely consistent with freedom of conscience'. From 1844 to 1857, 120 British schools were established in north Wales alone. There would be 300 throughout Wales by 1870, with an estimated 35,000 pupils. The National Society also launched a major effort to compete, and educational provision expanded dramatically in the next two decades. 'There was a sort of education mania in Wales at that time'.

But educational politics were more complicated than a simple duel between Church and chapel. For example, should any schools receive state grants or aid? Both National and British Societies had since the 1830s accepted government inspection in exchange for government financial assistance. This raised concerns that state grants of any kind might involve the first step towards later subversion and outright control by the established Church. 'Voluntaryists' rejected even the assistance of the British Society. In Wales, this became essentially a matter of conflict between southern voluntaryists like Henry Richard, David Rees and Ieuan Gwynedd; and northern supporters of the British schools, like Hugh Owen and Lewis Edwards.

The expansion of education also led to a political and cultural crisis. In 1846, William Williams, the Welsh-born MP for Coventry, called for an official inquiry into the state of education in Wales. As eventually framed, the commission viewed its business in terms that would be extremely controversial: not only to enquire into Welsh education, but 'into the means afforded to the labouring classes of acquiring a knowledge of the English language'. The emphasis on English is scarcely surprising: only in 1835, Macaulay's celebrated *Minute* on Indian education had asserted the absolute need for English proficiency as a means to escape the destructive and worthless culture of traditional Asia. But the Commissioners might have taken warning from the debates that followed Macaulay's statement. Charles Williams-Wynn had opined that any 'attempt at forcing the natives to adopt (English) would . . . produce a complete reaction', a view he based on several European examples – but above all, that of Wales. In the 1840s, the linguistic biases of the education Commissioners would produce exactly the counter-productive consequences foreseen by Williams-Wynn, causing the first real eruption into mass public debate of questions of Welsh language and national identity. And it would also help to establish the idea that the nonconformists of Wales were in effect the true representatives of the nation and its real values.

THE BLUE BOOKS

The Commissioners charged with examining Welsh education reported in 1847 in two large blue volumes. The report immediately became the subject of violent controversy, and the affair was given a title that placed it in the realm of mythic struggle. Medieval Welsh legend told of an ancient Saxon betrayal, the 'Treason of the Long Knives', and the title was readily changed to fit the new situation. This was instead the 'Treason of the Blue Books', *Brâd y Llyfrau Gleision*. The problems with the Report were many. Anglican witnesses had been disproportionately called and quoted; and the

commissioners had felt competent to make gratuitous and offensive
generalisations about Welsh honesty and morality, in matters of
sexual behaviour, perjury and petty crime. (In Flint, fornication was
rife; but at least it took the form of mere promiscuity, and not the
'recognized and systematic institution as in other counties of north
Wales'!)

But the central problem would still have been valid even if the
cheap insults had been withheld. The Commissioners felt that Wales
was in many respects a primitive and ignorant culture, and these
problems arose because its people were imprisoned by the Welsh
language. This was 'a peculiar language isolating the mass from the
upper portion of society', and only that elite could stimulate
progress. As Lord Acton would write in 1862, 'the Celts are not
among the progressive, initiative races, but among those which
supply the materials rather than the impulse of history, and are either
stationary or retrogressive'. The Celts of the British Isles thus
'waited for a foreign influence to set in action the rich treasure which
in their own hands could be of no avail.'[2]

Despite all the economic progress of Wales, the population
remained enmired in virtual barbarism:

> Whether in the country, or among the furnaces, the Welsh element is
> never found at the top of the social scale, nor in its own body does it
> exhibit much variety of gradation.

The Welsh workman never becomes clerk or agent:

> Equally in his new, as in his old, home, his language keeps him under the
> hatches, being one in which he can neither acquire nor communicate the
> necessary information. It is a language of old-fashioned agriculture, of
> theology, and of simple rustic life, while all the world about him is
> English.

He is completely isolated from all influences, 'save such as arise
within his own order'.

> He is left to live in an underworld of his own, and the march of society
> goes so completely over his head that he is never heard of, excepting
> when the strange and abnormal features of a Revival, or a Rebecca or
> Chartist outbreak, call attention to a phase of society which could
> produce so contrary to all we elsewhere experience.

Tragically, any mental effort on the part of the Welsh was
misdirected into questions of theology, and even his religious life

2. Quoted in Eric Williams, *British historians and the West Indies* (Port of Spain,
Trinidad 1964), 32–33.

was alien from that of his superiors. Within this dark land, this Kafiristan-across-the Wye, there was no real culture, unless this title could be granted to the simple world of 'preaching – prayer meetings – Sunday schools – clubs – biddings – funerals – denominational magazine (his only press)'.

These charges could be answered in many ways. A radical could easily rewrite this account into a wholly positive and laudatory account of a national community dominated by plebeian traditions of cooperation and solidarity, where the shared language reduced to a minimum the temptations to collaborate with class exploiters. But among contemporary authors, other themes were prominent. Journalists and pamphleteers were now goaded into a triple defence of Welsh society, the language, and of Protestant nonconformity; and all three gained substantially from the exchange. There were vigorous responses and denunciations from nonconformist writers like Ieuan Gwynedd (1820–1852), or from Lewis Edwards in *Traethodydd*; and the ensuing controversy marked early ventures into public life for a number of the later leaders of Welsh Liberalism, including Henry Richard. However, Anglican critics of the Report were also driven to patriotic defences that came close to accepting the equation between Welshness and nonconformity. Probably the best example was Sir Thomas Philipps' vast study of *Wales: the language, social conditions, moral character and religious opinions of the people* (1849). In such a work, arguments were buttressed by the new social science made possible by the torrent of government statistics that had begun in the previous decade, and it can be said that this debate marks the beginning of social investigation in Wales.

THE POLITICS OF EDUCATION

The Blue Books placed the Welsh language in the forefront of debate, as a source of local conflict as contentious as the common British topics of state aid or religious instruction. Through much of the nineteenth century, schools of most types had tended to penalise the use of Welsh, often through physical punishments or stigmas like the celebrated 'Welsh Not', a plaque borne by the Welsh-speaker, until the point that it earned him or her a beating. This legendary device may or may not have been used as systematically as stories suggest, but it reflects a real policy; and the 'Not' was a perennial grievance. It was as hated in popular memory as were political evictions in the countryside, or the Depression-era Means Test in the industrial towns. In some areas, the punishment for speaking Welsh applied to all settings and circumstances, not merely in school time. Until the 1840s, this sort of victimisation was little challenged, as it was so apparent that children should indeed be highly encouraged to learn the English language if they wished to advance. After the Blue Books, the role of Welsh in education became a lively issue, with the added dilemma of what the role of the language should be in adult society.

In 1870, Gladstone's Liberal ministry produced an Education Act that further complicated educational arrangements. Existing voluntary schools were not interfered with, but areas in which these arrangements were not sufficient would erect new schools subject to public authority. They would be rate-supported, and administered by elected school boards. In Wales, naturally enough, these elections provided yet another arena for religious and political conflict: in Caernarvonshire, for instance, for an attack on the authority of Lord Penrhyn.

The Forster Act of 1870 inflamed denominational issues by providing aid to National schools. This also raised the question of religious instruction in schools, which divided the nonconformists themselves. Some believed that education was meaningless without a religious framework. Others felt that denominational biases were bound to impinge, and that religion should be excluded from a secular school system. Henry Richard's position was that this area should be left to the Welsh Sunday Schools, one of the distinctive national institutions. Ironically, the very fervour of Welsh religiosity led many of its activists to positions on education not unlike those of Continental sceptics and anticlericals. By the turn of the century, Welsh conflicts over the Anglican role in education would frequently resemble French battles over the Catholic hold on the schools.

State aid, religious instruction and the Welsh language would all be recurring topics in Welsh educational politics for many years, but they would be debated in an atmosphere of much greater respect towards Welsh national aspirations than had prevailed in 1847. In 1873, Gladstone himself had appeared at the Mold eisteddfod and spoken respectfully of Wales and Welsh, quite a breakthrough for the 'peculiar language', the 'drawback' that had been so forthrightly condemned in 1847. And his administration was making serious efforts to secure the appointment of Welsh-speaking Welshmen as Judges and Bishops.

The changed climate was apparent in 1880, when the Aberdare committee studied Welsh education. This time, Welshmen were well represented in the investigation, and Henry Richard was one of the five committee members. Naturally, the conclusions of the study were wholly different from those of the Blue Books. Wales was recognised as a distinctive nation with its own religious traditions, a proud cultural heritage, and a language that was emphatically worth retaining. It was also in this decade that the use of the Welsh language in the schools began to achieve widespread support. From 1885, a 'Society for the Utilisation of the Welsh Language' (*Cymdeithas yr Iaith Gymraeg*) was formed to demand the teaching of Welsh in bilingual districts. The group noted that experiments of this kind were perfectly common in European states like Switzerland, Belgium and the Austrian Empire; but there were still many opponents. The *Western Mail* saw it as a truism that Wales' 'low social and educational condition is due to the prevalence of the Welsh language . . . .It is only those who have money and leisure who can afford to learn two languages'. Not until 1907 was a sort of victory achieved, when new regulations for elementary schools provided for the use of Welsh in the curriculum.

By 1889, the Welsh Intermediate Education Act provided what appeared to be a solution for long-running complaints, and one which was influential on English practice. Under the new measure, schools would be controlled by the new county councils, democratic bodies heavily dominated by Liberals and nonconformists. Schools would be undenominational, and funded by a mixture of local rates and Treasury aid. By 1914, there were almost 100 such 'county' secondary schools, many of the highest quality. This happy compromise appeared to have resolved most of the serious problems; but as we will see, tranquillity did not last long.

LANGUAGE AND CULTURE

The outrage caused by the Blue Books was perhaps a natural reaction, but it was undoubtedly increased by the time at which the controversy occurred. In Wales, the decades after 1820 were a time of cultural rediscovery and innovation, consolidating and popularising the radical advances of the age of Iolo and Owain Myfyr. This was the age of poetic competitions at numerous local eisteddfodau, based above all in the industrial areas. Betwen 1824 and 1900, there were well over 200 such competitions in the communities of Merthyr, Dowlais and Aberdare.

Such events were marked by work from major poets like *Eben Fardd* (1802–1863) or *Ceiriog* (1833–87). Probably the greatest of them all was *Islwyn*, William Thomas (1832–78), the author of the lengthy 'The Storm', which now has a reputation far above what it achieved in the author's lifetime. Poetry enjoyed an enormous vogue, and the winners of the national eisteddfod competitions (of which more shortly) became national celebrities. Of course, verse which conforms to strict metrical standards may be weak as poetry, and there was lively debate towards the end of the century about the real merit of much of this work; but the enthusiastic reception of the Victorian writers suggests that literature was a genuine mass enthusiasm.

We have already observed the strong Anglican and clerical element in the cultural revival before 1840, and in the early *eisteddfodau*. From the 1840s, however, nonconformists were much more strongly represented at these gatherings, and in every aspect of literature, music and scholarship. Welsh prose also flourished. Naturally enough, for contemporaries of Dickens and Eliot, this was also a notable age for the Welsh novel. Apart from the work of Gwilym Hiraethog, the other great name is Daniel Owen (1836–95), author of *Rhys Lewis* (1882–5), *Enoc Huws* and others.

Though by no means all the writers of the age were nonconformists, much of the work was done in a dissenting ambience. Daniel Owen was 'discovered' by Roger Edwards, and *Rhys Lewis* was serialised in *Y drysorfa*; Islwyn was a Methodist preacher. Towards the end of the century, Silyn Roberts and John Puleston Jones were both nonconformist ministers, members of a common breed of preacher-poets. Perhaps the most distinguished representative of this age was *Elfed*, the Rev. H. Elfed Lewis (1860–1953), a Carmarthenshire man who served a Welsh congregation in King's Cross from 1904 to 1940. He has been described as 'poet, popular preacher, spiritual leader, hymn-writer and ardent eisteddfodwr. A former Archdruid';[3] and he was active in every Welsh patriotic movement from the time of Gladstone to the 1950s.

Nonconformist dominance was particularly evident in the new musical culture which emerged in the nineteenth century, and which rapidly created the myth of the 'land of song'. Traditional Welsh music had been linked to the aristocratic culture of the bards, and had largely perished by 1750. The Methodist triumph was accompanied by extensive work in hymn-writing, some execrable, but

3. A.G. Prys-Jones, *Story of Carmarthenshire*, (Swansea: Christopher Davies, ii, 291.

much of literary quality. Choral singing became a fundamental part of chapel services, though more rational groups like the Unitarians despised these vulgar manifestations. In the 1830s, a movement towards choral excellence began in two Merthyr Tydfil congregations, Soar and Pontmorlais. This became bound up with the temperance movement, whose meetings were often accompanied by hymn-singing and choral competitions, and there were 'festivals of choirs' by the 1850s. The new enthusiasm for music spread to the Swansea valley by this time, and to the Rhondda by the 1870s. Local federations of 'choral unions' were now formed.

To meet the demand, there emerged a popular musical publishing industry; and works were specially composed: Joseph Parry is perhaps the best known of this creative generation. By the 1870s, performances had become elaborate affairs with large choirs and full orchestras, presenting either Welsh oratorios or mainstream classics like Handel and Mendelssohn. Musical competitions began to form an important role in the eisteddfodau in the 1840s; and from the 1870s onwards, the Welsh choir became a fundamental part of popular culture.

PATRIOTISM AND THE PAST

Cultural self-confidence reinforced patriotism. We have already seen that there was by the 1830s great enthusiasm for historical study, focusing on the heroic middle ages and the days of the independent Welsh kingdoms. From 1836, the Welsh Manuscripts Society began publishing some of the major sources of Welsh history, including the *Book of Llandaff* and the *Heraldic visitations*. In 1846, the journal *Archaeologia Cambrensis* commenced publication, and this laid the foundation for the Cambrian Archaeological Association. Major scholars of the mid-century included Richard Williams Morgan, John Williams *ab Ithel*, and Harry Longueville Jones. There were also many excellent local studies by antiquaries like G. Grant-Francis (on west Glamorgan) and G.T. Clark. It was in 1856 that the national anthem was composed, with its appeals to bygone warriors and princes of the 'old land of my fathers'.

The new antiquarians undertook much sound historical work, and had a familiarity with original sources that remains deeply impressive today. Welsh squires and antiquaries also made early use of photography in recording and depicting remains. On the other hand, most found no paradox in seeking to revive such ancient manifestations of Welsh culture as the eisteddfod, with all its druidic trappings. In 1858, ab Ithel was the chief sponsor of the 'Great Llangollen Eisteddfod', a farcical and rather corrupt event that was more Barnum than bardic. It was also marked by a clash with the excellent scholar Thomas Stephens of Merthyr, who applied modern critical standards to Welsh literature, and even debunked the myth of Madoc. The mood of the time was definitely with the credulous ab Ithel; and his success pioneered the modern phenomenon of the eisteddfod as a manifestation of national culture and community, an occasion for debates and orations that might have widespread political significance. When we also recall the enormous growth in dissenting strength and self confidence from the late 1850s, we can appreciate the power of the culture that the Blue Books were seeking to denigrate and destroy.

THE UNIVERSITY MOVEMENT

From the 1850s, a series of campaigns united the political forces of Liberalism and nonconformity with the movement for cultural revival and regeneration. Once again, education was a major cause, but this time it was the movement for a Welsh university that generated most excitement. This reflected the Liberal faith in the potential of education to improve and uplift, but there was also a distinctive Welsh component of national pride and cultural aspirations. The first institutions of higher education were teachers' training colleges, established from the 1840s. By the end of the century, there were four: two under Church control, at Carmarthen and Caernarvon; also the Normal College at Bangor, and a women's college at Swansea. By far the most important of these was Bangor, which enjoyed the reputation of a truly national institution well into the twentieth century. In addition, there were denominational colleges like those at Bala and Trefecca; and the Anglican college of St Davids at Lampeter obtained the right to grant degrees in 1865. Finally, the old Carmarthen Academy survived, as the (rather distinguished) Presbyterian College. By 1842, this was connected to the University of London.

But a true Welsh university remained an aspiration. Schemes emerged in the mid-1850s, with Hugh Owen as the leading advocate for a 'Queen's College for Wales'. A committee was formed in 1863, and enthusiasm was stirred at what was now Wales's national cultural event, the national eisteddfod of 1863, held at Swansea. The movement was funded by contributions from the public: there were at least a hundred thousand offerings, most of the order of a few shillings. A site was chosen at Aberystwyth – equally inconvenient for both north and south Wales – and the college opened in 1872, with 25 students. Though non-sectarian, the Welsh and nonconformist character of the university college is suggested by its first principal, serving from 1872 to 1891. This was Thomas Charles Edwards, a representative of the Methodist dynasty. After a difficult beginning, Aberystwyth flourished, as did new colleges at Cardiff (1883) and Bangor (1884). In 1893, they all became part of a new federal system with the authority to confer degrees: the long awaited University of Wales, with Lord Aberdare as the first Chancellor. By 1900, the University had 1300 students. (In 1920, a fourth college was added at Swansea.)

The last quarter of the nineteenth century was an exciting time for Welsh culture, with important work being undertaken not merely at Oxford (as so often in the past three centuries) but in the new Welsh University. In 1877, Sir John Rhys (1840–1915) was appointed Professor of Celtic at Oxford; and in the same year, he delivered the lectures later published as *Lectures on Welsh Philology*. This can be taken as a convenient starting date for the modern study of Celtic languages, with wide implications for the study of history, archaeology and folklore. In a 50-year career, Rhys edited many of the major manuscripts of Welsh history, employing the best techniques of contemporary Continental scholarship.

His example was followed by other friends and pupils, most visibly by the patriotic circle formed at Oxford in 1886 as the *Cymdeithas Dafydd ap Gwilym*. A leading member was Sir John Morris-Jones (1864–1929), later Professor of Welsh at Bangor. He combined a triumphant poetic and literary career with a rigorous eye for precise and scholarly approaches to Welsh diction, grammar and tradition. It was Morris-Jones who, in the 1890s, traced the long and disreputable story of the invention of the gorsedd and many of the eisteddfod traditions. Other leading scholars of the time included Sir Owen M. Edwards (1858–1920), another of the *Dafydd* group; and J.E. Lloyd. In 1913, Lloyd's *History of Wales* finally provided a sound basis for our knowledge of Welsh history before 1282, with a strong patriotic and even nationalistic emphasis. By the 1890s, the work of such men had encouraged the publication of a wave of literary and artistic journals on Wales and its language. In 1907, Wales acquired a National Library (at Aberystwyth), and a National Museum, at

Cardiff. It was also in these years that a new generation of poets broke free of the rigid constraints imposed by the Victorian eisteddfodic tradition. Writers like Silyn Roberts, W.J. Gruffydd and T. Gwynn Jones first earned celebrity in the first two decades of the century, and dominated the literary scene for a generation.

SPORT

The high culture of Wales therefore became more and more identified with a national cause. But sport also provided a focus of national loyalty, with little regard for class background. In the early nineteenth century, religious 'enthusiasts' had virtually eliminated many of the traditional games and pastimes in which Wales had once been so rich. They had not succeeded in most of the industrial areas, where amusements were aggressively proletarian, and were doubly shocking in their association with betting. Prize fighting and more orthodox boxing enjoyed an immense vogue in the south-east into the 1930s.

Nothing 'patriotic' could be seen in this; but from the 1870s, there developed an enthusiasm for the public school game of rugby. Initially a pastime for the professional and upwardly mobile, it soon achieved a vast following among industrial workers, above all miners. It was swiftly condemned by nonconformist leaders, who saw the 'black ball' as yet another novel sin from Glamorgan and Monmouthshire. By the 1890s, however, rugby became the national sport of Wales. The Welsh team won the Triple Crown in 1893, and six times more between 1901 and 1912. The game stirred real patriotic emotion, and the 1905 victory over the New Zealand All Blacks resulted in an outpouring that can best be described as messianic. The trappings of the game also entered popular culture as virtual national symbols; the song *Sospan Fach* became a second national anthem in parts of the south.

THE NEW NATIONALISM

By the 1860s, there was a subtle change in the character of the causes at the heart of Welsh political life. Most were essentially identical to the issues cherished by English Liberalism – peace, temperance, individual rights – but the Welsh causes increasingly took on a national flavour. There was a distinctive cultural dimension that was becoming increasingly difficult to ignore, even before the growing influence of Irish models under Gladstone. The Liberals annexed this new national awareness, and the Anglican 'patriots' of the 1840s already seemed hopelessly out of date. By the sixties, it seemed obvious that Welshness and dissent were natural allies; indeed, that they were both manifestations of a fundamental cultural identity.

This became apparent in the 1870s with demands for a law that would respect specifically Welsh traditions of nonconformist sabbatarianism. In 1881, a Sunday closing bill for public houses was passed after Parliament received supporting petitions from 267,000 people in Wales, as well as the votes of 28 out of 30 Welsh MPs (Monmouthshire was excluded from the measure until 1921). Welsh Sundays thus remained 'dry' till 1961, and subsequent local referenda on the issue have precisely defined the changing boundaries of rural, Welsh-speaking, nonconformist, Wales. Professor Kenneth Morgan has remarked on the importance of this measure, the first since the interregnum to apply a distinctive legal principle to Wales but not England.

The alliance of cultural, religious and Liberal causes is suggested by the careers of two men who each in their way were pioneers (or precursors) of modern nationalism. One was Robert Ambrose Jones, *Emrys ab Iwan*, a writer who actually coined the Welsh term for Home Rule, *ymreolaeth*. A Methodist minister, he attacked his denomination for its failure to promote Welsh language and culture. His older contemporary was Michael D. Jones (1822–1898), son of the first principal of the Independent college at Bala. After the near inevitable spell in the United States, he returned in 1850 and entered the ministry. From 1853, he headed the Independent College himself. However, his main fame lay outside denominational achievements. Jones was a classic nonconformist radical, who was bitterly opposed to the domination of Tory landlords, and who sought to reform Welsh society. Naturally enough, Sir Watkin Williams-Wynn was one of his bugbears, and the two were long-standing enemies. But Jones went further than most contemporaries by seeing emigration as a likely and desirable means of escaping injustice and poverty. He was the vital sponsor of the idea of a 'Welsh Colony', which would become a new and purer Wales outside the bounds of Britain.

A WELSH COLONY

The notion of a Welsh settlement was not original. Newfoundland had been the intended site of 'Cambriol' under James I, while Quaker and Baptist exiles between 1680 and 1710 had begun the two century long love affair between Wales and Pennsylvania. If Charles II had not overruled him, William Penn had actually chosen the name 'New Wales' for his planned colony. In the 1790s, radicals had attempted to found a new Cambria on the free soil of Kentucky or (yet again) Pennsylvania; and Brazil had seemed to offer promise in the 1840s.

Most Welsh settlements overseas emerged not from political idealism, but rather the rational economic choice to seek a better living. However, the good pay available to a largely skilled work force permitted them to recreate and sustain a Welsh environment with considerable authenticity. In the United States, there was a sizeable Welsh publishing industry, and the newspaper *Y drych* was widely read from the 1850s. An emigrants' manual of 1866 surveyed dozens of Welsh communities throughout Pennsylvania, in Pittsburgh, Johnstown, Danville, Scranton, Pottsville and so on.[4] Typically, the Welsh were to be found where there were rolling mills, blast furnaces, coal mines or slate quarries, and their wages were described in awed terms. Prosperity permitted the establishment of numerous Welsh chapels – sometimes Methodist, Independent and Baptist all in one town. Ebensburg, typically, 'is a very Welsh place where there is an abundance of religious services, and several chapels in the town and in the country'. In the coal counties of Carbon and Luzerne, 'the Welsh are very numerous'. Often, the language was still spoken, and eisteddfodau flourished in centres like Carbondale, 'the Athens of the Welsh'. On the other hand, there was a disturbing trend whereby the older communities lost their identity in a few generations, leaving only some crumbling Welsh Bibles to show their origins. Even in friendly America, it seemed that Welsh culture could not long endure.

In the 1860s, idealistic hopes turned to the land of Patagonia, which offered many advantages. It was virgin land, on which a wholly Welsh settlement might resist contamination indefinitely. And while outside the official sway of the British Empire, it was in a country where British influence was strong if help were ever needed;

4. Phillips G. Davies, 'The state of Pennsylvania: from Bromley and Jones, Instructions for the emigrant', *Pennsylvania History*, 335–346.

and it stood within easy reach of the Queen's naval bases. The Argentines sensed an excellent bargain, and offered settlers 2000 hectares of land per family, in the hope of securing firmer title to the land thus settled on the Chubut river. All seemed promising for the creation of the new Wales, *y Wladfa*, and 153 pioneers set sail from Liverpool in 1865.

Patagonia has enjoyed a degree of historical attention in Wales far beyond what it merits from the scale of the enterprise. At most, the settlement never had more than two or three thousand people of Welsh origin, in contrast to the tens of thousands who could be found in contemporary Ohio or Pennsylvania, to say nothing of Canada, Australia or even England. And while the settlers on the Chubut constructed around themselves a distinctively Welsh world of chapels and newspapers, it is unlikely that they did so any more systematically than their counterparts in north America. While the large-scale settlement of America soon lost its Welsh heritage in the Anglophone melting-pot, so the Patagonians were subject to the enormous pressure of Hispanic culture.

Also, the utopian roots of the scheme show clearly, in the worst sense of 'utopianism'. In setting forth to colonise one of the most barren and difficult landscapes in the world, the settlers paid little attention to bringing with them either the expertise or the materials they would need for survival. (The turning point of the colony's history came after a few years, when one settler discovered the essential and rather basic skill of irrigation.) Not until the late 1880s was the colony out of danger; and that was the point at which the colonists began to encounter an Argentine government less concerned with the niceties of the nonconformist conscience than their British counterparts. Military conscription and sabbath enforcement both proved contentious, as did the enforcement of Argentine educational standards and practices. It would be difficult to describe the Chubut settlement as a success; except in that it offered Welsh patriots at home a dream of an alternative and purer nation.

THE MEANING OF 1868

By the 1860s, the Liberal political leadership of Wales had acquired experience and self-confidence as the result of a dozen major campaigns, buoyed by the eruption of nonconformist strength; and they had also tasted success with the movements for a Welsh colony and a national university. They also had the satisfaction of feeling part of the international movement which had won the victory of evangelical democracy in the American civil war. It now remained to transform radical and democratic sentiment into real political power, and that implied parliamentary success. In 1866, Henry Richard and John Carvell Williams orchestrated the campaign by the Liberation Society to mobilise nonconformist voters through the formation of local registration societies. The expansion of the franchise provided by the second Reform Act led to a Liberal breakthrough in the 1868 elections.

In Liberal tradition, 1868 often appears as a near-miracle in Welsh politics, a sudden upsurge of the forces of righteousness on the lines familiar from the religious revivals. In reality, Liberalism of quite a radical kind was by no means as weak before 1868 as this might suggest. In Glamorgan, for example, all five constituencies had been in Liberal hands from 1857, and industrialist Members like H.H. Vivian and Lewis Dillwyn were strong friends of dissenters and their rights. Walter Coffin, a Unitarian coal-owner, had been elected for Cardiff in 1852 in a classic struggle between the nonconformists and the commercial men on the one hand, and the forces of privilege and the Castle on the other. In industrial seats like Merthyr, even a Member who was a powerful industrialist might find himself under real and effective pressure from his radical constituents. In 1852, Richard Davies the nonconformist had stood unsuccessfully for Caernarfon borough, and dissenters were prominent in other campaigns in the decade: notably in Merionethshire in 1859.

The 1868 election altered the balance of power in Wales, but not its fundamental nature. In 1865, there were 18 Liberals and 14 Conservatives in Parliament; in 1868, the numbers were respectively 23 and 10. Not until 1880 did the Liberals begin their effective 40 year one-party dominance of Wales, when they increased their holdings to 29 out of 33 seats. But several Liberal victories in 1868 stand out in particular, above all the election of Henry Richard in Merthyr Tydfil. As a Welsh-speaking nonconformist of humble birth and radical views, Richard was widely seen as a dramatic departure in the history of Wales' parliamentary representation. On the other hand, it should be stressed that Richard's epic triumph here was not won at the expense of an oppressive squire or Tory industrialist. His enemy was H.A. Bruce, Lord Aberdare, a powerful Liberal who served as Home Secretary in Gladstone's first ministry, and who would be strongly identified with Welsh cultural and educational causes.

Richard's appeal was frankly and aggressively directed to the 'real people' of Wales, and not to the 'English-speaking and propertied class'. Support was mobilised through the nonconformist chapels and the clergy, and Richard's rhetoric used 'Welsh' and 'nonconformist' as synonyms:

> The nation of Wales has never yet been represented in the House of Commons . . .The people who speak this language (the Welsh), who read this literature, who own this history, who inherit these traditions, who venerate those names, who have created and sustained and worked those marvellous organisations – Have they not a right to say We are the Welsh nation?[5]

Naturally enough, Richard's electoral meetings concluded with enthusiastic singing of that new battle hymn, *Hen wlad fy nhadau*, which had enjoyed such an enormous vogue at recent national eisteddfodau.

It was important for the character of Liberalism that the victory occurred in Merthyr. Most of the nonconformist leaders were not associated with the new industrial Wales emerging in the south-east: Gwilym Hiraethog and Gee were from Denbighshire, SR from Montgomeryshire, Richard from Cardiganshire, Michael D. Jones from Merionethshire. Their causes were above all those of the countryside and the small towns, rather than the class issues and grievances of the mines and factories. Richard's election, like the success of the nonconformist press, shows that idealistic populist Liberalism did have an appeal in industrial Wales.

Another notable victory occurred in Caernarvonshire, where the defeated candidate was the son of Lord Penrhyn. In Denbighshire, Thomas Gee managed the Liberal campaign against the high Tory Sir Watkin Williams-Wynn. Though Sir Watkin was re-elected, his new colleague in the Commons was George Osborne Morgan, a radical Liberal who shared all Gee's concerns about Welsh, nonconformist and educational causes. (Morgan drove a Biddulph of Chirk Castle into third place.) Elsewhere in Wales, Richard Davies won Anglesey and another nonconformist took Cardiganshire; though it is worth noting that 20 of the Liberal MPs were not nonconformists, and some were considerable landlords in their own right. The triumph of radical Liberalism in Wales began in 1868, but it was not fully accomplished for decades. (By 1895, the Welsh parliamentary contingent included 16 Welsh-speakers, and 21 nonconformists.)

5. Quoted in Raymond Grant, *The parliamentary history of Glamorgan 1542–1976* (Swansea: Christopher Davies, 1978), 181–183.

More important than the actual election of 1868 was the aftermath, when high Tory squires began the eviction of several tenants who had voted the wrong way. Evictions of this sort were not new, but the scale in mid-century was remarkable. The 1859 election had been followed by major evictions on the Peniarth and Rhiwlas estates in Merionethshire, a grievance all the more deeply felt because the landlord in question was a Ritualist. After 1868, there were 70 or so documented evictions in the counties of Carmarthen and Cardigan, and many on Caernarvonshire and other northern estates like Gwydir (the lands of Lord Willoughby d'Eresby). Other Liberal voters found their rents increased. A great deal of fiction surrounded the intimidation, and exaggeration suited everybody's purpose. Liberals sought martyrs; Tory landlords thought that stern actions might serve as a warning (some issued notices to quit that were subsequently withdrawn). But conflicts like this poisoned relations on many estates for decades. They also served to suggest a direct link between Liberalism, nonconformity, and the rights of tenants: a propaganda lesson that could scarcely have been achieved by decades of pamphleteering.

Finally, the evictions became a political issue at Westminster through the agitation of nonconformist leaders like SR and Michael D. Jones. This was not the first time that Welsh issues had entered national politics, but 1868 marked the beginning of a half-century in which the affairs of Wales would often be among the most contentious matters for the national government.

CHAPTER SIXTEEN
Liberal Wales 1868–1920

Between 1790 and 1868, a survey of the parliamentary history of Wales would give little or no idea of the changes taking place in the wider society and economy. The great majority of Welsh MPs were from exactly the same sort of families that had controlled the parliamentary seats for centuries. If there was a change from the late eighteenth century, it was perhaps a movement towards greater oligarchy, even tighter domination by a few wealthy houses, who were often aristocrats. In the first half of the century, Lords Cawdor and Dynevor ruled Carmarthenshire; Pembrokeshire was under Lords Kensington and Milford, and the Owens of Orielton; the Marquesses of Bute regarded Cardiff as virtually in their gift. Both Anglesey and Caernarvonshire were in the hands of the Bulkeleys and the Pagets. Merionethshire was represented from 1796 to 1832 by Sir Robert Williames Vaughan of Nannau.

Moreover, this landed supremacy survived the 1832 Reform Act with little damage, and the continuity into mid-century is striking. In Flintshire, the county constituency was dominated from 1554 to 1861 by 13 generations of the Mostyns of Mostyn. Sir Roger Mostyn served from 1761 to 1796, Sir Thomas from 1799 to 1831. He was eventually succeeded in the estate by Edward Lloyd, who sat from 1832 to 1837, and from 1842 to 1854. The family were created Lords Mostyn in 1831. Edward's son Thomas served from 1854 to 1861; and on his death, the Mostyn interest gave way to that of Lord Grosvenor, who sat until 1880. During the latter years of the Mostyn dominance, their main rivals were the Tory gentry house of the Glynnes of Hawarden, and Sir Stephen Glynne served from 1837 to 1842.

In neighbouring Denbighshire, three Sir Watkin Williams-Wynns sat as MPs from 1796 to 1885. Three other Williams-Wynns controlled the Montgomeryshire representation from 1799 to 1880. Considering such a lengthy succession of landed gentry and aristocrats, we might easily forget that this was supposedly a time of major electoral reform and democratisation. The Williams-Wynn interest was at least broken by the successive Reform Acts of 1867 and 1885, reinforced by the Ballot Act of 1872; but even these measures could not stop C.R.M. Talbot of Margam from representing Glamorgan from 1830 to 1890.

The 1832 Act did not fundamentally alter the composition of Welsh parliamentary representation, nor did it change the idea that electoral competition was essentially unhealthy. In the eighteenth century, it had been the highest boast of a landowner that he had been elected by the common consent of the constituency, without causing expense or division. Between 1832 and 1868, it was common for a majority of seats in a general election to be uncontested. Only five of 32 candidates were opposed in 1847, 1857 or 1865, four in 1859. In 1857, there were contests only in two county seats (Flintshire, and Glamorgan's two constituencies), and two boroughs (Denbigh and Haverfordwest). Not until 1868 were there actual contests in a majority of Welsh constituencies. In this perspective, Flintshire was one of the *more* democratic seats, where voters frequently had the opportunity to exercise their ballots. No less than five of the nine elections between 1832 and 1865 were contested in this county, a quite exceptional figure.

Nor did 1832 create a mass electorate. Between the first two Reform Bills, the proportion of Welsh people who could vote never rose above five per cent of the total, and only in 1865 did the electorate surpass 60,000. But the emphasis on social harmony and the avoidance of conflict prevented even the enfranchised few from casting their votes more than rarely. In 1859, only 4352 actual votes were cast throughout Wales, almost half of these in one seat, Cardiganshire. The absence of a secret ballot (before 1872) meant that a small electorate could be monitored and intimidated as easily as in 1770 or 1570.

THE TORY TRADITION

An increasingly Liberal and dissenting population was represented in Parliament by landowners who were generally Conservative. It was in 1869 that C.R.M. Talbot wrote of Glamorgan, 'All the great landowners in the county, except myself, are Conservative in politics'. The statement would be true of most Welsh counties, though there were Whig exceptions: the house of Glynllifon in Caernarvonshire, the Edwardes' in Pembrokeshire. The Conservative cause in particular counties was often dominated by a handful of landowners, or even by one magnate, like Bute in Glamorgan or Penrhyn in Caernarvonshire. Especially in rural Wales, landlords continued to be prominent Tories into Edwardian times: in Pembrokeshire, for instance, the county Conservative Association was headed by squire George Bowen of Llwyngwair. The continuation of the political *ancien regime* owed much to the power of the landlords, whose authority was based in the last resort on their ability to punish and reward.

Seeing Conservatism as the result of coercion was a natural component of Liberal and nonconformist propaganda, but it is simply inadequate. Under the much democratised electoral system in operation between 1886 and 1914, the Welsh Conservatives rarely fell below 30 per cent of the vote, and they approached 40 per cent in 1895. This reflects a real appeal to some sections of the population, but also the development of party organisation. The Liberals could base themselves in the chapels, as Labour would later rely on the unions; but what was available to the Tories?

Since the 1790s, there had been ad hoc associations to defend property rights against radicals, successively directed against Levellers, Chartists and anti-tithe agitators. These were often sponsored by magnates like Lord Penrhyn, but they attracted membership from much lesser landowners as well as commercial men. The Reform crisis announced the beginning of a new phase in party organisation. In 1832, the Bute family sponsored a Tory newspaper, *The Glamorgan, Monmouth and Brecon Gazette, and Merthyr Guardian.* In 1835, Glamorgan acquired a Conservative Association under the auspices of powerful landowners like the squires of Fonmon, Dyffryn and Rheola. Like similar bodies elsewhere, this was chiefly intended to use the new franchise to maximum advantage. It was in the rather comparable situation of 1869 that there appeared the most influential Tory paper, the *Western Mail*, later stigmatised as the organ of the south Wales coal-owners.

Elsewhere in Wales, we often find Conservative papers and journals emerging in response to reform agitation from a Liberal press. In 1810, the *Carmarthen Journal* challenged the Whiggish *Cambrian*. Probably the most successful example was a riposte to the west Wales radical paper, *Y diwygiwr*. From 1835 to 1865, the reformist journalism of David Rees was regularly met with the sarcastic assaults of *Yr haul*, an aggressive pro-Church paper edited by the volatile David Owen (Brutus).

The defence of the established Church was a central tenet of the Tory cause, and the Church in Wales offered a sizeable body of support as well as a means of presenting Conservative arguments. Religious loyalties might even bring other groups to support Tory views on specific issues. We have already seen that the earlier Methodists were often Conservative on social issues. Questions involving toleration of Catholics were divisive for the nonconformists, above all where Irish affairs were concerned. In 1837, the Conservative candidate for the county of Glamorgan won after a campaign based on his Liberal rival's support for 'O'Connell, Popery and the Repeal of the Corn Laws'. (Ironically, the Tory was Lord Adare, who would himself convert to Catholicism in the 1850s.) 'Conservatism', broadly defined, might have widespread appeal.

There were also Conservative business interests, though Victorian coal and iron masters were generally Liberal. Shipping interests in particular were likely to have a Tory streak, and three shipping magnates were among the Conservative MPs who held Cardiff so firmly between 1910 and 1929. In addition, common business interests might serve to link professional families to local landed estates, and we often find solicitors and agents at the head of the Tory cause. In Edwardian times, the south Glamorgan Conservative association was dominated by two lawyers, Robert Griffiths and Samuel Stockwood.

Finally, the Liberal emphasis on temperance gave the drink industry a vested interest in the Conservative Party. Brewers might be generous contributors to party funds; but more significant at local level were the publicans, proprietors of the buildings that were the main social centres in many communities. It would be over-simple to depict Welsh Conservatism as simply the tool of landlord, parson and brewer; but few could deny that that might be a powerful combination.

TOWARDS DEMOCRACY?

But electoral reform was having an impact, to the disadvantage both of the old landowner MPs and the Conservative cause. Parliamentary representation had increased in industrialised and more populous parts of the country, like Glamorgan. From its ancient two seats, Glamorgan's parliamentary strength rose to five in 1832, six in 1867, and ten by 1885. Also, population growth alone meant that the electorate increased between 1832 and 1867, even without franchise changes. The county of Glamorgan had 6759 voters by 1865.

Post-Reform MPs differed from their predecessors more than might initially appear. There were several constituencies, above all in the south-east, which were regularly represented by members of industrial or commercial families. As early as 1814, Glamorgan had been briefly represented by Benjamin Hall, who was primarily an ironmaster (his son served for Monmouth in 1832). After the Reform Act, industrialist representation became the norm for the new borough seats of Merthyr Tydfil and Swansea. The Guests in Merthyr, the Vivians and Dillwyns in Swansea, gained a position in their seats that was quite as secure as anything demonstrated by the Bulkeleys or Mostyns in theirs. The Baileys were another industrial family who were frequently elected for seats like Monmouth or Breconshire. Such new MPs represented different economic interests, and they were likely to share the religious concerns of their mainly nonconformist electorates; but the addition of a few ironmasters or copper tycoons scarcely marked a transition to a new democracy. Also, there was by mid-century a considerable fusion between the interests of older landowners and new industrialists, and magnates like the Talbots of Glamorgan or Pennants of Caernarvonshire straddled both categories.

1832 marked only the first stage in the democratisation of Welsh politics: much more significant were the changes effected by the legislation of 1868 and 1885–86. As a result of the 1867 Reform Bill, the Welsh electorate grew from 62,000 to 127,000. By 1885, the figure was 282,000; by 1910, 425,000. It was the changes of 1885 that permitted the entry of thousands of industrial workers on the electoral rolls. By 1900, 16 of the 34 Welsh constituencies had electorates in excess of 10,000 (all but four of these were located in the industrial south, in Glamorgan and Monmouth). In 1865, as in 1832, less than 5 per cent of Welsh people could vote. By 1868, the figure was 9 per cent, rising to a new plateau of 18 per cent between 1885 and 1918. However, the enfranchisement of women in 1918 radically changed matters, raising the total electorate to 1.17 million. Voters comprised 45 per cent of the people in 1918, 62 per cent by 1929 and almost 75 per cent today.

Alongside the growth of the electorate, we also note the increase of electoral conflict, and thus the opportunity to exercise the right to vote. In the mid-nineteenth century, one seat in seven might be contested. By 1885, the figure was six out of seven; and by 1910, every seat was fought. As the nineteenth century progressed, far more people actually got a chance to cast a ballot. Between 1841 and 1865, no Welsh election involved a national total of votes in excess of 13,000. In 1885, 205,000 votes were cast. In 1910, the figure was 378,000; in 1929, 1.32 million.

LIBERAL WALES

From 1868, Welsh MPs were much more truly representative of the voters, and had to be responsive to the wishes of a larger cross-section of the communities they served. In the context of the age, this meant that Welsh politics now moved sharply towards the causes that had achieved mass support in the previous three decades: to radical Liberalism, to nonconformist causes, and to a recognition of distinctive Welsh interests that was patriotic, if not strictly nationalistic. Through most of Wales, victorious Liberalism was founded on a patriotic front of professionals and dissenting clergy, together with the votes of tenant farmers and industrial workers, united in opposition to Tory landlords and parsons.

Gradually, the new forces also changed the composition of the representatives themselves. In 1860, the typical Welsh MP, Liberal or Conservative, was probably a substantial landowner and a Churchman; by 1900, he was much more likely to be a solicitor or businessman, a nonconformist, and quite probably a Welsh-speaker. In this profile, if in little else, Lloyd George was quite typical of his generation. When C.R.M. Talbot died in 1890, his successor in mid-Glamorgan was a nonconformist solicitor. With Liberals so likely to be returned, the focus of conflict then shifted to the process of selecting the Liberal candidates themselves, and the nonconformist presence was strongly felt. In Merionethshire in 1885, the slate workers led a vigorous campaign to demand that the Liberal candidate be specifically a Welsh nonconformist; and this led to a third party candidacy when the party mainstream was obdurate. In the Rhondda, such a conflict led to the election of *Mabon*, William Abraham, a Welsh nonconformist who served as miners' agent, and who marks the beginning of 'Lib-Lab' candidacies in Wales.

From 1880, Wales was politically a fortress for the Liberal Party.

In Robert Blake's revealing phrase, the Conservatives were so utterly outgunned, they seemed 'like White expatriates in a Black world'.[1] Between 1880 and 1920, the Conservatives rarely held more than four Welsh seats at any one time, compared to 29 or 30 Liberals. In 1906, they were obliterated from the electoral map. The Liberals generally took between 45 and 55 per cent of Welsh votes, compared to 30 or 35 for the Conservatives. Between 1885 and 1945, there were 81 parliamentary elections in the three counties that constitute Gwynedd: of these, precisely two resulted in the election of Tory members. In the new county councils which emerged after 1889, the Liberals regularly held two-thirds of the 600 or so positions, and the Conservatives only had a tenuous and sporadic control in one area, Brecon and Radnor. Liberal majorities were often embarrassingly huge – in 1904, they won Merionethshire by 52 seats to 3. In addition, the councils acted as training grounds for political leadership.

From the 1880s, the Liberals could do no wrong. They were able to score regular victories over the ancient landed magnates in all their ancient strongholds: the Williams-Wynn interest, wounded in 1868, was now demolished in Montgomeryshire, and Thomas Gee defeated Sir Watkin in the county council elections. Already powerful, the Liberals became invincible in the aftermath of the 1904 religious revival. Some of the specific results were staggering. In south Glamorgan, which incidentally includes the old hundred of Ogmore, the defeated Tory was Major Wyndham-Quin, heir to the Earl of Dunraven. He was beaten by William Brace, President of the South Wales Miners' Federation. It is difficult to know if this result was less evocative than the contest in south Monmouthshire, where the Conservative was Frederick C. Morgan of Tredegar, the first of his house to lose the county since 1659. His nemesis was Sir Ivor Caradoc Herbert, an eminently respectable squire of ancient lineage, who later became Lord Treowen. But he was a Catholic. Even when Liberal dominance faded after the First World War, it was to be replaced not by a revived Toryism, but by the juggernaut power of the Labour Party.

---

1. Robert Blake, *The Conservative Party from Peel to Thatcher* (London, Fontana, 1985), 48.

THE WELSH PARTY

This great age of Liberalism also witnessed the flowering of specifically Welsh politics. In the last quarter of the century, the emergence of a new type of Welsh MP led to the creation of a political caucus overtly modelled on the Irish parliamentary party. The Irish party was given greater obstructive force by its sheer numbers, but the Welsh Liberals might dispose of 25 or 30 votes that could be indispensable for a government majority. It therefore made sense to use this power to pursue Welsh interests and demands, possibly in alliance with others on the parliamentary fringe. Irish and Social Democratic Members were obvious possibilities, while it was at this time that Scottish home rule became a serious part of the Liberal political agenda. From 1886–1887, Welsh political interests were coordinated by new Liberal Federations for North and South Wales.

By the 1880s, Henry Richard had been joined in Parliament by a number of like-minded Liberals. Among the older MPs, the most experienced progressives included two west Glamorgan men, Sir H.H. Vivian and Lewis Ll. Dillwyn, both of whom had served since the 1850s. However, the newer members were a younger and different breed: there were eight nonconformists from Wales in 1880, 25 by 1906. Characteristic of the new type of Member were men like Alfred Thomas, an industrialist who was also president of the Welsh Baptist Union; David A. Thomas, the nonconformist coal magnate; or the Methodist solicitor David Randell.

The generation of the 1880s included at least three men who would in their times be seen as being virtual national leaders. The first was Stuart Rendel, who entered Parliament for Montgomeryshire in 1880, defeating the Williams-Wynn interest. He succeeded Henry Richard as the effective leader of the Welsh party until his elevation as Lord Rendel in 1894. Rendel was a close associate of Gladstone, and he led the Welsh caucus through an era in which the country's affairs were often at the centre of British politics. In view of the pacifist strand in Welsh Liberalism, it is ironic that Rendel owed his wealth to the armaments industry. 'The first great British arms salesman', he was thus a leading 'merchant of death'.

Tom Ellis served as Member for Merioneth from 1886 until his early death in 1899 (he was 40), and both in his life and posthumously he enjoyed immense popularity as a radical leader of 'true' Wales, the land of Welsh-speaking nonconformists, of small tenants and farmers. (He was elected in a contest with the Tory squire of Nannau and Hengwrt.) Like Rendel, he was also firmly connected to the Liberal mainstream, and became Chief Whip in 1894. He is one of Wales' great 'lost leaders'. Had he lived, he would assuredly have been a central figure in the Liberal government of 1906. He was active in all the great Welsh controversies of the 1890s: the tithe war and the 'land question', educational controversies, and disestablishment. These were familiar Liberal issues; but what was different about Ellis' era was that the question of national autonomy was finally moved towards the top of the agenda, in the form of home rule or devolution of power.

Last among this group was the most celebrated, David Lloyd George, who by 1910 was often described as being virtually synonymous with Welsh nonconformity. He first attained celebrity in the Llanfrothen case of 1888, when an Anglican parson refused to allow a Methodist quarryman to be buried in the parish churchyard. Lloyd George represented the family, and built on the case to secure election for Caernarvon borough in 1890. Defeating Lord Penrhyn's agent, he retained his seat until becoming Earl of Dwyfor in 1945. Long a folk-hero in much of Wales, his family became almost a Liberal dynasty. His daughter Megan Lloyd George was Wales' first woman MP, who held Anglesey from 1929 to 1951. His son Gwilym served for Pembrokeshire from 1922 to 1924 and again from 1929 to 1950.

Lloyd George's career is too well known to require elaboration here: he served as Chancellor of the Exchequer from 1908 to 1915, and was Prime Minister from 1916 to 1922. However, two points might be made about the peculiar importance of his Welsh background. Firstly, he approached national politics with a distinctive imperial vision, a broader, more critical, and perhaps more historical sense of the meaning of empire and sovereignty. No matter how invincible modern empires seemed, they might still encounter formidable opposition in the stubborn nationalism of subject peoples. After all, the Romans had once built a fortress at Caernarvon to dominate the Welsh; yet today, Welsh-speaking children played in its ruins, and Roman might had passed into the oblivion that had also consumed the Latin language. What appeared inevitable today might be equally transitory, while it was the culture which endured:

> Let no man despise Wales, her language or her literature. She has survived many storms; she has survived many empires. Her time will come. When the last truckload of coal reaches Cardiff, when the last black diamond is dug out of the earth of Glamorgan, there will be men then digging gems

of pure brilliants from the inexhaustible mines of the literature and language of Wales.[2]

In addition, much of Lloyd George's success was founded on an ability to apply to the wider British sphere the oratory and rhetorical principles he had learned in early Welsh conflicts. Like Ellis, he continued throughout his career to hit home time and again at the same familiar body of semi-mythical incidents – events such as the evictions of the 1860s. Welsh Liberalism flourished in part by its ability to interpret and present social and economic problems in simple populist terms of oppression by landowners and the Church. Lloyd George was a master of introducing English audiences to this type of rhetoric, attacking English peers and Tories in the way that had worked so well in rural Wales, and using the rich rhetorical tradition of the chapel and the itinerant preacher. As propaganda, Lloyd George's war speeches were hailed by one highly qualified critic as 'powerful . . . positively amazing . . . the most wonderful performances'. Hitler continued:

> Precisely in the primitiveness of his language, the primordiality of its forms of expression, and the use of easily intelligible examples of the simplest sort lies the proof of the towering political ability of this Englishman.[3]

POLITICAL NATIONALISM

But the Welsh leadership had discovered far more than the uses of oratory and caucus organisation. From the mid-1880s, they were influenced by new intellectual currents of an explicit nationalism that was seeking political expression on the Irish model, at a time when Irish demands for land reform were acquiring such direct relevance for rural Wales. At the 1886 eisteddfod, Michael Davitt appeared alongside Michael D. Jones and Lloyd George. Cultural nationalism was also gaining strength under the leadership of the new generation of historians and literary scholars. Ellis' successor in the Merioneth constituency was Owen M. Edwards. In 1891, Edwards had begun the influential journal *Cymru*, which vigorously promoted the myth

2. Quoted in D.M. and E.M. Lloyd, *Book of Wales* (London, Collins, 1953), 86. This account of the Liberal leadership draws heavily upon the work of Kenneth O. Morgan, and so (inevitably) does the remainder of this chapter. Especially valuable is his *Wales in British politics 1868–1922* (University of Wales, 1970).

3. Adolf Hitler, *Mein Kampf*, edited and translated by D.C. Watt, (London, Hutchinson 1974), 433.

of rural nonconformist society as the true bastion of Welshness. Another contemporary was Beriah Gwynfe Evans, who began a new phase in Welsh drama with his play on the appropriate topic of *Owain Glyndŵr* (1879: the play was revived in Caernarvon in 1911 as a commentary on the investiture of the new Prince of Wales).

We have already noted that a society for the promotion of Welsh in education emerged in 1885. The following year, a more important movement was formed: *Cymru Fydd* ('The Wales that is to be', or 'Young Wales'). This had close links to the new university, where Tom Ellis had been one of its earliest students. Welsh exiles were in the forefront, and the first *Cymru Fydd* societies were formed in Liverpool and London. The journal *Cymru Fydd* appeared from 1888 to 1891, to be followed by *Young Wales* from 1895. The movement was supported by many veterans of traditional radical struggles, above all by Thomas Gee; but it had its greatest appeal to the generation that knew only the successful populism of the 1880s. The slogan 'Home Rule for Wales' gained popularity from about 1887, and Ellis called for a separate Welsh legislature at a meeting held in Bala in 1890. Lloyd George further envisioned a nationalist movement intertwined with radicalism and socialism. Nonconformity was not so much a part of the new programme, it was rather the fundamental assumption behind the whole scheme. From 1891, *Cymru Fydd* branches spread throughout Wales, and the movement began to secure the selection of its candidates on the Liberal ticket.

The new movement posed many questions. Should the major emphasis of the Welsh MPs be on specifically Welsh issues, or should these be treated as part of a common British or even European dimension? Should nationalism take priority over traditional Liberalism and radicalism? If the movement was as radical as it claimed, were its leaders committing treason when they accepted government office? This last became a divisive question when Ellis accepted a position in Gladstone's new ministry. And the strength of the parliamentary movement rested on its alleged ability to threaten the government with a 'Welsh Revolt'; but even if this were possible, was it not suicidal to wreck a Liberal administration for its supposed moderation? When the parliamentary insurrection came in 1894, it was a pallid and divisive matter of four MPs (Lloyd George, D.A. Thomas, Herbert Lewis and Frank Edwards) resigning the Liberal Whip over the government's slow progress to Welsh disestablishment. *Cymru Fydd* was a long way from becoming Sinn Fein.

Among recriminations, *Cymru Fydd* fell apart by 1896, though its influence lingered for many years. Appropriately, in the light of its

Irish influences, a major force in the movement's destruction was the Welsh version of the Ulster question. Individualist nonconformist populism was suitable for Merioneth or Cardiganshire, but inappropriate to Glamorgan or Monmouthshire. These areas had long controlled most of the economic activity in Wales, but at the end of the century, they were charging ahead of the other counties. And for Cardiff and the Rhondda, imperialism and even some types of war made excellent economic sense. The Liberalism of the south-east was thoroughly different from that of the rest of Wales, and would be for the foreseeable future.

Moreover, in any future Welsh state, Glamorgan and Monmouthshire would probably be able to out-vote all the other shires combined; if that could not be achieved by Glamorgan alone. In a free Wales, Merionethshire for example would almost certainly be subject to a more direct and less sympathetic rule from Cardiff than anything currently emanating from London. Could that be avoided? Partition might be one answer, as might an American-style solution of granting one vote per county in a future assembly or parliament; but all the solutions had massive drawbacks. By 1911, the six least populous Welsh counties totalled 300,000 people between them; Glamorgan had 1.1 million. As home rule was discussed during and after the 1890s, it became obvious that there were critical divisions between the two regions, questions of personal style and political tradition no less than economic interest. *Cymru Fydd* came to be seen not so much as the party of Wales, but of north Wales and of Lloyd George's populists; while D.A.Thomas portrayed himself as the advocate of industrial Wales. The schism of 1896 is a fascinating precursor of the later rejection of nationalism, in 1979.

But for all the problems, the idea of nationalism had been placed on the political agenda. In 1890, Alfred Thomas proposed a Welsh Secretary of State. In 1892, he introduced a National Institutions (Wales) Bill, which appears tame by modern standards. This would involve a Secretary of State, a national council and a number of government departments, including one administering education. The Bill achieved little, and further progress was lost in the wreckage of *Cymru Fydd*.

A second home rule movement developed in 1910, under the leadership of E.T. John, MP for Denbighshire East, and Beriah Gwynfe Evans. Once again, this was partly a response to the current concern with Irish home rule; and as in Ireland, the movement was halted by the outbreak of war. John's Bill of 1914 only reached its first reading. However, at least John recognised the need for an organisational framework to support his campaign. He based his movement on the *Undeb y cymdeithasau Cymraeg* (Union of Welsh Societies), founded in 1913; and from 1914, his ideas found expression in the journal *Welsh Outlook*, founded by Thomas Jones and the younger David Davies of Llandinam. This framework kept nationalist ideas alive during the war years, and John dreamed of a 'Welsh Nationalist Labour Party'. However, this movement foundered in the early 1920s, with the north-south issue remaining central.

In fact, these later movements faced even greater difficulties than the *Cymru Fydd* era. First, the dominance of the south-east had become even more pronounced: of 36 Welsh MPs in 1918, 23 were from Glamorgan and Monmouthshire. And at least the battles of the 1890s had occurred within the nominal framework of one Liberal Party. From 1910, the south had become a hotbed of industrial militancy and syndicalism, reflected in the election of Labour MPs (there were ten by 1918). Independent Wales would be dominated not only by the south, but by 'the Bolsheviks of the South'.[4] Resolving the dilemma of cultural duality would prove fundamental to any hopes for home rule; and in future decades, there would be inevitable conflicts between the ideals of nationalism and democracy.

The 'national question' had at least been posed, and many of its implications were explored; but it was certainly not the only issue in late Victorian and Edwardian Wales. Far more important were some very traditional problems: tithes and the land question, debates on religion and disestablishment, and on education.

LAND

The rise of radical Liberalism in the 1880s coincided with a bleak time for Welsh agriculture. The depression which began in Britain in the 1870s initially had only a limited effect in Wales, chiefly in advanced regions like the north-eastern counties and south Pembrokeshire. Few areas depended directly on corn, and those that did were increasingly cushioned by pastoral farming. From 1886, however, the turndown in prices hit the livestock farmers, who did not recover until after 1896. On great estates like Nanteos, the level of arrears reached new heights between 1883 and 1885 and again between 1893 and 1895. Many areas were hard hit, so the slump

---

4. Kenneth O. Morgan, *Wales in British politics*, 293.

further stimulated emigration: either overseas, or to the coalfields of the south-east. It was the crisis of these years which decimated the rural Catholicism of north Monmouthshire, and uprooted communities which had survived three centuries of penal laws. Generally though, the vast majority of the victims were nonconformists. The small independent farmer was almost an icon for Welsh radicalism, and the sufferings of such people were well within the comprehension of radical leaders. Interestingly, the campaign paid little attention to labourers' demands for higher wages from those very farmers, though distress in the countryside did in fact lead after 1889 to moves towards unionisation, in Anglesey, Caernarvonshire and south Pembrokeshire.

The farm crisis now became a major issue in Liberal politics: it also inevitably acquired religious and political overtones. The evictions of 1868 had drawn attention to the issue of security of tenure and the control of rents; and there was much interest in the Irish Land Act of 1881, which established tribunals to regulate such matters. Davitt's Irish Land League was emulated by a Welsh organisation headed by Thomas Gee (1887), which adopted Irish demands like compensation for improvements. The economic crisis gave new importance to the issue of the tithe, a radical grievance since at least the 1650s. At a time when farmers were struggling to pay rents, this seemed an additional charge, arising from a religious structure that was rejected by most of those who paid it. Moreover, the tithe was of its essence a surtax on improvements. From 1883, a tithe protest movement arose, orchestrated by leaders like Evan Jones of Mostyn, an Independent minister who was an associate of Michael D. Jones. Evan Jones (*Pan*) was one of the first to advocate nationalisation as a solution for the crisis.

From 1887, discontent took a more active form, and when some Denbighshire farmers refused payment of the tithe, they were distrained. As in Ireland, evictions and distraints were often accompanied by protests and collective action. An Anti-Tithe League was headed by Howell Gee, son of Thomas, and the movement was supported by the Liberal press, by Welsh papers like the *Baner*, the *Celt* and the *Cenedl*; but most of the protests arose independently of any official organisation or sponsorship. There now began a 'tithe war' centred in northern counties like Denbighshire, Montgomeryshire and Caernarvonshire, but with incidents in Anglesey, Merioneth and Cardigan. This has been compared to the Rebecca movement in the south, and it is interesting to speculate what might have become of that earlier insurrection if popular action had been reinforced by a caucus of militant MPs. The riots were often severe, especially at Llangwm (Montgomery) in May 1887 and at Mochdre (Denbigh) in June. Amlwch and Bodffordd in Anglesey were the setting for violence, as was Meifod in Montgomery, and disturbances continued into 1895.

This was politically dangerous for the Welsh Party, as MPs like Lloyd George or Ellis might alienate English Liberals by their support of overtly illegal acts. Rendel was especially cautious on the matter. However, the land issue was a pressing one for supporters, and several Bills were introduced. In 1887, Bryn Roberts proposed a package on the Irish model: compensation for improvements, arbitration for fair rents, and regulation of evictions. This got nowhere, but Ellis and others maintained pressure. In 1892, the activists received the weighty support of Gladstone, who in a speech at Beddgelert denounced the cruelty and selfishness of the Welsh landlord class. The following year, a Royal Commission investigated landholding in Wales. Its report (1896) stimulated calls for change, but the issue gradually faded from the political mainstream as economic conditions improved from the end of the decade.

DISESTABLISHMENT

More enduring as a source of conflict was the question of the Church. By the 1880s, it was commonly believed that some 80 per cent of the Welsh people were nonconformist, and therefore not members of the established Church of England. Resolving this paradox seemed to require changing the legal status of the Church in Wales, as had been accomplished with the minority Church in Ireland in 1869. Disestablishment (Liberation) had been a common idea among Welsh radicals since at least the 1830s, and it had gained strength in the aftermath of the 1859 revival. Pressure for Liberation was mobilised by meetings and demonstrations that often achieved huge numbers, as at Swansea in 1862, Caernarvon in 1883 or in both these towns in 1912.

The Liberal Party was the obvious agent and beneficiary of such a movement, despite the qualms of more traditional Whig leaders. For disestablishment was in many ways a truly radical measure, involving as it did a direct attack on established property rights. The sum from the secularised endowments of benefices would be some £230,000 according to the Bill proposed in 1895; £173,000 under the scheme of 1912. There was also a growing nationalist attack on 'the Church of England in Wales'. Merely discussing the proposal tended to support the idea of Wales as a separate legislative entity, which in law it was not – yet. On the other hand, most of the actual controversy arising from the Welsh Bills took place in the rest of the United Kingdom, outside Wales. (It was the archetypical English F.E. Smith who spoke of 'a Bill which has shocked the conscience of every Christian community in Europe'.) Within Wales, there was overwhelming sentiment in favour of reform, and the only debate concerned the best means of implementing it.

In 1870, disestablishment had been proposed, but with little hope of success. The new Welsh Liberal Party that emerged after 1885 faced very different prospects, and a motion in 1886 failed only narrowly. Of 30 Welsh Members 27 voted for disestablishment. Several other motions failed in the following years, and the issue reached the dimensions of a major crisis in Gladstone's final ministry. In 1892, a Welsh Church Suspensory Bill offered limited disestablishment; in 1894–5, a fuller measure led to the mutiny of Lloyd George and the 'Four', who resigned the Liberal Whip. This Bill was in fact a radical measure, described as 'plunder and sacrilege' by a Tory member. Especially sensitive were the property clauses. Tithes would pass to the county councils, and the proceeds of disendowment would pass to educational and cultural enterprises. Curates and public patrons would not be compensated for their losses.

This measure failed, like its predecessors; and reform had to wait for the elections of 1906, and the new Liberal government. Once again, the Church establishment seemed doomed. The Liberals had an enormous majority; 25 of the Welsh MPs were nonconformist, and Lloyd George was a highly placed member of the administration; while the French disestablishment of 1905 offered an exciting precedent for British politics. In light of this, it is striking that Welsh disestablishment took so long. It was a perennial parliamentary topic from 1909 to 1913, and the coming of war resulted in the postponement of implementation until 1920. The new Bills did not demonstrate excessive radicalism: in fact, the property provisions of the 1909 Bill were more moderate than those of 1894–5, though there was to be a Welsh Council with the authority to dispose of the secularised endowments.

Unfortunately for the Welsh radicals, their favourite measure became enmired in the savage party politics of these years, when Conservatives saw the established order as under ruthless attack, and were accordingly determined to resist reforms on which they might earlier have compromised. Disestablishment therefore became part of a Liberal package which would require constitutional change to put into effect. Ultimately, the Welsh Bills may have benefited from the poisoned political atmosphere. By the time of the decisive vote in 1914, there was little enthusiasm or commitment to be found against the change, least of all in a country facing outright civil war over Ireland. It was almost by default that the Bill was passed in 1914. Suspension for the duration of the war was no more than a final insult, and formal disestablishment came in 1920. Far from being crippled by the loss of its position, Welsh Anglicanism survived the transition remarkably well; and new dioceses were created at Monmouth (1921) and Swansea and Brecon (1923).

EDUCATION

Last among the great Liberal issues of these years was education, and the issue of the Church-controlled schools. By the turn of the century, these were almost matched in number by the Board schools, but the Church still played a large role in education, especially in rural areas. From the late 1880s, there were several schemes to provide additional aid to the Church schools, and all met fierce Welsh opposition. One 1897 Bill was greeted by Tom Ellis with terms like 'outrageously and comprehensively bad . . . vicious'. In 1902, Balfour's Education Bill proposed a sweeping reform of the system, abolishing the distinction between Board and Church schools. All would be financed from the rates. Local authorities could inspect voluntary (non-provided) schools.

This Act led to a massive campaign of passive resistance and non-implementation known as the 'Welsh Revolt'. From 1903 to 1905, this was the dominant issue in Welsh politics; and of course, the coming of the 1904 revival could only further inflame sentiment. County councils refused to administer the Act, particularly the clauses granting rate-aid to Church schools. After initial wavering, only Breconshire and Radnorshire were tempted to comply. The Conservative government responded with what became known as the 'Coercion of Wales Act', of 1904, which permitted the Board of Education to take over operation of the Education Act where a local authority was in default. Grants would then be transferred to the Board. To Wales, this was 'the act of tyranny'. By 1905, all the Welsh counties were in default.

The attempt at intimidation laid the foundations for the parliamentary triumph of 1906, but Liberals also benefited in the county councils. Resisters (Progressives) heavily defeated compliers (Sectarians) – in 1904, by four to one. The campaign gave Lloyd George an unassailable power-base in nonconformist Wales, and appeared to elevate him to a position of national leadership unparalleled in modern times. One of the most remarkable aspects of the war was the frequent tendency to create national conferences and protest meetings, like the Cardiff convention of June 1904, or the successor at Llandrindod Wells two years later. These obviously resembled the national councils that Lloyd George had advocated in other circumstances: in 1895, for instance, to administer tithes. It almost looked like a Welsh political nation was coming into being without an explicit home rule measure. For once, Lloyd George was not greatly exaggerating when he spoke in 1904 of 'national revolution'.

Even the new Liberal government could not solve the crisis at a stroke, and in 1907 it found itself threatening to coerce some Welsh authorities who refused to provide required aid to Church schools. In 1906, a new Bill proposed to meet most of the grievances by placing all public elementary education under the appropriate local authority, and only non-denominational religious instruction would be provided. Welsh affairs would be controlled by a Welsh Council drawn from county and other local authorities, which proved to be a controversial proposal. This measure went down to defeat, though in 1907 the government did create a Welsh department in the Board of Education (Owen M. Edwards was the first chief inspector of schools under this body, which actively supported the interests of Welsh culture). Further changes were attempted, but ultimately, the Welsh authorities found that they could in essence live with the 1902 Act. This did give a fair degree of public supervision and control, and the Church role declined without legislation. As with disestablishment, success came through exhaustion rather than outright victory.

DECLINE AND FALL

The 'strange death of Liberal England' is a well-known phenomenon. The eclipse of Liberal Wales was equally sudden, but it was very predictable. Late nineteenth century radicalism had been a wide-

ranging package of idealistic measures that were perhaps incompat-
ible with the practical problems of long tenure in national
government. In time of war, it was necessary to jettison many
cherished ideas about individualism, local control, and non-violence.
As in the Boer War, the rhetoric of imperialism could seize Wales at
least as completely as that of pacifism. In 1914, the country
responded to the outbreak of war with considerable enthusiasm, and
some 280,000 men would serve, a proportionately higher number
than either England or Scotland. Lloyd George proved to have the
authoritarian and dirigiste instincts required by the new situation,
and he was able to draw on his Welsh acquaintance to find many
faithful satraps in government (it can be argued that Kenneth O.
Morgan perpetrates a slur against Sicilians by naming this band a
'Welsh Mafia'). It was Lord Rhondda who did so much to resolve
the supply crisis that threatened imminent defeat in 1916–1917.
Thomas Jones, 'T.J.', was another follower, a progressive academic
of Fabian and imperialist bent, whose *Welsh Outlook* series
epitomised so many political trends of the age.

The new spirit even invaded the home of pacific Liberalism, the
eisteddfod. At the gathering of 1915, Lloyd George stirred much
enthusiasm by his paean to the martial glory of Wales in days gone
by; a spirit that was now usefully directed to the protection of the
small nations of Europe. In 1917, it was found that the announced
winner of the bardic chair, *Hedd Wyn* of Trawsfynydd, had just been
killed in action, provoking a patriotic display of mourning quite
equal to any English outpouring over Rupert Brooke.

But Welsh Liberalism and nonconformity were by no means as
united as these bizarre pictures would suggest. Limited anti-war
sentiment did exist, both in Liberal and in some (though not all)
Labour circles. Conscription was a bitterly divisive issue, and in 1916
four Liberals voted against the measure (E.T. John, Tom Richards,
'Mabon', and W. Llewelyn Williams). Journals like *Y deyrnas* (the
Kingdom) and *Y wawr* (the Dawn) expressed traditional radical and
pacifist views. After 1918, there was growing concern among Welsh
Liberals about the maintenance of the wartime coalition, and by 1922
it was clear that Lloyd George's leadership had been a mixed blessing
for the Liberal Party.

THE LIBERAL PARADOX

But neither the war nor the leadership question caused the downfall of Liberal hegemony. Welsh Liberalism fell because it was supplanted by the Labour Party; and the chief question here is why this succession took so long to occur. Nineteenth century Wales had demonstrated to an extreme degree the contradictions of Liberalism. The dominance of nonconformist issues in the party platform allowed the creation of alliances and coalitions that seem quite extraordinary to anyone accustomed to the class-conscious politics of more recent years. A number of Liberal Members in this age were 'radical' in political terms, but their economic interests placed them definitively in the camp of the 'haves'. David Davies of Llandinam was a classic example: a magnate who built many of the railways in mid-Wales, he pioneered coal mining in the Upper Rhondda, and developed the Barry dock. This buccaneering capitalist was Liberal MP for Cardigan borough from 1874 to 1886, and a leader in that county's first county council in 1889.

Liberal voters in Cardiganshire may have had little first hand knowledge of the workings of industry in the south-east; but many Liberal industrialists were returned by the constituencies where their enterprises were based. Lewis Ll. Dillwyn held a Swansea constituency from 1855 to 1892, and was firmly radical on the key issues of the day: Church disestablishment, the injustice of tithes, and 'the removal of all religious disabilities'. In 1886, he introduced a disestablishment motion with a speech that was overtly nationalistic. Dillwyn represented one of the greatest industrial families in Wales, with major interests in metallurgical and chemical enterprises, and he certainly was not eccentric or unique in his role as a politically radical industrialist. Several of his most powerful contemporaries were equally wealthy, and active in Liberal and nonconformist causes. It is not surprising that they themselves were able to hold 'radical' opinions, but it can seem remarkable that their large democratic electorates were prepared to accept such wealthy employers as their true spokesmen.

In the Merthyr constituency, Dillwyn's Liberal colleague was D.A. Thomas, who served from 1888 to 1910. He was popular with his Merthyr electors, possibly as much so as the other town MP, the Socialist Keir Hardie. Thomas was unquestionably radical in contemporary terms, and he joined the parliamentary revolt of 1894. In terms of class politics coming to the fore around 1900, Thomas was clearly on the side of the possessing classes: in fact, his life reads like an example from a work by Lenin. Yet this Liberal paradox was slow to become glaringly apparent.

It is not difficult to understand the centrality of the religious issue for the rural population of 'Welsh' Wales; but it is remarkable to find the same concerns among the industrial areas of the south-east. Put another way, we might consider the case of a miner working for a great corporation like Ocean Coal Company, feeling the privation caused by the workings of the sliding scale: why did issues like disestablishment or sectarian education seem so fundamental, when there would appear to have been so many other more pressing matters? The same question might be asked of a Merionethshire quarryman, whose employers were as fervently Liberal as their Caernarvonshire counterparts were Tory.

Two reasons can be suggested for the enduring popularity of Liberalism. The first is the importance of paternalism in the industrial enterprises of the south-east. We naturally tend to focus on the outbreaks of conflict and violence, but the degree of social harmony was often surprising. For the new worker, the early industrial plants would have represented a remarkably familiar institution in what otherwise appeared a radically new landscape. Like the great house of old, the works and its owner provided justice or arbitration, work and welfare. It was the centre at which social life and benefit clubs would be organised. Thus the industrialist, a Dillwyn or Guest, would often fulfil the role once occupied by a squire or landlord, and the resemblance would be enhanced when the employer mobilised several hundred of his workers to swamp the electoral opposition.

Second, nonconformist issues and causes predominated because of the pre-eminence of the chapels and the dissenting denominations as organisational forces in almost every community in Wales. Apart from the pulpit, a political message could be conveyed by any of a number of related associations, by Temperance societies or the Liberation Society. Activities were coordinated by district federations like the Swansea Free Church Council, or the 'Nonconformist Election Committees' of Merthyr and Aberdare, that secured Henry Richard's victory in 1868. In 1885, the Monmouthshire Baptist Association typically urged members to 'be loyal to their consciences and to the Saviour in the polling booth . . . and not to fail to record their votes in favour of the Liberal candidates'.[5] And of course, the Welsh Liberal press was overwhelmingly nonconformist.

5. T.M. Bassett, *Bedyddwyr Cymru* (Swansea: Ilston House, 1977), 295.

By 1900, there was in place a network of propaganda and electoral mobilisation that would put to shame most secular political machines. Until the end of the century, there could be no rival to this among the working and middle classes. This was most apparent in parliamentary elections, but nonconformist power was also evident from other elective offices that had a more immediate impact on everyday life: the Boards of Health, Boards of Education, Poor Law Guardians and the Burial Boards. Until the early twentieth century, working-class electorates in communities like Merthyr and Aberdare consistently returned the nonconformist petty bourgeoisie to these offices. Nonconformist clergy were the largest single occupational category among the elected representatives.

Only after 1900 did this change, for a number of reasons that are probably inseparable. First was the rise of militant labour organisation, in the coalfields and the transport industry. Measures like the Taff Vale decision made it essential to secure political power in order to maintain union organisation and activity, and unions now began to provide an independent electoral structure. At the same time, chapels began to decline in industrial Wales, or at least, they lost their monopoly on political expression. In consequence, Labour began to emerge as a major force, and the Liberal monolith was shattered.

It was perhaps natural that the rise of Labour would destroy the traditional Liberal dominance of industrial Wales. However, the rural seats that were once so firm have also been lost. In 1945, the Liberals held seven seats through north and mid-Wales, and the national party leader was Clement Davies, MP for Montgomeryshire. In 1951, the party fell to only three seats, and it has never exceeded that total since. In 1966, they held only Montgomeryshire; in 1979, only Cardiganshire. And this despite dramatic fluctuations in electoral support, from barely five per cent in 1959 to 23 per cent (for the Alliance) in 1983. The old Liberal strongholds fell initially to the Labour Party, though later to other beneficiaries – often to Plaid Cymru, who could claim to be the true successors of Lloyd-Georgean ideas of radicalism, populism and rural nonconformity.

CHAPTER SEVENTEEN

'Red Wales' – The Socialist Tradition

For most of this century, Wales has been regarded as an extremely radical part of the British Isles, the home of militant unionists, of socialist or communist activists. This stereotype is composed of several different images, including the Tonypandy riots of 1910, the hunger marches of the 1930s, and the career of Nye Bevan. The story of 'Red Wales' has been as richly productive of myths as anything in the development of puritanism or nonconformity. Not even his popularity as national war leader could diminish the widespread perception in Wales that Winston Churchill was fundamentally an enemy, the man who sent in the troops to fire on the miners at Tonypandy. The years from 1909 to 1914 play a role in the traditions of Welsh labour akin to that of the Great Revival in nonconformist memories: both movements have their saints and demons.

THE REVIVAL OF TRADE UNIONISM

Trade unions would be a powerful force in twentieth century Wales, but this was scarcely an ancient tradition. Organisation in the 1850s and 1860s had been sporadic and rather weak, and conflicts had a defensive and even desperate quality; but matters changed in the following decade. From 1871, a new national ironworkers' union led by John Kane spread through the south-east. It had 110 branches by 1874, when there was a tinplate strike. However, the union was torn by internal feuds and expulsions. These were at least in part nationalistic, with a 'Red Dragon' revolt demanding an autonomous

Welsh movement. On the other hand, there were also more general conflicts between the national movement and local branches, with finances a lively topic of debate.

The low levels of coal miners' wages in Wales compared to other areas also led to union activity, with national federations in evidence. An Amalgamated Association of Miners was formed, which at its height claimed 42,000 members. In 1871, a suggested wage-cut of ten per cent was countered by a demand for an equivalent increase in pay: a dramatic departure, which led to a three month coal strike involving some 11,000 workers. In January 1873, 16,000 men were out; and the largest strike of all began in February 1875. These repeated conflicts exhausted and ruined the union financially: the 1875 strike led not only to defeat, but a wage cut of 12.5 per cent. Moreover, the employers had taken warning from these events, and organised their efforts through a new Monmouthshire and South Wales Coal Owners' Association, inspired by W.T. Lewis. One by-product of the new militancy occurred in 1874, when Thomas Halliday was a miners' candidate in the election for the Merthyr/Aberdare constituency. Though he was defeated, his 5000 votes represented a respectable 25 per cent of the poll.

In the next two decades, the centres of activity would lie outside the mines, above all in the engineering and rail industries. The Amalgamated Society of Engineers had branches at Cardiff, Swansea, Barry and Newport by the 1890s, a southern and coastal pattern that was common to these early organisations. There was a strong Welsh element in the Amalgamated Society of Railway Servants (ASRS), which was strong at Cardiff and Barry; and activist J.H. Thomas would go on to play a leading role when the National Union of Railwaymen was formed in 1913. The Associated Society of Locomotive Engineers and Firemen (ASLEF) was also represented at Neath and Pontypool. In 1890, the ASRS mounted a strike on the Taff Vale railway, and militancy attracted support. By 1897, almost 40 per cent of the rail workers in the south-east were members of ASRS. In 1900, it was a decision against this organisation which made unions liable for torts committed on their behalf: this was the celebrated Taff Vale judgement, which threatened the whole basis of union activity.

From the late 1880s, Wales was affected by the 'new unionism', and in 1887, the TUC met at Swansea. There was a major expansion of trades councils. By 1893, these were to be found at Swansea, Cardiff, Newport, Barry, Neath, Pontypridd and Merthyr Tydfil. There were new unions representing dockers and labourers, and strikes by these groups as well as seamen and building workers. The Welsh Artisans' Association was formed in 1888. This activity reached its height in 1891–1892, at Cardiff, Newport and Swansea. However, the movement rapidly faltered, in part because of the industrial depression, which wrecked the tinplate industry. A new iron and steel-workers union was crippled by the depression of these years, and the Tinplate Workers' Union collapsed in 1899.

SLATE AND THE RISE OF INDUSTRIAL CONFLICT

Geographical dispersal, enduring ideals of paternalism and class cooperation, all tended to hinder the emergence of mass action and socialist politics. The transition from collaboration to union militancy was slow and difficult, but the nature of the process can perhaps be best traced from one industry, the extraction of slate. This is appropriate because the quarrymen were long regarded as one of the most loyal and deferential work-forces, whose loyalty to nonconformity was little contaminated by adherence to more hedonistic lower class subcultures of the sort found in the south-east. Yet at the end of the nineteenth century, these dutiful and well-behaved workmen were engaged in some of the longest demonstrations of union militancy and solidarity ever witnessed in Wales. Their story is in no sense representative, as every industry had its own distinctive currents; yet certain common themes can be identified.[1]

In the second half of the nineteenth century, slate was a booming and generally prosperous industry employing some 14,000 men in Caernarvonshire and Merionethshire. The slate workers belonged to a large industry dominated by a few vast concerns; but they were far from being proletarianised. The new mining industries depended on labour drawn from what rapidly became tight-knit towns and villages, with well-defined common values. In the case of slate, the values of the industry and the community emphasised the power which the worker had over his own fate. In the slate regions as elsewhere, the conflicts from the 1870s concerned issues that are difficult to quantify: community values, autonomy, the control of one's labour that marked off the worker from a mere drudge. *Chwarae teg* (fair play) may have been an imported term, but it

1. Merfyn Jones, *The North Wales Quarrymen 1874–1922* (University of Wales 1981).

summarised something precious to the Welsh. Many of the bitterest conflicts arose from defensive actions taken against perceived threats to elementary fairness and justice.

Far from being a 'hand', the slate worker was in reality more like a small independent contractor. Slate was produced by practices that involved a great deal of skill and even intuition, which made the work unsuitable for outsiders: 'the rock does not understand English'. The slate worker was part of a small crew which negotiated rates with the employer according to the difficulty of the rock to be worked. There were also strongly embedded customary rights, often concerning the use and allocation of time. Meal-breaks were a near-sacred opportunity for cultural and social exchange in the *caban*; while workers freely took time off according to their perceptions of need, perhaps during a religious holiday, or else a community event like the harvest. The quarry managers had little knowledge of or sympathy for such traditions. Accordingly, they tried from the 1870s to introduce rigid rules fit for a 'factory' system, and to enforce compliance by fines.

From the 1860s, the slate workers began to form unions, but they were slow to seek active confrontation with the magnates, like Lord Penrhyn and Mr Assheton-Smith. When a strike did occur at the Penrhyn quarry in 1874, the workmen followed the old puritan tradition of blaming the advisers to the Crown rather than the sacred figure of the King: thus the demand was for a thorough change in management, which was achieved. For a decade, the quarrymen had a great deal of power over the workings of the company. Also in this year, the North Wales Quarrymen's Union was formed.

However, the success of 1874 was short-lived. Four times in the next three decades, there were devastating strikes and lockouts, which commonly arose from management attempts to curb the independence and near-craft status of the workers: to replace the 'bargain' (contract) system; to prevent unofficial holidays; to forbid mass meetings. From the late 1870s, the employers also attempted to cut wages, to reflect a slump in the industry. There were conflicts at Dinorwic in 1885–1886, at Llechwedd in 1893. In the Penrhyn quarries, a lockout that began in September 1896 lasted almost a year, and resulted in almost total victory for the employers. Another lockout of catastrophic proportions lasted from 1900 to 1903. Each new defeat cut the size of the union, by the late 1890s to near-extinction. But the successive waves of battle also changed the consciousness of the slate workers to a far more thorough rejection of the status quo in the industry, to a more advanced recognition of common class interests. The supposed tranquillity of the quarrymen also perished. In 1901 and 1902, troops and police were summoned to quell serious rioting at Bethesda, the centre of the Penrhyn dispute. As so often in Welsh disputes, the common targets were blacklegs and 'bootlickers' (cynffonau).

COAL

In the early twentieth century, the focus of labour conflict would move decisively to the south, above all to the coal industry, and we will find many points of resemblance to the slate conflicts. Here too, workers were attempting to secure a fair share of a booming and obviously profitable industry, and at the same time to secure as much control as they could over their work and their lives. Both in Bethesda and the Rhondda, the conflicts involved the values of whole communities, no matter how recently they had emerged.

On the other hand, the coal industry differed in many respects from slate. For Bethesda, it was easy to view the disputes in terms of a conflict between nonconformist workers and an oppressive Tory landlord like Lord Penrhyn (who even lived in a pseudo-medieval castle). Penrhyn did everything that was expected from Liberal mythology: he supported the Anglican cause, and penalised those employees or tenants who voted against him. In a dispute like this, it was easy for Liberals like Lloyd George to support industrial unionists; but coal was different. The leading coal owners included some of Liberalism's firmest supporters and best fund-raisers, men who might themselves be strong nonconformists. It was an urgent necessity for labour to seek an independent political voice separate from the broad Liberal party. Also, the colliers were in a vast industry far more central to the imperial economy.

The southern coalfields were employing 150,000 men by 1900, 250,000 by 1914. The events of the 1870s had left the miners in a difficult position, which left them on the defensive for many years. Wages were determined on the basis of the notorious sliding scale (1875–1903), which related payment to the price received for coal. This was an inherently disastrous system for the workers, as it encouraged overproduction to keep prices at a minimum. This meant both low wages, and threats to safety. Colliery accidents killed at least 1000 a year in the south Wales coalfield between 1900 and 1914: in 1910 and 1913, the figure exceeded 1700. Between 1874

351

and 1914, nearly 2600 died from underground explosions alone. Mortality rates were improving by the early twentieth century, but it remained a dangerous occupation; and even by 1914, there were only 15 mine inspectors for all 624 pits.

The sliding scale was supervised by a joint committee of labour and management, the dominant figures being respectively W.T. Lewis, later Lord Merthyr; and the miners' agent, Mabon, William Abraham. Mabon was a crucial figure in the labour movement, who represented the Rhondda in Parliament from 1885 to 1920. However, he was an arch-conciliator, with real distaste for the new militancy. By 1893, less than a third of the south Wales miners were unionised.

But matters were changing. In 1893, the Hauliers' strike was a bitter conflict which evoked shades of the Chartist era. As in the 1830s, different works were brought into conflict by marching gangs of workers; and this was the first use of troops in south Wales since the Newport rising. In August 1893, there was a colliers' mass meeting at the Rocking Stone, Pontypridd, a place rich with the druidic memories of William Price. This was later seen as the symbolic beginning of the new union activity in the pits. From the end of the decade, there were demands for intensified action, culminating in the strike of 1898 which was explicitly directed against the working of the sliding scale.

Six months of appalling hardship resulted in a complete defeat for the miners. However, 1898 marked the real turning point in industrial relations on the coalfields. It was in this year that the South Wales Miners Federation was born from the consolidation of seven existing unions. This was the SWMF, the 'Fed', which was affiliated to the Miners Federation of Great Britain. (In 1945, this in turn became the National Union of Mineworkers.) Within a year, the SWMF had over 100,000 members, and it soon had 200 lodges. It also had clear political ambitions, and would by 1902 be seeking to place its members in Liberal seats throughout south Wales. The Taff Vale judgement reinforced this belief in the central role of political action, and its urgent necessity.

Hitherto, Wales had played little part in the political Labour movement. By 1897, Independent Labour Party (ILP) branches were to be found only at Cardiff, Treharris, Merthyr and Wrexham; but the movement expanded greatly after the failure of the 1898 strike, the event that brought Keir Hardie to Wales. By 1905, there were 27 branches throughout south Wales, and the party had begun winning local and school board elections. In 1900, Labour also won a famous victory at Merthyr Tydfil, where Hardie was elected for Parliament.

In 1911, the *Merthyr pioneer* became an active organ for socialist opinion. The political activities of the SWMF would mean that Labour representation expanded dramatically. In 1899, Mabon was effectively the lone 'Lib–Lab'; by 1906, there were six labour representatives in Parliament, including four SWMF men. In addition to Merthyr, the group held Gower, west Monmouthshire, Rhondda, south Glamorgan and Denbigh. Among those elected were William Brace and Tom Richards, both pioneers of the SWMF.

The substance of Labour politics was also changing. Mabon, for example, was solidly in the Liberal tradition, and in 1900, he declared the basic points of his programme to be: 'first, disestablishment and disendowment of the Church; secondly, abuses of voluntary schools; and thirdly the great question of temperance'. It is instructive to compare Mabon's electoral propaganda with that of Keir Hardie. In 1906, the latter issued an address to his electors, in which he still recited many of the traditional pieties: the abolition of religious instruction in state schools; 'Prohibition or public control of the sale of liquor'; disestablishment in England and Wales; and home rule all around, for Wales and Scotland as well as Ireland. On the other hand, Hardie's programme was far more systematic and substantial than anything offered by Mabon. It included abolition of the House of Lords, universal suffrage (for men and women); and the abolition of extremes of wealth and poverty through 'socialist measures'.

Labour as a movement stood an excellent chance of maintaining and developing the political foothold established in 1906; but what should be the relationship of the different groups? The affiliation of the MFGB to the Labour Party was debated for several years, and was defeated in a vote of the membership in 1906; although even at that point, the south Wales miners supported the move. Affiliation eventually came in 1908; and by 1910, Wales had five MPs under the Labour ticket.

INDUSTRIAL CRISIS 1909–1914

The relationship between the Liberals and the Labour movement deteriorated in consequence of growing industrial conflict, above all, in the southern coalfields. This was remarkable, because Welsh miners had earlier been regarded as among the less militant in the industry. However, the battles between 1909 and 1914 created many new traditions, not least of the frequent exercise of mass democracy to determine vital political and economic questions. The ballots of the Fed's membership were among the largest democratic exercises hitherto witnessed in Wales. Also, the insurrection against the coal owners had as its particular targets some of the leading Liberal industrialists, like D.A. Thomas. The 'Lib-Lab' compromise was coming to an end.

From 1908, industrial relations in south Wales were transformed by a new wave of militant union activity that demonstrated the influence of revolutionary and syndicalist thought. In 1908, 6000 men struck the Powell Duffryn mines. In 1909, the Plebs League was formed, and it began to carry out propaganda in the Rhondda and Aberdare. Also vital was the influence of the Central Labour College, founded in 1909. Radical papers like the *Industrial Syndicalist* and *Justice* both found a wide readership.

However, the growing struggles were not caused by 'outside agitators'. There were structural problems in the industry quite as disruptive as earlier battles over the sliding scale. This was a labour-intensive industry in which wages were immediately linked to output. From the 1890s, geological factors were reducing the productivity of the Welsh pits, while the eight-hour day made it more difficult for the individual miner to earn a living wage. At the same time, the employers were under increasing pressure to cut costs to maintain profitability. As in the slate industry, conflict focused not on overall wages, but on customary rights and payments, such as the extra 'con' (consideration) for working in 'abnormal places'. These were difficult parts of the mine, which simply could not produce the same output as other areas. Extra piece-work payments provided compensation for this work; but in 1908, a deeply resented court judgement held that these payments were ex gratia, a gratuity, and therefore not legally enforceable. This decision, by Judge Bryn Roberts, was in its way almost as significant as Taff Vale. The employers now tried to cut back on the 'consideration', as well as other cherished customary rights such as access to waste wood.

The leadership of the SWMF urged conciliation, but there was a stoppage in the Cambrian pits in late 1910. At the height of the movement, perhaps 30,000 men were involved; and as the strike progressed, there were calls for a general strike in the industry as a whole (these were defeated by 77,000 to 45,000 votes). The Cambrian strikers were defeated, but only after a desperate year, and the upsurge of extreme militancy among the miners. In the SWMF, the moderate leadership were defeated, and men like Mabon,

Richards and Brace found themselves displaced by radicals like C.B. Stanton, George Barker and Vernon Hartshorn. The strike was run by an Unofficial Reform Committee in direct challenge to the SWMF. The URC included a definite syndicalist presence, represented by W.H. Mainwaring and Noah Rees.

Social conflict was at its height in late 1910, with frequent acts of sabotage against collieries, against strike-breakers and the trains which were attempting to bring them in. As so often in mine strikes, a lethal element is added by the access of both sides to explosives; and there was a bomb attack on the house of the manager of the Britannic Colliery at Gilfach Goch. Attempts to defend the workings of collieries naturally led to conflicts between strikers and police, and in turn to further radicalisation. One such battle at Llwyn-y-Pia led in turn to riots at Tonypandy in November 1910, in which a miner was killed.[2] Tonypandy produced the unforgettable propaganda image of mounted troops patrolling the area. As militants pointed out, they were only performing their basic function of defending the assets of the possessing class. Troops were reinforced by a thousand police, a hundred of whom were mounted.

Tonypandy is a classic illustration both of the power of myth in Welsh history, and of the attempts by recent historians to unravel these claims. A prime example is the role of Churchill. In reality, the government in which he served as Home Secretary did indeed dispatch troops, which Churchill initially halted. He ordered their use later, but his actions can hardly be seen as rash or hot-headed. Nor were the troops directly involved in the events which led to the death of a miner. Presumably, the Churchill legend was reinforced by confused memories of events in Llanelli the following year, and of Churchill's aggressive defence of the status quo in 1926. Attention has also been paid to the extensive looting which occurred in Tonypandy. Some writers justify the heavy hand of the authorities by noting the apparent breakdown of law and order, and the plunder of shops by criminals and 'mob' elements. In contrast, sympathetic historians stress the highly selective nature of the looting, and see it as a form of revenge against the property of unpopular local magnates. Both government and workers emerge rather differently in light of recent scholarship; but nothing has changed the image of the Tonypandy protests as a serious movement that seemed to presage wider and more violent insurgency in years to come.

In 1911, the URC moved closer towards becoming the true

2. David Smith, 'Tonypandy 1910' *Past and present* 87 (1980) 158–184.

leaders of the SWMF, as militants won election to the executive. Mainwaring now joined with Noah Ablett and Will Hay in drafting the revolutionary manifesto, *The miners' next step*. This was pure syndicalism, envisaging an industrial unionism that would achieve the goals outlined by James Connolly: 'to build up an industrial republic inside the shell of the political state'. When this was accomplished, the shell would crack, and the new democratic order would emerge fully formed. This influential pamphlet stated as its fundamental policy that:

'The old policy of identity of interest between employers and ourselves be abolished, and a policy of open hostility installed'

The overall objective was:

'Every industry thoroughly organised . . . to fight, to gain control of, and then to administer that industry. The coordination of all industries on a Central Production Board (to oversee production and distribution according to need) . . . leaving the men themselves to determine under what conditions and how the work should be done' . . . . 'Any other form of democracy is a delusion and a snare'

There were many socialists and radicals in these years who were drafting blueprints for a pure and just society. Few, though, had a plausible hope of the mass support of 150,000 workers in one of the most powerful industries in the world. Ideas of this sort were publicised through newspapers like the *Rhondda Socialist* (which soon became the *South Wales Worker*); and through the branches of the Industrial Democracy League, founded in 1912 by Ablett, Hay, A.J. Cook and others.[3] By 1913, the Welsh coalfields had become the leading national centre of anarcho-communist activity.

The rank and file leadership were successful in transforming the nature of the struggle from a specific issue (abnormal places) to a more general demand for a national minimum wage. In early 1912, this was the basis of a national coal strike throughout Great Britain. However, three years of industrial combat had taken their toll in morale no less than savings; and south Wales was one of the early areas to vote for a return to work, by a majority of 62,000 to 31,000 votes. Despite this setback, the radicals remained a force in the further disputes of 1913 and 1914, and into the conscription conflicts of the war years. The movement was perhaps stimulated by the

3. This account is based generally on Bob Holton, *British syndicalism 1900–1914* (London Pluto 1976); James Hinton, *Labour and Socialism* (Wheatsheaf 1983); Arthur Marwick, *The Deluge* (London Macmillan 1973); and Herbert and Jones, *Wales 1880–1914*.

disaster at Senghenydd colliery in 1913, when 439 men were killed: yet more proof of the constant dangers the miners encountered in their struggle to earn a living.

Industrial conflict was not confined to the mines. In fact, the violence of the colliery dispute was actually exceeded in the great rail strike of 1911. In August, a transport strike at Llanelli involved the seizure and sabotage of rail installations, and the halting of the Irish Mail. Soldiers sent in to restore communications fired on the crowd, killing two, and then launched a bayonet charge. The repression succeeded in the short term, but the funerals of the slain turned into a harrowing display of grief by all sections of the community; and there were reprisals against the magistrates believed responsible for summoning troops. Looting was widespread. Four other men were killed when an ammunition truck exploded during an assault on the goods yard. Llanelli, even more than the Rhondda, fully justifies descriptions like 'proto-insurgency'. These insurrections involved unionists of all types in addition to the workers whose grievances were at the source of the conflict. Solidarity was evident at Cardiff in the seamen's strike of the same year, with the involvement of other city unions. In August, protest in several industrial areas expressed itself in the particularly unsavoury form of anti-Jewish riots.

Militancy received a setback with the outbreak of war, but this was far from fatal. We have already noted that Lloyd George led the Liberals to regard the war as a crusade for democracy and the small nations, and anti-war activism was strictly limited. Socialist internationalism fared as poorly as Liberal pacifism. The union radical C.B. Stanton actually embarked on a Mussolini-like transition to superpatriotic jingoism, the 'independent Labour' platform on which he served in Parliament from 1915 to 1922. Ironically, he succeeded Keir Hardie at Merthyr. However, the mining areas continued to preserve a belief in the centrality of class interest.

Throughout the war, the south Wales coalfields gave the British government some of their worst domestic nightmares. The SWMF contract with the employers was due to expire in April 1915, and the miners demanded a war bonus. A strike was planned for July, and threats of draconian penalties under the new Munitions of War Act were ignored. (The vote was 95,000 votes to 52,000.) The miners had read the government correctly, and the strike succeeded, the first of several such confrontations. Ablett, Cook and other leaders from the traditional URC continued to push for militant action, especially over the issue of conscription. Major strikes were narrowly averted in 1917 and 1918. Collectivist radicals also won an indirect victory in terms of the direction of government policies after 1916. Despite heavy payments to the Liberal Party by the coal-owners, the government in effect took over the working of the mines under the Defence of the Realm Act, apparently setting an encouraging precedent for post-war social ownership. The mines remained in public hands from 1916 to 1921.

The miners' movement survived the war with less damage than might have been expected, but the years from 1919 to 1921 were a time of crisis. In January 1919, the union made ambitious demands over wages and hours, in addition to urging the nationalisation of the industry. These were referred to a Royal Commission under Lord Sankey, who treated the issues raised with great respect, even in so controversial an area as nationalisation. The report was presented in August, and was promptly rejected by the Prime Minister, Lloyd George. The strike had thus been postponed to a time far less advantageous for the miners, while the government no longer faced the danger of a simultaneous challenge from miners, transport workers, engineers and even police. In 1921, the pits were returned to the coal owners.

The numerical strength of the SWMF reached its height in 1921, with 200,000 members (the North Wales Miners' Association had a further 15,000). This was also the year in which the south Wales miners pressed the MFGB to affiliate with the Moscow-based Red International of Trade Unions. This suggests an aggressive confidence that would rapidly dissipate in the deteriorating conditions of the next decade. In 1921, there was a three month lockout throughout south Wales, and soldiers could again be seen patrolling the valleys. The failure of rail and dock workers to support the miners, and thus to honour the historic 'Triple Alliance', was seen as perfidy. The date of the decision, April 15, 1921, entered the miners' mythology as 'Black Friday'. Despite these defeats, union militancy would revive, for instance with the rank and file 'Minority Movement' of 1924–1926; and the leaders of the union were often Rhondda men and veterans of the great strikes, like Noah Ablett, Vernon Hartshorn and others. Glamorgan produced several general secretaries of the MFGB: Frank Hodges (1918–24), Arthur Cook (1924–1931) and Arthur Horner (1946–58). But a vital change had occurred, as the coal industry was no longer the buoyant flagship it had been in 1910. It was now entering a period of serious and possibly terminal depression, and the coal owners moved to the offensive, to claw back whatever concessions they could from the workforce. The employers embarked on a campaign of aggressive class militancy quite as enthusiastic of that of the syndicalists of earlier years.

From 1924 to 1926, the centres of conflict were to be found in the anthracite regions, and there was violence in a strike at Ammanford in 1925. In 1926, however, the employers' offensive culminated with demands for deep cuts in workers' pay and conditions. A strike was scheduled for May 3 in that year, which evolved into the national general strike that so many had sought or feared. May 12, however, the TUC committed what the miners considered to be the ultimate treason, and ended the stoppage. The Welsh colliers remained on strike until December 1926, when they were forced back in a catastrophic defeat, conceding the employers' demands.

This marked the beginning of one of the darkest periods for the SWMF; and in 1931, the Schiller award established mine wages at what were widely regarded as starvation levels. The union's membership fell from 136,000 in 1925 to 60,000 in 1932. There was now even a threat from complacent company unions (Spencer Unions), a relatively new threat in the coalfields. This challenge was not defeated until the mid-1930s, with the 'staydown' and boycott campaigns of 1935–1936. Not until the leadership of Jim Griffiths (President from 1934) did the SWMF begin to repair some of the worst damage of the depression years, and undertook a substantial internal reorganisation.

These conflicts also brought industrial struggles into the political arena. Forcible action obviously led to battles with the police and courts. However, unlike in previous years, there was now a sizeable band of Labour magistrates in the coal areas, and they were likely to sympathise with the union. Cases were thus charged with more serious offences such as riot, so that they could be brought before higher (and less sympathetic) tribunals. Nor would most members of the general public act against the union by serving as witnesses, so trials arising from labour battles were often decided on the basis of police evidence alone. Celebrated mass trials followed the riot between union men and blacklegs at Bedwas in 1933, and a battle between the county police (the 'Glamorgans') and miners at Trelewis in 1935. In the popular view, the police were increasingly depicted as brutal strike-breakers and perjurers, while the courts acted as simple agents of the employers. As in the years before 1914, economic conflict promoted political militancy.

A History of Modern Wales 1536–1990

COMMUNISM AND THE UNITED FRONT

A crisis as profound as that of the early 1930s might have gone far towards uprooting the radical tradition established in the coalfields in the prosperous years. However, there were tokens of recovery, or at least of organisation to resist the total destruction of these communities. One sign of resistance was the local strength of the Communist Party, which had had some support in south Wales since its foundation in 1920. At this time, radical study-groups had emerged in many of the mining communities, often coordinated by former students of the Central Labour College. These groups, Marxist with a definite syndicalist bent, provided a basis for local political action; and Nye Bevan served his political apprenticeship in the 'Query Club' of Tredegar. Some clubs affiliated with the ILP, but many others joined the communists. After the MacDonald defection of 1931, the party won followers disillusioned both by Labour, and by the possibility of achieving change through peaceful means.

The party began contesting Welsh seats in 1929, when Arthur Horner took nearly 6000 votes in Rhondda East, or 15 per cent of the total vote. Other candidates at Ogmore and Caerphilly were less successful, and thereafter communist attentions were focused on Rhondda East. In three elections between 1931 and 1935, the communists increased their share to almost 40 per cent of the vote against the Labour Member W.H. Mainwaring. In 1945, Harry Pollitt took 46 per cent of the vote, and cut Mainwaring's majority to under a thousand. This made it one of the few seats in Britain where the communists were in a sense the official opposition; but the seat never provided the party with a Welsh breakthrough equivalent to that of Keir Hardie in 1900.

Parliamentary politics aside, the communists worked in the unions and in community pressure groups like the unemployed workers campaign. In 1936, Arthur Horner succeeded the moderate Jim Griffiths as president of the SWMF. The Welsh organiser for the National Unemployed Workers' Movement (NUWM) was Horner's friend Lewis Jones from Clydach Vale in the mid-Rhondda, a veteran of the Central Labour College. A CP member jailed during the General Strike, he became a communist county councillor in Glamorgan in 1936. He also wrote the minor classics, *Cwmardy* and *We live*, which portrayed industrial struggles as 'a war that will never end while there are masters and men in the same world'.[4] Jones

4. Lewis Jones, *Cwmardy* (London: Lawrence and Wishart 1978), 310.

360

represented the heroic image of the dedicated militant, a picture consolidated by his early death in 1939, exhausted by his propaganda efforts on behalf of the Spanish republic.

In the winter of 1934–1935, the communists were also active in drumming up opposition to the new Act which proposed to trim welfare payments by limiting local discretion, and by tightening the Means Test. This campaign culminated in a day of protest on February 3, sponsored by the Fed and the NUWM, together with the ILP, CP, and elements of the Labour Party. 300,000 are believed to have participated across the region. In Merthyr, a women's group sacked the local office of the Unemployment Assistance Board. The campaign apparently achieved its objective, and the new payment scales were suspended within days (though they would be reinstated in November 1936). In March, there were other protests against public assistance offices, and a battle at Abertillery led to yet another mass riot trial. From 1933, both communists and Labour leftists proposed the creation of workers' defence groups or militias to repel police assaults. As so often, they were influenced by Continental example, and the experience of Germany and Austria. Internationalism led over a hundred south Wales miners to enlist in the republican cause in the Spanish civil war.

The communists never seriously challenged Labour in the valleys, but their ideas did have a profound influence on the wider culture of many a depressed community. The English press delighted in recounting horror stories of such 'Little Moscows', where Anglican clergymen were spat at in the streets. Maerdy and Nantyglo were notorious for such radicalism. More seriously, the staunch militancy of CP members like Lewis Jones offered an example to other parties on the Left, who were seeking drastic solutions in an era of extreme crisis. One response was to seek political unity with other Left parties, despite suspicions about their wider goals. The ILP had disaffiliated from Labour in 1932, and its supporters sometimes sought tactical alliances with the communists; which accelerated the decline of the party. In 1934, the ILP lost their seat at Merthyr to the Labour candidate, S.O. Davies, himself a socialist militant from the miners' union.

The victory against the new Unemployment Assistance law in 1935 was won through the actions of what we can only call an unofficial popular front; and the following year, the South Wales Council of Action was seen as a model of the united front organisation coming into vogue. Between 1934 and 1936, groups to the left of Labour were key organisers of the hunger marches, which mobilised many thousands of unemployed men, and especially women. By 1938, the communists were even attempting to draw nationalists into the broad front against fascism and poverty.

The best evidence of the socialist culture that flourished even in the darkest years of the depression comes from the libraries of the miners' institutes.[5] In 1930, a Carnegie Trust report remarked that the First World War had marked the shift of power in the industrial villages from the chapels to the miners' union and to these institutes. Their collections were often vast and well-used, all the more avidly during times of unemployment. Tredegar – which loaned 67,000 volumes in 1926 – was in a category by itself, but there were hundreds of smaller collections. The content of the libraries was diverse – in 1923, Bargoed Workmen's Institute subscribed to 60 periodicals of all persuasions - but there was inevitably a strong radical content. At the Cambrian Miners' Institute (Clydach Vale), the most frequently borrowed books between the wars included works by Edward Carpenter, Marx, Freud, Herbert Spencer, the Webbs, as well as a life of Stalin. By far the most popular were M.P. Price's *Reminiscences of the Russian Revolution*, W. Paul's *The State: its Origin and Function* and works on psychology and psychiatry by A. Tridon and A.G. Tansley. We note that Trotsky's history of the Russian revolution was extremely popular until 1931: at which point he fell out of favour in both Moscow and south Wales.

THE TRIUMPH OF LABOUR

1922 marked the breakthrough in the emergence of Labour as the dominant party in Wales. The party held ten Welsh seats in 1918, 18 in 1922, 25 in 1929. The number of Welsh Liberal seats dropped correspondingly, to 11 in 1924, 10 in 1929. In local government, Liberals were often to be found allying with Conservatives on anti-Labour 'ratepayers' tickets: but to little avail. The Labour share of the national vote – barely 18 per cent in January 1910 – reached 40 per cent by 1922, and it remained above that level for six decades. This pre-eminence grew steadily until in 1966 the party took 32 of 36 Welsh seats: not quite a triumph of 1906 proportions, but more than enough to qualify it as the national party of Wales. In fact, the Labour share of the Welsh vote from 1945 to 1966 was usually

5. Hywel Francis, 'The origin of the South Wales Miners Library', *History workshop journal* 2(1976), 183–205.

around 60 per cent, a figure never reached by the Edwardian Liberals. In the early 1950s, Labour also began to make inroads into old Liberal heartlands like Anglesey, Merioneth and Caernarfon. 'Red Wales' appeared to be an indisputable reality.

Labour's roots were to be found in the industrial south-east. The struggles of 1911, the disasters of 1926 and 1932, the victory of 1945, all served to attach industrial Wales indissolubly to the Labour Party. The parliamentary victories were one part of this hegemony. Between 1918 to 1979, 24 of the Welsh seats were to be found in south-eastern Wales, here defined as the traditional counties of Glamorgan and Monmouthshire, together with the south-eastern corner of Carmarthenshire. Within this area, there might have been three safe Conservative seats – in Cardiff, and in rural Monmouthshire. With these exceptions, south-eastern Wales from Llanelli to Newport has long demonstrated rock-solid loyalty to the Labour Party, and has rarely provided less than 20 members of the parliamentary party. (The 'belt' is neatly defined by the boundaries of the south Wales coalfield.)

This political strength was based on far more than sentiment. For many years, the Labour Party had become a fundamental part of the network of institutions on which daily life depended in much of industrial Wales, as essential as the union, the 'Fed', or the Coop. Just as the Party and the union developed swiftly in the years after 1900, so also did the cooperative societies. The first society in Wales was founded in Aberdare, in 1860. The south Wales branches of the movement had almost 20,000 members in 1892, 118,000 by 1915. There were also local institutions broadly cooperative in nature, like the Medical Aid Societies maintained by popular subscription in towns like Tredegar.

Labour MPs often emerged through one or more of these institutions. Of course, there were outsiders from the earliest years, but it is remarkable how many fitted the stereotype: a man who worked in the mine or on the shopfloor, but who educated himself through individual efforts in night classes and the miners' library. From this, he worked his way up to an official position in the union and the cooperative society, served as a councillor, and eventually entered Parliament. A few even had credentials in great strikes such as the Cambrian dispute, a background equivalent to 'Eton and the Guards' in other contexts. Both the Rhondda MPs fell into this category: W.H Mainwaring (1933–1959) and Will John (1920–1950). Jim Griffiths (Llanelli 1936–1970) was a former President of the SWMF. Labour succeeded in completely identifying the interests of the Party with those of the community – if indeed we could speak of these as different things. By 1939, 13 of 18 Labour MPs in south Wales were nominated by the SWMF.

Labour support in the south-east has been so firm as to be almost a standing joke, with the legendary 20,000 majorities regularly reported in Aberafan or Ebbw Vale. Even in 1987, after years of agonising about the crisis of Labour, there were still nine constituencies in this area where the Party won in excess of 60 per cent of votes cast. Vast majorities were accompanied by firm job security for Labour politicians, for whom 30 year parliamentary careers were by no means unusual. The generation that came to power in the Depression often maintained their hold into the Wilson era. This included legendary figures like S.O. Davies (Merthyr Tydfil 1934–1972), Ness Edwards (Caerphilly 1939–1968), and Aneurin Bevan (Ebbw Vale 1929–1960). Since 1929, Aberafan has been represented by just two Labour men. This was also a powerful generation – Ness Edwards, Nye Bevan and Jim Griffiths all served as ministers in the Attlee government.

The loyalty of this Welsh 'red belt' has withstood many storms. In 1931, with the parliamentary Labour Party ceasing to exist over much of England, south-eastern Wales returned a phalanx of 16 MPs. This was disappointing in comparison with later results, but in the context of the time it was miraculous. At another low point in Labour fortunes, in 1983, Labour won 17 of 24 seats in the south-east, which appears to be the irreducible base of support in the area. Elsewhere in Wales, we find such determined adherence to the Party only in the extreme north-east of the country, in what are now the two constituencies of Wrexham, and Alyn and Deeside; and even these became marginal in 1983. The importance of the red belt has increased as the strength of Labour nationwide has faltered. Moreover, all the leaders of the Labour Party since 1974 have represented Welsh seats – James Callaghan (Cardiff South-East), Michael Foot (Ebbw Vale) and Neil Kinnock (Islwyn).

The Labour Party came to be seen as the heir of the militant traditions that had been so powerful in the first quarter of the century. However, the Party found itself ruling a society very different from the expansive optimism of the great years of coal and steam. The original goals of socialism had been to promote universal and democratic access to the benefits of life; but this vision now had to be, at least, postponed. In the 1920s and 1930s, the Welsh economy all but collapsed, and Labour found itself not leading its supporters in a march of social progress, but of defending them against still greater immiseration. A theory founded on distributing the fruits of abundant prosperity had to come to terms with the painful task of managing decline.

CHAPTER EIGHTEEN

Economy and Society 1920–1990

GWALIA DESERTA

From 1870 to 1914, the Welsh economy had grown at a dizzying rate; from the 1920s, the image is almost of a film suddenly thrown into reverse, as the country entered a period less of slump than of deindustrialisation. Wales now paid the full price for its excessive reliance on coal, and thus on the permanence of the technologies based on coal. At the 1913 peak, the south Wales coalfield produced 56 million tons of coal, 70 per cent of which was directed to export. In the whole of Wales, mining and quarrying together accounted for over 270,000 men by 1921, or 30 per cent of the total employed. By 1929, Welsh coal production stood at 48 million tons, and it fell below 35 million by 1932. The coal industry suffered a series of disasters. In 1925 and 1926, the economy was hit by a series of problems – battles over tariffs and the gold standard, the over-valuation of sterling, the ending of the coal subsidy, industrial conflict. Coal was hard hit because of its reliance on export markets. Oil replaced coal in many types of industry, above all shipping, while the growth of electric power reduced demand.

The coal owners had failed in the good years to invest in the mechanisation of the production process, which now placed the industry at a severe disadvantage to its aggressive overseas competitors. By the 1930s, south Wales was the 'sick man' among the coal regions, with the lowest productivity, the highest production costs and the smallest profits; and the smallest proportion of coal cut or conveyed by machine. By 1945, coal production stood at 20 million tons, and Wales had only 112,000 miners.

Obviously, the decline of mining had a severe impact in the

uplands of the south-east, where in the 1920s the industry had accounted for 50 or 60 per cent of total employment; but coal was not the only industry thus affected. Unlike earlier crises (such as the tinplate disaster of the 1890s) it was no longer possible for workers cast out of one industry to find employment elsewhere in the region. Decline was general. The British share of the contracting world market in tinplate fell from over 60 per cent in 1929 to only 51 per cent by 1935, a loss mainly due to German and Italian competition.

Steelmakers suffered from their failure to keep up with methods of strip mill production pioneered in the United States; though individual areas were hit even harder by long-term trends not directly connected with the depression. The traditional iron working areas had already been in real difficulties since the 1870s, with the move to coastal sites. Most of the legendary Merthyr works were gone by 1900, and Cyfarthfa finally closed in 1920. This only left Dowlais, and the Guests already had a new plant near Cardiff, at East Moors. In 1930, Dowlais too shut down, with the loss of 3400 jobs. In 1929, the closure of the Ebbw Vale steelworks cost 10,000 jobs.

Industrial failure spread its effects further afield through the slowdown in transportation and shipping. The south Wales ports all experienced major contractions in business after 1929. Building and construction reached a virtual standstill by the early 1930s. Without economic activity, retailing was crippled, and in south Wales this especially damaged the Coops. Apart from the coal and metal areas, there were other local woes to be suffered, such as the 1926 closure of the naval dockyard at Pembroke Dock.

The impact of the crash also must be understood in contrast to the recent prosperity. Take for example the borough of Merthyr Tydfil. In 1913, there were 84,000 people there, and unemployment was below 2 per cent. There were 24,000 miners, 3500 steelworkers and 4500 'all others'. By 1921, the number of employed miners was 16,000; by 1934, it was 8000. In 1939, the population of the borough stood at 61,000. The depression served to remind people of how tenuous and perhaps unnatural was the growth of such huge concentrations of population in these remote and barren areas. When in 1936 the Prince of Wales visited the deserted Dowlais works, he made a point that was brilliant in its simplicity: 'Something must be done for these people. After all, they were brought here for this works'. The visit earned him real popularity in Wales, where he became a Good Englishman, perhaps a successor to Gladstone; and a counterpoint to the Churchill who sent the troops against the miners. Vernacular history was adamant (and incorrect) in believing that this display of possible radicalism had caused the ruling class to force the new King's abdication shortly afterwards.

There was no one day on which the world ended, and decline was staggered – coal faltered in 1923, while steel remained fairly steady until 1930 – but disaster was general by the opening years of the thirties. Between 1923 and 1934, the number employed in Wales fell by 26.2 per cent, well in excess of either Scotland or England. Welsh unemployment rose from almost 20 per cent in 1927 to a high of 37.5 per cent by 1932. By the end of 1933, there were at least 208,000 unemployed in Wales. In particular regions, the effects were even worse. By 1932, Glamorgan and Monmouth both had unemployment rates above 40 per cent. Anglesey was as badly placed, while the Breconshire figure exceeded 50 per cent. Even when matters improved a little by 1937, 20 per cent rates were common for most of the Welsh counties. The overall figure was 22.3 per cent, at a time when rates in southern and midland England were below eight per cent. In the whole decade, this was the only point at which Wales briefly lost its position as the bleakest region, when Northern Ireland unemployment nudged marginally ahead.

Once a job was lost, it was likely that the ensuing period of unemployment would be long, often several years. Women workers suffered harshly, in contrast to the abundant work opportunities of the war years. By the 1930s, the best options appeared to be in domestic service, the only field for which official training programmes were available. Even this work might not be available in Wales itself: by 1931, there were 10,000 Welsh women working as domestics in London alone.

SOCIAL EFFECTS

Glamorgan and Monmouthshire had the highest proportions of people receiving poor relief in the whole United Kingdom, with the sole exception of County Durham. Perhaps worse than the fact of unemployment was the treatment given to the displaced by official agencies. There was in Wales a long tradition of resisting the worst excesses of the Poor Law, often by overt defiance. At first, local authorities attempted to ignore official policies, and simply overspent to meet social needs. In 1927, the Bedwellty Board of Guardians was so deeply in the red that the government intervened to appoint a new

Board with more stringent standards about outdoor relief, and granting assistance to single men. Public expenditure was curbed, but at a high social cost.

In the next decade, concern chiefly focused on the means test required to receive relief. Whatever the principle of the test, it was seen in practice to subject the poor to the constant surveillance of official busybodies seeking signs of petty extravagance. Also unpopular was the provision of the new Unemployment Assistance Act introduced in 1935, whereby the earnings of adult or adolescent children could cause a cut in the earnings of an unemployed family. The Poor Law was a deeply felt indignity, and the rage and frustration it engendered were demonstrated by the popular revolt of early 1935.

The effects of the economic crash worked their way through the whole of society. Mass unemployment and general stagnation had devastating effects on the tax and rate base for government and public service, destroying the ability of government to provide and maintain services. In the mining areas, it was common for rates to triple between 1920 and 1934. Poverty also dried up the voluntary contributions which were essential for the maintenance of other public services, above all the hospitals, but also other charitable and religious bodies. Sporting organisations disintegrated, most visibly the rugby clubs formed with such pride at the turn of the century. In the words of Dai Grenfell, MP for Gower, 'We are losing our population, and the resources which would enable us to meet our community responsibilities'.[1]

Given the massive importance of nonconformity in Welsh society, we should emphasise here the serious effects on the chapels. They had already been in decline before 1920, with the rise of rival social and leisure attractions, and the emergence of radical socialist politics – both apparent in urban and industrial Wales. But chapel membership was hard hit by the interwar depression and attendant emigration, and the 1935 bicentennial of the great revival was celebrated with less fervour than might have been expected earlier.

From a 1905 peak of over 520,000, nonconformist membership fell to 391,000 by 1955. The years since 1930 have witnessed a lengthy plummet in adherence that would leave disused chapels as one of the characteristic features of the landscape. The story is summarised by one of the most distinguished chapels, Capel y Cymer in the Rhondda. Formal membership here reached a peak of

1. Quoted in T. Herbert and G.E. Jones, *Wales between the wars* (Cardiff 1988), 40.

500 in 1906, but this ignores the numbers of 'hearers', *gwrandwyr*; and in 1895, seating had been extended to accommodate a congregation of 1050. The hearers virtually disappeared during the 1930s, leaving a shrinking core of members: 312 by 1930, 187 by 1940, 40 by 1960. The denomination that did best from these years was the one most used to persistent hardship: and Catholicism would be one of the minor success stories of modern Welsh history. Today, the church is some 140,000 strong.

The crisis manifested itself in public health, never an area in which the Welsh boom-towns had excelled. In the 1930s, hunger was an ever-present reality, with real malnutrition in the hardest hit mining regions. In 1937, the death-rate in Rhondda was in excess even of poor London boroughs like Stepney. Poverty opened the way to diseases like scarlet fever and rickets, with the most obvious deterioration being apparent in tuberculosis. This had long been known as the 'Welsh disease', with the highest incidence in England and Wales to be found in six or seven shires of rural Wales. In Edwardian Wales, there had been campaigns to end this evil, but improvements were brought to a sudden halt in the 1930s, when public health stagnated or worse. In 1939, a committee headed by Clement Davies found that tuberculosis was still at its worst in Wales, especially in the north and west; and still far worse than the British average. Psychological complaints such as depression and alcoholism were equally devastating.

Even worse, there appeared to be no hope for improvement at any point in the future. If there was to be some sort of revival, then the current disasters would blight the future of Wales for decades to come:

> If prosperity does not return very quickly, it will return to find two kinds of men – old men, too old to work, and thousands of young men who have never in their lives done a day's work . . . the best hope for a Welsh collier nowadays is to develop into an hotel worker on the promenade in Brighton[2]

(Rev. John Roberts of Cardiff, 1936)

One solution was emigration, and a sudden reversal of the incredible population growth of the early years of the century. Population decline set in after 1921, so that the number of people by 1940 was probably no greater than what it had been in 1911. From the 1920s to the 1950s, the population fluctuated between 2.4 and 2.6 million; and the 1921 peak was not reached again until the early

2. Quoted in T. Herbert and G.E. Jones, *Wales between the wars* (Cardiff 1988), 43.

1960s. Some 450,000 emigrated from Wales between 1921 and 1939, mainly from the industrial south, with the English south-east and midlands as major destinations. Some found good jobs in engineering or car factories; others faced destitution. On the streets of London, a group of beggars needed only to show a placard inscribed 'Welsh Miners' to explain how they had reached this degradation. (Idris Davies' poem on the glories and disasters of 1926 concludes with 'Dai and Shinkin/ as they stood on the kerb in Charing Cross Road' a few years afterwards.)

The population of the Rhondda alone may have fallen by 30 per cent by 1940. By 1951, Mountain Ash, Rhondda and Aberdare had all lost in excess of 15 per cent of their 1931 populations. But emigration was not enough. In 1939, Political and Economic Planning took the crisis to its logical step, by suggesting that euthanasia might be appropriate for communities that were already dying. Merthyr should be abandoned, and its inhabitants moved to a new town in the Vale of Usk or coastal Glamorgan.

By the mid-1930s, Wales appeared to be a society in dissolution. In 1934, most of Glamorgan and west Monmouthshire received official designation as one of four regions hit hardest by the depression; a policy codified in the Special Areas Reconstruction Act of 1936. This scheme was intended to bring aid, by encouraging businesses to locate new ventures in the depressed areas. Incentives would include relief on rent, rates and taxes. The principle was good, and a similar plan would be valuable after 1945; but at the time, this was grossly inadequate.

It is difficult and even tasteless to seek a more positive side to these disasters, but the crisis also involved a fundamental industrial restructuring that was of benefit to some. Parts of Wales did rather well from just these years, and Deeside boomed with the expansion of steel, textiles (notably synthetics), and light manufactures. Between 1931 and 1951, population growth of 20 per cent or more was recorded in a number of north-eastern districts, including Hawarden, Connah's Quay, Buckley, Wrexham, Flint and Mold: surprising given the continued unemployment even in these areas. Holywell grew by 50 per cent. The two counties of Denbigh and Flint had a combined population of 262,000 in 1921, 323,000 by the 1940s: a 23 per cent increase at a time when most other regions were stagnating or declining.

The overall decline in the populations and economies of Welsh counties also serves to mask local growth. From the late 1930s, recovery in much of England increased the demand for leisure facilities, with consequent growth in the resorts of Rhyl and Llandudno. And the desire for retirement properties and second homes promoted the redevelopment of coastal areas like Pembroke-shire and Gower.

Even in the south-east, there were pockets of – if not prosperity, then at least survival. The Special Areas designation excluded the regions of Swansea, Cardiff and Barry. Cardiff in these years was far better off than centres like Merthyr, if we measure by criteria like numbers of cars, telephones and radios per capita. The city was a technological generation ahead of areas just 15 or 20 miles away. In 1923, Cardiff acquired a radio relay station (by 1937, this was the basis of the Welsh Home Service). There must also have been enough internal demand in the south Wales economy to permit the minor leisure booms that occurred in the 1930s, for instance in sport and the cinema. Swansea also did fairly well, and even benefited from the growth of the car industry that did so much to aid the reconstruction of the English midlands. The new car plants needed nickel, which they obtained from this traditional non-ferrous centre. Wales now began its career as an oil centre, with the Anglo–Persian oil refinery at Llandarcy (1922).

From the late 1930s, there were pockets of recovery even in the south. In 1938, an industrial estate which opened at Treforest foreshadowed the success of this kind of development in stimulating local growth. There was rationalisation and consolidation in the steel and tinplate industry, laying a foundation for growth in the next two decades. Between 1938 and 1945, the tinplate industry became heavily concentrated in west Wales, between Llanelli and Gorseinon; and steel enterprises grew at East Moors and around Port Talbot. Also in 1938, a modern strip mill opened at Ebbw Vale; the following year, Merthyr Tydfil received desperately needed assist-ance in the form of a new ICI plant. By 1939, there were still 600,000 insured workers in Wales, though only 35 per cent worked in the coal or metal industries. 20 per cent were employed in engineering or manufactures, 15 per cent in the retail and distributive sectors.

In World War II, south Wales was certainly not beyond the reach of German bombers – 1000 civilians died in raids in 1941 alone, most spectacularly in the Swansea attacks of February; but sites here were preferable to those in the Home Counties. In consequence, there were several large scale Royal Ordnance Factories in Wales, notably at Bridgend and Hirwaun. The former provided the basis for a later industrial estate that helped make Bridgend a real economic centre from the 1950s onwards.

RECONSTRUCTION 1945–1973

After 1945, the reconstruction of British industry was a primary goal of the new Labour government. In addition, the Party had firm roots in south Wales, so action here was urgent. The intellectual environment of the time favoured central planning and direct investment, with nationalisation seen as a major first step. Coal was nationalised in 1947, steel from 1951 to 1953. Also, the government supported corporate consolidation to promote efficiency and investment. The merger of Richard Thomas and Baldwins in 1945 gave the new concern control of two-thirds of the pack-mills which made Welsh tinplate. In 1947, several major companies combined to form the Steel Company of Wales, with its showcase at Port Talbot.

The new Abbey works here, opened in 1951, demonstrated the hopes of the planners. It had excellent facilities for transportation by land and sea, and it represented massive investment in new plant as opposed to reliance on outmoded equipment. By the late 1960s, the Abbey works employed almost 20,000 people, making Port Talbot the latest in a long series of Welsh boom communities, successor to Merthyr and Aberdare in the nineteenth century, the Rhondda in the early twentieth. The Abbey had enormous marshalling yards, and a new deepwater port would improve communications still further. Port Talbot also exemplified the new rational approach to economic planning in the 1950s and 1960s. Welsh steel was to be concentrated in just four enormous and efficient plants: Port Talbot, Llanwern (1962), Ebbw Vale and Shotton. There were also cold reduction plants conveniently located nearby, at Margam, Velindre and Trostre. This represented a strategic plan to preserve Welsh hegemony in steel and tinplate.

The Attlee government presided over a real revival in Welsh industry, an expansion that was reinforced by subsequent developments in the 1960s. This was important in that it assisted the region come to terms with the end of the old economy based on mass employment in coal. Far from abandoning the Welsh pits, the National Coal Board made new investments in the region. The emphasis was now on productivity and efficiency, with a concentration on fewer and larger collieries. By 1953, south Wales was still producing almost 21 million tons from 115 pits, including 85 per cent of the total British production of anthracite. But the workforce was steadily contracting: there were 130,000 miners in the early 1950s, only 25,000 by 1981. By this time, there were 34 pits in the south, producing 7.7 million tons. The only surviving collieries in the north-east were at Point of Ayr and Bersham, employing 1200 men between them. In the north, slate approached terminal crisis.

The government role was not exhausted by the new direction in the heavy industries. Improving on the old Special Area idea, the Attlee government offered tax relief and grants through an Industrial Development Certificate earned by firms locating in depressed areas; and there were real successes between 1946 and 1949. In Merthyr Tydfil, three major enterprises opened factories, but in activities different from the traditional industries, including aircraft control equipment and Triang toys. Other plants opened in the old depressed areas, making goods as diverse as rubber, plastics and synthetic textiles.

Some of the new industries were extraordinarily successful. By the 1960s, the opening of a huge oil port at Milford Haven and a new refinery at Llandarcy made Wales a European centre of the petroleum industry. Together with the Baglan Bay petrochemical complex, this growth was of special benefit to the Swansea Bay region, which seemed to be emerging as a centre of European importance. Just as travellers had once remarked on the infernal displays of smoke and fire around Merthyr, so Swansea Bay by the 1960s was lit at night by its ring of steelworks, chemical plants and oil refineries. Swansea also gained a foothold in the car industry, with the Ford assembly plant.

Despite the decline of coal, there were many areas of economic growth between 1945 and 1970. The number working in service or white-collar industries in Wales doubled, to 345,000, with particular impact on the cities of Cardiff and Newport. The concentration of official Welsh agencies in towns like Cardiff expanded the opportunities for bureaucratic employment; and by the 1980s, the service sector represented almost 60 per cent of employment in Wales. Regional policies favoured the relocation of national agencies to 'provincial' areas like Wales: the Royal Mint came to Llantrisant; Companies House to Cardiff; the Driver Vehicle Licence Centre to Swansea. This sort of growth also drew more women into the work force. Women comprised a third of insured workers in the late 1960s, 42 per cent by the early 1980s.

Swansea and Bridgend flourished, as did areas of the north east, like the Marchwiel trading estate. Some installations opened in non-traditional industrial areas like Anglesey, where there was a new nuclear power station as well as a Rio Tinto Zinc aluminium plant. This sort of growth did much to make up for the steep decline in agricultural labour in these years. However, rural development may have been set back by the closure of many marginal rail lines in the

1960s. The 'Beeching axe' was severely wielded in Wales, where total mileage fell from 637 to 363.

As the rural infrastructure contracted, so a new network of communications secured the dominance of the south-east, through its connections to western England. In the last quarter of a century, the Severn bridge and the extended M4 motorway have brought Cardiff and Newport virtually within commuter distance of London; while the emerging Bridgend-Newport corridor has experienced dynamic industrial growth even while other areas have declined. Less dramatic but also important was the new heads of the valleys road, opened in 1964. Government planning brought a wholly new town to Monmouthshire in the form of Cwmbran, initiated in 1952. Another scheme to create a new town in mid-Wales was abandoned, only to be replaced by intensive growth around Newtown.

THE CRISIS IN COAL AND STEEL 1973–1990

The expansive years since 1945 were not without their problems, including a growing political alienation which will be noted below; but life was palpably improving for most citizens. After 1973, there was a gradual reversion to problems and crises that most had thought banished with the 1930s. As the British economy declined, the older industrial areas were severely affected, and there began a new wave of closures and layoffs. In Merthyr, most of the enterprises that had saved the town after World War II departed in the 1970s. Most difficult to accept, 'restructuring' was now targeted against towns and plants that had once been the golden hopes of the Welsh economy, especially in the steel industry.

The new crisis was clearly in prospect from the mid-1970s, with the closure of the works at Ebbw Vale and East Moors. However, the election of the Thatcher government in 1979 was followed by rapid industrial decline. In the mid-1970s, the British Steel Corporation had 63,000 employees in Wales, a number which collapsed to 19,000 by 1983. Shotton closed, losing 9000 jobs; Port Talbot and Llanwern contracted to what appeared near-extinction. The impact of the blows was cushioned somewhat by large redundancy payments, but these could do little to prevent long-term social problems in the affected communities.

The contractions in mining and manufacturing were severe:

	Total employed	Extractive industries	Manufacturing	Services
1972	973	75	412	486
1978	1015	64	395	556
1982	899	58	295	546

(All figures in thousands)

Between 1979 and 1982, Wales lost 130,000 jobs. By the end of 1981, Wales had 170,000 known unemployed, with a further 44,000 in rather tenuous job creation programmes. Despite some recovery, officially recorded unemployment stood at over 17 per cent by 1986, making this clearly part of the 'have-not' half of the British Isles.

To take a specific example, Port Talbot had stood on the frontier of innovation and prosperity. In the 1980s, however, it was a symbol for other perennial features of the Welsh landscape: of unemployment and social decay, of industrial obsolescence and uncompetitiveness. The steelworks had only 5000 employees by 1985, and cutbacks in other industries had also contributed to produce a local unemployment rate in excess of 20 per cent. A social science more developed than that of the 1930s traced the impact of the new depression in a number of contemporary indices: the growth of alcoholism and suicide, of social disruption and family breakdown. Port Talbot may have been better placed than some other towns, such as Pembroke Dock and Tenby, where 30 per cent unemployment was recorded by 1983. In Anglesey, one of the most recent areas of industrial growth, unemployment reached 21 per cent at this time, with the closure of the Holyhead drydock and reductions elsewhere.

Industrial decline affected the traditional industries most severely: indeed, it almost seemed as if the government were vindictively targeting the most familiar and venerated landmarks of the Welsh economy. The coal industry was in a special status here, because of its century-old role as the foundation of Wales. By the 1980s, there were only 20,000 miners, and this decline in itself marked a social and political revolution. Miners generally need little instruction in the importance of cooperative values and labour solidarity, and they are likely to support traditional socialist parties and policies. The Labour Party had very different prospects in 1920, in a country with 270,000 miners, than it could expect in the 1990s. By 1970, the NUM was sponsoring only two Labour MPs from the region, S.O. Davies and Gwilym Davies. Most tragic was the collapse of the old

Miners' Institutes with their superb libraries, a dissolution mitigated only by the work of the South Wales Miners' Library opened in 1973.

In this context, the great miners' strike of 1984–1985 marked a painfully symbolic ending to the era of mass labour politics. Welsh miners' communities had supported the strikes of 1972 and 1974, and they were loyal to the National Union of Mineworkers' leadership under Arthur Scargill, but Welsh events were peripheral to the main battlegrounds in Yorkshire and the north midlands. The irrelevance of the Welsh pits was a striking illustration of the decline of the industry. Tragically, it was only in Wales that this savage conflict involved loss of life, when three strikers were involved in an incident that led to the death of a taxi-driver carrying a strike-breaker to work. Not long after the failure of the strike, the Welsh miners were again at the forefront of conflict, but this time in the once unthinkable position of disobeying the NUM. To open the new pit at Margam in Glamorgan, the Coal Board demanded flexible working practices, which the local union conceded over the protests of the national leadership. The politics of coal had changed completely. Equally dramatic was the failure by Welsh unions to halt decline by industrial action. A steel strike failed as utterly as would the miners' conflict of later years.

THE 1980s

As in the 1930s, the situation seemed grim in many parts of Wales, and it was perhaps worst in the areas where the expectations of the 1950s had collapsed most totally. But there were also positive signs, which belied the atmosphere of despair that characterised 1980 or 1981. A glance at the shopping centres of Cardiff, Newport or Swansea makes it apparent that although unemployment might be high, there is still substantial demand for durables and luxury goods. Wales shared the general consumer prosperity throughout Great Britain, manifested by the ubiquitous taste for what would once have been inconceivable luxuries: for electronics and computers, much wider selections of imported wine and foods. At the same time, the growing towns continued to absorb and gentrify hitherto rural villages, as suggested by the soaring house prices of Gower and the Vale of Glamorgan.

This prosperity came in part from the much greater productivity secured from the old heavy industries, and the Margam pit represented new investment. There were also several centres of substantial growth based on high-technology industries. Wales benefited from the workings of regional policies which focused investment on the less prosperous areas: the Welsh Development Agency had been established in 1975. In addition, the country made good use of its own intellectual resources. Swansea attempted to build an innovation centre which could apply the expertise of the University College, and a high-technology centre emerged at Newport. Pilkington's established a groundbreaking fibre-optics plant in the north-east, while innovative computer-based industries were widespread around Cardiff, Swansea and Wrexham.

Multinational companies showed enthusiasm for setting up new enterprises among such a placid and relatively low-paid labour force. Between 1972 and 1988, the Japanese alone invested in 21 new enterprises, creating 5000 jobs. Over 1000 people worked at the Sony factory at Bridgend (opened 1973). However, there was a quid pro quo, as the Japanese demanded rationalised working practices and single-union contracts. Also, the Japanese were tempted by the location of Wales within the European Community, so that goods manufactured here would be immune from any future protectionist measures.

Entry to the Community in 1973 benefited Wales in many ways. It allowed access to funds intended for the promotion of agriculture and fishing, as well as special aid for depressed areas. Politically, the European link raised new possibilities for devolution. Wales might not achieve complete sovereignty, but could it not exist as an autonomous unit within the European context, on a par with Ireland or England? In historical terms, Welsh culture has often been outward looking and European, rather than merely imitating English models.

TOURISM

Wales also took advantage of the boom in tourism, leisure and 'heritage', the packaging of historical sites for popular consumption. This became a growth industry in the 1980s, with a rash of leisure parks, country parks and newly opened country houses, like Margam and Erddig. Even the failed industrial past could be packaged, with museums commemorating coal or slate mines.

Tourism brought income to hotels and eating establishments, and many a quiet country pub transformed itself into a restaurant of some quality. By the late 1980s, Wales was as successful as Scotland in attracting visitors from within the British Isles. Foreign tourists remained fewer, but even so, Wales accounted for perhaps 600,000 a year. The national eisteddfod alone drew over 120,000 visitors. On the other hand, the emphasis on leisure and tourism also had its controversial side. As we will see, the enormous popularity of Welsh holiday homes led to a hostile reaction from nationalist activists, culminating in a widespread arson campaign.

One aspect of 'heritage' was a rediscovery of ancient place-names and territorial units as arcane as anything to be found in a newly independent land of the Third World. In the 1970s, Carmarthenshire once more became part of 'Dyfed'. Even the ancient commotes were rediscovered, so that the Llandeilo area was once more described as 'Dinefwr', the 'Kingdom of Cennen'. Partly this was a triumph of advertising, but the nature of the publicity raised interesting questions about Welsh perceptions of their past. For two centuries, Welsh tourism has faced the paradox that many of the most glorious and visible monuments are tokens of conquest, often garrisons for occupying armies; and a Welsh patriot must appreciate the ambiguity of celebrating Caernarvon or Conway Castles as signs of national pride.

The new industry resolved this dilemma by adopting an aggressively nationalistic view of the Welsh past, and it presented a version of that history which better resembled Irish conditions. Dinefwr Castle is trumpeted as the seat of an independent Welsh lord of Deheubarth holding off tyrannical English invaders; while at Llandovery ('the scene of earlier Welsh rebellions'), a tourist leaflet proudly notes that 'many a rebel met his end below the castle mound'. Carreg Cennen becomes the 'impregnable bastion of the Welsh princes'. There is no suggestion here that the worst dangers faced by the Welsh lords might come from other equally Welsh magnates, as part of a struggle over dynastic succession and control of Westminster. Endlessly malleable Welsh history seemed to be in the midst of yet another of its great transformations.

THE NEW POLITICS

Wales in the 1980s seemed to be becoming a radically different country. A country with only marginal activity in coal and steel would have been barely conceivable only a few years previously. In politics, the 1980s witnessed the culmination of a real restructuring away from the one party dominance of the previous half-century. In the next chapter, we will examine the growth of nationalism and the rise of the 'national question' in political life. However, it is possible to exaggerate the real impact of the nationalist cause, which was arguably a response to the decline of Labour, rather than its cause. The decline of the Labour Party was in large measure a result of its near-absolute hegemony in the 1930s and afterwards. This led to complacency and stagnation, while the economic growth of the 1950s and 1960s provided abundant opportunities that could be used or abused by local authorities and political parties. The result was widespread official corruption, and still worse, the common perception that these practices were all but universal. This laid a foundation for real malaise and frustration with the Labour political establishment.

In the 1960s, a 'new Wales' shared in the optimism of the wider United Kingdom. It was a time of building and redevelopment, providing many thousands of jobs, many in the public sector. This gave particular importance to the activities of local authorities as employers and as suppliers of contracts. In addition, the new prosperity of much of Wales helped revive aspirations of social mobility thwarted by the crisis years. For the local councils in the industrial areas, almost all Labour, the expansion of education at all levels acquired the status of an article of faith. Close in importance was public housing. A building boom in council houses was followed by a wave of urban redevelopment across much of Wales, partly to restore and improve decaying town centres. This movement was caught up in the insane property boom which reached its height in the late 1960s.

Local politics were of paramount importance in this prosperous new society. In a typical town in the industrial south, members of the party bureaucracy enjoyed immense power through the tenure of offices in unions and councils, and they often had close relationships with local business and the media. Links with Parliament and the national party might also give considerable influence in securing government projects for the local area, as well as positions in the many authorities directing matters as various as broadcasting, higher education or cultural affairs. In short, much of south Wales was in effect a one-party state, with enormous discretionary power and wide patronage in the hands of a party elite. (It is difficult to avoid using terms like nomenklatura and apparatchik, which seem so appropriate.) Patronage was the cement of this political order, far more than it had been in the time of the eighteenth century gentry. Official power could now be used to bestow jobs and houses for the ordinary citizen, enormous business opportunities for the wealthy. Historians of the turn of the century are fond of discussing south Wales as 'American Wales': but there can be few areas where analogies between the two cultures are as close as the evolution of the Welsh bosses and party machines after 1945.

Contacts between the various overlapping elites were apparently formed and consolidated through membership in freemasonry, a movement with 26,000 members organised in some 300 lodges. This was perfectly proper and even laudable in itself, but the lodges allowed the formation of discreet links between local elites in government, business, law, media, police and education. Many of the local government scandals can be traced back to these informal networks. It may be that this situation was not new, and that earlier Liberals had also taken full advantage of such power in government; but it was the Labour Party in which abuses became most glaringly apparent, in a series of trials between 1975 and 1980.

Through the 1960s, abuses in patronage and the granting of contracts were well-known in particular communities, though not officially recognised. Rumour acquired an importance more characteristic of a totalitarian country, while the gap between public suspicion and official reporting led to a severe loss of confidence in the media. In 1975, one of the largest scandals developed from an anonymous pamphlet about corruption in Swansea, subsequently followed up by a television programme and the investigations of the courageous muckraking magazine, *Rebecca*. (It remains unclear whether the original charges reflected the contemporary campaign by some governmental agencies to discredit and destabilise the Labour Party nationwide.[3]) Charges focussed on the council role in a number of vast redevelopment schemes currently overwhelming older neighbourhoods. In the next two years, the Swansea case led to the conviction of several, including the Labour leader on the Swansea council. In 1976, Labour lost its hold of the council in an electoral massacre. They were replaced by the anti-corruption Ratepayers,

3. The chronology of the scandals fits remarkably well with the events portrayed in books like David Leigh, *The Wilson plot* (New York: Pantheon, 1988).

whose leader was himself convicted of similar charges within a few years.

The Swansea scandal was closely reflected by events in Port Talbot, where the key issue was a 16 million pound redevelopment scheme that affected some 350 acres of the town centre. Charges here were essentially the same: receiving money and favours in exchange for contracts or official assistance. This affair claimed two former mayors among others from the Labour elite. Also in these years, the anti-corruption purges claimed one of their most powerful victims in Ernest Westwood, a prominent member of the Glamorgan county council.

In May 1976, the corruption issue played an instrumental role in devastating Labour defeats in local council elections. The party lost control of eight centres, including Cardiff, Barry, Caerphilly, Merthyr Tydfil, Newport, Port Talbot and Wrexham. Corruption seemed pervasive – so much so that few were surprised when the Jeremy Thorpe scandal of 1976–9 allegedly involved criminal misdeeds by a number of west Glamorgan businessmen (all were in fact acquitted).

What caused the greatest public impact was not so much the specific charges, but the suggestion that they reflected the standard operating practice of the area, a view supported by *Rebecca*'s wide-ranging allegations between 1975 and 1982. Influence existed to be sold, and there was little concept of the public good. Furthermore, the scandals raised questions about the motives underlying the great rebuilding of the Welsh towns, and its devastating social impact. In Swansea, this was termed 'the second Blitz', recalling the disaster of 1941. Had it all been undertaken purely for private profit? The role of the miners' pension fund in financing such a development was still more controversial. The affairs were a particular condemnation of the Welsh media, which had for decades let such blatant criminality run riot without the slightest comment or investigation.

British historians have often tended to see official corruption as a regrettable digression from 'normal' political development, an issue better covered by the criminologist or the sensationalistic press. Before the work of scholars like Alan Doig and Geoffrey Searle, it was scarcely a reputable topic for research. But in Wales at this time, corruption played a role that is difficult to grasp from reading the press, all the more so given the extreme nervousness of British papers in face of the libel laws. The scandals themselves were critical to Labour decline in the 1970s. Local parties throughout Britain were riven after 1975 by challenges from left and right, from 'militants' and 'moderates': in Wales, morale was already near collapse even before these ideological debates reached their zenith. Corruption cases provided the essential background for the upsurge of Plaid Cymru support in industrial and urban Wales, and for the mass defection of Labour's youth membership. They would also contribute to the reluctance of much of Wales to accept devolution into the hands of the party machines of the south. Finally, scandals may well have contributed to the 1974 partition of Glamorgan into three units, thus fragmenting the patronage empire of the old county council.

In the long run, no one party reaped an electoral harvest from the failures of Labour. However, these events go far towards explaining the remarkable phenomenon of the Conservatives winning sweeping victories in Welsh elections since the 1970s, at a time of apparent mass discontent with the policies of a Conservative government. Was this a political shift parallel to the economic realignment? To put this in long-term context, the Liberals between 1906 and 1924 fell from 28 Welsh seats to 11. Over a similar period, between 1966 and 1983, Labour contracted from 32 seats to 20. The decline is not as steep, but we are justified in asking whether 'Labour Wales' has gone the way of its Liberal predecessor.

The Conservative tradition in Wales has long remained remarkably firm, with an appeal to the electorate that has often been underestimated. In the last half-century, the Conservative vote has run steadily between 25 and 32 per cent. There have also been a steadily growing number of dependable Conservative seats in Wales: in eastern Gwent and south Glamorgan; in Pembrokeshire; and along the northern coastal strip east of Bangor. From a low of three in 1966, the Tories have usually held at least eight seats through the last two decades; and that total grew to a remarkable 14 in 1983, the best Tory result since 1874. While the Labour vote declined, there was also an increase in the number of parties which would realistically be seen as plausible rivals to Labour, including Plaid Cymru and the Liberals (the 'Alliance'). Wales effectively has had a four-party system for the last 30 years. There were thus an increasing number of electoral contests where (say) a generally anti-Conservative vote was widely split, permitting the election of a Conservative member. In politics as in the economy, many traditional Welsh stereotypes perished in the Thatcher era.

Of the parties challenging Labour hegemony from the late 1960s, only the nationalists represented a wholly new parliamentary force. Even the 'national revival' of the 1890s occurred within the framework of the existing British party system, and did not result in the formation of an overt separatist movement. It is tempting to suggest that the apparent rise of political nationalism symbolised a new national consciousness, a new sense of identity emerging from the break-up of an older imperial Britain. As we will see, nationalism has indeed been influential in modern Wales, but a Welsh national entity appears as remote a prospect as ever.

CHAPTER NINETEEN
A Nation Once Again?

It is possible to be a strong advocate of Welsh culture and language without supporting national independence. In 1667, Charles Edwards published the influential *Hanes Y ffydd ddi-ffuant* (History of the genuine faith), which argued to the contrary that the loss of political independence had been the essential prerequisite to bringing the Welsh people the Gospel in their own language. Culture and religion both benefited from the Act of Union; and both were apparently flourishing three centuries after Henry VIII. In the 1890s, it was a vibrant and expansive Wales that rejected home rule as an irrelevant move which would usher in more problems than it could solve. More recently, concern about the precipitous decline of language and culture has led many to seek political nationhood as the only solution to what may be a terminal crisis.

The crisis has many dimensions, but linguistic decline is perhaps the most serious. In 1891, the first linguistic census suggested (on rather controversial evidence) that the number of Welsh speakers was about a million, or half the population. There were also some 16 per cent of Welsh people who were believed to be monoglot. By 1911, the figure for Welsh speakers was little changed, but explosive population growth had reduced the proportion to about 40 per cent. There were already worrying signs of vulnerability. Almost half the Welsh speakers lived in the industrial south-east, where they were exposed to turbulent social change, heavy English and Irish immigration, and the anglicising influences of mass culture. Depression and subsequent emigration caused a sharp deterioration, most dramatically in the industrial regions. The proportion of Glamorgan residents speaking Welsh fell from 44 per cent in 1901 to 32 per cent in 1921, and 17 per cent in 1961. The current figure is below ten per cent.

After 1945, each subsequent census showed the language to be on the decline at a national level, to perhaps 30 per cent in 1950, 25 per cent in 1970, barely 20 per cent in the 1980s. Even worse, the 1960s figures suggested that Welsh was increasingly the language of the over-40s. It is possible to question the basis of these figures, which derive from the self-assessment of those questioned, and some researchers have seen the census figures as unintentionally understating the true extent of Welsh. But the general picture was clearly one of decline. Where would it stop? By, say, 2050, would Welsh go the way of Cornish? Wales seemed destined to become a mere zone of western Britain, with traditional Welsh culture kept alive only to amuse tourists.

Of great symbolic importance here was the Sunday closing issue. For most of the twentieth century, Wales was strictly 'dry' on Sundays, in accordance with the moral imperatives of traditional nonconformity. As with any form of prohibition, there were enormous loopholes, and the restrictions seemed increasingly irrelevant in a more secular age. The 1961 Licensing Act permitted local referenda on a county or county borough basis to determine if Sundays should remain dry. The results showed in stark form the growing isolation of 'traditional' Liberal Wales with its temperance ideals. In 1961, 'wet' Wales included the whole of the industrial south-east, in addition to Flintshire, Breconshire and Pembrokeshire. Further referenda have been held at seven-year intervals since that point, and these have progressively reduced the dry areas to the Welsh-speaking core: most of Gwynedd, Cardiganshire and west Carmarthenshire. As in the nineteenth century, temperance is still the badge of Welsh and nonconformist Wales, but this is now a mere remnant of what it once was.

Associated with linguistic and religious decline was a perceived

Table: 19.1 The Administrative Regions of Wales

County	Population(thousands)	Administrative Centre
Gwynedd	225.1	Caernarvon
Dyfed	323.1	Carmarthen
Clwyd	376	Mold
Powys	101.5	Llandrindod Wells
Mid-Glamorgan	540.4	Cardiff
West Glamorgan	371.9	Swansea
South Glamorgan	389.2	Cardiff
Gwent	439.6	Cwmbran

crisis in rural Wales. From 1974, local government reorganisation had divided Wales into eight counties, and the three counties that now constituted north and west Wales were (by British standards) strikingly underpopulated.

Between them, Gwynedd, Powys and Dyfed had 71 per cent of the total land area of Wales, and 23 per cent of the population, with an average population density of 115 per square mile. Powys is far the most sparsely populated county to be found in England or Wales, although it contains no less than three of the old geographical shires. In the whole region of west and north-west Wales, there were only nine towns with more than 10,000 people; only one of these (Llanelli) had more than 20,000.[1] There were still thriving rural communities, but they were subject to many threats, above all, emigration and poverty.

Government played a rather sinister role. For a bureaucrat in London or Cardiff, these empty spaces seemed to represent an almost unpopulated hinterland, an appropriate home for reservoirs or for nuclear power stations like those built at Trawsfynydd and at Wylfa Head in Anglesey. Pacific Wales also acquired a distinctly belligerent landscape, with crucial US military facilities at Brawdy and Caerwent, RAF stations at Valley and St Athan, SAS training grounds in the Brecon Beacons, and German Panzers on the Castlemartin artillery range. The country was deemed suitable for overflights by hedge-hopping warplanes.

Overcrowded England found many possible uses in this 'wilderness'. The desolate landscape was ideal for recreation and tourism, for establishing national parks, and for purchasing holiday or retirement homes. All these developments accelerated the decline of the rural structures that were essential for the preservation of the language. And just as perceptions of crisis were becoming acute, the coming of television promoted the cultural homogeneity of the British Isles to an unprecedented degree. Technology threatened to achieve what the 'Welsh Not' could never have done.

Any attempt to resolve the cultural crisis by political action would need to confront the razor-sharp divisions between different regions or sections of Wales, the conflict on which Liberal home rule schemes had foundered in the 1890s. In the modern era, linguistic change has complicated the picture still further. One useful framework for understanding the contemporary situation is the

1. The largest towns in this category were Bangor, Conway, Llanelli Holyhead, Llandudno, Aberystwyth, Carmarthen, Milford, Pembroke. None was in Powys.

'three Wales model', that is based on surveys examining self-identification.[2] First, inhabitants of Wales are divided as to whether they see themselves as British or Welsh. These groups are further analysed according to knowledge of the Welsh language. Three regions then emerge. There is *Y Fro Cymraeg*, of Welsh-speaking Welsh people, six constituencies concentrated in the rural north and west. There is 'British Wales', overwhelmingly English-speaking, extending in a broad swathe along the English border, but including most of Pembrokeshire. This area of 17 constituencies also includes Cardiff, Newport and the coastal south-east. Finally there are the 15 seats of 'Welsh Wales', essentially the southern Red Belt; where people describe themselves as Welsh, though they often do not speak the language.

The implications for nationalism are serious. An independent Wales might well be viable, on the analogy of the many small nations to be found around the world, the little 'five foot five' countries like Norway, Denmark or Switzerland. But was any kind of separate political identity really possible for *y Fro* alone? Or if there was to be a united Wales, should the whole country be subjected to the values and interests of this area? Welsh nationalism was a risky weapon to be used in defending language and culture.

THE ORIGINS OF PLAID CYMRU

In 1936, a sensational incident drew attention to what would eventually become a powerful force in Welsh politics. As a protest against a proposed RAF bombing range at Pen y Berth, near Penrhos on the Llyn peninsula, a group of Plaid Cymru members launched an arson attack against the site. The three – Saunders Lewis, Lewis Valentine and D.J. Williams – promptly gave themselves up, and used the ensuing trials as a forum for their views on pacifism, Welsh nationalism, and the need for direct action when morally necessary. The action attracted considerable support; Lloyd George was one of many who criticised the government for moving the trial to the Old Bailey, far from what might well be a sympathetic Welsh jury.

Plaid Genedlaethol Cymru (National Party of Wales) had been formed in 1925, when a group of patriotic activists met in the

2. The model is used extensively in John Osmond ed., *The national question again* (Gomer Press 1985).

northern resort of Pwllheli during the national eisteddfod. There were several reasons for the new concern about Welsh identity. In the late nineteenth century, it had seemed likely that Irish home rule would be followed by similar if less far-reaching recognition for national aspirations in the other Celtic lands of the British isles. After the Irish settlement of 1922, it became apparent that this was not going to occur in Wales. A Speakers' conference had discussed devolution, but a resulting Bill had easily been talked out. The repeated failures of E.T. John to secure election on a Nationalist platform between 1922 and 1924 suggested public apathy towards the 'national question'.

Also, the rapid decline of the Liberal Party threatened a radical change in traditional alignments in Wales. By 1924, there were only 11 Welsh Liberal MPs, a total which fell to three by 1951. Liberal Wales was succeeded by Labour hegemony, a leftward shift that was troubling for the largely conservative nationalists of Plaid. At the same time, concern for cultural integrity was manifested in societies intended to promote the Welsh language. The *Urdd Gobaith Cymru* (League of Welsh Youth: 1922) was one of the more enduring, and this had 50,000 members by 1934.

The precursor to Plaid was the *Mudiad Cymreig*, (Welsh Movement), founded in 1924 by a clique that included Saunders Lewis, Ambrose Bebb and G.J. Williams. Heavily influenced by the model of De Valera's Sinn Fein, and perhaps by Mussolini, the group was to act as a clandestine society observing strict rules of secrecy. Lewis himself planned to establish secret training camps, and goals included the 'extermination' of the English language in Wales. The following year, the leaders of this bizarre sect annexed some other patriotic groups, and Plaid was born. (It thus predated the Scots National League of 1927, and the modern SNP which emerged in 1928.)

Plaid was deeply divided on the questions of its aims, a conflict that can be summarised in terms of rival cultural and constitutional goals. In its early years, the organisation emphasised the defence of the Welsh language and the culture which sustained it. These were the particular emphases of the founder, H.R. Jones, and of Saunders Lewis, his successor as leader from 1926 to 1939. For Lewis (1893–1985) in particular, constitutional or political questions came a poor second to ensuring that the Welsh language survived in what he perceived as a humane society. It was only after his time in office, about 1945, that Plaid was transformed from a pressure group to a modern party.

Saunders Lewis's social views were diametrically opposed to those

of the industrial radicals of the day. They recognised the vital
significance of industry as a new force in human affairs, and sought
to control this power in the name of the working class. By contrast,
Lewis followed English writers like Hilaire Belloc in total opposition
to industrialism, 'factoryism', socialism, capitalism, mass society and
the profit motive. He sought to cure the ills of the south by
deindustrialisation, finding his model in an idealised and decentralised neo-medieval world of small property holders. To quote a 1934
manifesto, 'Agriculture should be the chief industry of Wales and the
basis of its civilisation'. The crash was final proof of the ruin of the
specious ideals of the Enlightenment and the rational nineteenth
century:

> In the beginning, it wasn't like this we saw things;
> We thought that it was only the redeeming ebb and flow, the
>   thrifty dislocation
> That our masters blessed as part of economic law,
> The new scientific order that had cast out natural law. . . .
> Then, on Olympus, Nineteen twenty nine,
> At their infinitely scientific task of guiding the profits of fate,
> The gods decreed, with their feet in the Aubusson carpets,
> And their Hebrew snouts in the quarter's statistics,
> That the day had come to restrict credit in the universe of
>   gold.
> Earth's latest gods did not know
> That they had breached the last floodgates of the world. . . .
>
>   From Saunders Lewis, 'The Deluge 1939'
>   translated by Gwyn Thomas.

The party was following a Rightist nationalist tradition that had
been developing in Wales since the 1880s. Under the nonconformist
assault, Anglican writers had become increasingly influenced by
European (especially French) views which saw Liberalism as a
cynical bourgeois ploy to stir up the poor against the natural elites in
society and the Church. Welsh Liberal calls for non-denominational
education were seen as part of a covert attack on all religion. The
new Right developed a systematic critique of most aspects of the
modern world: mass society, majoritarianism and democracy,
industry and urbanisation. Against this, they extolled the traditional
organic community of the countryside, a theme that fitted remarkably well with Welsh radicalism; and the Welsh Right was strongly
nationalistic in affairs of Church and state. From the 1880s to the
First World War, we frequently find such views expressed in Church
journals such as *Yr haul* or *Y cyfaill eglwysig*.

In the 1920s, this Rightist tradition was a strong influence on nationalists like Saunders Lewis and Ambrose Bebb. Lewis converted to Catholicism in 1932, and Bebb was an advocate for Mussolini and Franco. Plaid was denounced as a near-fascist sect by a number of patriotic writers like Thomas Jones and W.J. Gruffydd, while the party was challenged from the Left by the rival nationalist group, *Gwerin*, (the People), based at University College, Bangor. Nationalistic and pacifist considerations both contributed to Plaid's opposition to World War II, a policy that was easily misinterpreted as opposition to the Allied war effort. In 1941, Lewis' pamphlet *Byd a Betws* denounced the war.

Undoubtedly, some of the nationalists were motivated by strongly anti-English sentiment. In the 1940s, the Germans hoped to exploit these, and believed that Welsh nationalists would provide fervent fifth columnists. They were disappointed, but there were individuals whose nationalist opinions drove them close to treason. It still remains unclear how far agents like Arthur Owens and his circle were the Abwehr spies and saboteurs they appeared to be, or if they were in fact double-agents in the employ of the British Security Service.[3]

Saunders Lewis' social thought was utterly and unashamedly irrelevant, if not hostile, to the interests of the bulk of the Welsh people, including many Welsh speakers, the majority of whom still lived in the advanced areas of the south-east. He opposed carrying out propaganda in the English-speaking areas. Was Welsh nationalism only intended for the seven or so constituencies where rural Welsh speakers formed a substantial part of the population? If so, the movement was assuredly doomed to form a tiny minority, even within Wales. By contrast, Lewis' colleague D.J. Davies wished to convert the anglicised parts of Wales in order to create a true national movement.

As so often before and since, the definition of Welshness thus posed questions that the nationalist groups have never fully resolved. It was also in just these years that the southern 'outsiders' evolved a culture of great power in the poetry of Vernon Watkins, Dylan Thomas, David Jones, Idris Davies, Alun Lewis and many others, the prose of Jack Jones and Lewis Jones. They would appear to most to be Welsh writers of the highest quality, but are depicted slightingly as 'Anglo-Welsh', apparently an inferior category.

3. For different views on this question, compare Nigel West, *MI5* (New York: Stein and Day, 1982); and Lauran Payne, *German military intelligence in World War II: the Abwehr* (New York: Military Heritage Press, 1984), 78–92.

Emphasis on the language and rural values made nationalism irrelevant to the thriving culture of urban and industrial Wales.

Equally divisive was the question of socialism. Lewis and his successors all tended to be 'radical', in the sense of being populists, pacifists and internationalists. An excellent example was Gwynfor Evans (Plaid party leader 1945–1981). However, Evans and his like often espoused views that were anathema to the proletarian radicals of a town like Aberdare or Llanelli, with Plaid's 'Liberal' (or even worse, petty-bourgeois) hostility to proletarianisation and the overpowerful state. In 1927, a Plaid pamphlet stated that 'Class warfare is a popular idea in Wales today simply because the nation, the proper object of group loyalty, has been suppressed'. Once again, it was D.J. Davies who offered a more realistic vision of an independent Wales, which took some account of economic realities. In the 1930s, it was Davies who addressed the charge that the economically ruined Wales of the time could ever stand on its own. Quite the contrary,

> Wales is poor because under an alien imperialist government, seeking alien interests, her resources have been unused, disused and misused.[4]

The solution was to find and exploit new sources of wealth, under new social and economic arrangements. Already in the 1930s, the question of socialist policies thus divided Plaid in a way that has become painfully familiar to the modern movement.

LABOUR AND THE 'NATIONAL QUESTION'

From 1929, Plaid began contesting constituencies, perhaps one or two in each election, and never scoring more than a thousand votes or so. The party's internal debates were strictly marginal to Welsh politics before the 1960s, but 'the national question' was a more central matter. From the 1920s to the 1970s, the true national party of Wales was Labour, and issues of cultural identity would be long debated. In the early decades of this hegemony, the Party was too concerned with economic and international questions to focus on what appeared the peripheral question of Welsh nationalism. In 1945, the Labour triumph provided the opportunity of significantly

---

4. Quoted in Charlotte Aull Davies, *Welsh nationalism in the twentieth century* (New York: Praeger 1989), 68.

restructuring every aspect of British life; and there was some pressure for changing the status of Wales.

The 1945 manifesto had offered several proposals, including the establishment of a Secretary of State for Wales; while the construction of a north-south trunk road would promote development, and provide greater unity within the country. But the following years were disappointing. Not until 1964 was a Secretary of State appointed, though this was scarcely a major advance towards autonomy. Also, the new nationalised enterprises seemed to be deliberately constructed to avoid recognition of a Welsh identity. North Wales electricity supply, for example, was the province of MANWEB, the 'Manchester and North Wales Electricity Board'. Even the south Wales coalfields were part of a region in 'south-western' Britain.

Welsh MPs were divided on 'national' issues, and some of the most influential, like Aneurin Bevan and Ness Edwards, were strong 'jacobin' centralists who saw nationalism as a diversionary issue. Others had both idealistic and practical concerns. They recognised that Wales might have distinct interests; but more seriously, they wished to avoid a challenge from political nationalism. Economic hardships were serious, and protesters against Labour were unlikely to turn to the Conservative Party. However, the Liberal heritage might reassert itself if given a new nationalist platform. Troubling here was the example of Scotland, and the immensely popular 'Covenant' movement of 1949 and 1950.

In response to nationalist pressure, tiny as it was, some rudimentary 'national' institutions emerged; though most smacked strongly of what a later generation would name 'tokenism'. In 1942, the use of Welsh was permitted in the courts, and from 1944, there was a 'Welsh Day' in the House of Commons. More significant were the moves that came from the Labour Party itself. In 1948, there was a Welsh Council for Labour. In 1949, an advisory Council for Wales was formed under the chairmanship of trade unionist Huw T. Edwards, and this body attracted considerable attention as the potential nucleus for later growth.

In 1951, Wales showed itself once again to be firmly non-Conservative, electing only six Tories out of 36 MPs; yet of course, the new Westminster government continued to rule without recognising any separate identity for the country. This divorce between central authority and local sentiment increasingly raised questions about the Welsh role within a larger Britain. Fringe publications like the *Welsh Republican* began to obtain a wider hearing, and the Labour Party in particular debated issues of devolution, though well short of outright independence. From 1950, there was a 'Parliament for Wales Campaign' chaired by Megan Lloyd George, but drawing support from elements of all parties. In 1955 the controversial MP for Merthyr, S.O. Davies, introduced a far-reaching home rule bill. The following year, a petition for a parliament attracted a quarter of a million signatures: the movement was also supported by five Welsh Labour MPs. The Conservatives offered conciliation, but little substance. Cardiff was declared the capital of Wales, and in 1951, there was a minister for Wales; though the office was always held jointly with another 'real' Cabinet position. In 1957, the office was awarded on a full time basis to Vivian Lewis, a figure of little substance in Welsh affairs.

The 'parliament' proposals were divisive for the Welsh parties: for the Liberals, but most pointedly for Labour. Debate was intensified in 1959 by the angry resignation of Huw T. Edwards from the Council of Wales. This helped push the Labour Party towards acceptance of an increased national dimension. With the support of the Welsh Council of Labour, the Party came out in favour of a Secretary of State for Wales and a Welsh Office.

From 1963, Labour was discussing Welsh strategies considerably more adventurous than the unquestioning unionism of recent years, with a Secretary of State and an elected Welsh council. There were influential supporters of some degree of devolution, like Emrys D. Jones, Secretary of the Party in Wales, or Jim Griffiths, first Secretary of State for Wales in the 1964 Wilson government. Another was Gwilym Prys Davies, who wished to fuse the radical traditions of urban and rural Wales into a powerful new coalition. In 1964, therefore, Labour was approaching the zenith of its power in Wales with a considerable willingness to explore new solutions to Welsh problems. The new Secretary of State would ultimately be responsible for some important functions, including health, education, transportation and some aspects of economic planning. From 1971, the Welsh Office was located in Cardiff; by the late 1980s, the department had a budget in excess of three billion pounds, and a staff of 2300. In 1966, Labour supported the creation of an Assembly for Wales, and a Welsh TUC emerged in 1973.

THE RISE OF NATIONALISM

It was precisely at the height of Labour's electoral power in Wales that the nationalist challenge appeared to threaten a complete overthrow of its position. The suddenness of this change was quite as dramatic as the earlier ascent of radical Liberalism in 1868, or of socialism after 1910. In the mid-1960s, Plaid Cymru was widely regarded as a joke in much of Wales, a quixotic movement that had little to do with real politics. Surely it could never rival the awesome strength of Labour?

In 1959, Plaid contested 20 seats, and won 77,000 votes: not disgraceful, but scarcely enough to pose a challenge in any constituency. Between 1966 and 1968, however, the party achieved a series of startling by-election successes; and the movement's defeats were if anything more surprising than its victories. It was just possible that a resolutely Welsh constituency like Carmarthenshire might be sufficiently eccentric to return a candidate with the immense personal appeal of Gwynfor Evans, as occurred in July 1966. Gwynfor (as he was universally known) was after all following Megan Lloyd George, and succeeded in attracting much traditional Liberal support. But the Labour enemy he defeated was no alien carpetbagger: it was Gwilym Prys Davies, who had worked hard to promote Welsh interests over the years.

Still more remarkable were the contests in industrial Glamorgan in the following two years, when Plaid secured swings in excess of 25 per cent, though without winning further seats. Plaid received 40 per cent of the votes in Rhondda West (1967) and Caerphilly (1968). This achievement raised speculation that virtually any of Wales' 36 seats might fall, to the particular chagrin of the Labour Party. In 1972, a by-election in Merthyr Tydfil gave Plaid second position with 37 per cent of the vote. In the 1970s, the party also won stunning victories in local and council elections across the towns of 'Welsh Wales', and it took control of the borough council in Merthyr.

Even for those in Wales who were not enamoured of Plaid as a party, their achievement was still exciting. The 1966 Carmarthen election caused a thrill comparable to that of major sports triumphs. The British media began treating Wales as an area of serious political interest, as opposed to an inevitable Labour fortress, and the phenomenon of nationalism was the subject of much journalistic investigation. More important, there were many towns and cities where it finally became apparent that the Labour machine could be challenged and defeated, after decades of virtual one-party rule. This revolution could be accomplished not by a step as drastic and unthinkable as voting Conservative, but in turning to one of Plaid's many articulate and attractive local candidates.

Almost certainly, the Plaid successes were largely misread, particularly in the south, where the central issue had not been nationalism. In the 1960s, people voted against Labour (rather than *for* Plaid) as a protest against economic policies. There was also increasing outrage at the successive local government scandals associated with Labour, though the media underplayed this element. Newspapers and television thus reinforced the picture of an upsurge in national consciousness, with Plaid as its vehicle, and the bombers as a genuinely dangerous fringe. This nationalist movement appealed to younger voters, and it attracted many of the energies that elsewhere went into radical movements like ecology and feminism. Plaid was an early practitioner of the community politics that would so often be advocated in the 1980s.

Plaid Cymru never fulfilled its early promise, but its achievements were striking. The party's support in general elections fell gradually, from a peak of 175,000 votes in 1970 to a mere 124,000 in 1987: 11.5 per cent of the Welsh vote compared to 7.3 per cent; but this was sufficient to establish them as a parliamentary presence. Since 1974, they have always held either two or three Welsh constituencies. Carmarthen fell to Gwynfor Evans once more in 1974, though it returned to Labour in later years. Much more reliable was the nationalist fortress in the north-west. Since 1974, the party has always held Caernarfon and Merionethshire (Meirionydd Nant Conwy), respectively the seats of Dafydd Wigley and Dafydd Elis Thomas. The taking of Anglesey (Ynys Môn) in 1987 essentially gave Plaid the whole of traditional Gwynedd, with the exception of the east Caernarvonshire strip that makes up the Conwy constituency. The achievement owed much to the vagaries of the British electoral system, which favours a party with a strong local base over one that has more widely disseminated support. In both 1983 and 1987, the Liberal/SDP Alliance won about a fifth of the Welsh vote in each election, and gained respectively two and three seats: the same as Plaid, which received under eight per cent.

The rise of Plaid raises important questions about the potential of Welsh nationalism, but also about its limitations. The party attracts a protest vote in addition to its nationalist core, but the 'disaffected' are not likely to provide a firm base. When Liberal (Alliance/Democrat) support crumbled in the late 1980s, defectors transferred their loyalty not to Plaid, but to the ecological Green Party, which suddenly emerged in the 1989 European elections with almost as many Welsh votes as Plaid. In fact, the upstart Greens outpolled Plaid in three of the four Welsh Euro-constituencies, with only North Wales preventing total humiliation.

Tracing Plaid support over the years tells us much about the nature of regionalism within Wales. Plaid is now as firmly embedded in *Y Fro Cymraeg* as is Labour in the Red Belt; but it seems equally unlikely that either party will advance far beyond their respective bastions to win support throughout Wales. (On the other hand, it is likely that Plaid will win southern victories in protest against a future Labour government.) In 1987, Plaid earned 15 per cent or more of the vote in five constituencies, which provided 56 per cent of the total Plaid support. These five seats – the three they held, plus Carmarthen and Ceredigion – neatly delineate the *Bro*, where temperance ideals remain strong. By contrast, this 'Welsh National' party could earn only three per cent or less of votes in 20 of the 38 constituencies. Even among Welsh speakers, Plaid in 1987 attracted less support than did any of the three 'unionist' parties, including the Conservatives.

Every election in the 1980s (national, local, European) seemed to show the existence of a loyal Plaid core, of between 120,000 and 150,000 voters, heavily concentrated in the north and west. Nationalist sentiment thus appears to be passionately held in a few limited areas, while it is seen as irrelevant or worse to a sizeable majority of the population. This was resoundingly demonstrated by the attempts of Westminster governments in the 1970s to meet what appeared to be the aspirations of the Welsh people, by granting a measure of devolution.

DEVOLUTION AND THE REFERENDUM

The Labour Party in the late 1960s found itself in disarray in the face of the Plaid menace, and the fervent unionism associated with leaders like George Thomas was easily portrayed as servility or worse by the nationalist press. On the other hand, flexibility was vital in confronting the most significant Welsh upsurge since Edwardian days. Welsh events were also affected by the success of Scottish nationalism, which appeared to be on the verge of sweeping a sizeable majority of that country's parliamentary seats. In 1968, the

Labour government established the Kilbrandon Commission to examine possible constitutional changes in Scotland and Wales. When this reported in 1973, it recommended elected assemblies for both countries: at best a limited autonomy well short of the independence claimed by Plaid (or the SNP).

Between 1974 and 1976, the Kilbrandon proposals drew nearer to implementation with White Papers, and a Scotland and Wales Bill followed in 1976. The proposed Scottish assembly would have wide-ranging powers, and early schemes suggested that no less could in fairness be given to the Welsh authority. Devolution for Wales would be based on an elected assembly of 80 members, with control over the areas currently in the charge of the Welsh Office: education below university level, health and social services, development and industry, and local government. The Westminster parliament would retain a right of veto, and the assembly would have no new fund-raising power.

The 1976 Bill soon ran into serious difficulties, and the legislative effort ground to a halt in 1977. Opposition to devolution was fierce. Unionists included not only Conservatives, but also Labour politicians like Neil Kinnock and Leo Abse. Unionist opponents made free use of the stereotypes so common in both industrial and rural Wales. Southerners dreaded rule by rural nonconformist fanatics, who were likely to penalise non-Welsh speakers in the allocation of jobs, no less than in the amenities of everyday life. These Celtic purists had already succeeded in a wholesale trans-formation of place-names and road-signs, substituting 'authentic' Welsh forms for local (and comprehensible) usage: it was a portent of cultural aggression. In north and west Wales, there was fear of tyranny by the overwhelming numbers to be found in the south, the land of corrupt machines and ultra-leftist agitators. Nationalists, moreover, complained that the measure went nowhere near far enough for the crisis facing the culture.

The parliamentary opponents waged a lengthy guerrilla war against Welsh devolution, a campaign made possible by the minority status of the Labour government of the time. The Act eventually became law in 1978, but it still faced obstacles: above all, the requirement of a referendum before devolution could be imple-mented. Still more controversial, passage of the Bill could only be achieved if 40 per cent of the registered electorate voted in the affirmative. In fact, this was an unnecessary obstacle. The referen-dum was held on March 1, 1979, and it resulted in an overwhelming defeat for devolution. From a 59 per cent turnout, only a fifth of voters (some 240,000 in all) supported the measure. Support for devolution was strongest in Dyfed and Gwynedd; but even here, the Nos triumphed by majorities of (respectively) 72 per cent and 66 per cent. Nationalist political demands were removed from the political agenda as suddenly as they had appeared in 1966. The 'National Question' appeared to have found an answer: Wales was part of the United Kingdom.

DIRECT ACTION

The political and constitutional debates of the 1950s and early 1960s often demonstrated a resentment at official neglect of Welsh identity or interests, but it was inconceivable that nationalistic passions might be excited over issues like the appointment of a Secretary of State for Wales. These were matters relevant only to the corridors of Westminster, or to the equally closed (and perhaps irrelevant) circles of the Labour Party bureaucracy in Wales. By contrast, there were other issues at this time which did stir visceral reactions, which brought the question of national identity to the forefront of political life; and which brought violence into that conflict. And these were emphatically not ended by the 1979 defeat.

In terms of the earlier debates within the nationalist movement, these were cultural rather than constitutional issues, though the two would always be difficult to separate. Water was one such emotive issue. As early as 1952, a small leftist group blew up a pipeline linking the Claerwen dam in mid-Wales with the city of Birmingham. The act seemed incomprehensible to the British public, if only because they viewed water as self-evidently a limitless natural resource beyond the realm of political conflict. Reservoirs were indisputably needed, and where better to put them than in the open spaces of the Welsh hills?

In Wales, however, there was a different perception of the Claerwen dam and its counterparts: that the water needs of Birmingham had caused the destruction of yet another irreplaceable part of the Welsh heartland. The land of Wales was not the wilderness portrayed by the statistical tables; it was the proper home of the traditional rural community, that was also the immemorial mainstay of the Welsh language and its associated culture. In the 1950s, issues of water supply and reservoirs provided a focus for nationalist agitation. The Tryweryn affair involved Liverpool corporation's purchase of a Merionethshire valley for redevelopment, a process that would involve the destruction of the village of Capel Celyn. Through the mid-1950s, the effort to save Tryweryn created a rare unanimity in Welsh politics. It also made a celebrity of Gwynfor Evans, who led the opposition. Nevertheless, the valley was flooded and the dam built.

THE LANGUAGE MOVEMENT

1962 marked a turning point. In a moving radio lecture, *Tynged yr iaith* (the fate of the language), Saunders Lewis drew attention to the state of the Welsh language, and called for the energies of the nationalist movement to be concentrated entirely on rescuing a culture in crisis. Given this urgent perception of decline, there were several possible courses of action, and all seemed to involve direct action, even if not initially as forceful as that undertaken by Lewis and his colleagues back in 1936. Within months of the radio address, *Cymdeithas yr iaith Gymraeg* (the Welsh Language Society) began a new campaign to promote bilingualism throughout Wales; most visibly by demanding the use of Welsh on official forms and road-signs. When authorities were slow to yield over these issues, activists began a campaign to paint over English names on signs (usually in patriotic green).

Cymdeithas yr iaith used illegal activities to promote its cause, but never as a movement resorted to terrorism. The road-sign campaigners were in theory directed not to obliterate instructions in such a way that accidents could result. Other groups felt that both *Cymdeithas yr iaith* and Plaid were too moderate for the current situation, which required desperate action. By the 1970s, this extreme wing included a movement like *Adfer*, from the Welsh word 'to restore'. This group wished to save at all costs the Welshness of the heartland areas. 'British Wales' was in effect dismissed as already lost – and so was 'Welsh Wales', a more controversial sacrifice. The *Bro*, the Welsh areas of north and west, would be a monolingual Welsh state, and all measures would be taken to prevent land passing to outsiders or 'invaders'. For a group like this, bilingualism was a grossly inadequate compromise.

Other groups openly advocated violence and armed struggle. In 1963, protests against the Tryweryn dam resulted in the formation of a 'Movement for the Defence of Wales', *Mudiad Amddiffyn Cymru*, or

MAC. They attacked dam and power installations, but were rapidly apprehended. However, the example of militant action was powerful. Graffiti throughout Wales began to boast of an organisation called the Free Wales Army, together with its badge of the 'White Eagle of Snowdon'. It may have begun as a joke, but from 1965, there were uniformed groups who claimed indeed to be the FWA of legend. FWA leaders like Julian Cayo Evans became well-known media figures, and some engaged in at least the planning of direct attacks against water supplies and public buildings. Whatever the substance of this specific movement, the FWA set a perilous example. Avowedly militant and separatist organisations mushroomed, under a bewildering range of initials, and the vogue for uniformed demonstrations posed a direct challenge to the state by flouting the public order legislation of the 1930s. To put this in contemporary context, it must be recalled that this Welsh movement was at its height before the rise of the far more deadly conflict in Ulster. It was widely accepted that for Britain at least, serious political violence was a matter of the distant past. Even in contemporary Europe, the Welsh events found parallels only in the south Tyrol.

Open terrorism was at its height between 1966 and 1969, when there were dozens of bomb and arson attacks throughout Wales. Popular targets were water pipelines and dams (notably in 1966, at the new Clywedog dam), but there were raids on military facilities like Pembrey air force base, and administrative offices in Cardiff. The pace and seriousness of the violence increased from late 1967, with the decision of John Jenkins to reform MAC, and to begin a more professional bombing campaign, far removed from the publicity stunts of the FWA. The sense of crisis reached a height in 1969, as the investiture of the Prince of Wales at Caernarvon drew near. Intensive police activity resulted in the arrest or close surveillance of all known militants; and the leaders of both MAC and FWA were all in custody by the end of the year.

Terrorism in Wales faded in the 1970s, though this cannot be wholly attributed to the effectiveness of the police response. More significant was the apparent success of Plaid Cymru in seeking national autonomy through constitutional means. And as devolution reached its apparently inevitable triumph, so there was a linguistic revival of sorts among younger middle class Welsh people, the upwardly mobile who can form so central a part of any political movement. Children were likely to bear Welsh Christian names; Welsh bookshops and publishing enterprises flourished, as did folk music; and there was an enormous vogue for Welsh-language schools. This was all encouraging; though cynics suggested that the last phenomenon was not entirely a demonstration of patriotism. It was simply the best way of preserving an elitist middle-class environment for children who would otherwise have to be sent to a comprehensive school.

But optimism ended in 1979. It now appeared obvious that constitutional movements were not going to win even the rather pallid devolution promised by the Callaghan government, to say nothing of full-fledged independence. Two decades of Plaid Cymru moderation had collapsed. Also, the vote seemed to confirm extremist claims that the real and pure Wales of the *Bro* could only save itself by drastic measures: had not the rest of Wales voted away its national identity? In the words of one of the more extreme militants,

> (There is a) Christian proposition that life is sacred. No individual or nation has the right to commit suicide. In the face of a declared intention to destroy the life of a nation, a minority has not only the right but a Christian obligation to seize control to prevent that life being snuffed out. . . . .A nation, the individual and unique creation of God himself, has twice within the decade (the Common Market and the Devolution referendum) demonstrated its determination to destroy itself.[5]

NATIONALISM RECONSTITUTED 1979–

The defeat of devolution also ushered in the new Conservative government, which undertook economic policies that at least in the short term seemed disastrous for Wales. Closures and cuts resulted in an upsurge of political radicalism in many parts of Britain, but in Wales the economic crisis also aggravated the national question. The economic damage appeared to result directly from government policies, and from decisions in which overwhelmingly non-Tory Wales had no say.

The defeat of the referendum changed Welsh affairs, but assuredly did not end nationalist or pro-language politics. Two issues in particular caused controversy in Wales in the years immediately following the referendum, though both were the culmination of

5. Derrick Hearne, *The ABC of the Welsh revolution* (Talybont, Dyfed: Y Lolfa, 1982), 28.

grievances dating back for decades. One was the purchase of houses in Welsh villages by outsiders (usually English), who would then renovate them and use them as holiday homes. There were said to be 20,000 such homes by the late 1970s. This was a grievance because such an incursion appeared to dilute still further the linguistic purity of those *Bro* communities that were the strongholds of the language. Also, the purchase of second homes was said to push up prices, increasing homelessness and emigration among local residents. Protests against such sales had been organised by *Cymdeithas yr iaith* as early as 1972, but the struggle now became more violent. In December 1979, one such second home fell victim to an arson attack, and this marked the beginning of an intense campaign. By 1988, there had been 130 of these acts throughout north and west Wales. Occupations and other protests were often directed at the estate agents who undertook the business. 'Wales is not for sale' joined the repertoire of popular graffiti.

Another conflict with the state loomed over the issue of a separate Welsh television channel. When a fourth channel was planned, it was proposed that this would for Wales be a Welsh-language service. In 1979, minister William Whitelaw announced that this would not in fact be granted; and enormous protests followed over the next two years. At the height of the protests, in the autumn of 1980, thousands were declaring their willingness to go to prison rather than pay television licences. Gwynfor Evans even adopted the Irish republican tactic of threatening a fast until death if the demands were not granted. The government succumbed, and the new channel opened in 1982 as S4C, *Sianel 4 Cymru*.

These were also the years in which Welsh radicals began to explore once more the implications of a nationalism based on revolutionary and socialist traditions, a topic always close to the heart of John Jenkins. In 1974, for example, he had agreed with *Adfer* that 'there *must* be a heartland, a power base for the culture'; but at the same time,

> *Cymraeg* (Welsh) must be seen to be the language of the social revolution, not the discourse of a folk museum. The workers of the conurbations must be educated to equate nationalism with socialism, and the Welsh language as the avant-garde of that movement.[6]

In 1979, there had been an influential socialist manifesto, *Sosialaeth i'r Cymry* (Socialism for the Welsh People), which asked of Plaid,

6. John Jenkins, *Prison letters* (Y Lolfa 1981), 100.

What characteristics other than compromise, cowardice, vacillation, gradualism and opportunism could we expect from a party whose leadership and many of its most influential members are petty bourgeois, nonconformist and pacifistic?

The old leaders were simply 'The Rural Right'. Out of this debate came in 1980 the Welsh Socialist Republican Movement, with some 300 members; its newspaper was *Y faner goch*, the Red Flag. In 1981 and 1982, events both in Wales and in Britain at large encouraged the growth of new nationalist militant movements. There was also a revival of terrorism: 13 bomb and arson attacks were recorded between 1980 and 1982 in all parts of Wales, to say nothing of the ongoing holiday home campaign. Targets included offices associated with the Conservative Party, as well as army recruiting offices and economic centres.

Responsibility for some attacks was claimed by WAWR – 'Dawn' in Welsh, from an acronym for the 'Workers Army of the Welsh Republic'. Others boasted that MAC had revived, or that the campaign was the work of the 'Sons of Glyndwr'. Even John Jenkins was in the news again. Released from prison in 1976, he was much quoted as a spokesman for the cause of militancy. In 1981, a paramilitary march on 1960s lines commemorated the 'martyrs' of Abergele, two MAC activists killed by the premature explosion of a bomb they were in the process of planting on the eve of the 1969 investiture. Taken together, the Irish parallels were becoming unnerving.

The official response was draconian, and abuses of police powers were now added to the lengthy list of nationalist grievances. In 1978, an unhappy precedent had been set in Carmarthen when a trial of *Cymdeithas yr iaith* supporters had involved the vetting of a jury on political grounds: members had been selected on the strength of their English names and origins. Special Branch surveillance and sabotage was commonly encountered by WSRM. In the crisis of 1980–1982, there was a series of mass round-ups of suspects, often with minimal regard for even the limited legal rights permitted by British courts. One such purge involved the arrest of some 50 nationalists and leftists in the 'Operation Fire' investigation of 1980. In 1983, charges against WSRM activists led to the controversial 'Cardiff Explosives Trial'. This lengthy political case resulted in the acquittal of several of the defendants in circumstances that suggested serious qualms about police behaviour and evidence.

Plaid Cymru, a parliamentary party with a sizeable following, found itself divided by the ferment of ideas and debates that characterised these years. As with the Liberals of Tom Ellis' day, sympathy for protesters had to be tempered by political and legal considerations. Also reminiscent of the Liberal Party of days gone by was the schism over socialism, the old conflict between the Red Dragon and the Red Flag. This was inevitable if Plaid was not to be forever confined to the *Bro*, a region of a region, as feared by Plaid leaders like Phil Williams. In the 1980s, large sections of Plaid accepted socialist solutions, often accompanied by theories of decentralisation and community control. In contrast, a more traditional 'cultural' and anti-socialist wing of the movement seceded as 'the Covenant Society of the Free Welsh'.

The apparent vigour of Welsh nationalist politics masks insuperable divisions. In the aftermath of 1979, it seems unthinkable that the whole of Wales will ever gain even quasi-autonomy. Wales must be seen in a British context, and we have to ask whether militant separatism or language activism can ever have more than a peripheral nuisance value. This is ironic, in that no recent evidence contradicts the radicals in their basic belief that Welsh language and culture are in serious peril, and the country may in another century find itself *Di-Gymraeg*, 'Welshless'. This must raise questions about the whole direction of modern Welsh history.

Nobody in recent years has seriously advocated the extirpation of the Welsh language, and contemporary European ideals favour the cultivation of linguistic diversity in a free marketplace of tongues.[7] But there are special issues when dealing with languages that cannot survive in that marketplace; and defending the Welsh language means confronting troubling political and philosophical questions. Can any policies or actions save the culture? Languages can be brought back from the edge of extinction, as demonstrated by the staggering success of the Hebrew revival in the present century; but this occurred in what must surely be regarded as the unique circumstances of the state of Israel.

By contrast, the Welsh have a long and proud tradition of defeating a wide variety of linguistic solutions imposed for their alleged future benefit. Even if such actions were possible at this relatively late stage, would any society be justified in implementing them against the wishes and interests of an overwhelming majority of the Welsh people. What is the value of a culture? How does that

7. European parallels to the Welsh problem are many. From a large literature, see for example the summary of the Breton situation presented in Theodore Zeldin, *France 1848–1945: intellect and pride* (Oxford 1980), 54–67; or in John Ardagh, *France in the 1980s* (London: Penguin 1982).

compare with the price of democratic freedoms and majority rule? Is a language worth preserving in the museum environment of a *Gaeltacht*? Is there not a stage at which attempts at artificial resuscitation should be abandoned? And perhaps most troubling of all: are Welsh people to be accorded different social worth according to their linguistic background?

CHAPTER TWENTY
Historical Writing in Wales

THE TRADITION

In 1709, an Anglican cleric named Francis Davies was undertaking some research on the treatment of dispossessed clergymen in Glamorgan during the interregnum. Much of his work involved what we would today call oral history, but he also sought out what documents he could to confirm the picture he formed. While visiting the widow of one of the Puritan sequestrators, he found records which, he believed, gave a peculiarly damning picture of the financial maltreatment which the Anglicans had received. On a second visit, however, the woman 'obstinately refused' any further chance to consult these papers. Davies and his friends immediately assumed that she had been silenced by nonconformists, who were supporters of the dissenting martyrologist, Edmund Calamy.

Throughout Welsh history, contemporary politics have often been shaped by partisan interpretations of past events. The druids, the Celtic church, the Edwardian conquest, recusants and Jacobites, all have had their uses for different groups at various times, often in bizarre contexts. The consequences of such politicised history have rarely been as lethal as in Ireland, but certain themes recur in both countries: both commemorate their martyrs, and deplore their alleged traitors. In the religious realm, studying the eras of persecution and martyrdom was an important element of Welsh historiography into the present century.

The 'Calamy faction' denounced in the 1709 story would carry a great deal of weight in later historiography. It was Henry Richard who said that 'the nonconformists of Wales are the people of Wales', in a phrase quoted approvingly by Gladstone; and issues of religious origin have naturally done much to shape Welsh historical study. For much of the last century, by far the greatest part of historical research undertaken in Wales was directed towards aspects of religious development, especially in the area of Dissent.

Such an interest had an importance far beyond the academic realm, as religious history acquired great significance for practical politics. In the eighteenth and nineteenth centuries, the nonconformists had made much of their martyrs, the ejected clergy of 1662 and the other victims of the post-Restoration purges; to say nothing of earlier heroes like John Penry. The ejected clergy were extravagantly commemorated in gatherings in 1862, an event which helped the mobilisation of contemporary nonconformist radicalism through the Liberation Society. And in 1912, further assemblies and demonstrations recalled the events both of 1662 *and* 1862, in an attempt to maintain the parliamentary momentum towards the disestablishment of the Welsh Church. Anti-Popery activists, meanwhile, made frequent reference to martyrs like Bishop Ferrar.

In secular politics too, martyrology had its impact. In the nineteenth century, it was a common electoral theme that some Tory candidate was descended from the persecutors of the 1660s, and would be equally cool towards the rights of modern dissenters. The memory and mythology of persecution may have done much to shape the traditions of secular politics, in which martyrdom at the hands of the rich and powerful was so common a theme. From Dic Penderyn in 1831 to the tenants dispossessed after the 1868 election, to the victims of the tithe wars of the 1880s – all joined a secular pantheon which owed much of its power and prestige to the existing religious traditions.

This also served to place contemporary events in a long historical perspective – and overwhelmingly, the beneficiaries were those parties who claimed to represent the common people, the Liberals and later Labour. In 1868, Sir Thomas Love Jones-Parry won the Caernarvonshire county seat for the Liberal Party. To celebrate, his friend Edward Breese presented Parry with a book inscribed with a triumphant inscription about 'the year when the county . . . threw off the fetters of Toryism and elected a Liberal Member'. The volume was a lengthy account of the trial, execution and dying speeches of the 'fanatic' regicides executed in 1660, including Colonel John Jones. Is the suggestion that 1868 was in a sense revenge for 1660? The first 'Love Parry' – an ancestor – had been named about that time by his father, a Roundhead officer. The conflicts and martyrs of the seventeenth century were never far from the political consciousness of Victorian Wales.

The character of Welsh historiography is usefully illustrated by a textbook known as *Famous Welshmen*, a volume of short biographies prepared by a committee of the Welsh department of the Board of Education. The book was published in 1944 for the use of secondary schools up to GCE level; but frequent reprints ensured that the book remained in use at least into the 1970s. Naturally, we would not expect first-rate historical scholarship in a work intended for such a level, but what is striking is the perspective that emerges about the important trends in Welsh history at this time.

In contemporary England, comparable books of 'celebrities' could usually be criticised for their over-emphasis on high politics, on military and colonial adventurers. In Wales, by contrast, the slant was far more towards spiritual pioneers, to matters of religion, culture and education. Of 40 'famous Welshmen' born between 1680 and 1840, at least 25 were clergy, all but two of these Dissenters. In about 30 cases, the main field of activity involved religious evangelism and preaching, cultural and poetic activity, or else educational endeavours. No less than five were musicians or hymnodists (this group includes the one woman, Ann Griffiths). Of the remaining celebrities, most were known for political activities, but all were very much from the same mould: radicals and Liberals who attacked oppressive landlords, while simultaneously promoting the essentially nonconformist agenda on matters like disestablishment, pacifism and educational reform.

Equally striking would be a list of Welshmen who failed by these standards to achieve fame: after the Reformation, there are no aristocrats, no military leaders, no Conservatives; and not even any trade unionists – the radicalism favoured here is populist and democratic, not collectivist. The Liberal and Dissenting view of Welsh history would probably find no more complete expression than this. And 'Welshness' appears to be selectively defined: of the 40, none derived from the uplands of Glamorgan or Monmouthshire; and none was active there for more than brief visits. The book offers only two industrialists, both untypical: David Davies of Llandinam, and Robert Owen.

This ephemeral textbook deserves notice not because it was so widely used or influential, but because it epitomises so many of the peculiar strengths and weaknesses of Welsh historiography. If we look at the useful and distinguished *Dictionary of Welsh Biography* (originally published in Welsh in 1953, then translated and revised in 1959), we will indeed find accounts of many of the industrialists,

union leaders and military men who were so conspicuously un-
famous by the standards of the earlier textbook. However, the
entries in the volume overwhelmingly concern those active in the
fields of religion, culture and education, with the emphasis very
much on nonconformist religion and culture in the Welsh language.
We therefore have elaborate entries on preachers or poets of strictly
marginal and local reputation, even when next to nothing survives of
their writings or sermons; while the material on ruling elites is
sketchy at best. The Tory writer H.M. Vaughan sardonically
referred to this as the 'Rev, John Jones of Cwmscwt' school of
history.

The *DWB* must be understood in terms of its original goal, to
rectify perceived omissions in the *Dictionary of National Biography*,
where elite figures are better covered. However, the book still gives
the impression that only the Liberal and nonconformist leaders are
truly part of the nation. Conversely, there is relative neglect of the
Williams-Wynn family, despite their enviable political power in a
number of counties. In the *DWB*, most of the prominent members
of the family receive only brief notice in a collective genealogical
article on the house. Even this omits distinguished squires like that
Sir Watkin Williams-Wynn, a Conservative bastion in mid-Victorian
north Wales, who achieved infamy as the arch-enemy of Henry
Richard, Michael Jones, S.R., and George Osborne Morgan.
Needless to say, all these are firmly established in any account of the
pantheon of Victorian Wales.

These religious and political biases cannot be attributed to any
deliberate wish to falsify or slant history. Instead, the distinctive
emphases reflect the natural interests and concerns of the sort of
people who undertook much of the historical research during the last
century. The traditional Welsh approach is also in some ways
refreshing. There is no question here of having to struggle to justify
a democratic view of history 'from the bottom up', as this has long
been virtual orthodoxy. On the other hand, the different emphasis
must be appreciated if we are to understand the current directions of
historical work in Wales.

In the nineteenth and early twentieth centuries, Wales had a range
of antiquarian scholars similar to those of any English region,
working on the histories of particular counties, of boroughs or
parishes, or of great events like the civil wars. G.T. Clark, J.H.
Matthews, J.A. Bradney, Alfred N. Palmer, all were highly diligent
researchers whose work is well worth consulting today. However,
by far the greater volume of research at this time was being directed

not to gentle or 'high' politics, but to Dissent. In 1861, Thomas Rees published an influential but aggressively sectarian *History of Protestant nonconformity in Wales* (revised edition 1883). In the twentieth century, nonconformist historical societies and their journals established themselves long before academic or merely 'secular' studies. The Welsh Baptists were publishing Historical *Transactions* from 1906; the Independents produced *Y cofiadur* from 1923. The *Journal* of the Calvinistic Methodist Historical Society was edited by the able antiquary Morgan Hugh Jones from 1916 to 1930. By the 1920s, the Catholics were exploring their traditions in the Cardiff periodical, *St Peter's Magazine*.

No less than journals, book-length studies bear witness to this almost obsessive study with the early origins of later religious divisions. In the 1920s, there were historians studying social and economic aspects of Welsh history, but the most prolific writers were sectarian scholars such as Thomas Richards, author of works like *The puritan movement in Wales 1639–1653* (London 1920); *Religious developments in Wales 1654–1662* (London 1923); *Wales under the penal code 1662–1687* (London 1925); or *Piwritanieth a pholitics* (Wrexham 1927). He also published over 30 articles on related topics. In later years, nonconformist history attracted other major Welsh historians, like Gomer M. Roberts and R. Tudur Jones. Distinguished additions to this tradition include Jones' *Hanes annibynwyr Cymru* ('History of the Welsh Independents', Swansea 1966) and T.M. Bassett on *The Welsh baptists* (Swansea: Ilston House 1977).

Older works like the Richards volumes offer the modern historian an invaluable resource, but they also pose serious problems. The books, while not uncritical, are written with strong sympathy for the Puritans and the rightness of their cause, and with a 'puritanical' eye for opposition from the Anglican and unconverted. Also, there is a sense in which we simply know too much about the dissenting ministers and Methodist preachers so assiduously described in these books, or in every volume of the various sectarian journals. Over the years, the researchers have examined the minutiae not merely of the major figures like Howell Harris, but of many hundreds of individuals of strictly local and ephemeral importance. This can easily give the impression that Dissent was a far more powerful force in Wales in (say) 1720 than was really the case. It might also suggest that Dissent was a stronger force than in areas of England, where there might just be less intensive later research. In 1968, there appeared a major *Bibliography of the history of Wales*, which betrays at every point this religious preoccupation. For the period 1714–1789, there are roughly 450 entries of which almost 300 fall under the category 'Religion and education'; and a third of these concern Methodism alone.

FURTHER READING

Religious debates have been central to Welsh history, but it is now possible to approach other aspects of the story. In the last half century, Wales has been fortunate in its academic historians, especially those who have more than justified the hopes of the founders of a national university. It was above all the emergence of the University of Wales as a centre of research that has established the rich tradition that exists in Welsh history today. This is particularly strong in matters of social history, of ethnic and class consciousness; and it has demonstrated an enviable awareness of the nation's wider European context.

The discussion of further reading is complicated by a number of issues. In order to be comprehensive, it would be necessary to refer to many general works on British history, which happen to include much important material on Wales and the Welsh, and where the entries are often by some of the authors described below. The *History of parliament* volumes are an obvious example; but such works will be cited only rarely. Also, in a general work of this nature, the emphasis will be on books rather than journal articles, though these latter are essential for any more detailed study. There are at least 20 historical journals of substance published in Wales, including the flagship *Welsh history review*, and any detailed bibliography should really include virtually everything published in these in the last two or three decades.

Also problematical is scholarship written only in Welsh. There are some important studies in this category, but only a handful will be cited here. This is unfortunate, because some of the detailed local case-studies in particular are excellent. There are biographical studies of key figures in Welsh history, such as *Iolo Morgannwg*, by G.J. Williams (University of Wales Press 1956). Williams also wrote a fundamental report of the development of the Welsh literary tradition in his account of Glamorgan, *Traddodiad llenyddol Morgannwg* (Cardiff: University of Wales Press 1948).

HISTORICAL WRITING 1930–1960

During the 1930s and 1940s, there emerged an impressive generation of Welsh historians whose work laid the foundations for much that was to follow. There were several distinguished scholars – William Rees, Emyr Gwynne Jones, Glyn Roberts, Iorwerth Peate, Sir Frederick Rees, and others; but for our present purposes, three names in particular stand out as major influences on the history of modern Wales. All influenced many pupils, but they also left published work which remains in active use to the present day. This account will focus on their books, but much of value was also published in journals like the *Transactions of the honourable society of Cymmrodorion* or the *National Library of Wales Journal*. The first was R.T. Jenkins, author of two volumes which portrayed the history of Wales from 1700 to 1843 (*Hanes Cymru yn y bedwaredd ganrif ar Bymtheg* (Cardiff 1933) and *Hanes Cymru yn y ddeunawfed ganrif* (1931: both were reprinted in 1972). Jenkins was also the guiding force behind the project that produced the *Dictionary of Welsh Biography* in the 1940s and 1950s.

Also of the first quality was the work of David Williams, whose main areas of interest concerned the radical and protest movements of the early nineteenth century; but whose descriptions of those events also offer an amazingly complex portrait of the wider social context. All these works remain essential reading, and Williams exercised a powerful influence on later scholars like Gwyn A. Williams and D.J.V. Jones. His works include *The Rebecca riots* (University of Wales Press 1955); *John Frost, a study in Chartism* (Cardiff: University of Wales Press 1939); and the chapter on 'Chartism in Wales' in *Chartist studies*, ed. Asa Briggs, London 1959. In 1950, Williams also published a *History of modern Wales* (updated and revised edition with I.G. Jones, University of Wales Press 1977).

Third among this group was A.H. Dodd, author of a remarkable series of articles in the 1940s and 1950s on the 'high' politics of Stuart Wales, work which is still too little known by English historians of the period. His books include *Studies in Stuart Wales* (1952, revised edition 1971) and two invaluable local studies – *A history of Wrexham* (ed. 1957) and a *History of Caernarvonshire* from the thirteenth century to 1900 (Caernarvonshire Historical Society 1968). Dodd had earlier published an excellent guide to the process of industrialisation in *The Industrial Revolution in North Wales* (1933, University of Wales Press 3rd edition 1971). A still valuable counterpart was published in 1950

A History of Modern Wales 1536–1990

by A.H. John in *The industrial development of South Wales* (Cardiff, University of Wales Press 1950).

Welsh history in mid-century was in a flourishing state. In addition to the work of scholars like Dodd and Williams, there were major projects afoot to publish the basic source materials for that history – family papers, records of the central government concerning Wales, records of Welsh recusants and dissenters, manuscript narratives, and so on. From as early as 1910, we have an important series under the title of *West Wales historical records*; from 1932, the South Wales and Monmouthshire Record Society had made such sources accessible to a wider public, often superbly edited and annotated by scholars of European reputation like William Rees. In 1929, the Board of Celtic Studies of the University of Wales Press began similar undertakings for both the medieval and early modern periods.

By the late 1950s, the work of scholars like these had provided a firm foundation for Welsh historical scholarship, and had suggested many directions for research. In 1959, the translated *DWB* provided an indispensable reference for students of Welsh history; and in 1962, the thriving scholarship of these years found a new focus in a journal, the *Welsh history review*. Local and county historical journals began in the late nineteenth century. By 1960, every county had its historical magazine – *Brycheiniog, Ceredigion, Morgannwg*, and so on. Larger counties like Glamorgan had several local journals in addition.

NEW CURRENTS 1960–1990

The 1960s and 1970s more than fulfilled the promise of these early years, and we will note especially the books of scholars like Kenneth O Morgan, Glanmor Williams, I. G. Jones, D.J.V. Jones, David Howell, Gwyn Williams, Gareth E. Jones, Prys Morgan, and many others. While the older journals continued successfully, there now appeared a series of even more specialised periodicals to meet new research interests: *Llafur*, on Labour history; *Maritime Wales*; *The Welsh historian*; the *Cambrian law review*; the *Journal of Welsh ecclesiastical history*, and others. Historical concerns were also prominent in the pages of journals of more general cultural interest, like *Planet*. The new scholarship resulted in a number of single volume attempts at a history of modern Wales after the model pioneered by David Williams and R.T. Jenkins. Readable examples

414

include Gareth E. Jones, *Modern Wales: a concise history 1485–1979* (Cambridge 1984); Hugh Thomas, *A history of Wales 1485–1660* (University of Wales Press 1972); E.D. Evans, *A history of Wales 1660–1815* (Cardiff 1976); David Gareth Evans, *A history of Wales 1815–1906* (Cardiff 1989); John Davies, *Hanes Cymru* (London: Allen Lane, 1990); and Gwyn A. Williams, *When was Wales?* (Penguin 1985).

One of the more remarkable endeavours in contemporary Welsh studies has been the *Glamorgan county history*, a work that serves almost as a history of Wales in miniature. (It will be cited hereafter as *GCH*.) From inception in 1936 to completion in 1988, the 50 or so contributions to these six volumes provide a fascinating sampling of the broad interests and varied methodologies of two generations of Welsh historians and social scientists. For present purposes, the most important volumes are those which cover *Early modern Glamorgan* (volume 4:1974), *Industrial Glamorgan* (5:1980) and *Glamorgan society 1780–1980* (6:1988). The *Pembrokeshire county history* also offers rich pickings: see for example the volume edited by B.E. Howell on the *Early Modern Period, 1536–1815* (3:1987).

GENERAL HISTORIES

In fact, the historical research of this period was so rich and diverse as to make essential some kind of general overview, a more substantial synthesis that could provide signposts for the next generation. In the 1980s, two attempts were made at new comprehensive histories of Wales, and they are the obvious starting point for any further research into the Welsh past. The first of these series has been jointly published by Oxford and the University of Wales Press. Volumes produced to date include G.H. Jenkins, *The foundations of modern Wales: Wales 1642–1780* (1987); Glanmor Williams, *Wales 1415–1642: recovery, reorientation and reformation* (1987); and Kenneth O. Morgan, *Rebirth of a nation: Wales 1880–1980* (1981). All are distinguished pieces that fully meet their goal of summarising existing research while at the same time making important new contributions to the field. All, incidentally, have excellent bibliographies.

Very different in conception is the series published by the University of Wales Press for the Open University in Wales, all under the editorship of Trevor Herbert and Gareth E. Jones. Each volume consists of five or so essays by a number of writers with different approaches – social, economic, religious and so on; and each essay is followed by an extensive selection of relevant documents. The editors provide a framework for understanding the period, together with questions for discussion. These books are aimed at an audience much less accustomed to traditional academic assumptions, and popular appeal and interest are maintained without sacrificing academic integrity. Among the stimulating and often enjoyable books in this series are *Tudor Wales* (1988); *The remaking of Wales in the eighteenth century* (1988); *People and protest 1815–1880* (1988); *Wales 1880–1914* (1988) and *Wales between the wars* (1988).

The reader interested in pursuing a particular issue or individual will obviously find material in one of these comprehensive accounts: and *GCH* should probably be reckoned here alongside the two 'New Histories of Wales'. As reference books, we naturally have the *DWB*, but there are also works like *The Oxford companion to the literature of Wales*, edited by Meic Stephens (Oxford UP 1986). On political history, we have works of reference like Arnold J. James and John E. Thomas, *Wales at Westminster* (Gomer Press 1981: on Welsh parliamentary history from 1800 to 1979) or their *Union to Reform* (Gomer 1988), which covers the years from 1536 to 1832. The volumes on the buildings of Welsh counties, published by the *Royal commission on ancient and historic monuments* are also valuable for matters of social and economic history. *The national atlas of Wales* was edited by Harold Carter (University of Wales Press 1980), and naturally contains much historical material. L.J. Williams, *Digest of Welsh historical statistics* (Cardiff: University of Wales Press, 1985) is a goldmine. The 1962 *Bibliography of the history of Wales* has been superseded by a new fiche version edited by Philip Henry Jones (University of Wales).

TUDOR AND JACOBEAN WALES

In addition, an outline of the major books on particular topics will suggest the current state of research in Welsh history, the chief concerns of current scholarship. To begin with the Tudor period: one of the most celebrated historians of contemporary Wales is Glanmor Williams, whose many publications include *Welsh Reformation essays* (University of Wales Press 1967). He also wrote very readable contributions to *GCH* on social, economic and political topics, no less than religious questions. On political issues, significant studies include Penry Williams, *The Council in the Marches of Wales under Elizabeth I* (Cardiff: University of Wales Press 1958); Gareth E. Jones, *The gentry and the Elizabethan state* (Swansea: Christopher Davies, 1977) and G. Dyfnallt Owen, *Wales in the reign of James I* (Royal historical society 1988). *Class, community and culture in Tudor Wales* (Cardiff: University of Wales, 1989) is a series of social history essays edited by J. Gwynfor Jones. He has also published a collection of sources under the title *Wales and the Tudor state* (Cardiff: University of Wales, 1989).

For the social and cultural world of Tudor Wales, major sources include the work of antiquaries like George Owen in Pembrokeshire and Rice Merrick in Glamorgan. See B.G. Charles, *George Owen of Henllys: A Welsh Elizabethan* (Aberystwyth: National Library of Wales 1977); and the edition of Rice Merrick's *Morganiae archaiographia* by Brian Ll. James (Cardiff: 1983). This latter was the first publication by the reformed South Wales Record Society, which has gone on to publish sources and documents on many periods of Welsh history.

THE EARLY MODERN ECONOMY

The economic history of Tudor and Stuart Wales is brilliantly covered in volumes four and five of the *Agrarian history of England and Wales*, both edited by Joan Thirsk (Cambridge: volume four, 1967); and volume five, parts one and two, 1984–1985). This is one of the rare histories of 'Britain' where Wales achieves extensive coverage by some excellent contributors. The existing volumes cover the period from 1540 to 1760, and describe topics such as farming regions, landlords and estate management, and vernacular housing. Matthew Griffiths offers a local case-study in *Penmark and Porthkerry: families and farms in the seventeenth century Vale of Glamorgan* (Department of extra-mural studies , University College, Cardiff 1979).

On early industrial development, there is a spectacularly thorough compilation by William Rees, *Industry before the Industrial Revolution* (two volumes, University of Wales Press 1968), the product of some 50 years of research. This covers the highly active industrial development of the region in every period from the middle ages until the end of the eighteenth century. Books on early industry tend to focus on the iron and coal regions of the south-east, so it is useful to have a book like J. Geraint Jenkins, *The Welsh woollen industry* (Cardiff: University of Wales Press 1969), which deals chiefly with mid-Wales.

'THE PEOPLE ABOVE'

The booming Welsh historical world of the last three decades has often been deeply influenced by the current concerns of English scholarship – about crime and social protest, or class and deference in the industrial age. Given the wave of county and gentry studies originally inspired by the alleged rise (or fall) of the gentry in the century after the Reformation, it was not surprising that the Welsh squires would soon find themselves the subject of attention. This genre began with Howell A. Lloyd's excellent account of *The gentry of south-west Wales 1540–1640* (University of Wales Press 1968). More recent contributions on the later Stuart and Georgian periods include Philip Jenkins, *The making of a ruling class: the Glamorgan gentry 1640–1790* (Cambridge 1983) and David Howell, *Patriarchs and Parasites* (Cardiff: University of Wales Press 1986). One essential reference work is J.R.S. Phillips, *The justices of the peace in Wales and Monmouthshire 1541–1689* (Cardiff: University of Wales 1975).

Among these 'elite' studies we might also count heraldic and genealogical works. These are scarcely popular among academic historians today, but they can often offer valuable source material in addition to any intrinsic interest. Between 1910 and 1929, Francis Green published many of these family studies in *West Wales historical records*. Major Francis Jones has published dozens of such studies of particular families over the years, well represented in his *Historic Carmarthenshire houses and their families* (Carmarthenshire Antiquarian Society 1987).

The high politics of Stuart and Georgian Wales have never really been fashionable, despite the magnificent precedent set by A.H. Dodd. Important work on eighteenth century elections was undertaken by Peter D.G. Thomas in a dissertation that never, alas, appeared in book form. However, he published a number of detailed county studies in the historical journals of the respective shires in the late 1950s and early 1960s (see for example 'The parliamentary representation of Merionethshire in the eighteenth century', *Journal of the Merionethshire historical and record society*, 3(2), 1958; and many others). Carmarthenshire county and (notably) borough politics were the subject of important studies by Glyn Roberts, reprinted in his *Aspects of Welsh history* (University of Wales Press 1969).

THE TOWNS

Roberts' study of Carmarthen is an important reminder of the rather patchy nature of urban studies in Wales. There are some excellent case-studies, and much of the material in Ralph A. Griffiths ed., *Boroughs of medieval Wales* (Cardiff: University of Wales Press 1978) in fact concerns sixteenth century conditions. Other works to note include A.H. Dodd, ed., *A history of Wrexham* (Wrexham 1957) and Elis Jenkins ed., *Neath: a symposium* (Neath 1974). Borough politics are rarely treated in detail, and the guilds in particular deserve attention. The lack of long-term studies of town politics is unfortunate because of the continuing role of the towns as centres of Protestantism, Dissent and Methodism.

On later periods, John Davies, *Cardiff and the Bute estate* (University of Wales Press 1981) is a model account of the relationship between an aristocratic landed estate and the city which it dominated – indeed, created. Michael J. Daunton offers a parallel view of the city in *Coal Metropolis: Cardiff 1870–1914* (Leicester UP 1977).

RELIGION AND POLITICS 1640–1780

For the politics of the seventeenth century and the mid-century crisis, the most valuable source is certainly Dodd's *Studies in Stuart Wales*. There is also much of use in some of the older accounts of these events in books like Norman Tucker, *North Wales in the Civil War* (Denbigh 1958), or some of the articles reprinted in J.F. Rees, *Studies in Welsh history*. The remarks made above about the limitations of the older nonconformist works should not detract from their unquestionable value as source material. Richards in particular had an encyclopaedic grasp of the available resources; and it is difficult to approach the critical years of the 1650s except through studies of the 'saints'. Valuable here are G.F. Nuttall, *The Welsh Saints* (Cardiff University of Wales Press 1957) and R. Tudur Jones, *Vavasor Powell* (in Welsh: Swansea 1971).

On the religious history of the eighteenth century, G.F. Nuttall also published an account of *Howell Harris 1714–1773, The last enthusiast* (Cardiff: University of Wales Press 1965), which successfully places him in the wider British and European contexts. However, the most important current work is that of Geraint H. Jenkins, not least in *The foundations of modern Wales,* cited above. Other major works by Jenkins include *Literature, religion and society in Wales 1660–1730* (University of Wales Press 1978); and his *Hanes Cymru yn y cyfnod modern cynnar 1530–1760* ('History of Wales in the Early Modern Age' University of Wales Press 1988). David Walker edited an important *History of the Church in Wales* (Church in Wales 1976), which is strong on Dissent as well as the establishment.

THE ECONOMIC TRANSFORMATION

On the process of industrialisation in the eighteenth and nineteenth centuries, the older books by Dodd, John and Rees are all valuable. More recently, we have Michael Atkinson and Colin Baber, *The growth and decline of the South Wales iron industry 1760–1880* (Cardiff: University of Wales Press 1987); Colin Baber and L.J. Williams, eds., *Modern south Wales: essays in economic history 1780–1950* (University of Wales Press 1986); and Pat Hudson ed., *Regions and industries: a perspective on Britain's industrialisation* (Cambridge, 1989). Case-studies include C.W. Roberts, *A legacy from Victorian enterprise* (Gloucester: Alan Sutton, 1983). Naturally, the relevant volumes of *GCH* also provide much useful material about the process and impact of industrialisation; while Wales is well covered in the *History of the British coal industry* by M.W. Flinn, Roy Church, William Ashworth et al. (five volumes projected: Oxford 1984–).

While Wales was radically changed by the coming of industry, much of the land naturally remained rural and agrarian, and this older society is ably described in David Williams' account of the Rebecca movement. There are powerful studies by David Howell, *Land and people in nineteenth century Wales* (Routledge and Kegan Paul 1978) and David Jenkins, *The agricultural community in south-west Wales* (Cardiff: University of Wales Press 1971).

POLITICAL RADICALS 1780–1850

Welsh history offers fertile ground for anyone interested in the social and political consequences of industrialisation. The prolonged and severe social crisis of the early nineteenth century has been the subject for several fine historians; and all the works by David Williams cited earlier remain well worth reading. More recently, we have Gwyn A. Williams, *The Merthyr rising* (Croom Helm 1978), which is fundamental to our understanding of the period. Gwyn Williams' other books include *The search for Beulah land: the Welsh and the Atlantic revolution* (London: Croom Helm, 1980); and there is much of interest in the essays presented to him in Clive Emsley and James Walvin ed., *Artisans, peasants and proletarians 1760–1860* (Croom Helm 1986).

Another current writer who stands firmly in the honourable tradition founded by David Williams is D.J.V. Jones, author of *Before Rebecca: popular protest in Wales 1793–1835* (London: Allen Lane, 1973); *The last rising: the Newport insurrection of 1839* (Oxford 1985) and *Rebecca's children: a study of rural society, crime and protest* (Oxford 1989). The late eighteenth and early nineteenth centuries remain a source of fascination, in part because of the individuals of European or transatlantic consequence produced by Wales in that period. There is a biography of one such in Whitney R.D.Jones, *David Williams, the anvil and the hammer* (Cardiff: University of Wales Press 1986).

THE LABOUR MOVEMENT 1850–1990

The history of labour organisation and militancy has inevitably been a major source of attention for historians of nineteenth and early twentieth century Wales, and this interest was inevitably refreshed by the growth of radical history in the 1970s. In Wales, the major manifestation of this was the lively journal *Llafur* (despite the title, published in English). This bears many resemblances to the English *History workshop journal*, especially in its endeavour to synthesise and reconcile issues of class, ethnicity and gender. Labour and industrial topics have also been a real emphasis in the *Welsh history review* in recent years.

There have been some important books in this tradition. Among the most highly regarded of recent years was Merfyn Jones, *The*

A History of Modern Wales 1536–1990

North Wales quarrymen 1874–1922 (University of Wales Press 1981). Other significant contributions include Jean Lindsay, *The great strike: a history of the Penrhyn quarry dispute of 1900–1903* (David and Charles 1987); David Smith ed., *A people and a proletariat: Wales 1780–1980* (Pluto 1980); Hywel Francis and David Smith, *The Fed: a history of the South Wales miners in the twentieth century* (Lawrence and Wishart 1980).

Traditionally, labour history in Wales tended to concentrate on the coal and steel areas, with the slate industry a more recent emphasis. In the 1980s, there was growing interest in less celebrated sectors of the economy. We now have P.J. Leng, *The Welsh dockers* (Ormskirk: Hesketh, 1981); A.Y. Jones and D. Beddoe, *The Welsh maid: a study of Welsh women in domestic service 1919–1939* (London 1988) and David A. Pretty's account of farmworkers' unions in Wales from 1889 to 1950 in *The rural revolt that failed: farmworkers' trade unions in Wales 1889–1950* (University of Wales Press 1989). There are also books on more general working-class or union history, that nevertheless have a great deal of Welsh material. See for example Jane Morgan, *Conflict and order: the police and labour disputes in England and Wales 1900–1939* (Clarendon 1987), and S. MacIntyre, *The little Moscows* (1980).

VICTORIAN AND EDWARDIAN WALES

Labour and radical history have never had to struggle to justify their existence in the Welsh academic world – at least, not in the last half century. More conventional approaches to mainstream political and social history were less in evidence before the 1960s, and especially until the 1963 publication of Kenneth O. Morgan, *Wales in British politics 1868–1922* (University of Wales Press third edition 1980). To apply a much over-used term, this was a seminal work. It was followed by numerous other books and articles by this prolific author, some of which are essential for our understanding of Wales at the turn of the century.

I.G. Jones was another historian attracted primarily by the society and politics of nineteenth and early twentieth century Wales. Some of his most important articles are to be found in two collections: *Explorations and explanations: essays in the social history of Victorian Wales* (Llandyssul: Gomer Press 1981); and *Communities* (Llandyssul: Gomer Press 1987). There is also an important festschrift to

422

Professor Jones, in Geraint H. Jenkins and J. Beverley Smith, eds., *Politics and society in Wales 1840–1922* (University of Wales Press 1988).

The social and political history of the period can be addressed through books like Cyril Parry, *The radical tradition in Welsh politics: a study of Liberal and Labour politics in Gwynedd 1900–1920* (1970). For temperance as an issue in nineteenth century Wales, see W.R. Lambert, *Drink and sobriety in Victorian Wales 1820–1895* (University of Wales Press 1984). Patagonia is discussed in Glyn Williams, *The desert and the dream: a study of the Welsh colonisation of Chubut 1865–1915* (University of Wales 1975). There is a large literature on the Welsh settlement in North America. See for example Rowland T. Berthoff, *British immigrants in industrial America 1790–1950* (Cambridge, MA: Harvard University Press 1953); or Alan Conway ed., *The Welsh in America: letters from immigrants* (Minneapolis: University of Minnesota, 1961).

NONCONFORMITY

For the religious history of the nineteenth and twentieth centuries, there is much important and accessible work, such as E.T. Davies, *Religion in the Industrial Revolution in South Wales* (Cardiff: University of Wales Press 1965, new edition 1987); and *Religion and society in the nineteenth century*, by the same author (Llandybie: Christopher Davies, 1988). Valuable source material is reprinted in I.G. Jones and David Williams, eds., *The religious census of 1851* (Cardiff: University of Wales Press 1977). Though not academic history in the conventional sense, there is useful material in the works of nonconformist hagiographers. Eifion Evans, for example, published a series of studies such as *Daniel Rowland and the great evangelical awakening in Wales* (Banner of Truth Trust 1985); *Two Welsh revivalists: Humphrey Jones, Dafydd Morgan and the 1859 revival in Wales* (Evangelical Library of Wales 1985) and *The Welsh revival of 1904* (Evangelical Library of Wales 1969).

More substantial is R. Tudur Jones' excellent book (in Welsh) on the 1904 revival: *Ffydd ac argyfwng cenedl: hanes crefydd yng Nghymru 1890–1914* ('Faith and national crisis: a history of religion in Wales 1890–1914', Swansea: John Penry Press, 1982). A useful book for understanding the later history of nonconformity is *Chapels in the valley: a study in the sociology of Welsh nonconformity* by D. Ben Rees

A History of Modern Wales 1536–1990

(Upton, Merseyside: Ffynnon, 1975).
The topic of education was closely tied to religion, and featured in many of the same debates. There is a sizeable literature here, but L.J. Williams and G.R. Hughes, eds., *The history of education in Wales* (Swansea 1978) provides a point of entry. See also Gareth E. Jones, *Controls and conflicts in Welsh secondary education 1889–1944* (Cardiff: University of Wales Press 1982).

MODERN POLITICS

For most of the last century, the two major political forces in Welsh life were the Labour and Liberal parties and the traditions they represented. The rise of nationalism has often appeared to threaten that, though any 'national awakening' on those lines remains an unfulfilled dream. There is a fine collection of essays edited by John Osmond under the title *The national question again: Welsh political identity in the 1980s* (Gomer Press 1985), which provides a good introduction for any discussion of recent political developments. Nationalist and separatist movements are described in *The Welsh nationalist party 1925–1945: a call to nationhood* by D. Hywel Davies (University of Wales Press 1983); and Charlotte Aull Davies, *Welsh nationalism in the twentieth century: the ethnic option and the modern state* (New York: Praeger, 1989). There is a Welsh-language account in *Cymru'n deffro: hanes y Blaid Genedlaethol 1925–1975* ('Wales Awakens – a History of the National Party 1925–1975' – a series of essays edited by John Davies: Y Lolfa, 1981). The practical politics and dilemmas of modern nationalism are discussed in D. Foulkes et al *The Welsh veto: The Wales Act 1978 and the referendum* (University of Wales Press 1983). It was in 1983 that a Welsh Political Archive was established at the National Library of Wales, and we can expect some important publications from this centre in coming years.
It is impossible to draw a line between historical study and contemporary politics, and we can scarcely know what current issues will appear to have significance in ten or 20 years' time. However, there are a number of works (often polemical or journalistic in nature) which give the flavour of contemporary debates about nationalism and language struggles. In so doing, they raise enduring questions about state powers and individual rights. See Ned Thomas, *The Welsh extremist: a culture in crisis* (London: Gollancz 1971). Roy Clews, *To dream of freedom* (Talybont, Dyfed: Y Lolfa,

1980) is a sympathetic history of the 'Free Wales Army' and related militant movements in the 1960s. The leader of M.A.C., the most active terrorist group in this wave, was John Jenkins, whose *Prison letters* (ed., Rhodri Williams. Y Lolfa: 1981) have been published. John Osmond, *Police conspiracy* (Y Lolfa 1984) discusses one of the many controversial prosecutions of political offenders in these years. There are contemporary manifestos of militant Welsh republican separatism by authors like Derrick Hearne, in *The rise of the Welsh republic* (Y Lolfa 1975) and *The ABC of the Welsh revolution* (Y Lolfa 1982).

SOCIAL SCIENCE

The problem of deciding exactly when history comes to a full stop also determines our selection of social science books on contemporary Wales. Many of these provide essential material for understanding Welsh society and the economy over the last three or four decades, and can thus be read as historical texts as much as contemporary analyses. In 1950, Alwyn D. Rees published his account of *Life in a Welsh countryside* (University of Wales), which inspired a whole genre of rural community studies drawing on the insights of sociology and anthropology. Ronald Frankenberg studied a *Village on the border* (London: Cohen and West,1957), Isobel Emmett published *A north Wales village* (London: Routledge Kegan Paul 1964); while Elwyn Davies and Alwyn D. Rees, ed., *Welsh rural communities* (University of Wales 1960) offered several such case-studies, all with a strong awareness of the historical dimension. Enduring – apparently eternal – geographical patterns would also be discussed in D. Huw Owen, ed., *Settlement and society in Wales* (University of Wales Press 1989).

Particularly useful among recent works are: Gareth Rees and Teresa Rees ed., *Poverty and social inequality in Wales* (London: Croom Helm 1980); Ian Hume and W.T.R. Pryce, *The Welsh and their country* (Gomer Press 1986); and Kenneth D. George and Lynn Mainwaring, *The Welsh economy* (University of Wales Press 1988). The annual review *Contemporary Wales* surveys social and economic studies. Apart from their intrinsic interest, social and economic questions naturally have a strong 'national' and cultural dimension in contemporary Wales. This emerges clearly in most of the works cited here, as in the articles collected by Glyn Williams, ed., in *Social and cultural change in contemporary Wales* (London: Routledge and

Kegan Paul 1978). J.W. Aitchison and Harold Carter published *The Welsh language 1961–1981: an interpretative atlas* (University of Wales Press 1985), a vital source for cultural and linguistic debates.

THE NATIONAL QUESTION

The rise of nationalism intensified interest in questions of ethnicity, regionalism and national development – in short, what exactly Wales was: nation, principality, region, anomaly? This sort of literature was far from new, but 'the British Question' became something of a vogue in the 1970s and 1980s. In historical terms, this implied growing concern with movements of unification within the British Isles, and the state of the respective Celtic cultures facing the pressure for political unity. Social science concepts were often mined heavily to grasp these processes; and inevitably, Wales was usually treated alongside Ireland and Scotland. Among a large number of studies we might single out Michael Hechter, *Internal colonialism: the Celtic fringe in British national development* (London: RKP, 1975); Victor Edward Durkacz, *The decline of the Celtic languages* (John Donald 1983); Keith Robbins, *Nineteenth century Britain: integration and diversity* (Oxford: Clarendon 1988); and Hugh Kearney, *The British isles: a history of four nations* (Cambridge 1989). Meic Stephens, *Linguistic minorities in western Europe* (Llandyssul: Gomer 1976) offers a European context for Welsh debates and Welsh examples are used by E.J. Hobsbawm in his survey of *Nations and nationalism since 1780: programme, myth, reality* (Cambridge University Press 1990).

Even when the 'British Question' was not addressed so directly or comprehensively, the issues of that debate were very much present in books like Glanmor Williams' *Religion, language and nationality in Wales* (University of Wales Press 1979), or Tony Curtis ed., *Wales: the imagined nation: essays in cultural and national identity* (Bridgend 1986). The intriguingly titled *Wales! Wales?* by Dai Smith (Allen and Unwin 1984) seeks to define Welsh culture and local cultures. It emphasises that the world of the south-eastern industrial valleys is perhaps as distinct from the rest of 'Welsh' Wales as from England, with all that that implies for a separatism that presupposes a unified Welsh entity. Which Wales?

CULTURAL DIMENSIONS

This central concern with culture as a force determining the nature and limits of community means that poetry, music and literature are fundamental to appreciating the changing nature of the wider society. In the works of the best historians, like Glanmor Williams, 'cultural' material is wholly and sucessfully integrated with accounts of politics or religion. Useful starting points for understanding the development of Welsh culture are Prys Morgan, *The eighteenth century renaissance* (Swansea: Christopher Davies 1981); and the magisterial *History of Welsh literature* by Thomas Parry (translated by H.I. Bell: Oxford 1955). R. Brinley Jones and Meic Stephens edited an important series of monographs on *The writers of Wales* (Cardiff 1970). Biographies of note include W. Moelwyn Merchant's *R.S. Thomas* and Bruce Griffiths' *Saunders Lewis* (both University of Wales Press). For more recent developments, see Meic Stephens ed., *The arts in Wales 1950–1975* (Cardiff: Welsh Arts Council 1979); and Eric Rowan, *Art in Wales 1850–1975* (Cardiff: University of Wales Press 1978). There is a fine essay on 'Wales and Film' in Herbert and Jones ed., *Wales between the wars*, cited above.

In discussing aspects of popular culture, we should certainly include here David Smith and Gareth Williams, *Fields of praise: the official history of the Welsh Rugby Union 1881–1981*, a book that casts light on many aspects of Welsh social and political history.

The study of popular culture and 'folk-life' has long been a strong suit among Welsh historians. In recent years, there have been numerous studies of buildings, architectural styles and landscapes, all of which naturally provide a necessary framework for social and economic history. Examples include J.B. Hilling, *The historic architecture of Wales* (Cardiff: University of Wales Press 1977); Eurwen Wiliam, *Historic farm buildings of Wales* (John Donald 1986) and Peter Smith, *Houses of the Welsh countryside* (second edition, HMSO 1988). In the Penguin *Buildings of Wales* series, we have Richard Haslam on *Powys* (1979) and Edward Hubbard on *Clwyd* (1986).

DESIDERATA

Having identified some of the areas of real strength in Welsh history, we might also note a few regions of relative weakness. Gaps are to be found even in topics where much ink has been spilled, such as the social, economic and political foundations of the great eighteenth century revivals. Often, the work exists in journal articles, but systematic approaches are called for. Studying the changing sociology of the nonconformist ministry over the last three centuries would be of great interest, and might say a great deal about sectarian and theological differences. The same point could be made about the changing economic base of the chapels in general, for example in the great building years of the late nineteenth century. A detailed book-length analysis of the politics and sociology of one major chapel over a century or so would be a wonderful contribution, especially in a congregation where the deacons were also prominent in politics, government or business.

The study of official administration is not well advanced; and much remains to be said about the Conservative political tradition. Politics at county council level remain fairly obscure, though important. Labour history is well explored, but there is little comparable on those class-conscious militants, the employers and their organisations. In view of the critical role played by groups like the coal owners and the shipping men, this is an amazing lacuna. Much remains to be done on Welsh business history and its political ramifications: a history of the last two centuries of freemasonry might do much to illuminate both.

'Middle-class' affairs in all periods demand attention. Surely there are now enough case-studies to develop a general account of Welsh urban politics? The professions offer a fairly open field, with a crying need for social and political studies of groups like the solicitors, doctors and journalists. Without such a basis, it is difficult to understand the changing fate of nonconformity or middle-class liberalism between about 1880 and 1930, to say nothing of modern local government and the magistracy. Long before that, lawyers and stewards played a critical role in party organisation and industrial development, as well as religious revivalism.

Courts, judges and barristers have also played a recurring role in politics and industrial conflict from the Taff Vale judgement onwards, and a systematic study would be invaluable. There is a useful biography of *Judge John Bryn Roberts* (by Jack Eaton: University of Wales 1989), which explores his reputation as the 'union smasher of the boss class'. In earlier periods, the Welsh judges have not attracted the attention they deserve: the standard work (by W.R. Williams) is almost a century old.

Criminality also remains to be studied in much greater depth, but not simply by mining the loaded and rather questionable official statistics. These tell us a great deal about changing bureaucratic practices and priorities, but little about crime and deviancy as they really existed. D.J.V. Jones has shown what can be achieved here, and other periods of Welsh history are beginning to be subjected to similar analysis. Something must also be said about official corruption and upperworld criminality, topics that appear immune from standard archival investigation; though oral history approaches would seem fruitful here. A history of political patronage in modern Welsh society would be enlightening.

Gender is a glaring issue in current historiography. There have been articles by authors like Dot Smith in the *Welsh history review* and *Llafur*, but gender issues have not attained the central place in labour and radical scholarship that we find in some countries. Women obtained little attention in most of the recent attempts at 'New Histories' of Wales published in the 1980s; though Deirdre Beddoe's article in Herbert and Jones, *Wales between the wars* is an impressive exception (see also Jones and Beddoe, *The Welsh maid*, cited above; and Deirdre Beddoe's *Welsh convict women* (Barry 1979).

The relative lack of study is all the more startling when we consider the role of women in religious dissent and revivalism in Wales. To appreciate this, we need only consider the abundance of female names among the recusant rolls; or the dominance of women like the Countess of Huntingdon, Madam Bevan and Lady Charlotte Edwin in the Methodist sects of the eighteenth century. Ann Griffiths was one of the greatest hymn-writers of the movement. Women predominate in the great 'invention of Welshness' in the early nineteenth century. Lady Charlotte Guest and Lady Llanover are the best known, but Angharad Llwyd was a leader of the 'Old Clerical Patriots'. In modern literature, Kate Roberts is one of the best Welsh prose writers of the current century. In understanding the scarcity of women in the literature, we can only assume that gender issues have taken a poor second place to questions of class and nationality.

Maps

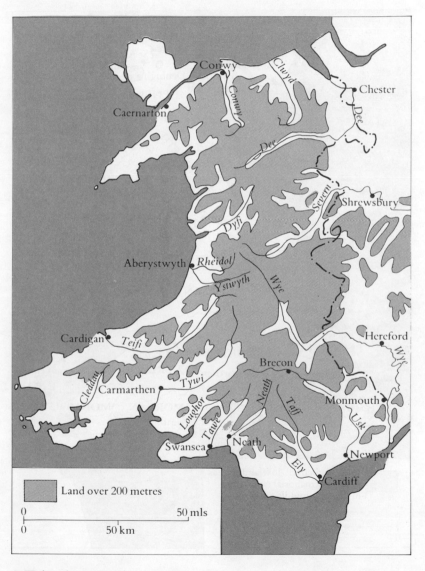

1 Wales: the geographical context

The "anglicized" lowlands: areas
of intense manorial cultivation
in the high middle ages.

0   50 mls

0   50 km

2 Early modern Wales

3 The hundreds

4 The Welsh towns 1550–1750

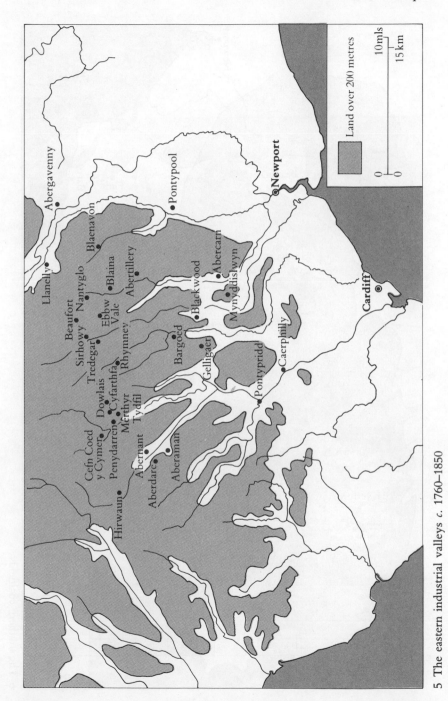

5 The eastern industrial valleys *c.* 1760–1850

Land over 200 metres

10mls
15 km

Abergavenny

Pontypool

Newport

Llanelly

Beaufort
Nantyglo
Blaenavon
Blaina
Abertillery
Abercarn
Mynyddislwyn
Blackwood

Ebbw
Vale

Sirhowy
Tredegar
Rhymney
Bargoed
Gelligaer
Pontypridd
Caerphilly

Cardiff

Cefn Coed
y Cymer
Dowlais
Cyfarthfa
Merthyr
Tydfil
Penydarren

Abernant
Aberaman
Aberdare
Hirwaun

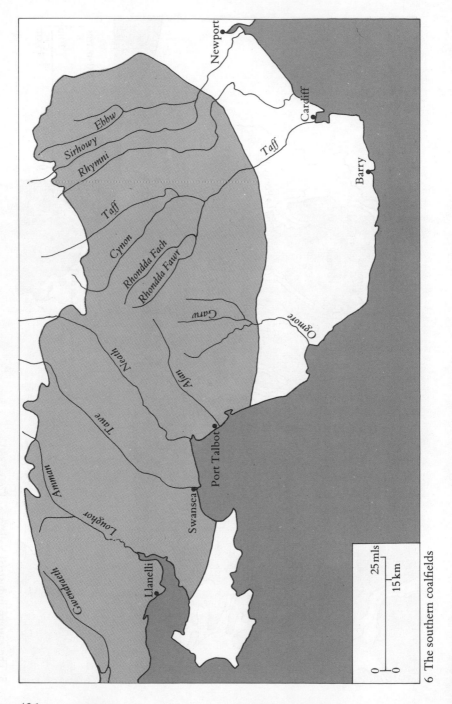

6 The southern coalfields

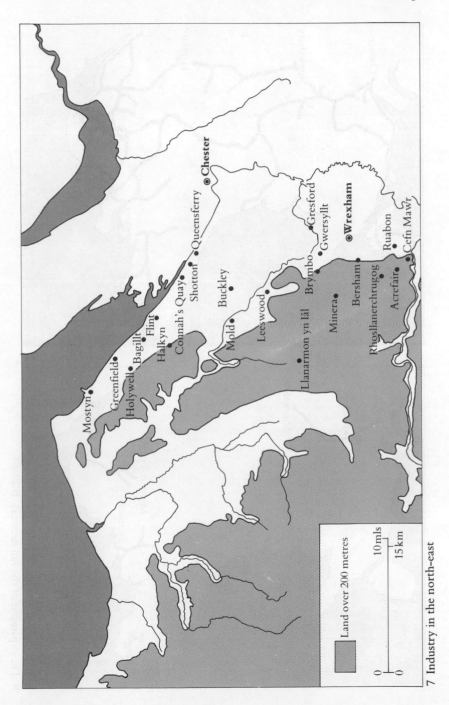

7 Industry in the north-east

Land over 200 metres

10mls
15 km

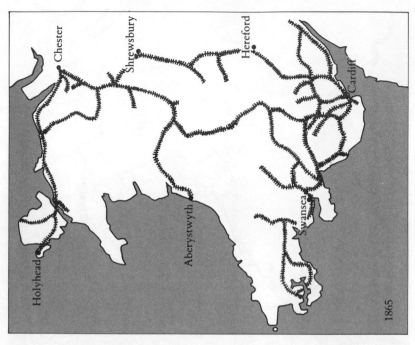

1865

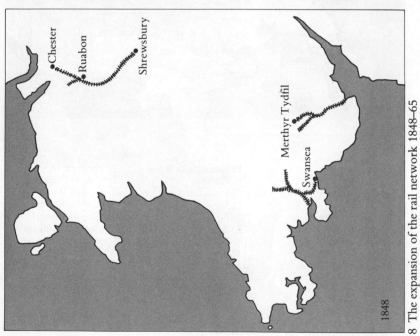

1848

8 The expansion of the rail network 1848–65

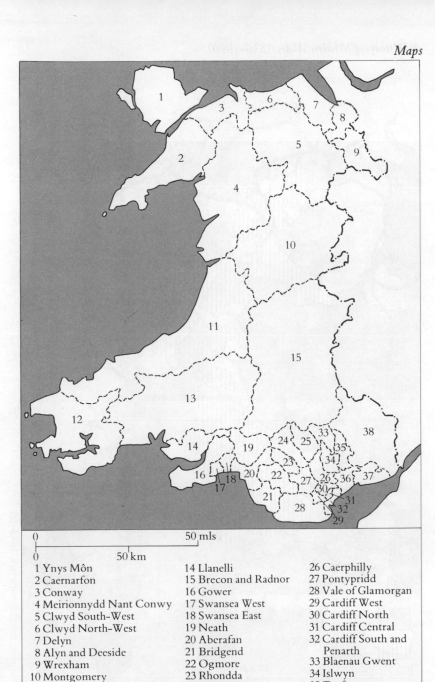

0   50 mls

0   50 km

1 Ynys Môn	14 Llanelli	26 Caerphilly
2 Caernarfon	15 Brecon and Radnor	27 Pontypridd
3 Conway	16 Gower	28 Vale of Glamorgan
4 Meirionnydd Nant Conwy	17 Swansea West	29 Cardiff West
5 Clwyd South-West	18 Swansea East	30 Cardiff North
6 Clwyd North-West	19 Neath	31 Cardiff Central
7 Delyn	20 Aberafan	32 Cardiff South and
8 Alyn and Deeside	21 Bridgend	Penarth
9 Wrexham	22 Ogmore	33 Blaenau Gwent
10 Montgomery	23 Rhondda	34 Islwyn
11 Ceredigion and	24 Cynon Valley	35 Torfaen
Pembroke North	25 Merthyr Tydfil	36 Newport West
12 Pembroke	and Rhymney	37 Newport East
13 Carmarthen		38 Monmouth

9 Welsh parliamentary constituencies 1990

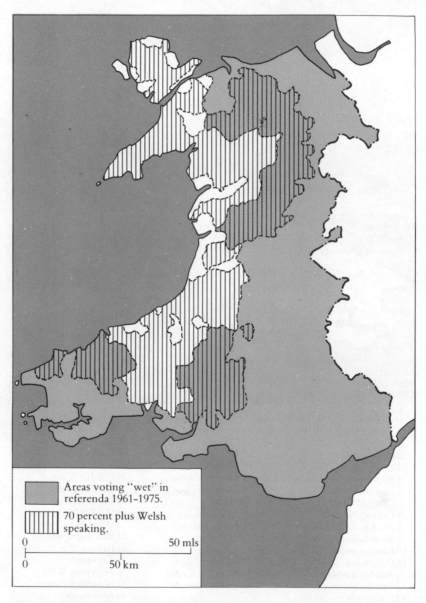

Areas voting "wet" in referenda 1961-1975.

70 percent plus Welsh speaking.

0   50 mls

0   50 km

10 The changing definition of Wales: language and temperance

Index